PARLIAMENTS AND THE EUROPEAN COURT OF HUMAN RIGHTS

Parliaments and the European Court of Human Rights

ALICE DONALD
and
PHILIP LEACH

OXFORD
UNIVERSITY PRESS

OXFORD
UNIVERSITY PRESS

Great Clarendon Street, Oxford, OX2 6DP,
United Kingdom

Oxford University Press is a department of the University of Oxford.
It furthers the University's objective of excellence in research, scholarship,
and education by publishing worldwide. Oxford is a registered trade mark of
Oxford University Press in the UK and in certain other countries

First Edition published in 2016

Published in the United States of America by Oxford University Press
198 Madison Avenue, New York, NY 10016, United States of America

British Library Cataloguing in Publication Data
Data available

Library of Congress Control Number: 2016934607

ISBN 978–0–19–873424–6

Alice Donald

I dedicate my work on this book to the memory of my dearly loved partner of almost twenty years, Nigel Rogers (18 December 1957–18 January 2013). He contributed immensely to my academic endeavours, and his ideals have been an inspiration throughout.

For their friendship and encouragement, warmest thanks are owed to my colleagues Joshua Castellino and Elvira Dominguez-Redondo—and to Philip Leach, a colleague of quiet brilliance and integrity and the most inspiring and supportive of co-authors.

Lastly, I would like to express my heartfelt thanks to my parents, Trevor and Diana Donald; my brother, Paul Donald; my sister-in-law, Fiona Roberts; and my children, Nathan and Ruby Rogers.

Philip Leach

In loving memory of my father, Frank Leach (1 May 1935–1 January 2016).

I would like to dedicate this book to my mother, Marion Leach. I should also put it on record that it has been an utter joy and privilege to co-author a book with the remarkable Alice Donald.

Sincere thanks also to my inspirational colleagues at EHRAC and at Middlesex University.

Foreword

In recent years, our understanding of the roles which national parliaments can play in the practical implementation of human rights norms and decisions has developed significantly, energized by considerable political and academic interest and scrutiny. When the forty-seven Council of Europe member states met in Brussels in March 2015, for a high-level conference on the 'Implementation of the European Convention on Human Rights, our Shared Responsibility', the governments explicitly acknowledged the value of parliamentary involvement, alongside the executive and the judiciary. The Brussels Declaration urged governments to take steps to improve the awareness of the work of the European Court of Human Rights amongst members of parliament and to involve parliaments in a more transparent 'implementation dialogue', which of course should not be the preserve of governments alone.

During my time as President of the Parliamentary Assembly of the Council of Europe, I have been emboldened in my view that the Assembly can and does play an important role in strengthening the democratic legitimacy of the Council of Europe's human rights mechanisms, including the Court. The Assembly was the continent's first supranational parliamentary body, and, in the words of the signatories to the 1949 Statute, it provides a 'means through which the aspirations of the European peoples may be formulated and expressed, the governments thus being kept continually in touch with European public opinion'.

One of the important areas of focus for the Assembly continues to be the implementation of judgments of the European Court—and the Brussels Declaration was highly supportive of our work in this field. In September 2015, the Assembly published a further Recommendation on the implementation of judgments, based on a report by my colleague Klaas de Vries, who described the scale of outstanding problems as alarming. The Assembly deplored the lack of political will of particular states to implement judgments of the European Court fully and rapidly, and urged the Committee of Ministers to take firmer measures with states that do not comply, including using the 'infringement proceedings' mechanism.

I therefore warmly welcome this important study by Dr Alice Donald and Professor Philip Leach which tackles and elucidates these themes. They cast their spotlight on five European states (Ukraine, Romania, the UK, the Netherlands, and Germany), providing an important depth of analysis. Crucially, however, they also situate their country studies within the broader political, legal, and academic contexts and discussions, thus analysing the institutional and political pressures on the Convention system ('backlog' and 'backlash') and the perceptions, of some commentators, of a crisis of democratic legitimacy within the European human rights system. It is also significant that they address recent debates about the extent to which the European Court is inclined to take account of the extent of any prior review by national parliaments, in assessing the proportionality of restrictions on European Convention rights—thus, can deference be 'earned' and does this represent a deepening of the concept of subsidiarity?

For all of these reasons, I highly commend this book to my European parliamentary colleagues in particular, and to anyone (practitioners, scholars, students) with an interest in the European regional human rights system.

Anne Brasseur
President, Parliamentary Assembly of
the Council of Europe (2014–16)

Acknowledgements

We are grateful to all those who gave interviews during our research and were so generous with their time and insights. Thanks are also due to the following for helpful advice on sections of the book: Ed Bates, Dmytro Kotliar, Günter Schirmer, Roman Schmidt-Radefeldt, and Anne-Katrin Speck. For research and translation assistance at various stages, we would also like to express gratitude to Nicola Bruch, Nicole Bürli, and Laurie van Dalm.

When work on the book began, both authors were based at London Metropolitan University. We are especially grateful to Aruna Dudhia for her excellent administrative support in the early stages of the research. In 2013, we moved to Middlesex University, and we are pleased to have the opportunity to express our thanks to colleagues in the School of Law—and especially the Dean of the School, Joshua Castellino—for the stimulating, supportive, and collegiate environment that welcomed us.

The research underpinning this book was funded by the Nuffield Foundation: we are grateful to the Foundation for its generous support, and to Sharon Witherspoon, Teresa Williams, and Alison Rees for their assistance throughout. In May 2015, a conference hosted by the Polish Senate, and funded by the Nuffield Foundation, provided a valuable opportunity to invite speakers from various Council of Europe institutions and member states to Warsaw to debate the themes of the book. We are grateful to Dominika Bychawska-Siniarska and Iuliia Cheromukhina of the Helsinki Foundation for Human Rights (Warsaw), and the staff of the Senate, for assistance in organizing the conference. Thanks are also due to the speakers: Dr Adam Bodnar, Dr Başak Çalı, Justyna Chrzanowska, Daniel Florea, Katarzyna Gonera, Zdravka Kalaydjieva, Egbert Myjer, Senator Michał Seweryński, Fredrik Sundberg, Christian de Vos, Dr Almut Wittling-Vogel, and Mirosław Wróblewski. To two other speakers at the conference—Andrew Drzemczewski, Head of the Legal Affairs and Human Rights Department at the Parliamentary Assembly of the Council of Europe, and Murray Hunt, Legal Adviser to the Joint Committee of Human Rights in the UK parliament—we owe special thanks for conversations and correspondence generously shared over several years which have been invaluable in shaping our understanding of the themes underlying this book. Andrew also assisted us on 27 June 2013 to present our research findings to the Committee on Legal Affairs and Human Rights and Committee on Political Affairs and Democracy of the Parliamentary Assembly, to whose members we are grateful.

Warm thanks are also due to Merel Alstein and Emma Endean at Oxford University Press for their patient support and care at seeing the book through to publication.

Contents

Table of Cases

COMMITTEE OF MINISTERS RESOLUTIONS AND MEMORANDA

EUROPEAN COMMISSION OF HUMAN RIGHTS

EUROPEAN COMMITTEE OF SOCIAL RIGHTS

EUROPEAN COURT OF HUMAN RIGHTS

NATIONAL JURISDICTIONS

Germany

United Kingdom

Table of Legislation

EUROPEAN CONVENTION ON HUMAN RIGHTS

OTHER INTERNATIONAL INSTRUMENTS

UNITED KINGDOM LEGISLATION

Statutes

List of Abbreviations

AIV	Advisory Council on International Affairs (*Adviesraad Internationale Vraagstukken*) (Netherlands)
BVerfGE	*Bundesverfassungsgericht* (Federal Constitutional Court) (Germany)
CDDH	Steering Committee for Human Rights (*Comité Directeur pour les Droits de l'Homme*)
ECHR	European Convention on Human Rights
ECommHR	European Commission of Human Rights
ECtHR	European Court of Human Rights
EHRC	Equality and Human Rights Commission (UK)
EU	European Union
FCO	Foreign and Commonwealth Office (UK)
FDP	Free Democratic Party (*Freie Demokratische Partei*) (Germany)
GC	Grand Chamber
HRTF	Human Rights Trust Fund
IACtHR	Inter-American Court of Human Rights
ICCPR	International Covenant on Civil and Political Rights
JCHR	Joint Committee on Human Rights (UK)
NGO	Non-governmental organization
NHRI	National human rights institution
NIHR	Netherlands Institute for Human Rights
NIM	National Institute of Magistracy (Romania)
NJCM	Netherlands section of the International Commission of Jurists (*Nederlands Juristen Comité voor de Mensenrechten*)
OSJI	Open Society Justice Initiative
PACE	Parliamentary Assembly of the Council of Europe
PPSD	Parliamentary Project Support Division of the Parliamentary Assembly of the Council of Europe
PVV	Party for Freedom (*Partij voor de Vrijheid*) (Netherlands)
RIS	Romanian Intelligence Service
SPD	Social Democratic Party (*Sozialdemokratische Partei Deutschlands*) (Germany)
SVP	Swiss People's Party (*Schweizerische Volkspartei*)
VVD	People's Party for Freedom and Democracy (*Volkspartij voor Vrijheid en Democratie*) (Netherlands)

1

Introduction

Origins and Methodology

The role of parliaments in interpreting, applying, and monitoring the implementation of human rights norms and standards has been described as 'an idea whose time has come'.[1] In recent years, both scholarly and political interest in the parliamentary dimension of the state's obligation to protect and promote human rights has flourished.[2] Within the Council of Europe, where this book's primary focus lies, attention to the parliamentary role has been driven largely by the need to strengthen the efficiency and effectiveness of human rights implementation at the domestic level—an imperative which, it is widely recognized, parliaments have both the power and obligation to pursue, in tandem with the executive and judicial branches of the state.[3]

Allied to the efficiency and effectiveness imperative is a normative concern that human rights, and especially *international* human rights regimes, lack democratic legitimacy.[4] Whether such a 'democratic deficit' exists, and if so, how to redress it, are matters of contestation. Increasingly, the dichotomous understanding of judicial and political actors as antagonists, each vying with the other to have the final say on human rights questions, has given way to convergence behind the idea that all branches of the state—the executive, parliament, and the courts—are the 'inseparable and intersecting constituents of ... democratic systems'[5] and partners in the shared endeavour of protecting and realizing human rights. Yet the 'democratic critique'[6] has not been silenced and, indeed, has grown to a crescendo in the

[1] Dr Hywel Francis MP, Welcoming remarks to a seminar organized by the Parliamentary Assembly of the Council of Europe (PACE) on 'The Role of National Parliaments in the Implementation of Judgments of the European Court of Human Rights', Portcullis House, Westminster, 14 October 2013 (on file).

[2] See, especially, Murray Hunt, Hayley Hooper, and Paul Yowell, eds., *Parliaments and Human Rights: Redressing the Democratic Deficit* (Oxford: Hart Publishing, 2015).

[3] See, for example, Parliamentary Assembly of the Council of Europe (PACE) Resolution 1823 (2011), National parliaments: guarantors of human rights in Europe, 23 June 2011, para. 1.

[4] See, especially, Andreas Føllesdal, Johan Karlsson Schaffer, and Geir Ulfstein, eds., *The Legitimacy of International Human Rights Regimes: Legal, Political and Philosophical Perspectives* (Cambridge: Cambridge University Press, 2013).

[5] David Kinley, 'Finding and Filling the Democratic Deficit in Human Rights', in Hunt, Hooper, and Yowell, eds. (n 2): 29, 32.

[6] Murray Hunt, 'Introduction', in Hunt, Hooper, and Yowell, eds. (n 2): 1, 3.

UK where, at the time of writing, the government has not ruled out withdrawing from the European Convention on Human Rights (ECHR or 'the Convention') if it fails to secure reform allowing it to opt out of judgments of the Strasbourg-based European Court of Human Rights (ECtHR or 'the Court').[7]

The twin imperatives of, one the one hand, efficiency and effectiveness and, on the other hand, legitimacy have combined to focus attention on the most effective institutional arrangements for human rights protection, both at the domestic and international levels. This discussion is increasingly, and properly, preoccupied not by abstract determinations about whether political or judicial actors have superior attributes for decisions regarding the meaning and scope of human rights, but by both practical and normative questions about how parliaments, executive bodies, and courts—both national and international—interact: that is, how they 'speak to' and 'listen to' each other so as, variously, to regulate, monitor, incentivize, or defer to each other's decisions and actions.

This book contributes to this burgeoning area of scholarship and practice by examining the role of parliaments in the implementation of judgments of the ECtHR and, more broadly, the relationship between parliaments and the Convention system in both its practical and normative dimensions. Detailed analysis focuses on five states: Ukraine, Romania, the UK, the Netherlands, and Germany (see 1.2.2). We are concerned with both the institutional and political dimensions of the parliamentary role, since human rights implementation and oversight depends upon both the capacity and the will of parliamentarians. In respect of capacity, the book documents the development of parliamentary structures and mechanisms for human rights implementation and explores their effectiveness and their interaction with other branches of the state, as well as with civil society, national human rights institutions, and Council of Europe bodies. We are also concerned with the extent to which parliamentarians view it as their remit to interpret, apply, or monitor the implementation of human rights norms and standards. In respect of will, we examine the political dynamics of compliance with Convention standards and ECtHR judgments and the incentives and disincentives that condition the political response to judgments. As political actors, parliaments not only advance implementation but also, in some instances, complicate or obstruct it. Notwithstanding this complexity, our central argument is that invigoration of the role of parliaments in Council of Europe states is crucial to alleviating pressures on the European Convention system of both an institutional and political nature.

[7] 'Cameron Refuses to Rule Out Leaving European Convention on Human Rights', *The Guardian*, 3 June 2015. In November 2015, the parliamentary Joint Committee on Human Rights (JCHR) invited the Justice Secretary, Michael Gove, to confirm, inter alia, that the government had ruled out both withdrawal from the Convention and ending the UK's obligation under Article 46(1) ECHR to abide by the final judgment of the ECtHR in any case to which they are a party; see letter from Harriet Harman MP, chair of the JCHR, to Michael Gove, 4 November 2015. At the time of writing, no response from the government has been published on the JCHR's website.

1.1 Institutional and Political Pressures on the Convention System

The efficiency/effectiveness and legitimacy imperatives identified above are of pressing concern within the Council of Europe and its main constituent bodies—the Court, the Committee of Ministers (the inter-governmental arm), and the Parliamentary Assembly (PACE). The source of this concern—and the consequent emphasis on strengthening the parliamentary role—is not hard to identify. The Convention system has in recent years faced pressures which have been encapsulated in two words: backlog and backlash.[8] These pressures, both institutional and political, have distinct origins but have combined in such a way as to create existential fears for the future of the Convention system, hitherto regarded by some as an 'unparalleled success story'.[9]

1.1.1 The backlog

The backlog refers to the accumulation of applications at the Court, which reached a staggering 160,000 in September 2011.[10] This mountainous backlog was the basis of the argument made by certain politicians,[11] academics,[12] and figures formerly associated with the Court[13] that the Court should play a 'constitutionalist' role, delivering—whether on the basis of stipulated criteria or judicial discretion—fewer judgments relating only to large-scale violations, structural, or systemic problems, or important questions of the interpretation and application of the Convention. This proposed reform, which would effectively curtail the right of individual application, has not found favour either among states,[14] the Court,[15] the Parliamentary Assembly,[16] or civil society organizations.[17]

[8] Julie Fraser, 'Conclusion: The European Convention on Human Rights as a Common European Endeavour', in Spyridōn I. Phlogaitēs, Tom Zwart, and Julie Fraser, eds., *The European Court of Human Rights and Its Discontents: Turning Criticism into Strength* (Cheltenham: Edward Elgar Publishing, 2013): 192, 193.

[9] Johan Karlsson Schaffer, Andreas Føllesdal, and Geir Ulfstein, 'International Human Rights and the Challenge of Legitimacy', in Føllesdal, Schaffer, and Ulfstein, eds. (n 4): 1, 5.

[10] European Court of Human Rights, *Annual Report 2012* (2013) 6.

[11] See David Cameron, 'Speech on the European Court of Human Rights', 25 January 2012, in which the Prime Minister argued that the ECtHR should not act as a 'small claims court'.

[12] Fiona de Londras, 'Dual Functionality and the Persistent Frailty of the European Court of Human Rights', *European Human Rights Law Review* 1 (2013): 38.

[13] Luzius Wildhaber, 'Rule of Law: "Constitutional Court" or "Guardian of Individuals"?', Proceedings of the MultiRights Annual Conference on 'The Long-Term Future of the European Court of Human Rights', organized by PluriCourts under the auspices of the Council of Europe, Holmenkollen Park Hotel, Oslo, Norway, 7–8 April 2014 ('MultiRights Annual Conference 2014'): 92.

[14] Steering Committee for Human Rights, Committee of Experts on Reform of the Court (DH-GDR) Draft CDDH report on the longer-term future of the system of the European Convention on Human Rights, DH-GDR(2015)R9 Addendum, 20 November 2015, paras. 89–93.

[15] European Court of Human Rights, Preliminary Opinion of the Court in Preparation for the Brighton Conference, 20 February 2012, para. 25.

[16] PACE Resolution 1856 (2012), Guaranteeing the authority and effectiveness of the European Convention on Human Rights, 24 January 2012, para. 2.

[17] Joint NGO statement, 'The Brighton Declaration Must Strengthen Human Rights Protection in Europe and Preserve the Integrity and Authority of the European Court of Human Rights', 13 April 2012.

Moreover, such arguments are undermined by the fact that, since 2011, the Court has achieved a remarkable reduction in its docket, due largely to changes introduced since 2010 under Protocol No. 14 of the Convention to streamline its processing of applications and, more contentiously, tighter admissibility criteria and stricter procedural conditions for applicants. As of 31 October 2015, there were 66,500 pending applications.[18] A substantial proportion of these are repetitive cases arising from systemic or structural violations of the Convention in a handful of countries (principally, Ukraine, Russia, Turkey, and Italy).[19] Having cut the size of its docket by more than half in a matter of four years, the Court has adopted a strategy to reduce the remaining backlog[20] to fewer than 20,000 cases by the end of 2016, and steadily dispose of the remainder within the following eight years, while at the same time dealing expeditiously with new applications, which are expected to remain at around 60–70,000 annually.[21] Elimination of the backlog, however, is dependent on the provision of a temporary additional budget of some €30 million, and it remains to be seen whether states will be forthcoming with this financial support.[22]

Another indicator of the health of the Convention system is the number of the Court's judgments that remain unimplemented, often for many years. At the end of 2014, 10,904 non-executed judgments[23] were pending before the Committee of Ministers, the executive arm of the Council of Europe with formal responsibility for supervising the execution of ECtHR judgments.[24] This figure was the second small year-on-year decrease but it was still higher than 2011 and almost three times the number a decade earlier. Moreover, 2014 saw a slight increase in the number of non-executed cases under the 'enhanced' supervision of the Committee of Ministers (such as those involving structural or systemic violations of the Convention),[25] and

[18] European Court of Human Rights, Pending Applications Allocated to a Judicial Formation, 31 October 2015.

[19] Steering Committee for Human Rights, Committee of Experts on Reform of the Court (DH-GDR), Drafting Group 'F' on Reform of the Court (GT-GDR-F), Presentation to the 3rd meeting by the Registrar of the European Court of Human Rights, GT-GDR-F(2014)021, 24 September 2014, 4, 8–9.

[20] Since 2012, the Court has defined the 'backlog' as consisting of cases which are not dealt with within deadlines set out by Council of Europe member states in the Brighton Declaration arising from the High Level Conference on the Future of the European Court of Human Rights, 19–20 April 2012. Para. 20(h) of the Declaration stipulates that the Court should deal with all incoming applications within one year of registration, either by rejecting them or communicating them to the respondent state, with an additional target of terminating the proceedings within a further two years.

[21] GT-GDR-F(2014)021 (n 19) 9–10.

[22] GT-GDR-F(2014)021 (n 19) 10. The Registrar of the Court indicated that around €30 million would be required over eight years from 2014 to equip the Court to process the most stubborn element of the backlog; that is, the roughly 18,400 cases that are well-founded but are neither repetitive cases nor cases designated as high priority.

[23] Committee of Ministers, *Supervision of the Execution of Judgments and Decisions of the European Court of Human Rights: 8th Annual Report of the Committee of Ministers 2014* (2015) ('8th Annual Report of the Committee of Ministers 2014') 27.

[24] Under Article 46(2) ECHR.

[25] Up from 6,707 in 2013 to 6,718 in 2014; 8th Annual Report of the Committee of Ministers 2014 (n 23) 30. For an explanation of the categories of cases that fall under 'enhanced' supervision, see 2.5.1.

a larger proportionate increase in those which had been awaiting execution for more than five years.[26] Some positive trends were also evident, such as the more rapid execution of judgments which became final after 2011, compared to older judgments, indicating that the revised working methods adopted by the Committee of Ministers since 2011 have had some effect (see 2.5.1).[27] Despite this positive indicator, the Committee of Ministers notes that certain cases reveal significant 'pockets of resistance', linked variously to entrenched social prejudice (e.g., concerning Roma or other minority groups), political considerations, or, more commonly, technical or economic obstacles to implementation.[28] The Parliamentary Assembly has deplored the lack of political will of certain states to fulfil their obligations under the Convention, and described the scale of non-compliance as 'alarming'.[29] Overall, the figures attest to the 'implementation crisis' identified by the Open Society Justice Institute as afflicting not only the European human rights system but also other regional and international human rights mechanisms.[30]

1.1.2 The backlash

The backlash, too, is not confined to Europe. Schaffer, Føllesdal, and Ulfstein venture that human rights regimes around the world 'increasingly face potentially disabling scepticism and critique, resentment and even resistance from many of the agents involved'.[31] The backlash has been most evident in the Inter-American human rights system: Venezuela has withdrawn from the system, accusing both the Inter-American Commission and Court of Human Rights of political interventionism.[32] At the time of writing, the Dominican Republic's continued membership of the Inter-American system is in jeopardy after a ruling by the Constitutional Tribunal declared that the country's accession to the jurisdiction of the Inter-American Court in 1999 was unconstitutional.[33] The governments of Bolivia, Nicaragua, Ecuador, and Brazil have also criticized the Inter-American human rights bodies as being 'a platform for US imperialism, an obsolete institution inadequate to contemporary geopolitical realities, or a biased judicial body exceeding its jurisdiction'.[34] In Africa, political resistance led by the Zimbabwean government

[26] Up from 128 in 2013 to 160 in 2014; 8th Annual Report of the Committee of Ministers 2014 (n 23) 11.

[27] 8th Annual Report of the Committee of Ministers 2014 (n 23) 10.

[28] 8th Annual Report of the Committee of Ministers 2014 (n 23) 11.

[29] PACE, Committee on Legal Affairs and Human Rights, Implementation of judgments of the European Court of Human Rights, Doc. 13864, 9 September 2015 (Rapporteur: Klaas de Vries) paras. 7, 46.

[30] Open Society Justice Initiative, *From Rights to Remedies: Structures and Strategies for Implementing International Human Rights Decisions* (New York: Open Society Foundations, 2013) 23.

[31] Schaffer, Føllesdal, and Ulfstein (n 9) 2.

[32] Organization of American States, 'IACHR Deeply Concerned over Result of Venezuela's Denunciation of the American Convention', 10 September 2013.

[33] Open Society Justice Initiative, 'Flawed Ruling in the Dominican Republic Threatens Human Rights Protections', 8 November 2014.

[34] Manuela Picq, 'Is the Inter-American Commission of Human Rights too Progressive?', *Al-Jazeera*, 9 June 2012.

led in 2012 to the Southern African Development Community's Tribunal being stripped of its mandate to hear individual human rights complaints.[35]

In the European context, challenges to the Convention system have emanated not only from illiberal states such as Russia,[36] but also those that pride themselves as being champions of human rights, democracy, and the rule of law, some of which have railed against external human rights supervision as an illegitimate constraint on their domestic democratic affairs. Critiques cohere around a number of now-familiar narratives. The most prevalent is the assertion that the ECtHR has used its dynamic interpretation of the Convention as a means of expanding its authority and jurisdiction, even to the point of 'human rights imperialism'.[37] This argument is primarily based on the propositions that the Convention, by being interpreted as a 'living instrument', is being applied in ways that would not have been foreseen by its drafters, or that the Court is taking an over-activist approach which interferes in an undemocratic fashion with decisions made by national authorities. Judgments which are perceived to constrain domestic decision-making on matters of crime, national security, and immigration have been especially contentious. Judgments concerning sensitive matters of religion or belief have also provoked a political backlash.[38]

The Court has endured particular obloquy in the UK. This has largely been expressed in bursts of political outrage against particular judgments. It made the Prime Minister David Cameron 'physically ill' to contemplate giving any convicted prisoner the vote, as required by the *Hirst* judgment in 2005,[39] which held that the UK's indiscriminate ban on prisoner voting was a disproportionate interference with the right to free elections under Article 3 of Protocol No. 1 to the Convention.[40] The Home Secretary, Theresa May, deplored the Court's 'crazy interpretation of our human rights laws' which had delayed the deportation of the terror

[35] Frederick Cowell, 'The Death of the Southern African Development Community Tribunal's Human Rights Jurisdiction', *Human Rights Law Review* 13(1) (2013): 153.

[36] A bill which would empower the Russian Constitutional Court to determine whether findings by international bodies on protection of human rights and freedoms (including those of the ECtHR) are to be implemented or not was passed on its first reading on 1 December 2015, with only three deputies voting against, and one abstaining. See Halya Coynash, 'Russia Moves to Legislate Impunity from International Law', Human Rights in Ukraine (website of the Kharkiv Human Rights Protection Group), 2 December 2015. On 8 December 2015, the Committee on Legal Affairs and Human Rights of the Parliamentary Assembly agreed to ask for an opinion on the matter from the Venice Commission (Committee on Legal Affairs and Human Rights, Synopsis of the meeting held in Paris on 8 December 2015, AS/Jur (2015) CB 08, 10 December 2015, 2).

[37] Lord Dyson, 'The Extraterritorial Application of the European Convention on Human Rights: Now on a Firmer Footing but is it a Sound One?', University of Essex, 30 January 2014, 2. See also Kanstantsin Dzehtsiarou, 'European Consensus and the Evolutive Interpretation of the European Convention on Human Rights', *German Law Journal* 12(10) (2011): 1730.

[38] See, for example, Susanna Mancini, 'The Crucifix Rage: Supranational Constitutionalism Bumps against the Counter-Majoritarian Difficulty', *European Constitutional Law Review* 6 (2010): 6, referring to the revolt by almost the entire political class in Italy against the Chamber judgment in *Lautsi v Italy*, No. 30814/06, 3 November 2009 (which was overturned by the Grand Chamber judgment of 18 March 2011).

[39] *Hirst v UK (No. 2)*, No. 74205/01, 6 October 2005 [GC].

[40] HC Deb, 3 November 2010, vol. 517, col. 921.

suspect Abu Qatada to Jordan until assurances had been obtained that he would not be tried there on the basis of evidence obtained by torture.[41] For his part, Dominic Raab MP, who was made Parliamentary Under-Secretary of State for Justice in the Conservative government elected in May 2015, lambasted the 'warped moral compass' of the Strasbourg Court following a ruling that for whole-life prison tariffs to be compatible with the Convention there must be a possibility of review within UK law—a judgment which in his view highlighted the need to 'insulate Britain from such perverse and arbitrary European rulings'.[42] Judgments that have prevented the deportation of foreign criminals on the grounds of their right to family life under Article 8 ECHR have also been asserted as the basis for keeping open the option of withdrawal from the Convention.[43]

Antipathy towards the ECtHR in the UK is fuelled by, and frequently confused with, scepticism about the European Union.[44] In this sense, hostility towards the Court may be viewed as a proxy for the concurrent yet unrelated crisis over the broader project of European political integration and its perceived democratic deficit.[45] It has been suggested that the Court presents an attractive target for British politicians seeking to satisfy Eurosceptic opinion since it tends not to 'answer back'.[46] The UK debate has also been distinctive in its insistence on the primacy of parliament vis-à-vis the ECtHR; critics have called for a 'democratic override' of Strasbourg judgments to which a majority in parliament is opposed (see 4.6).[47]

Some senior judicial figures have lent their weight to the critique of the ECtHR. In an influential lecture in 2009, the former law lord, Lord Hoffmann, argued that the Strasbourg Court 'lacks constitutional legitimacy'.[48] More recently, Lord Judge argued that 'the imposition of [the Court's] views on Parliament represents

[41] HC Deb, 8 July 2013, vol. 566, col. 24 (referring to *Othman (Abu Qatada) v UK*, No. 8139/09, 17 January 2012).

[42] 'Calls Grow to Boycott "Toxic" Human Rights Court', *The Telegraph*, 9 July 2013 (referring to *Vinter and Others v UK*, Nos. 66069/09, 130/10, and 3896/10, 9 July 2013 [GC]).

[43] Prime Minister David Cameron told the House of Commons on 3 June 2015 (n 7): '[O]ur plans, set out in our manifesto, don't involve us leaving the [ECHR]. But let's be absolutely clear. If we can't achieve what we need—and I'm very clear about that when we've got these foreign criminals committing offence after offence and we can't send them home because of their right to a family life—that needs to change. And I rule out absolutely nothing in getting that done.'

[44] Kanstantsin Dzehtsiarou and Alan Greene, 'Legitimacy and the Future of the European Court of Human Rights: Critical Perspectives from Academia and Practitioners', *German Law Journal* 12(10) (2011): 1707.

[45] Schaffer, Føllesdal, and Ulfstein (n 9) 11. See also Lord Neuberger, 'The British and Europe', Cambridge Freshfields Annual Law Lecture, 12 February 2014.

[46] Conor Gearty, 'On Fantasy Island: British Politics, English Judges and the European Convention on Human Rights', UK Constitutional Law Association blog, 13 November 2014.

[47] See, for example, Jack Straw, *Aspects of Law Reform: An Insider's Perspective* (Cambridge: Cambridge University Press, 2013) Chapter 2.

[48] Lord Hoffmann, 'The Universality of Human Rights', Judicial Studies Board Annual Lecture, 19 March 2009, para. 38. Lord Hoffmann added (para. 44): 'I have no objection to the text of the Convention being used as a standard against which a country's compliance with human rights can be measured for the purposes of … political criticism.… The problem is the Court; and the right of individual petition, which enables the Court to intervene in the details and nuances of the domestic laws of Member States.'

a dramatic and unconstitutional extension of judicial authority'.[49] The former President of the Court and UK judge, Sir Nicolas Bratza, lamented the fact that such interventions 'gave an air of legal respectability' to what had hitherto been 'essentially a political campaign to denigrate the Court and the Convention system as a whole'.[50] Indeed, the Justice Secretary Michael Gove told parliament in May 2015 that concern among senior judges about the relationship between the UK courts and the ECtHR was the reason why 'we need to look at the matter again'.[51] However, while critical judicial commentary about the ECtHR has dominated the headlines, the weight of senior judicial opinion (expressed in speeches extra-judicially) has, in fact, been favourable to the Court.[52] For example, in the view of Lord Phillips, the former President of the Supreme Court, 'Europe needs the Convention and Europe needs the Court. I have no hesitation in expressing my conclusion that Strasbourg is a powerful force for good'.[53]

In October 2014, the Conservative Party issued a document proposing fundamental reform of UK human rights law,[54] including making judgments of the Court merely advisory in respect of the UK and breaking the formal link between domestic courts and the ECtHR created by the Human Rights Act (HRA) 1998—reforms which the former Conservative Attorney General Dominic Grieve argues would make the Convention 'inoperable'.[55] The document stated that should it be unable to secure the Council of Europe's agreement for these unilateral reforms, 'the UK would be left with no alternative but to withdraw' from the Convention.[56] The option of withdrawal was not referred to in the Conservative Party manifesto for the general election in May 2015, which did, however, pledge to 'curtail the role of the European Court of Human Rights'.[57]

Criticism of the Court within well-established democracies has not been confined to the UK. Politicians and commentators in the Nordic countries have expressed concern about the effects of 'European judicial review' of domestic legislative acts, including that conducted by the ECtHR and (in respect of European Union law) by the Court of Justice of the European Union.[58] In March 2013, the

[49] Lord Judge, 'A View from London', *Counsel*, October 2014. See also Lord Sumption, 'The Limits of Law', 27th Sultan Azlan Shah Lecture, Kuala Lumpur, 20 November 2013.

[50] Sir Nicolas Bratza, 'The Convention, the Common Law and the Strasbourg Court—Apocalypse Now?', University of Nottingham, 12 March 2014.

[51] HC Deb, 28 May 2015, vol. 596, col. 291.

[52] Ed Bates, 'The Senior Judiciary on "Strasbourg"—More Supportive than Some Would Have You Believe', UK Constitutional Law Association blog, 28 May 2015.

[53] The Rt Hon the Lord Phillips of Worth Matravers, 'European Human Rights—A Force for Good or a Threat to Democracy?', Centre of European Law Lecture, King's College London, 17 June 2014, 13.

[54] Conservative Party, *Protecting Human Rights in the UK: The Conservatives' Proposals for Changing Britain's Human Rights Laws* (2014).

[55] 'Tory Plans Will Destroy Human Rights across Europe, Warns Dominic Grieve', *The Guardian*, 11 June 2015.

[56] Conservative Party (n 54) 8.

[57] Conservative Party, *The Conservative Party Manifesto 2015*, 58.

[58] Andreas Føllesdal and Marlene Wind, 'Introduction: Nordic Reluctance towards Judicial Review under Siege', *Nordic Journal of Human Rights* 27 (2009): 131; Jaakko Husa, 'Nordic Constitutionalism and European Human Rights. Mixing Oil and Water?', *Scandinavian Studies in Law* 55 (2010): 101.

right-wing Swiss People's Party (SVP) made a parliamentary submission raising the possibility of denouncing the Convention with a view to withdrawal, a move strongly rejected by the Swiss Federal Council.[59] The SVP has also sought to introduce a new clause into the Swiss Federal Constitution stating that the Constitution takes precedence over public international law.[60] The move was denounced by all other major parties;[61] however, the liberal Free Democratic Party introduced its own initiative to seek to oblige the ECtHR to focus on its 'core purpose' by further tightening its admissibility criteria, among other measures.[62] As explored in 8.2.1, contention about the Court and its influence with respect to the Netherlands gained momentum in 2010–12. In 2012, Joost Taverne of the People's Party for Freedom and Democracy introduced a private members' bill to amend Articles 93 and 94 of the Dutch Constitution, which provide for direct applicability of international legal norms and accord them a higher priority than domestic legal norms. The Taverne bill seeks to strip Dutch courts of their power to disapply acts of parliament in the event of conflict with self-executing provisions of treaty law, [63] thereby, the proposal argues, 'rebalancing democratically legitimate decision-making and judicial review'.[64] Since 2012, however, the 'critical wind' against the Court has subsided,[65] in part due to an effective pro-Strasbourg counter-mobilization in the Dutch Senate. A recent study examining the reception of the Convention in Belgium, France, Germany, the Netherlands, Sweden, and the UK concluded that '[in] Belgium, France, Germany and Sweden, the overall legitimacy of the Court and its judgments is hardly subject to debate'.[66] Nevertheless, antipathy towards the Court surfaced in France in 2015, when a member of the conservative Union for a Popular Movement tabled a resolution in the National Assembly calling on the government to negotiate with other Council of Europe states to review the composition and powers of the ECtHR and to ban applications to the Court by individuals convicted of terrorist offences.[67] The proposed resolution, which was not passed, called on the government to state that it would be ready to denounce the Convention if the desired reform was not secured.[68]

[59] 13.3237—Interpellation, Dénonciation de la Convention de sauvegarde des droits de l'homme et des libertés fondamentales, presented by Toni Brunner in the National Council, 22 March 2013.

[60] SVP, 'Volksinitiative zur Umsetzung von Volksentscheiden: Schweizer Recht geht Fremdem Recht Vor' ['People's Initiative to Implement Referenda: Swiss Law Takes Precedence over Foreign Law'], 12 August 2014.

[61] Sarah Lambrecht, 'HRA Watch: Reform, Repeal, Replace? Criticism of the European Court of Human Rights: A UK Phenomenon?', UK Constitutional Law Association blog, 27 July 2015.

[62] FDP, 'Bessere Vereinbarkeit von Völkerrecht und Landesrecht' ['Reconciling International Law and Domestic Law'], 17 June 2013.

[63] Lower House, Parliamentary Papers 2011/12, 33 359, Nos. 1–3 (the 'Taverne Proposal').

[64] Taverne Proposal, No. 3, Explanatory Memorandum, section 1.

[65] Janneke Gerards and Joseph Fleuren, 'The Netherlands', in Janneke Gerards and Joseph Fleuren, eds., *Implementation of the European Convention on Human Rights and of the Judgments of the ECtHR in National Case-Law: A Comparative Analysis* (Antwerp-Oxford-Portland: Intersentia, 2014): 217, 256.

[66] Janneke Gerards and Joseph Fleuren, 'Comparative Analysis', in Gerards and Fleuren, eds. (n 65): 333, 369. See also Barbara Oomen, 'The Rights for Others: The Contested Homecoming of Human Rights in the Netherlands', *Netherlands Quarterly of Human Rights* 31(1) (2013): 41.

[67] Motion for Resolution No. 2601, proposed by Mr Pierre Lellouche, 2 April 2015.

[68] A member state may withdraw from the Convention by a process of 'denunciation' (Article 58). This requires six months' notice to be given to the Council of Europe.

In summary, while antipathy towards the Court has surfaced outside the UK, it has tended to be sporadic, confined to the political margins, and/or expressed in response to specific judgments rather than challenging the underlying legitimacy or authority of the Court. In some instances, centrist parties have adopted a stronger rhetoric against the Court, apparently in response to pressure from populist right-wing parties. However, in no other Council of Europe state have proposals to weaken the Court or denounce the Convention become part of *mainstream* political discourse as they have in the UK. To this extent, the debate in the UK may be seen as an aberration; moreover, expressions of defiance towards the Court can in some instances be identified as the result of 'contagion' from the UK to other states.[69]

Paradoxically, at the same time as the Court is challenged for transgressing its mandate, it is also under fire for being ineffectual, in respect of its (now diminishing) docket crisis.[70] It is here that the backlog risks intensifying the backlash, in the sense that long delays in judgments being issued or implemented may erode the reputation of the Convention system as one that is able to deliver swift and effective justice.[71]

Criticisms of the competence, authority, and legitimacy of the ECtHR have been rebutted by senior figures in the Court,[72] among others.[73] They argue that the Court's dynamic interpretation of the Convention is common to many treaties (as well as domestic legal systems) and reflects an essential adjustment to changing social circumstances and to new or previously neglected or unrecognized threats to fundamental rights and freedoms. Moreover, it is argued that many of the Court's critics have lost sight of the origins of the Convention as a system for the *collective* guarantee of human rights, in which each state is exposed to the same possibility of scrutiny in return for the shared benefits of regional peace and stability and the effective protection of human rights across the forty-seven states of the Council of Europe.[74] In recent years, scholars have begun to pay systematic attention to the legitimacy and authority of the international human rights judiciary in general, and the ECtHR in particular—a debate explored in Chapter 4.

[69] Alice Donald and Philip Leach, 'Hostility to the European Court and the Risks of Contagion', UK Human Rights blog, 21 November 2013.

[70] Schaffer, Føllesdal, and Ulfstein (n 9) 5–6.

[71] This factor should not be overstated. Research on the perceived legitimacy of the ECtHR among domestic actors found that the normative performance of the Court plays a greater role in the assessment of its overall legitimacy than does its managerial performance, including in respect of the length of proceedings. See Başak Çalı, Anne Koch, and Nicola Bruch, *The Legitimacy of the European Court of Human Rights: The View from the Ground* (Department of Political Science, University College London, 2011) 13.

[72] Nicolas Bratza, 'The Relationship between the UK Courts and Strasbourg', *European Human Rights Law Review* 5 (2011): 505; Michael O'Boyle, 'The Future of the European Court of Human Rights', *German Law Journal* 12 (2011): 1862; Robert Spano, 'Universality or Diversity of Human Rights? Strasbourg in the Age of Subsidiarity', *Human Rights Law Review* 14(2) (2014): 1.

[73] Alice Donald, Jane Gordon, and Philip Leach, *The UK and the European Court of Human Rights*, Research Report 83 (Equality and Human Rights Commission, 2012); Dominic Grieve, 'Is the European Convention Working?', Rule of Law Lecture, Faculty of Advocates, Edinburgh, 21 September 2015.

[74] O'Boyle (n 72) 1867.

1.1.3 The view from the Council of Europe

The inter-related challenges described above have largely determined the priorities of the process within the Council of Europe of reforming the Convention system in the longer term. It has been repeatedly stated at the inter-governmental level that more effective domestic implementation of Convention standards and judgments of the ECtHR is the key to reducing the caseload of the Court and the accumulation of unimplemented judgments facing the Committee of Ministers.[75] In the Brighton Declaration of 2012, states for the first time laid emphasis on the necessity of *parliamentary* engagement in ensuring Convention compliance,[76] this dimension having been conspicuously absent in the 2011 Declaration at Izmir[77] and mentioned only perfunctorily in the 2010 Interlaken Declaration.[78] The Brussels Declaration of 27 March 2015 went significantly further than its predecessors in elaborating the ways in which parliaments can and should be involved within the domestic system of implementation,[79] and in recognizing the role of the Parliamentary Assembly in the supervision of the execution of judgments.[80] Senior judicial figures in Strasbourg have also acknowledged the 'pivotal' role of parliaments in the future of the Court.[81]

This imperative has been evident for considerably longer in the work of the Parliamentary Assembly, whose Committee on Legal Affairs and Human Rights has gone so far as to say that unless national parliaments assume a more dynamic role in the implementation of judgments, 'the key role of the Convention, its supervisory mechanism and the Council of Europe as a whole, in guaranteeing the effective protection of human rights in Europe, is likely to be put in jeopardy'.[82]

Scholarly attention has increasingly focused on the significance of domestic institutions as (potential) members of a 'pro-compliance partnership' and on compliance as an 'inherently domestic affair' (see 3.1).[83] Hillebrecht finds that strong institutionalized checks on executives have a positive and statistically significant effect on states' compliance with human rights judgments, suggesting that parliaments can play both a constraining and facilitative role in the compliance

[75] See, especially, Brighton Declaration (n 20) sections A and F; High-Level Conference on 'Implementation of the European Convention on Human Rights, Our Shared Responsibility', Brussels Declaration, 27 March 2015, section B.

[76] Brighton Declaration (n 20) paras. 9.c.ii, 29.a.iii, and 29.e.

[77] High Level Conference on the Future of the European Court of Human Rights, Izmir Declaration, 27 April 2011.

[78] High Level Conference on the Future of the European Court of Human Rights, Interlaken Declaration, 19 February 2010.

[79] Brussels Declaration (n 75) paras. B.1.b, B.2.a, B.2.f, B.2.h, and B.2.j.

[80] Brussels Declaration (n 75) paras. C.1.c and C.3.f. See also DH-GDR(2015)R9 Addendum (n 14) para. 53.

[81] Sir Nicolas Bratza, 'Future of the European Court of Human Rights—Role of National Parliaments', European Conference of Presidents of Parliaments, 20–21 September 2012, 12.

[82] PACE, Committee on Legal Affairs and Human Rights, Implementation of judgments of the European Court of Human Rights, Doc. 12455, 20 December 2010 (Rapporteur: Christos Pourgourides) 1.

[83] Courtney Hillebrecht, *Domestic Politics and International Human Rights Tribunals: The Problem of Compliance* (Cambridge: Cambridge University Press, 2014) 3.

process.[84] Notwithstanding this emphasis, relatively little scholarly attention has been paid either to the role of national parliaments in the implementation of judgments of the ECtHR or to the supervisory role of the Parliamentary Assembly. This is despite the fact that parliamentary involvement pertains both to the efficiency/effectiveness and legitimacy imperatives implied by critiques of the Convention system.

In order to address this omission, in 2012–15, the authors undertook a comparative study to elucidate and analyse models of parliamentary engagement in the implementation of Strasbourg judgments.[85] This book presents the findings of that study and situates them within debates between scholars of international law, international relations, political science, and political philosophy concerning the role of parliaments in the implementation of human rights norms and the broader relationship between democracy, human rights, and legitimate authority.

1.2 Methodology

The empirical part of the study employed a qualitative research methodology. Its scope was delimited in two ways; first, detailed investigation was confined to five states: Ukraine, Romania, the UK, the Netherlands, and Germany. Secondly, attention was principally focused on the role of parliaments in the implementation of ECtHR judgments, rather than in broader aspects of human rights implementation. This section discusses the advantages and limitations of these approaches.

1.2.1 Qualitative approach

The research comprised a total of ninety-two semi-structured interviews.[86] Within each of the five states, interviewees were purposively sampled to include: current or recent members of parliament; parliamentary legal advisers; government officials; judges and practising lawyers; national human rights institutions; civil society organizations; and academics. Interviews were also conducted with judges of the ECtHR and officials of the Committee of Ministers and the Parliamentary Assembly. In addition, the authors have had multiple opportunities to discuss the themes of the research with wider networks of parliamentarians, parliamentary staff, government representatives, and non-government organizations (NGOs) at various events held under the auspices of the Council of Europe, among others, in 2012–15.[87]

[84] Hillebrecht (n 83) 58.

[85] The authors are grateful to the Nuffield Foundation for funding this research.

[86] See Appendix for a list of interviewees. Interviews were mostly conducted face-to-face on an individual basis. A few were conducted by telephone or in small groups. In two cases, answers were supplied in writing. Interviews were recorded, transcribed, and manually coded for emergent themes. The book makes extensive use of quotations which illustrate key themes and perspectives. Some interviews were conducted on the basis of anonymity. Quotations are attributed with the consent of the interviewee.

[87] See 'Parliaments and the European Court of Human Rights', report of conference organized by Middlesex University and the Helsinki Foundation for Human Rights at the Senate, Warsaw, 12 May 2015; Steering Committee for Human Rights, Drafting Group 'F' on Reform of the

The intention was to gain an understanding of the 'micro-processes'[88] involved in implementing ECtHR judgments at the national level and the relationship between parliaments and Council of Europe bodies. Within each state, the authors examined the structures and processes used by parliamentary bodies in responding to adverse judgments of the Court. Questions encompassed the way in which parliamentarians interact, both formally and informally, with other domestic actors: the executive, the judiciary, national human rights institutions, and civil society organizations. Attention was paid to the difficulties and opportunities presented by the place of parliament within the respective legal and political systems. Interviews also covered the nature and extent of contact, both formal and informal, between parliamentarians and institutions of the Council of Europe. The authors discussed with interlocutors their assessment of the impact and effectiveness of the domestic arrangements for implementation. The study also explored the political dimensions of legislative deliberation about human rights judgments, given the inherent contestability of human rights in the political sphere. In the following chapters, we integrate the data obtained from interviewees with insights gleaned from a wide range of documentary evidence from parliamentary bodies, governments, and Council of Europe institutions, in addition to academic literature.

Qualitative methods provide a depth of insight into the views and experiences of interviewees which quantitative methods do not. A qualitative approach permits detailed analysis of the normative perspective of interlocutors, as well as the gathering of rich factual data. Qualitative methods also have the advantage of permitting interrogation of *why* interviewees think or act as they do, with sensitivity to context and personal experience. However, there are unavoidable limitations in the use of qualitative methods alone; mainly, the difficulty in ensuring that the data obtained is representative of the constituencies involved. Purposive sampling can mitigate but not remove these limitations and the scope of the research study has been delimited, and the findings qualified, accordingly.

It was not possible to deduce from this inquiry a blueprint for parliamentary *structures* that can be shown to be inherently more effective than others, as well as replicable across Council of Europe states. Indeed, we did not set out to identify such a model. Given the diversity of legal and political systems across the

Court (GT-GDR-F), Presentation to the 3rd meeting by Alice Donald, GT-GDR-F(2014)023, 24 September 2014; PACE, Parliamentary Project Support Division (PPSD), 'The Role of Parliaments in Implementing ECHR Standards: Overview of Existing Structures and Mechanisms: Background Memorandum', prepared by the Secretariat with the assistance of Dr Alice Donald, PPSD (2014) 22 rev., 8 September 2015; Alice Donald, 'The Role of National Parliaments', MultiRights Annual Conference 2014 (n 13): 178. In addition, Alice Donald attended a workshop for MPs from various Council of Europe states organized by the PACE Parliamentary Project Support Division in London on 14 October 2013, and facilitated workshops for parliamentary staff from several states in Strasbourg (4–5 September 2014) and for parliamentarians from several former Soviet states in Tbilisi (21 September 2015). Alice Donald and Philip Leach made a presentation to a Joint Hearing of the Committee on Legal Affairs and Human Rights and Committee on Political Affairs and Democracy in Strasbourg, 27 June 2013.

[88] Ryan Goodman and Derek Jinks, 'How to Influence States: Socialization and International Human Rights Law', *Duke Law Journal* 54 (2004): 621, 639.

forty-seven states of the Council of Europe, no such prescription is appropriate (see 3.4.2). Rather, our findings relate principally to the *functions* of parliamentary bodies in respect of the implementation of ECtHR judgments, and the *principles* that underpin them. Such functions and principles may be fulfilled using a variety of structures, the optimal configuration of which is dependent upon the particular national context. Moreover, structures and procedures can be deceptive and give an illusion of activity or commitment where little or none exists.[89]

A caveat should be inserted here in relation to the research methodology and the dynamic nature of the subject being investigated. Initial research interviews were conducted between March and June 2012; additional interviews were conducted at various points up to May 2015. Since the research began, there have been national elections in all five case study states and, in Ukraine, tumultuous events leading to continuing political instability (see 5.1). There have also been notable developments, such as the creation in several Council of Europe states of new parliamentary structures for human rights implementation (see 3.4). These developments posed a challenge to the research, in the sense that those interviewed early on were not in a position to comment on more recent developments. In order to mitigate this problem, the authors conducted several follow-up interviews, and/or corresponded with interviewees, in order to update specific factual information.

1.2.2 Selection of states

The selected states—Ukraine, Romania, the UK, the Netherlands, and Germany—were chosen in the first instance because each has some type of parliamentary structure or mechanism designed to monitor implementation of ECtHR judgments. As explored in Chapters 5–9, these structures and mechanisms take different forms, including national implementation legislation (Ukraine); specialized parliamentary committees or sub-committees (UK, Romania); mainstreamed or hybrid committee structures (the Netherlands, Ukraine, and Germany); and various methods of executive reporting to parliament (Romania, the UK, the Netherlands, and Germany). In this sense, the decision was made to concentrate on 'most likely cases'[90] where at least some parliamentary engagement in the process of implementation was likely to be present such that its motivation, dynamics, and effectiveness could be examined.

At the same time, the choice of states was designed to reflect diversity in respect of various criteria. First, the selected states differ in terms of their legal and political systems: they include civil and common law countries; monist, dualist, and hybrid legal systems; and presidential, semi-presidential, and parliamentary systems.[91]

[89] Open Society Justice Initiative (n 30) 16.

[90] Todd Landmann, 'Social Science Methods and Human Rights', in Fons Coomans, Fred Grunfeld, and Menno T. Kamminga, eds., *Methods of Human Rights Research* (Antwerp-Oxford-Portland: Intersentia, 2009) 39.

[91] Chapters 5–9 outline the constitutional, legal, and political systems in place for each state.

Table 1.1 Pending applications at the ECtHR at 31 December 2014

State	Pending applications allocated to a judicial formation	As a percentage of all pending applications
Ukraine	13,635	19.5
Romania	3,385	5
UK	1,243	2
Netherlands	329	0.5
Germany	335	0.5

Source: European Court of Human Rights, *Annual Report 2014 (Provisional version)* (2015) 166.

They include both newer and older members of the Convention in different regions of Europe.[92]

Using the latest available statistics, Table 1.1 shows the variation between the states in terms of the number of alleged human rights violations giving rise to applications to the ECtHR. Ukraine accounted for almost one-fifth of all pending applications before the Court, more than any other state, while Romania accounted for 5 per cent (down from 8% at the end of 2011).

Table 1.2 shows the total number of applications and judgments concerning each state since they ratified the ECHR, and the number of judgments that found at least one violation of the Convention ('adverse judgments'). From these figures, it is possible to identify the 'rate of defeat' for each state at Strasbourg. The rate of defeat reflects the proportion of applications brought against the state which eventually results in an adverse judgment. These figures belie the depiction of the Court as being overly intrusive in domestic affairs; rather, the low rate of defeat—less than 2 per cent for each of the five states—reflects the very high proportion of applications that are found inadmissible by the Court and the comparatively tiny number that eventually results in an adverse judgment.

From the final column in Table 1.2, it can be seen that, despite having joined the system more recently, Romania and Ukraine have been the target of significantly more adverse judgments than the other three states, and that each accounts for 7 per cent of all adverse judgments delivered by the Court.

Table 1.3 shows the difference in the states' respective records at 31 December 2014 in terms of both non-executed judgments and the average time taken to execute judgments in leading cases closed.[93] Again, it is evident that Ukraine, and to a lesser extent Romania, have worse records than the other states in respect of the

[92] The dates on which the respective countries ratified the Convention are as follows: Ukraine, 11 September 1997; Romania, 20 June 1994; UK, 8 March 1951; the Netherlands, 31 August 1954; Germany, 5 December 1952.

[93] Leading cases are those revealing a new structural or systemic problem in a respondent state, thus requiring the adoption of general measures. Leading cases also include pilot judgments and 'judgments with indications of relevance for the execution (under Article 46)'.

Table 1.2 Applications and judgments by respondent state 1959–2014

State	Total number of applications	Total number of judgments	Adverse judgments (i.e. judgments finding at least one violation)	'Rate of defeat' (percentage of applications that results in an adverse judgment)	Adverse judgments per state as a percentage of all adverse judgments of the ECtHR
Ukraine	70,605	1,002	987	1.3	7
Romania	56,683	1,113	1,004	1.8	7
UK	22,781	513	301	1.3	2
Netherlands	8,961	145	85	0.9	0.5
Germany	27,715	276	176	0.6	1

Source: The total number of applications is from European Court of Human Rights, *Overview: 1959–2014* (2015) 8. All other figures are from European Court of Human Rights, *Annual Report 2014 (Provisional version)* (2015) 176–7.

Table 1.3 Pending cases before the Committee of Ministers at 31 December 2014

State	Total number of cases	Total number of cases as a percentage of all pending cases	Average duration of the execution in leading cases closed (number of years, months)
Ukraine	1,009	9	7, 4
Romania	639	6	4, 1
UK	26	0.3	3, 5
Netherlands	11	0.1	4, 1
Germany	19	0.2	3, 6

Source: Committee of Ministers, *Supervision of the Execution of Judgments and Decisions of the European Court of Human Rights: 8th Annual Report of the Committee of Ministers 2014* (2015) 35–7 (total number of cases and total number of cases as a percentage of all pending cases), 49–50 (average duration of execution).

number of pending cases before the Committee of Ministers, and, in Ukraine's case, in respect of the average time taken to execute judgments.[94]

1.2.3 Focus on the implementation of judgments

The second way in which the scope of the study was delimited was the decision to focus principally on the role of parliaments in the implementation of ECtHR judgments, rather than in all aspects of human rights implementation. There is a range of ways in which parliaments are, or could be, involved in protecting and promoting human rights. These include the vetting of legislation and draft legislation for compatibility with human rights standards; post-legislative scrutiny to monitor how the law works in practice; ratifying or authorizing the ratification of international human rights treaties and ensuring that norms set forth in those treaties are translated into national law and implemented; monitoring the steps taken by governments to report to UN treaty monitoring bodies and to address the criticisms presented in the concluding observations of those bodies on state compliance with the treaties; overseeing the adequacy of the domestic institutional machinery for the protection and fulfilment of human rights and ensuring that sufficient resources are available for the system to function effectively; and undertaking thematic or topical inquiries.[95]

[94] Note, however, that where the overall number of pending cases is small, the average duration of the execution process is a fairly crude measure which might be affected by slow implementation in a single case.

[95] Inter-Parliamentary Union and Office of the United Nations High Commissioner for Human Rights, *Human Rights Handbook for Parliamentarians* (IPU and OHCHR: Geneva, 2005); Riccardo Pelizzo, Rick Stapenhurst, and David Olson, *Parliamentary Oversight for Government Accountability* (World Bank Institute, 2006); Committee on Legal Affairs and Human Rights, National parliaments: guarantors of human rights in Europe, Doc. 12636, 6 June 2011 (Rapporteur: Christos Pourgourides) para. 20.

In addition, parliaments may monitor the executive response to adverse human rights judgments and may debate and adopt legislative measures in order to ensure compliance with such judgments, and it is this activity with which this book is primarily concerned. The reason for this choice was partly methodological. As Çalı and Wyss observe, unlike human rights treaties, which generate general and non-time specific obligations, human rights judgments generate specific and 'temporally traceable' commitments, and moreover, commitments which are legally binding under Article 46(1) of the Convention.[96] The implementation of judgments is thus a particularly institutionalized form of human rights commitment, in which the role of specific actors is more than usually visible. (There remain, however, challenges to identifying causality and impact in relation to parliamentary activity, which are discussed at 3.7.) The priority we accord to this particular human rights function of parliaments also reflects the emphasis placed upon it by Council of Europe institutions, including the Committee of Ministers[97] and the Parliamentary Assembly.[98]

At the same time, parliamentary monitoring of adverse human rights judgments—whether those issued by domestic courts or by the ECtHR—should not be seen as a role that is essentially distinct from other aspects of parliamentary human rights activity. The various functions of parliament with respect to human rights are frequently, although not always, undertaken by the same body; typically, committee(s), sub-committee(s), or ombudsmen within a national parliament. Moreover, these bodies use some of the same mechanisms to monitor or debate the executive response to human rights judgments as they do to monitor or debate other aspects of executive activity; for example, oral and written questions; committee hearings; correspondence with ministers; calls for evidence; and (rarely) plenary debates. Additionally, parliamentary bodies may consider adverse human rights judgments, whether against their own state or another state, in the course of conducting rights-based legislative scrutiny or thematic inquiries, and not only in the immediate post-judgment phase.[99]

Indeed, the desirability of such a holistic approach to fulfilling human rights treaty obligations explains our use of the term 'implementation' as opposed to 'execution' to describe the steps taken by states in response to adverse human rights judgments. The two terms are sometimes used interchangeably but, although they overlap, they are not identical. Execution refers to the steps taken by a state to remedy violations of the Convention identified by the ECtHR in judgments against it. Implementation is a broader term which includes execution in the above sense, but also encompasses steps taken by a state in response to an adverse judgment against *another* state, where the same problem of principle exists within its own legal or administrative system.

[96] Başak Çalı and Alice Wyss, *Why Do Democracies Comply with Human Rights Judgments? A Comparative Analysis of the UK, Ireland and Germany*, SSRN eLibrary, 26 August 2009, 2.

[97] See Brussels Declaration (n 75).

[98] For example, the PACE Committee on Legal Affairs and Human Rights created a sub-committee to monitor this issue in 2015. In addition, since 2000 it has appointed a rapporteur on the implementation of judgments of the ECtHR, and has made this function of national parliaments the subject of numerous reports, resolutions, and recommendations (see 2.6.1).

[99] As, for example, the JCHR in the UK did in 2002–03 when, in the process of scrutinizing the Communications Bill (which became the Communications Act 2003), it referred extensively to the judgment in *VgT Verein Gegen Tierfabriken v Switzerland* No. 24699/94, 28 June 2001 (see 7.6.3).

In so doing, that state respects the authority of the Court to make the final, authoritative interpretation of the rights and freedoms defined in the ECHR—a principle known as *res interpretata* that has been repeatedly reinforced by the Parliamentary Assembly[100] and also acknowledged at the inter-governmental level.[101] This is justified on the ground that any judgment of the ECtHR that has relevance to the domestic practice of a state should be considered and applied without waiting for a case to be brought against that state alleging a violation of the Convention. The term implementation is also intended to convey a more proactive approach to Convention standards and Court judgments generally, including consideration of judgments in policy-making and in the process of drafting and scrutinizing legislation. This book uses the broader term implementation except when referring to the formal process of supervision of the execution of judgments by the Committee of Ministers.

The book also refers to another term, 'compliance', which is used interchangeably in much academic literature to describe the steps taken by a state to ensure conformity *either* with a particular judgment or decision (case-level compliance) *or* with the standards and obligations contained in a treaty (overall compliance). In general, this book uses the term implementation to describe the former; thus, states *implement* judgments of the ECtHR in order to ensure that they are in *compliance* with the Convention. In summary, according to this usage of terminology, the terms execution, implementation, and compliance overlap with each other but are not indistinguishable. Execution has the narrowest meaning, implementation is broader, and compliance is broadest.

1.3 Outline

This book is divided into two parts. Part I consists of Chapters 2–4, which explore the relationship between national parliaments and the Convention system in its broader institutional, political, and normative aspects. Part II consists of Chapters 5–9; these examine in detail the parliamentary role in (respectively) Ukraine, Romania, the UK, the Netherlands, and Germany. Chapter 10 concludes.

Chapter 2 considers the role of national parliaments from the perspective of Strasbourg. It also serves as a general introduction to the Convention system for readers who are unfamiliar with it. It explains the obligations on parliaments as state actors within the Convention system, and addresses recent developments with respect to the ECtHR's approach to redress and the continuing process of reform of the Court, highlighting their relevance for national parliaments. It explains and evaluates the formal process of supervision of the execution of judgments conducted

[100] PACE Recommendation 1991 (2012) Guaranteeing the authority and effectiveness of the European Convention on Human Rights, 24 January 2012, para. 2. See also Andrew Drzemczewski and Julia Lowis, 'The Work of the Parliamentary Assembly of the Council of Europe' in Hunt, Hooper, and Yowell, eds. (n 2): 309, 321 (text at n 57).

[101] Interlaken Declaration (n 78) para. 4.c; Brussels Declaration (n 75) para. B.1.d; DH-GDR(2015)R9 Addendum (n 14) paras. 37–42.

by the Committee of Ministers, and the increasingly active supervisory role of the Parliamentary Assembly. It identifies opportunities for greater parliamentary interaction with the Court, the Committee of Ministers, the Parliamentary Assembly, and other Council of Europe bodies.

Chapter 3 examines, from both a theoretical and empirical perspective, the role of national parliaments within domestic systems for the implementation of Convention standards and ECtHR judgments. It situates our theme in the context of theories of compliance that seek to explain states' varying degrees of compliance with international human rights norms and standards—and evidence as to how far ECtHR judgments *are*, in fact, complied with. Our approach is congruent with, and contributes to, a growing body of literature which explains human rights compliance as resulting largely from the way in which domestic actors appropriate or invoke international human rights norms or judgments in the context of political bargaining and collaboration. The chapter examines the structures and mechanisms adopted by parliaments in Convention member states for the conduct of human rights oversight, and assesses the advantages and disadvantages of different institutional models, as well as the principles and functions that are—or should be—common to all systems. The chapter also examines the mechanisms by which executives co-ordinate implementation and report to parliaments, given their dominant role as interlocutors of both the Court and Committee of Ministers. While taking into account the inherently political nature of the implementation process, the chapter considers the methodologies by which the effectiveness of parliamentary human rights bodies can be identified and evaluated.

Chapter 4 discusses the normative dimension of our topic: namely, the relationship between human rights, democratic governance, and legitimate authority. It explores whether, in fact, international human rights regimes (and the ECtHR in particular) have a 'legitimacy problem'—and, if so, what the nature of this problem might be, bearing in mind the distinction (and inter-relationship) between the normative, legal, and social dimensions of the concept of legitimacy. The chapter focuses in particular on the notion of *democratic* legitimacy, both in respect of institutional and procedural factors and the allocation of power between the Convention system and democratic decision-making at the national level. In this context the (potentially) legitimacy-boosting role of the Parliamentary Assembly is highlighted. The chapter reviews the relationship between the ECtHR and national parliaments, including the Court's engagement with the parliamentary process, and the ways in which the Court might facilitate or incentivize parliamentary involvement in the implementation of its judgments. Proposals for 'democratic override' of judgments to which a majority of parliamentarians are opposed are examined—and rejected.

Chapters 5–9 present our research findings on the five case study states. Each chapter examines the structures and processes by which parliamentary actors are involved in responding to adverse judgments of the ECtHR, and their relationship both with other domestic actors and Council of Europe institutions. These chapters refer in detail to the process of implementing specific judgments which are illustrative of particular research themes.

Chapter 10 synthesizes conclusions from Parts I and II, and suggests priorities for future research.

PART I

2

The Strasbourg System

Roles and Relationships

The role of national parliaments in the implementation of judgments of the European Court of Human Rights (ECtHR or 'the Court') based in Strasbourg needs to be understood in the context of the European Convention on Human Rights (ECHR or 'the Convention') system as a whole. The chapter is concerned with both the obligations and opportunities that parliaments have as state actors within the Convention system, both at the domestic level and in respect of their relationship with Council of Europe bodies.

This chapter examines, in 2.1, the nature of the obligations on states—including parliaments—under the Convention. The following sections, 2.2–2.4, are concerned with the Court. They examine, in turn, the implications for parliaments of the Court's practices and procedures in the pre-judgment phase; the Court's developing approach to redress; in particular, the shift in recent years from a mainly declaratory approach to one that can be more directive or prescriptive, notably by means of the 'pilot judgment' procedure; and the opportunities that exist for contact between the Court and national parliaments.

The formal process of supervision of the execution of judgments conducted by the Committee of Ministers, and the nature and extent of parliamentary engagement with that process, is discussed in 2.5. The increasingly active involvement in the supervision process of the Parliamentary Assembly of the Council of Europe (PACE), and the dual role and mandate of Assembly members is explored in 2.6. In 2.7, the role of other Council of Europe bodies is considered.

The effectiveness of the supervision system as a whole is evaluated in 2.8, while 2.9 addresses developments in Strasbourg that have implications for the role of parliaments: in particular, the continuing process of reform of the Convention system. Finally, 2.10 concludes.

2.1 States' Obligations under the Convention

The Convention imposes an obligation on the forty-seven Convention states (through Article 1) to ensure that everyone within their jurisdiction enjoys the rights and freedoms which are set out in it.[1] States are accordingly required to uphold those rights, regardless of an individual's nationality or residence,[2] or indeed any other characteristic. The 'jurisdiction' of states is considered to be 'primarily territorial'.[3] In other words, the Convention applies within the geographical territory of each state. However, in exceptional cases, acts by Convention states 'performed, or producing effects, outside their territories' can constitute an exercise of jurisdiction by them within the meaning of the Convention.[4] For that reason, the Convention can be said to have extra-territorial effect.[5]

According to the Convention, states must secure Convention rights within a system of 'effective political democracy'[6] that consists, inter alia, of an elected legislature[7] and an independent and impartial judiciary.[8] Parliaments are included in the general obligation to ensure that Convention rights are 'protected by the law'.[9] This obligation has both a negative dimension (requiring the protection of individuals against arbitrary state actions or omissions that infringe their rights) and a positive dimension (requiring the state to provide both substantive and procedural guarantees proactively to protect Convention rights).[10]

According to Articles 26 and 27 of the Vienna Convention on the Law of Treaties,[11] international treaties are binding upon states and must be implemented by them in good faith without the possibility of invoking a provision of national law to justify non-implementation. While it is the executive that formally represents the state before both the Court and the Committee of Ministers, it widely recognized that the obligation under Article 1 ECHR is binding on *all* branches of the state—executive, legislative, and judicial. This consensus is reinforced by a number of other treaties and interpretations of treaties, both within the Council of Europe[12] and at the United Nations (as we explore in more detail at 3.3).

It is the role of the ECtHR to ensure that states observe their obligations under the Convention.[13] It does so primarily through its adjudication of individual

[1] Article 1 ECHR: 'The High Contracting Parties shall secure to everyone within their jurisdiction the rights and freedoms defined in section 1 of this Convention.'

[2] See, for example, *D v UK*, No. 30240/96, 2 May 1997; *Amuur v France*, No. 19776/92, 25 June 1996.

[3] See, for example, *Bankovic v Belgium and Others*, No. 52207/99, 12 December 2001, para. 59; *Al-Skeini and Others v UK*, No. 55721/07, 7 July 2011 [GC], para. 131.

[4] See, for example, *Jaloud v Netherlands*, No. 47708/08, 20 November 2014 [GC].

[5] Marko Milanovich, *Extraterritorial Application of Human Rights Treaties: Law, Principles, and Policy* (Oxford: Oxford University Press, 2011).

[6] Preamble of the Convention, para. 4.

[7] Article 3 of Protocol No. 1 ECHR.

[8] See, for example, Article 6(1) and Article 10(2) ECHR.

[9] See, for example, Laurens Lavrysen, 'Protection by the Law: The Positive Obligation to Develop a Legal Framework to Adequately Protect ECHR Rights', in Eva Brems and Yves Haeck, eds., *Human Rights and Civil Liberties in the 21st Century* (Dordrecht: Springer, 2014): 69.

[10] Lavrysen (n 9).

[11] Vienna Convention on the Law of Treaties, 1155 UNTS 331.

[12] See, especially, PACE Resolution 1823 (2011), National parliaments: guarantors of human rights in Europe, 23 June 2011, para. 1; High-Level Conference on 'Implementation of the European Convention on Human Rights, Our Shared Responsibility', Brussels Declaration, 27 March 2015.

[13] Article 19 ECHR.

applications,[14] and, occasionally, inter-state cases.[15] Once they become final, judgments of the ECtHR are binding on the state party concerned (under Article 46(1) ECHR).[16] Again, it is widely recognized that this obligation applies to all branches of the state, including parliaments.[17]

The effect of a judgment in which the Court finds a violation of the Convention is to impose a legal obligation on the state in question not only to put an end to the breach, but also to make reparation for its consequences in such a way as to restore as far as possible the situation existing before the breach (a principle known as *restitutio in integrum*). Therefore, if *restitutio in integrum* is possible, it is for the state to ensure that it is carried out.[18] If, however, *restitutio in integrum* is in practice impossible, the state is free to decide *how* to comply with a judgment,[19] provided that those means are compatible with the conclusions set out in the Court's judgment.[20] Thus, states have considerable leeway as to how they honour their fundamental obligation under Article 1 ECHR.[21] Indeed, the European human rights system is founded on the principle of subsidiarity, according to which national authorities—governments, parliaments, and courts—have the primary responsibility for securing for everyone within their jurisdiction the Convention rights and freedoms. Article 13 ECHR reinforces the primary duty of states to secure the human rights set out in the Convention. It requires states to provide 'an effective remedy before a national authority' to any individual who claims that their rights under the Convention have been violated. Taken together, Articles 1 and 13 mean that it is first and foremost for the national authorities to uphold rights—or, when they have failed to do so, remedy any violation of the Convention. The discretionary space thereby created is one in which parliaments can and should operate, conducting oversight of executive action or inaction in the post-judgment phase and, where legislative reform is required, devising remedies which are workable and command consensus.

[14] Under Article 34 ECHR, the Court may receive applications 'from any person, non-governmental organisation or group of individuals claiming to be the victim of a violation' by a state of a Convention right.

[15] Article 33 ECHR. The inter-state process has, however, rarely been used. See Dean Spielmann, President of the ECtHR, 'The European Court of Human Rights as Guarantor of a Peaceful Public Order in Europe', Speech to Gray's Inn, 7 November 2014.

[16] Judgments issued by Chambers of the Court become final after the expiry of a three-month period, during which any party may, exceptionally, request that the case be referred to the Grand Chamber. If such a request is made, a panel of five judges considers whether the case deserves further examination because it involves a serious question affecting the interpretation or application of the Convention or a serious issue of general importance. In that event, the Grand Chamber will hear the case and deliver a final judgment. If the referral request is refused, the Chamber judgment will become final on that day.

[17] Brussels Declaration (n 12).

[18] See, for example, *Iatridis v Greece*, No. 31107/96, 19 October 2000 [GC], paras. 32–3.

[19] See, for example, *Selçuk and Asker v Turkey*, Nos. 23184/94 and 23185/94, 24 April 1998, para. 125.

[20] See, for example, *Scozzari and Giunta v Italy*, Nos. 39221/98 and 41963/98, 13 July 2000 [GC].

[21] See, for example, *Iatridis v Greece* (n 18) para. 33.

2.1.1 The interpretative authority of the Court's judgments

Although a judgment of the Court is only formally binding on the respondent state in that particular case, states are increasingly being urged to take account of judgments finding a violation of the Convention against other states. This is known as the 'interpretative authority' (or *res interpretata*) of the Court.[22] In its case law, the Court has emphasized that it is entitled to assess whether national authorities 'have sufficiently taken into account the principles flowing from its judgments on similar issues, even when they concern other States'.[23] As noted at 1.2.3, the principle of *res interpretata* has been repeatedly reinforced by the Parliamentary Assembly[24] as well as being acknowledged by governments.[25] The Committee of Ministers has not, however, acceded to the Parliamentary Assembly's request for it to address a general recommendation to states calling on them to reinforce, by legislative, judicial, or other means, the interpretative authority of the Court's judgments (see 2.5.4 for other general recommendations).

Systematic monitoring of ECtHR case law is no easy task. The problem is partly one of scale: in 2014, the Court delivered 891 judgments, 756 of which found at least one violation of the Convention (although this is a reduction from the peak in 2009 of 1,625 judgments, of which 1,504 were adverse judgments).[26]

Language barriers also need to be overcome. The working languages of the Court are English and French. In 2012, the Court initiated a project (funded by the Human Rights Trust Fund (HRTF)) to translate and disseminate case law 'of Europe-wide significance' in twelve target languages, supplemented from 2013 by outsourced translations in a further five languages.[27] The Court also makes available on its website sources of non-official translations from most Council of Europe states.[28] These translations of judgments are a valuable resource for domestic actors, including parliaments; however, they do not entirely resolve the problem of identifying case law of significance to particular non-respondent states, since it may be that a judgment that is not of Europe-wide significance nevertheless has implications for the legal order of particular states.

Once judgments of potential significance have been identified, a further challenge lies in transposing them from one national context to another. This process is complicated in view of the discretion or 'margin of appreciation' which the Court

[22] Committee of Ministers, Guaranteeing the authority and effectiveness of the European Convention on Human Rights, Doc. 13024, 18 September 2012.

[23] *Opuz v Turkey*, No. 33401/02, 9 June 2009, para. 163.

[24] See 1.2.3 at n 100.

[25] See 1.2.3 at n 101.

[26] European Court of Human Rights, *Annual Report 2014* (2015) 171; *Annual Report 2009* (2010) 145.

[27] The beneficiary states of the HRTF project (which ended in April 2015) were Albania, Armenia, Azerbaijan, Bosnia and Herzegovina, Georgia, Republic of Moldova, Montenegro, Serbia, the former Yugoslav Republic of Macedonia, Turkey, and Ukraine. In addition, the Court's Registry commissions translations of selected case law in Bulgarian, Greek, Hungarian, Russian, and Spanish. See European Court of Human Rights, *The Court's Case-Law Translations Programme: Aims, Achievements and Remaining Challenges*, April 2014.

[28] See the ECtHR's website at <http://www.echr.coe.int/Pages/home.aspx?p=caselaw/HUDOC/translations>.

affords to states in determining the necessity of the restriction of a right. The margin of appreciation is the doctrine by which the ECtHR, as a supranational court, accommodates differences between nations, acknowledging that national authorities are in principle better placed than the Court to assess the necessity of a restriction '[b]y reason of their direct and continuous contact with the vital forces of their countries'.[29] The task of transposing judgments between states therefore needs to take into account this variable and sometimes unpredictable factor.

Marten Breuer, an academic who has produced reports for the German government on cases against other states which might have implications for Germany, identifies further difficulties (see 9.5).[30] Most judgments are, by their nature, fact- and context-specific, and there is a need to determine in each case the true source of a violation, which may not be immediately obvious. [31] As Breuer observes:

> The Court says 'in that particular case the Convention has been breached' but this might be due to the fact that the internal law has been applied badly, so it's due to the executive or the judiciary that the right has been breached rather than the legislative branch. So it's really difficult to identify clear cases where the German order needs to be amended—it's very rare.

In practice, states' arrangements for monitoring ECtHR case law against other states in order to identify any implications for their own legal order vary considerably, to the extent that they exist at all. The parliamentary Joint Committee on Human Rights (JCHR) in the UK has expressed concern that the binding effect of Strasbourg judgments is limited in practice by states taking an 'essentially passive approach' to compliance with the Convention.[32]

The Dutch government performs this task in-house, while the German government commissions independent academics to produce an annual report on relevant judgments (see 8.4 and 9.5). The Polish Ministries of Justice and Foreign Affairs liaise with the Constitutional Tribunal and Supreme Administrative Court to identify and translate judgments against other states that are of relevance to Poland; forty such cases were translated in 2014.[33] By contrast, arrangements in Ukraine may be described as, at best, haphazard (5.5.2).

The governments of the Netherlands and Germany report annually to their respective parliaments on relevant judgments against other states, while the Swiss government also includes such information in its quarterly reports (see 3.5.2).[34] In the UK, the government has declined a request by the JCHR to inform the

[29] *Handyside v UK*, No. 5493/72, 7 December 1976, para. 48.

[30] Interview, 4 May 2012.

[31] See, however, 2.3.1 which examines the development by the Court of the 'pilot judgment' procedure as a means of dealing with structural or systemic violations of the Convention that may give rise to large numbers of repetitive cases.

[32] JCHR, Fifteenth Report of Session 2009–10, *Enhancing Parliament's Role in Relation to Human Rights Judgments*, HL Paper 85, HC 455 (2010), para. 188.

[33] Justyna Chrzanowska, Polish government agent before the ECtHR, 'Parliaments and the European Court of Human Rights', report of conference hosted by the Senate, Warsaw, 12 May 2015.

[34] Marten Breuer, Interview, 4 May 2012. See also JCHR, Fifteenth Report of Session 2009–10 (n 32) para. 189.

Committee regularly about relevant judgments against other states,[35] but does selectively bring to parliament's attention non-UK judgments of 'direct, immediate and obvious' significance (see 7.5).[36] Aside from the Netherlands, Germany, and Switzerland, we have found no instances of other governments reporting regularly to parliament about judgments against other states.

Nor have we found evidence of parliamentary bodies conducting such reviews of the ECtHR's case law on their own initiative. This is unsurprising; judgments against other states are rarely politically compelling, with cases such as *Salduz v Turkey*[37] (concerning the right of access to a lawyer prior to being interviewed by the police) being exceptional in prompting legislative reform in several jurisdictions.[38] Moreover, hard-pressed parliamentarians are likely to be unwilling to invest in an avoidably complex, time-consuming, and exploratory exercise. Nevertheless, the priority accorded to the Court's interpretative authority by Council of Europe institutions suggests that, at a minimum, parliamentary bodies should expressly *recognize* the principle of *res interpretata*, and scrutinize the adequacy of executive systems for monitoring judgments against other states and reporting to parliament on any judgments of significance for the domestic legal order.

2.2 Practices and Procedures of the Court in the Pre-judgment Phase

This section briefly explains a number of the Court's practices and procedures to which we refer in this chapter, and throughout the book.

In urgent situations, where an applicant's life is at risk, or where there is a substantial risk of serious ill-treatment, the Court may apply 'interim measures' (under Rule 39 of the Court Rules) in order to require a state to take particular steps to avert the risk. The Court will only invoke interim measures where there is a threat of irreparable harm of a very serious nature and where the harm threatened is imminent and irremediable. They have been most frequently applied in situations where applicants are threatened with expulsion to a country where they face a danger of torture or death. However, they are also applied in other situations, such as to safeguard the health of vulnerable detainees, and exceptionally to ensure that a detainee has access to a lawyer.[39] The stipulations which the Court issues under this procedure are legally binding on states.[40] Although applications for interim measures are frequently made, they are relatively rarely granted.[41]

[35] Joint Committee on Human Rights, The Government's Human Rights Policy and Human Rights Judgments, Oral Evidence HC 1726–I, Rt Hon Kenneth Clarke MP, Oral Evidence, 20 December 2011, Q23.

[36] Interview (anonymous), 10 July 2012.

[37] No. 36391/02, 27 November 2008 [GC].

[38] See, for example, the 'Salduz Watch' website maintained by the Legal Aid Reformers' Network.

[39] See, further, Philip Leach, *Taking a Case to the European Court of Human Rights*, 3rd edn. (Oxford: Oxford University Press, 2011) 2.48–2.63.

[40] *Mamatkulov and Askarov v Turkey*, Nos 46827/99 and 46951/99, 4 February 2005 [GC].

[41] For example, between 2012 and 2014 only 427 Rule 39 applications were granted (as regards all forty-seven states), out of a total of 5,489 requests (less than an 8% success rate). See 'Rule 39 requests

Many cases submitted to the Court are declared inadmissible (usually by a single judge or a committee of three judges) without the Court needing to ask the government in question to respond. This may happen, for example, where an application is clearly inadmissible because of the failure to exhaust domestic remedies, or where the six-month time limit within which to lodge a case at the Court has been missed. However, if a case cannot be dealt with in this way, it will be referred to the government for a response. This is known as the 'communication' stage of the proceedings. The Court will produce a summary 'statement of facts', and will also invite the government to respond to specific questions from the Court. These documents are posted on the Court's 'Hudoc' website. This is usually the first time in a case that information about the case is publicized.

The 'communication' of a case also triggers the third-party intervention procedure. Under Article 36 ECHR, the Court may invite states or 'any person concerned' to submit a written intervention, as a third party, in any case, 'in the interest of the proper administration of justice', or to participate in a hearing before the Court.[42] In practice, both states and a range of civil society organizations make use of this procedure for various reasons including, for example, to provide the Court with a broader perspective on the issue raised by the case, or comparative international standards and case law. For states, this process may represent an opportunity to provide the Court with further information considered relevant to a particular issue (but which might not otherwise have been presented to the Court). They are most likely to do so where the issue raised by the case is also relevant to the situation in the intervening state. For example, as we discuss at 8.2, the Netherlands government intervened in the case of *M.S.S. v Belgium and Greece*[43] (concerning the protection of asylum-seekers) because of the similarities in the Belgian and Dutch asylum systems. More controversially, as we discuss at 7.5, the UK government intervened in the case of *Saadi v Italy*,[44] in order to argue (unsuccessfully) that state authorities should be able to balance the risk that a deportee might suffer torture or inhuman or degrading treatment against the risk they are deemed to pose to national security.

An application before the Court may be resolved, prior to judgment, where the parties agree a friendly settlement (Article 39 ECHR).[45] If that happens, the Court then strikes the case out of its list of cases (and its execution is supervised by the Committee of Ministers). Such settlements can be advantageous to both applicants

granted and refused in 2012, 2013 and 2014 by respondent state', available at: <http://www.echr.coe.int/Documents/Stats_art_39_01_ENG.pdf>.

[42] Applications to intervene as a third party must be submitted to the Court within twelve weeks of the communication of the case (Rule 44 of the Court Rules).

[43] No. 30696/09, 21 January 2011 [GC]. Third-party interventions in that case were also submitted by the UK government, the AIRE Centre, Amnesty International, the Council of Europe Commissioner for Human Rights, the Office of the United Nations High Commissioner for Refugees (UNHCR), and the Greek Helsinki Monitor.

[44] No. 37201/06, 28 February 2008 [GC].

[45] See also Helen Keller, Magdalena Forowicz, and Lorenzi Engi, *Friendly Settlements before the European Court of Human Rights: Theory and Practice* (Oxford: Oxford University Press, 2010).

and respondent governments, and they can include, for example, an acknowledgement by the state that the Convention has been violated, an undertaking to pay damages (and costs) and even to investigate a particular situation, or revise relevant laws or policies. Allied to the friendly settlement process is a process by which the Court can strike out a case on the basis of a 'unilateral declaration' made by a government. If a government makes such a declaration in a case and the Court considers that the terms of the declaration are sufficient to resolve the case (whether or not the applicant agrees), then it may strike the application out of its list of cases (Article 37 ECHR).

Given that the conclusion of friendly settlements or the proffering of unilateral declarations may involve, in some cases, the adoption of policy positions which might be politically contentious, a case could be made for parliamentary involvement in the *formulation* of the positions taken by governments in the course of their interventions before the Court. Indeed, the JCHR in the UK has made such a case (see 7.5). There are, though, undeniable logistical difficulties, not least the relatively short period (twelve weeks after the communication of a case) within which an application to intervene must be submitted to the Court. However, the primary focus of this book is oversight of the implementation of ECtHR judgments and decisions, and we suggest that there are also questions about the potential for parliaments to monitor decisions resolved by way of friendly settlements and unilateral declarations. Our interlocutors in the UK government (see 7.5) acknowledge that there is a lack of accessible information about third-party interventions, which are not published by the ECtHR at the time of submission. Parliamentary or non-government actors can (at least in theory) obtain a copy on application to the Court's Registry, or may be made aware of the intervention if, exceptionally, an oral hearing is held, or if a press release is issued by the Court. There is, however, an additional problem—Court decisions striking out cases by way of a friendly settlement or as a result of a unilateral declaration have a much lower profile than judgments of the Court, and are therefore much less likely to be the subject of any external scrutiny. One way of addressing these lacunae, at least retrospectively, would be for governments to use their annual reports to parliament (see 3.5.2) to draw attention to interventions made in the previous year and the arguments underlying them.

2.3 The Court's Developing Approach to Redress

The clarity or prescriptiveness of a judgment of the ECtHR may be critical to its effective implementation. Both facets may help to answer the question: 'what is required by this judgment?' Since the mid-2000s the Court has begun to issue judgments in certain areas which are increasingly prescriptive in setting out what is required, both in terms of redress for the applicants ('individual measures') and also as regards wider changes to law or practice which the Court considers are needed to put an end to the Convention violation at issue ('general measures').

The Court's traditional approach to the issue of redress has been cautious; its judgments have therefore been 'essentially declaratory'.[46] Thus, in a case in which the applicant has successfully established that the Convention has been violated, the Court's usual approach is to issue a declaration to the effect that the Convention has been violated (with more or less detailed reasoning) and to exercise its discretion as to whether to award compensation (in the form of pecuniary and/or non-pecuniary damages) and legal costs. Restricting a judgment to the specific circumstances of a case may create uncertainty about how the legal principles invoked in the judgment may be generalized, obscuring the implications for broader legislative or policy change (see 2.1.1). In recent years, however, the Court has proved willing and able to go beyond its standard, declaratory approach in responding to particular types of Convention violations,[47] including the failure to compensate people who had lost property when it was nationalized,[48] unfair trials,[49] individuals unlawfully detained,[50] and unfair dismissal.[51] Accordingly, aside from the question of compensation, the Court may also order states to take particular measures, such as ensuring that property is returned, that trials are re-run, that detainees are released, or that people unlawfully dismissed are reinstated.

2.3.1 The pilot judgment procedure

Since 2004, the Court has developed and applied its 'pilot judgment' procedure in cases related primarily to large-scale systemic or structural violations of the Convention.[52] As such violations are often caused by defective legislation, pilot judgments are of great significance for the parliamentary role in implementation and may, indeed, expressly stipulate a legislative solution.[53]

46 See, for example, *Marckx v Belgium*, No. 6833/74, 13 June 1979, para. 58; *Assanidze v Georgia*, No. 71503/01, 8 April 2004 [GC], para. 202.

47 Philip Leach, 'No Longer Offering Fine Mantras to a Parched Child? The European Court's Developing Approach to Remedies', in Andreas Føllesdal, Birgit Peters, and Geir Ulfstein, eds., *Constituting Europe: The European Court of Human Rights in a National, European and Global Context* (Cambridge: Cambridge University Press, 2013): 142.

48 See, for example, *Papamichalopoulos and Others v Greece*, No. 14556/89, 31 October 1995; *Brumărescu v Romania*, No. 28342/95, 23 January 2001 [GC]; *Zwierzynski v Poland*, No. 34049/96, 2 July 2002; *Hirschhorn v Romania*, No. 29294/02, 26 July 2007; *Dacia S.R.L. v Moldova*, No. 3052/04, 19 February 2009; *Saghinadze and Others v Georgia*, No. 18768/05, 27 May 2010.

49 See, for example, *Lungoci v Romania*, No. 62710/00, 26 January 2006; *Maksimov v Azerbaijan*, No. 38228/05, 8 October 2009.

50 See, for example, *Assanidze v Georgia* (n 46); *Ilaşcu and Others v Russia and Moldova*, No. 48787/99, 8 July 2004 [GC]; *Aleksanyan v Russia*, No. 46468/06, 22 December 2008; *Tehrani and Others v Turkey*, Nos. 32940/08, 41626/08, 43616/08, 13 April 2010; *Fatullayev v Azerbaijan*, No. 40984/07, 22 April 2010.

51 See, for example, *Oleksandr Volkov v Ukraine*, No. 21722/11, 9 January 2013.

52 Philip Leach, Helen Hardman, Svetlana Stephenson, and Brad Blitz, *Responding to Systemic Human Rights Violations—An Analysis of Pilot Judgments of the European Court of Human Rights and Their Impact at National Level* (Antwerp-Oxford-Portland: Intersentia, 2010). The pilot judgment procedure was codified in 2011; see Rule 61 of the Rules of Court. All pilot cases are granted priority treatment (in accordance with Rule 41).

53 As in the case of *Greens and MT v UK*, Nos. 60041/08 and 60054/08, 23 November 2010, which required the UK Government to 'bring forward ... legislative proposals' (operative para. 6(a)).

The consequence of applying the pilot judgment procedure in a case is, firstly, the express identification by the Court of a systemic or structural violation of the Convention and, secondly, its stipulation of general measures in the operative part of the judgment in order that the respondent state should resolve the systemic issue. In a pilot judgment, the Court may also impose binding time limits (in its operative provisions) within which the specified remedial measures must be adopted by states, and it may adjourn the examination of all similar applications pending the adoption of the remedial measures.

A significant proportion of pilot judgments to date have concerned structural dysfunctions within states such as property-related matters,[54] the non-enforcement of domestic court judgments,[55] and the excessive length of legal proceedings.[56] Other issues which have been the subject of pilot judgments include prison conditions,[57] the situation of statelessness,[58] the loss of foreign currency savings,[59] and the disenfranchisement of convicted prisoners.[60]

The Court has ordered different forms of redress in the pilot judgments, and has stipulated varying time periods. As regards cases concerning the excessive length of domestic proceedings, the Court has required states to introduce an effective domestic remedy (or combination of remedies) within one year.[61] A similar form of general measures has been stipulated in cases concerning the non-implementation of domestic court judgments, either within six months[62] or one year.[63] In the latter, the respondent states were also required to provide redress to the applicants within one year, whereas in *Maria Atanasiu and Others v Romania*,[64] which concerned the applicants' inability to obtain restitution of their nationalized properties or to secure compensation, the state was permitted eighteen months within which

[54] See, for example, *Broniowski v Poland*, No. 31443/96, 22 June 2004 [GC]; *Hutten-Czapska v Poland*, No. 35014/97, 19 June 2006 [GC]; *Maria Atanasiu and Others v Romania*, Nos. 30767/05 and 33800/06, 12 October 2010; *M.C. and Others v Italy*, No. 5376/11, 3 September 2013; *Ališić and Others v Bosnia and Herzegovina, Croatia, Serbia, Slovenia, and The former Yugoslav Republic of Macedonia*, No. 60642/08, 16 July 2014 [GC].

[55] *Yuriy Nikolayevich Ivanov v Ukraine*, No. 40450/04, 15 October 2009; *Burdov v Russia (No. 2)*, No. 33509/04, 15 January 2009; *Olaru and Others v Moldova*, Nos. 476/07, 22539/05, 17911/08, and 13136/07, 28 July 2009; *Manushaqe Puto and Others v Albania*, Nos. 604/07, 34770/09, and 43628/07, 31 July 2012; *Gerasimov and Others v Russia*, Nos. 29920/05, 3553/06, 18876/10, 61186/10, 21176/11, 36112/11, 36426/11, 40841/11, 45381/11, 55929/11, and 60822/11, 1 July 2014.

[56] *Rumpf v Germany*, No. 46344/06, 2 September 2010; *Vassilios Athanasiou and Others v Greece*, No. 50973/08, 21 December 2010; *Dimitrov and Hamanov v Bulgaria*, Nos. 48059/06 and 2708/09, 10 May 2011; *Ümmühan Kaplan v Turkey*, No. 24240/07, 20 March 2012; *Michelioudakis v Greece*, No. 54447/10, 3 April 2012; *Glykantzi v Greece*, No. 40150/09, 30 October 2012.

[57] *Ananyev and Others v Russia*, Nos. 42525/07 and 60800/08, 10 January 2012; *Torreggiani v Italy*, Nos. 43517/09, 35315/10, and 37818/10, 8 January 2013; *Neshkov and Others v Bulgaria*, Nos. 36925/10, 9717/13, 21487/12, 72893/12, 73196/12, and 77718/12, 27 January 2015; *Varga v Hungary*, Nos. 14097/12, 45135/12, 73712/12, 34001/13, 44055/13, and 64586/13, 10 March 2015.

[58] *Kurić and Others v Slovenia*, No. 26828/06, 26 June 2012 [GC].

[59] *Suljagić v Bosnia and Herzegovina*, No. 27912/02, 3 November 2009.

[60] *Greens and MT v UK* (n 53).

[61] *Rumpf v Germany* (n 56) (see also *Sürmeli v Germany*, No. 75529/01, 8 June 2006 [GC]); *Vassilios Athanasiou and Others v Greece* (n 56); *Dimitrov and Hamanov v Bulgaria* (n 56).

[62] *Olaru and Others v Moldova* (n 55); *Burdov v Russia* (n 55).

[63] *Yuriy Nikolayevich Ivanov v Ukraine* (n 55).

[64] Above n 54.

to take the measures needed to resolve the issue (a deadline that was subsequently extended; see 6.6.3). In a case relating to pre-trial detention in Russia,[65] the Court ordered the state to grant redress within one year not only to the applicants in that particular case, but also to all the victims of inhuman and degrading conditions of detention in Russia's remand prisons who had lodged applications with the Court before the judgment was issued.

Allied to the pilot judgment procedure has been the Court's increasingly frequent use of so-called 'Article 46' or 'quasi-pilot' judgments. Like pilot judgments, these use directive wording in relation to systemic breaches of Convention rights, but not within the operative provisions.[66] The Court's more directive or prescriptive approach to redress in some areas inevitably has an impact upon the implementation process. Greater clarity or specificity in the judgments, especially as regards remedial measures, may mean that states are better able to comply: it will be clearer what exactly is required and accordingly there will be less 'wriggle room' for states to prevaricate as to how to respond. In the context of discussion about the long-term reform of the Convention system, governments have suggested that a more directive approach by the Court would be acceptable, or even welcome, in certain areas. These include the stipulation of individual measures which are narrow in scope;[67] and indications of general measures where the state has expressed a wish for the Court to make such indications.[68] Governments have also called for greater clarity in the Court's judgments in relation to, first, the elements which were 'actually problematic and constituted the direct source of the finding of the violation' and, secondly, the particular authority or authorities towards which the judgment is addressed (e.g., whether it requires a change in practice rather than legislation).[69] The Court itself notes that in certain types of case the parties could be invited to make submissions on the efficacy of identifying specific remedial measures in its judgment.[70] In exceptional cases, it adds, this could even be the subject of a distinct phase of the procedure before the Court, taking place after the main judgment has been given.

2.3.2 The implications for parliaments

It should be recognized that a higher level of specificity in Strasbourg judgments may not always be welcomed by national authorities, as there may be political objections to perceptions of a more prescriptive approach being adopted by the

[65] *Ananyev and Others* (n 57).

[66] There is also a third tier of judgments that address systemic violations of the Convention but do not explicitly apply Article 46 ECHR.

[67] As in the case of *Oleksandr Volkov v Ukraine* (n 51) (see also 5.2.1).

[68] See, for example, Steering Committee for Human Rights, Drafting Group 'F' on Reform of the Court (GT-GDR-F), Consolidated draft CDDH final report on the longer-term future of the Convention system, GT-GDR-F(2015)010, 15 May 2015, paras. 108–111.

[69] GT-GDR-F(2015)010 (n 68) para. 111.

[70] European Court of Human Rights, Contribution of the Court to the Brussels Conference, 26 January 2015, para. 14.

Court so as to narrow the discretionary space traditionally afforded to states. Such perceptions have indeed fuelled claims that the Court suffers from a 'democratic deficit' to the extent that it intrudes on the legislative and policy competence of democratically elected law makers (see 4.6). Our interviews with parliamentarians and government officials in the five states under review reflect the spectrum of responses indicated above, cautiously welcoming greater direction from the Court in certain circumstances but within limits demanded by respect for the principle of subsidiarity.

The former Romanian judge at the ECtHR, Corneliu Birsan, observes that judgments must be 'clear, educative, and specific' as to the nature and cause of the violation but that it is the role of politicians to resolve the general problems that underlie individual complaints.[71] The former Romanian government co-agent, Irina Cambrea, ventures that an overly prescriptive approach 'carries the risk of generating solutions which could be less adapted to domestic realities'.[72] Interviewees of all types in Germany caution against a greater degree of prescription than that presently used by the Court, since parliament is willing and able to 'do its legislative job'.[73]

Interviewees in the UK generally concur with these expressions of caution. For the Conservative peer, Lord Mackay of Clashfern, 'the less prescriptive Strasbourg is, the better. It must recognize the jurisdictional competency of the national parliament'.[74] The Court's judgments on prisoner voting rights, he adds, are a good example of the way in which 'the Court's doesn't tell you what you have to do but what you cannot continue to do'. A former legal adviser to the JCHR, Professor David Feldman, adds that while a more directive or even prescriptive approach might assist the oversight work of parliamentary human rights bodies, it would nevertheless 'be a very bad thing ... because ... politicians don't like being told what to do'.[75] In the view of Angela Patrick, a former assistant legal adviser to the JCHR, the discretion inherent in supervision mechanism, especially in cases involving the proportionality of restrictions upon non-absolute rights, means that 'generally the Court should not prescribe the policy replacement'.[76] However, the clarity and precision of judgments were vital attributes in order to identify appropriate remedies. Patrick commends the Court's approach of providing guidance that would assist implementation without being unduly prescriptive; for example, in the case of *S and Marper v UK*,[77] concerning the indiscriminate powers of retention of biometric data of persons suspected but not convicted of offences in violation of Article 8 ECHR (right to respect for private life), it had been helpful to the JCHR and its advisers that the Court had cited the Scottish retention scheme approvingly as the basis for an alternative regime (see 7.6.2). Conversely, in *Gillan and Quinton v UK*, in which Court held that stop and search powers contained insufficient safeguards to act as a curb on the wide discretion afforded to the executive (in violation of

[71] Interview, 25 June 2012.
[72] Written response from Irina Cambrea, 25 June 2012.
[73] Christoph Strässer, Interview, 21 March 2012.
[74] Interview, 14 March 2012.
[75] Interview, 25 April 2012.
[76] Interview, 8 March 2012.
[77] Nos. 30562/04 and 30566/04, 4 December 2008 [GC].

Article 8 ECHR), the Court had not provided guidance as to what an alternative system might look like. Patrick ventures that '[g]uidance about the kind of safeguards that might be integrated into a new system would have been helpful. [The Court] doesn't have to say "the system should look like this" but it might be constructive to say what the essential criteria are'.

Such criteria could take the form of the 'checklists' of principles which the Court has developed in respect of, for example, the quality of assurances required to assess whether an applicant faces a real risk of ill-treatment in a country to which he or she is to be removed.[78]

Interviewees in all states are less anxious about the Court being prescriptive as to time scales, since this is not perceived as intruding on the policy competence of national authorities; however, several interviewees venture that unfeasibly short deadlines risk bringing the process into disrepute. For example, the one-year deadline for a legislative solution in the pilot judgment in *Rumpf*, concerning the problem of overly lengthy domestic legal proceedings, was only met because the German government had already begun to draft legislation, of which the ECtHR was aware (see 9.3).[79] Deadlines set by the Court must therefore reflect the demands and complexity of the legislative process, an imperative that has also been recognized by domestic courts.[80]

2.4 Contact between the Court and National Parliaments

National parliamentarians, at least those who are not members of the Parliamentary Assembly, presently have little direct contact with the Court. Such contacts, for example by means of study visits, have the potential to widen knowledge and understanding of the Convention system beyond PACE delegates.

Another option that has been little explored is for judges of the Court to appear before the relevant committee of their national parliament on a regular (but not necessarily annual) basis. The purpose of such appearances would not be for the judge to account for his or her judicial performance, or to engage in substantive discussion of pending or decided cases, but rather 'to inform parliamentarians about the work of the Court and to give them, and the wider public, an opportunity to engage directly with the work of the Court and the issues currently facing it'.[81]

[78] See, for example, *Othman (Abu Qatada) v UK*, No. 8139/09, 17 January 2012, paras. 187–9.

[79] Almut Wittling-Vogel, Interview, 20 March 2012.

[80] In the case of *M v Germany*, No. 19359/04, 17 December 2009, concerning the retrospective and effectively indefinite prolongation of preventive detention of prisoners considered to be dangerous, seventeen laws (one federal law and one law in each of the sixteen constituent states) were necessary, in addition to other administrative measures (see 9.2). This occasioned the German Federal Constitutional Court, in a subsequent judgment on the same matter (No. 2 B v R 2365/09, 4 May 2011) to impose a deadline of just over one year, during which the impugned law (albeit with modifications determined by the court) continued to apply.

[81] Murray Hunt, Submission to the CDDH consultation, 'The Longer Term Future of the System of the European Convention on Human Rights and the European Court of Human Rights' (undated), para. 2.

In March 2012, in the first session of its kind in the UK, the (then) UK Judge and President of the Court, Sir Nicolas Bratza, appeared before the JCHR, along with the Court's (then) Deputy Registrar Erik Fribergh,[82] demonstrating that such appearances need not, as might be feared, unduly politicize the judicial role or undermine its independence. Sir Nicolas acknowledged that national judges, rather than parliaments, were the 'natural partners' of ECtHR judges, but added that he would encourage his fellow judges to engage in similar dialogue with their respective national parliaments 'if there is a body such as [the JCHR] with a particular commitment to the protection and furtherance of human rights'.[83]

We have not uncovered similar instances of ECtHR judges appearing formally before a national parliamentary body. Contact does, however, take place between PACE delegations and their respective ECtHR judges while in Strasbourg. The German delegation meets the German judge annually.[84] The former Dutch judge, Egbert Myjer reports doing so on a more ad hoc basis during his term.[85] The former Romanian judge, Corneliu Birsan, had maintained 'informal, but not institutional, contacts' with parliamentarians in Romania.[86] Speaking during his term as judge, Egbert Myjer detects an ambivalent attitude among his fellow judges to such meetings, especially at the national level:

> It depends a little on the kind of judge you are. I know some colleagues who don't want to have any contacts with parliamentarians.... I think I should be able to talk to parliamentarians and give them general background information but [in respect of specific cases] I won't give more information than is in the judgment because as judges we speak through our judgments, including dissenting opinions.

Another means by which a human rights committee might increase its engagement with the Convention system is to play a part in the selection of candidates for judges to the Court. Each judge of the Court is elected by the Parliamentary Assembly from a list of three candidates nominated during a national selection procedure.[87] Committee of Ministers Guidelines on the selection of candidates for the post of ECtHR judge suggest that, depending on national circumstances, members of the selection body may include members of relevant parliamentary committees as happens in Belgium, Croatia, Lithuania, Switzerland, the former Yugoslav Republic of Macedonia, and Ukraine.[88]

2.5 The Role of the Committee of Ministers

Within the Council of Europe system it is the Committee of Ministers which, according to the Convention itself, has the role of supervising the execution of ECtHR

[82] JCHR, Uncorrected Transcript of Oral Evidence from Sir Nicolas Bratza and Erik Fribergh on Human Rights Judgments, 13 March 2012.

[83] Oral Evidence from Sir Nicolas Bratza (n 82) Q137.

[84] Christoph Strässer, Interview, 21 March 2012.

[85] Interview, 27 June 2012.

[86] Interview, 25 June 2012.

[87] See 2.6.1 at n 158.

[88] Guidelines of the Committee of Ministers on the selection of candidates for the post of judge at the European Court of Human Rights—Explanatory Memorandum, M(2012)40 addendum final, 29 March 2012, para. 51.

judgments.[89] The Committee of Ministers is the executive organ of the Council of Europe, formally comprising member states' Foreign Ministers, with Ministers' Deputies or permanent representatives acting on a day-to-day basis. In order to fulfil its function of supervising the enforcement of ECtHR judgments, the Committee of Ministers holds four regular meetings (known as 'DH meetings') a year, with urgent cases being considered during other meetings where necessary. In practice, legal experts from ministries of justice and legal advisers in permanent missions participate in the decision-making processes as much as diplomats themselves.[90] The Committee of Ministers is assisted by a secretariat body, the Department for the Execution of Judgments of the ECtHR.[91] The Committee of Ministers also has a Steering Committee for Human Rights (CDDH), composed of representatives of the forty-seven member states. The CDDH oversees and coordinates the intergovernmental work of the Council of Europe in the human rights field, and advises the Committee of Ministers on all questions within its field of competence.

2.5.1 Implementation of individual and general measures

In order to assess the question of the effective implementation of a particular judgment, the Committee of Ministers will be required to consider both 'individual measures' and 'general measures' which arise. As noted at 2.3, 'individual measures' concern the payment of damages (and/or legal costs) to the applicant in the case,[92] as well as any other specific measures which would benefit the applicant. For example, individual measures may include the following: the reopening of domestic proceedings;[93] the lifting of an injunction;[94] an acquittal;[95] the cancellation of a criminal record;[96] release from custody;[97] the requirement to carry out an effective

[89] Article 46(2) ECHR provides that '[t]he final judgment of the Court shall be transmitted to the Committee of Ministers, which shall supervise its execution'.

[90] Başak Çalı and Anne Koch, 'Foxes Guarding the Foxes? The Peer Review of Human Rights Judgments by the Committee of Ministers of the Council of Europe', *Human Rights Law Review* 14(2) (2014): 301, 308.

[91] The Department for the Execution of Judgments is part of the Council of Europe's Directorate General of Human Rights and Rule of Law.

[92] The requirements for payment of just satisfaction (e.g., as to the amount, recipient, and deadline) are generally stipulated in the judgment; however, complex issues do sometimes arise, relating, for example, to the validity of powers of attorney, the applicable exchange rate, devaluations in the currency of payment, and the seizure or taxation of sums awarded. See Committee of Ministers, Monitoring of the payment of sums awarded by way of just satisfaction: an overview of the Committee of Ministers' present practice, CM/Inf/DH(2008)7 final, 15 January 2009.

[93] See, for example, *Unterpertinger v Austria*: Resolution DH(89)002, 18 January 1989; *Jersild v Denmark*: Resolution DH(95)212, 11 September 1995; *Sadak, Zana, Dicle, and Doğan v Turkey*: Interim Resolution ResDH(2002)59, 30 April 2002; *Lungoci, Caracas, and Bacso v Romania*: Resolution CM/ResDH(2013)68, 30 April 2013.

[94] See, for example, *Open Door and Dublin Well Woman v Ireland*: Resolution DH(96)368, 25 June 1996.

[95] See, for example, *Barberà, Messegué, and Jabardo v Spain*: Resolution DH(94)84, 16 November 1994.

[96] See, for example, *Marijnissen v Netherlands*: Resolution DH(85)004, 25 February 1985.

[97] See, for example, *Van Mechelen and Others v Netherlands*: Resolution DH(99)124, 19 February 1999; *Sadak, Zana, Dicle, and Doğan v Turkey*: Final Resolution ResDH(2004)86, 9 December 2004.

investigation into a disappearance and death;[98] the return of a plot of land;[99] or the revocation of a decision to expel.[100]

'General measures' are broader steps taken by the national authorities with the aim of preventing further similar violations, such as legislative, administrative, regulatory, or policy changes, and in rare instances constitutional reform. Thus, for example, general measures may involve: the introduction of new legislation;[101] consequential changes in the case law of the domestic courts;[102] the publication and dissemination of the judgment;[103] issuing instructions to the relevant domestic authorities;[104] or the education and/or training of public officials.[105] The imposition of general measures may also require the setting up of new domestic remedies to deal with violations already committed.

The Committee of Ministers applies a 'twin-track system' for the supervision of the execution of judgments: a standard procedure and an enhanced procedure.[106] Under this system, most cases are examined under the standard procedure. Cases which are subject to the enhanced procedure are those in the following categories: judgments requiring urgent individual measures; pilot judgments; judgments disclosing major structural and/or complex problems; and inter-state cases.[107]

2.5.2 Action plans and action reports

The Committee of Ministers has placed increasing emphasis on the provision of 'action plans' or 'action reports', which were introduced in 2004 and have become embedded in the supervision process since 2009.[108] Under both the standard and enhanced supervision procedures, states are required to provide an action plan or action report on the case as soon as possible and at the latest within six months

98 See, for example, *Gongadze v Ukraine*: Interim Resolution CM/ResDH(2008)35, 5 June 2008.

99 See, for example, *Driza and Manushaqe Puto and Others Group*, H/Exec(2013)2, 26 April 2013.

100 See, for example, *D v UK*: Resolution DH(98)10, 18 February 1998.

101 See, for example, *Urbarska Obec Trencianske Biskupice, Jenisova, Salus, and Sefcikova v Slovak Republic*: Resolution CM/ResDH(2013)87, 7 May 2013; *A and Others v UK*: Resolution CM/ResDH(2013)114, 6 June 2013.

102 See, for example, *Beaumartin v France*: Resolution DH(95)254, 20 November 1995.

103 See, for example, the Norwegian Supreme Court's activities to publish a summary and analysis in Norwegian of the ECtHR judgment in *Bergens Tidende v Norway*: Resolution ResDH(2002)69, 11 July 2002.

104 See, for example, *Assenov v Bulgaria*: Resolution ResDH(2000)109, 2 October 2000; *Saunders v UK*: Interim Resolution DH(2000)27, 14 February 2000.

105 See, for example, *Yagiz v Turkey*: Resolution DH(99)20, 18 January 1999; Interim Resolution CM/ResDH(2007)107 concerning the judgments of the ECtHR in the case of *Velikova* and seven other cases against Bulgaria relating in particular to the ill-treatment inflicted by police forces, including three deaths, and the lack of an effective investigation, 17 October 2007.

106 Committee of Ministers, Supervision of the execution of judgments and decisions of the European Court of Human Rights: implementation of the Interlaken Action Plan—Modalities for a twin-track supervision system, CM/Inf/DH(2010)37E, 6 September 2010.

107 The Committee of Ministers may also decide to examine any case under the enhanced procedure at the request of a member state or the Secretariat.

108 Committee of Ministers Recommendation CM/Rec(2008)2 to member states on efficient domestic capacity for rapid execution of judgments of the European Court of Human Rights, 6 February 2008, para. 6.

from the date upon which the judgment became final.[109] An action plan sets out the measures which a state intends to take to implement a judgment of the Court. An action report describes the measures which have been taken by a state to implement a judgment and/or explains why a state considers that no measures, or no further measures, are necessary. The Committee of Ministers describes action plans and reports as 'the practical expression of the principle of subsidiarity', which have injected 'transparency and dynamism' into the execution process.[110] The number of action plans or reports submitted by states in 2014 almost doubled compared to 2012.[111] Our interlocutors in the Council of Europe confirm that most states now comply with the six-month deadline for the provision of action plans or reports in relation to new cases, but that the quality of the plans is extremely variable, with some lacking detail or consisting largely of a critique of the judgment.

The Committee of Ministers notes that action plans and reports are 'key tools' which can contribute to enhanced dialogue between the executive and other actors, including parliaments and national human rights institutions (NHRIs).[112] It also proposes that action plans and reports should be written in non-technical language and be widely disseminated in national languages.[113] Action plans or reports are usually the first point in the implementation process at which a state must give a reasoned, public explanation for the action it proposes to take in response to a judgment. They can be revised and resubmitted at any time, meaning that the state can incorporate subsequent recommendations made by parliament or other domestic actors. In addition, the principle of subsidiarity implies that states should use action plans in part to keep the Committee of Ministers informed of any relevant parliamentary consideration of the measures proposed by it in response to a judgment.[114]

Given the increasing centrality of action plans to the process of supervision, routine provision of these documents to parliamentary human rights committees at the same time as they are submitted to the Committee of Ministers has the potential to strengthen the implementation process.[115] Christos Giakoumopoulos, Director of Human Rights in the Council of Europe's Directorate General Human Rights and Rule of Law, endorses this approach, although he clarifies that this should not go as

[109] Committee of Ministers, Action Plans—Action Reports, Definitions and Objectives, Memorandum prepared by the Department for the Execution of Judgments of the European Court of Human Rights, CM/Inf/DH(2009)29rev, 3 June 2009.

[110] Committee of Ministers, *Supervision of the Execution of Judgments and Decisions of the European Court of Human Rights: 8th Annual Report of the Committee of Ministers 2014* (2015) ('8th Annual Report of the Committee of Ministers 2014') 203.

[111] During 2014, the Committee of Ministers received 266 action plans and 481 action reports. For the same period in 2013, 229 action plans (158 in 2012) and 349 action reports (262 in 2012) had been submitted to the Committee; see 8th Annual Report of the Committee of Ministers 2014 (n 110) 41.

[112] Brussels Declaration (n 12) para. B.2.a.

[113] 8th Annual Report of the Committee of Ministers 2014 (n 110) 204.

[114] Joint Committee on Human Rights, Seventh Report of Session 2014–15, *Human Rights Judgments*, HL Paper 130, HC 1088 (2015), para. 6.4.

[115] Although action plans are published on the Committee of Ministers' website in advance of the meeting at which they are considered, this does not always happen as soon as they are received, a delay which might in some cases impede effective scrutiny of a state's response in the national parliament.

far as requiring formal parliamentary endorsement of an action plan or report since this could complicate the execution process unduly:

> [T]he idea of a [parliamentary] human rights committee reviewing an action plan as it is submitted to the Committee of Ministers is a good one.... The government should take the initiative and inform parliament. There is no reason to exclude the parliament from this discussion, in particular where legislative action needs to be taken in the framework of the execution of a judgment.[116]

However, to our knowledge, such practice has so far become routine in only one state: the UK (see 7.4.1).

Under the standard procedure for supervision, the involvement of the Committee of Ministers is limited to verifying whether or not action plans or action reports have indeed been submitted by states. Applicants (or their representatives) are entitled to communicate with the Committee of Ministers as to the payment of 'just satisfaction' or other individual measures.[117] In addition, the Committee of Ministers may consider communications about the execution of judgments from NGOs or NHRIs.[118] Action plans are subject to a preliminary assessment by the secretariat as to both the measures envisaged and the timetable proposed and contact is made with the national authorities if further information or clarifications are necessary. When a state informs the secretariat that it considers that all measures have been taken and that it has complied with its obligation under Article 46 ECHR, the action plan is turned into an action report. The secretariat will then make a 'conclusive assessment' of it (within six months). If the state and the secretariat agree on the measures adopted or implemented, the secretariat will propose that the Committee of Ministers adopts a final resolution closing the examination of the case.[119]

If a case is subject to the enhanced procedure, it is envisaged that the secretariat will engage in more intensive and proactive co-operation with the state, which may involve the provision of assistance in the preparation and/or implementation of action plans; the provision of expert assistance as regards the type of measures to be taken; or establishing bilateral or multilateral co-operation programmes (such as seminars or roundtables). Enhanced procedure cases may also be the subject of a debate, at the request of any state or the secretariat, or they can be the subject of a narrative decision, without the need for a debate. Cases may be transferred between the two procedures. For example, a case will be transferred from the standard to the enhanced procedure if there is serious delay in the implementation of an action

[116] Interview, 27 June 2013.

[117] Rule 9(1) of the Rules of the Committee of Ministers for the Supervision of the Execution of Judgments and of the Terms of Friendly Settlements, 10 May 2006. The Rule does not expressly permit the applicant to send communications relating to general measures, although this is not explicitly excluded.

[118] Rule 9(2) of the Rules of the Committee of Ministers for the Supervision of the Execution of Judgments and of the Terms of Friendly Settlements, 10 May 2006.

[119] In 2014, 1,502 final resolutions were adopted, almost double the number in 2011 and an all-time high; see 8th Annual Report of the Committee of Ministers 2014 (n 110) 52.

plan. More commonly, transfers are made from enhanced to standard supervision as a result of progress achieved in implementation.[120]

A case remains on the agenda of the Committee of Ministers until the respondent state has reported that the necessary action has been taken and the Committee of Ministers is satisfied that those measures are sufficient to comply with the judgment. At this point, the Committee of Ministers adopts a resolution stating that it has completed its task under Article 46(2) ECHR. If there is a justifiable delay in the execution of a judgment, the Committee of Ministers adopts an interim resolution which will note what steps have rapidly been adopted to limit, as far as possible, the number of new violations and indicates a timetable for further reforms needed in order to resolve the problem in question. If, however, there are problems with the execution of a judgment (or where there is uncertainty), the Committee of Ministers may issue further more strongly worded resolutions that urge the respondent state to take the steps necessary to comply with the judgment in question. In such resolutions, the Committee of Ministers may comment directly on the need for legislative action as a means of exerting pressure on national parliaments.[121] Where there are continuing systemic problems, the Committee of Ministers may issue a series of resolutions calling for further action to be taken by the authorities, as has been the case, for example, with applications concerning the excessive length of proceedings before the civil and administrative courts in Italy;[122] the failure to enforce final domestic judicial decisions relating to compensation for property nationalized under the communist regime in Albania;[123] and Turkey's failure to compensate refugees displaced from their homes in northern Cyprus.[124] The Committee of Ministers may take various other steps in order to assist in the effective execution of the judgment, such as declarations by the Chair, press releases, and holding 'high level' meetings.

2.5.3 Interpretation and infringement procedures

Two additional procedures relating to the implementation of judgments were introduced in 2010 (in accordance with Protocol No. 14 of the Convention). Firstly,

[120] 8th Annual Report of the Committee of Ministers 2014 (n 110) 10.

[121] See, for example, Committee of Ministers Interim Resolution DH(2007)74, 6 June 2007 on excessively lengthy proceedings in Greek administrative courts and the lack of an effective domestic remedy, which urged the Greek authorities to pass two Bills to remedy the respective violations.

[122] See, for example, Resolution DH(97)336, 11 July 1997; Interim Resolution DH(99)436, 15 July 1999; Interim Resolution DH(99)437, 15 July 1999; Interim Resolution ResDH(2000)135, 25 October 2000; Interim Resolution CM/ResDH(2010)224.

[123] Interim Resolution CM/ResDH(2013)115, Execution of the pilot judgment Manushaqe Puto and 11 other judgments of the European Court of Human Rights concerning the failure to enforce final domestic judicial and administrative decisions relating to the right of the applicants to restitution or compensation (whether pecuniary or in kind) for property nationalised during the communist regime in Albania, 6 June 2013.

[124] Interim Resolution DH(2001)80, 26 June 2001. This unusually strongly worded resolution reminded Turkey that 'acceptance of the Convention, including the compulsory jurisdiction of the Court and the binding nature of its judgments, has become a requirement for membership of the [Council of Europe]', and called on other member states to 'take such action as they deem appropriate' to ensure Turkey's compliance with the judgment in *Loizidou v Turkey*, No. 15318/89, 18 December 1996 [GC].

if the Committee of Ministers (by a two-thirds majority) considers that the supervision of the execution of a judgment is hindered by a problem of its interpretation, it may refer the matter to the Court for a ruling on the question of interpretation.[125] Secondly, if the Committee of Ministers (again by a majority of two-thirds) considers that a state 'refuses to abide by' a final Court judgment, it may, in exceptional circumstances, refer the question to the Court as to whether that state has failed to fulfil its obligations under the Convention, a so-called 'infringement' procedure.[126] If the Court finds a violation of Article 46(1) ECHR the case will then be referred to the Committee of Ministers for consideration of the measures to be taken. As Çalı and Koch observe, these Convention-based mechanisms carve out a potential role for the Court in the process of monitoring the implementation of judgments, a role to which it had previously been 'categorically opposed'.[127]

To date, the Committee of Ministers has used neither procedure. In respect of the infringement procedure, this is attributable partly to the lack of clarity about the meaning of the term 'refuses to abide by' in Article 46(4) ECHR. 'Refusal' might be interpreted to cover a range of circumstances including non-implementation, partial or long-delayed implementation, or situations of deadlock when a state considers that it has adequately implemented a judgment but the Committee of Ministers disagrees. The ambiguity of the term suggests that guidelines may need to be drawn up to clarify the situations in which the procedure might be invoked.

A more intractable obstacle is the lack of political resolve within the Committee of Ministers to sanction recalcitrant states.[128] Indeed, the mere mention of the infringement procedure appears to be viewed as problematic in the inter-governmental context.[129] The head of the Department for the Execution of Judgments has described the procedure under Article 46(4) ECHR as 'fairly cumbersome' and its potential use as having an uncertain outcome.[130] The Committee of Minsters has been subject to criticism by the Parliamentary Assembly for its failure to use all

[125] Pursuant to Article 46(3) ECHR.

[126] Pursuant to Article 46(4) ECHR. See Rule 11, Rules of the Committee of Ministers for the supervision of the execution of judgments and of the terms of friendly settlements, (adopted by the Committee of Ministers on 10 May 2006 at the 964th meeting of the Ministers' Deputies), Appendix 4, 10 May 2006.

[127] Çalı and Koch (n 90) 310.

[128] Dinah Shelton, 'Making Remedies in the European Court Consistent with International Law', Proceedings of the MultiRights Annual Conference on 'The Long-Term Future of the European Court of Human Rights', organized by PluriCourts under the auspices of the Council of Europe in Holmenkollen Park Hotel, Oslo, Norway, 7–8 April 2014 ('MultiRights Annual Conference 2014') 116.

[129] A draft version of the Brussels Declaration dated 2 February 2015 urged the Committee of Ministers to 'use, in a graduated manner, all of the tools at its disposal, including infringement procedures' (para. C.1.a; on file). However, the express reference to infringement procedures did not survive the inter-state negotiations; the final Declaration refers (para. C.1.a) to the need to 'continue to use, in a graduated manner, all the tools at its disposal, including interim resolutions, and to consider the use, where necessary, of the procedures foreseen under Article 46 of the Convention, when the conditions have been satisfied'.

[130] Steering Committee for Human Rights, Committee of Experts on Reform of the Court (DH-GDR), Drafting Group 'F' on Reform of the Court (GT-GDR-F), Presentation to the 3rd meeting by the Director, Human Rights, GT-GDR-F(2014)022, 24 September 2014, para. 17.

available means to deal with dilatory or defiant states. According to its rapporteur on the execution of judgments,

> [I]t is perhaps time for the Committee of Ministers to make use of the procedures set up in Article 46 paragraphs 3, 4 and 5 of the Convention and in particular the 'infringement procedure'. As long as they have not been used, it is impossible to assess their efficiency.[131]

Civil society organizations have repeatedly echoed such calls, especially in respect of cases concerning systemic, widespread, or gross human rights violations.[132] One NGO has proposed that the Committee of Ministers consider institutionalizing the infringement procedure in order to render it automatic in specified grave instances.[133] A judge of the ECtHR, Helen Keller, has further proposed that the requirement for a two-thirds majority be reduced in order to lower the political hurdle for invoking the procedure.[134]

2.5.4 General recommendations

In addition to monitoring the execution of specific judgments, the Committee of Ministers also issues general recommendations which establish basic compliance expectations to be met by all Council of Europe member states. Çalı and Koch note that the recommendations establish standards against which the behaviour of states can be assessed by the Department for the Execution of Judgments and increase confidence in the even-handedness and legitimacy of the supervision process.[135] Together with other non-case-specific activities of the Committee of Minsters (such as roundtable discussions) they may also assist states that are struggling with compliance on technical or capacity grounds.

Of particular relevance to our theme is the 2008 recommendation on the development of efficient domestic capacity for rapid execution of Court judgments.[136] This recommendation refers to the need to establish or strengthen both parliamentary and executive mechanisms and co-ordinate all national actors, with support at the highest political level.[137] However, governments were recommended to report

[131] PACE, Committee on Legal Affairs and Human Rights, Implementation of judgments of the European Court of Human Rights, Doc. 13864, 9 September 2015 (Rapporteur: Klaas de Vries) ('8th Rapporteur Report') para. 49.

[132] See, for example, Joint NGO Response to the draft Brussels Declaration on 'Implementation of the European Convention on Human Rights, Our Shared Responsibility', 27 March 2015. See also 'Request for initiation of infringement proceedings by the Committee of Ministers in relation to the judgment of the European Court of Human Rights in *Isayeva v Russia*, No. 57950/00, 24 February 2005' submitted by the European Human Rights Advocacy Centre and Memorial Human Rights Centre, 27 July 2012, under Rule 11 of the Rules of the Committee of Ministers, pursuant to Article 46(4) ECHR.

[133] Open Society Justice Initiative, Briefing paper on supervision of execution of Court judgments, submitted to Drafting Group 'E' on Reform of the Court, GT-GDR-E(2013)005, 13 May 2013, para. 10.

[134] Presentation by Judge Helen Keller, MultiRights Annual Conference 2014 (n 128) 148.

[135] Çalı and Koch (n 90) 319–20.

[136] CM/Rec(2008)2 (n 108).

[137] CM/Rec(2008)2 (n 108) para. i.

to parliaments on the execution of judgments only 'as appropriate', reflecting the Committee of Ministers' perfunctory approach to the parliamentary dimension of implementation which has only recently begun to shift to one that evinces more genuine commitment.[138]

2.5.5 Contact between the Committee of Ministers and parliaments

It is the government that represents the state during the process of supervision of the execution of judgments by the Committee of Ministers; therefore, at the national level the main interlocutors of the Committee of Ministers and its secretariat are government officials. Given the discretion inherent in the supervision mechanism, however, the executive may not adequately represent the views and interests of all state actors and therefore the execution process can become an arena in which differences emerge *between* state institutions. A question which consequently arises is how far the Committee of Ministers engages not only with governments, but also with national parliaments (or other non-executive actors) in respect either of its general activities to promote effective implementation or its supervision of the execution of specific judgments. The answer is that parliamentarians are involved to only a limited extent in either aspect of the Department's work.

In respect of its general activities, the Department for the Execution of Judgments has developed targeted co-operation programmes in particularly problematic areas (supported by the Council of Europe's HRTF). Since 2009, such activities have related to, among other issues, non-enforcement of domestic court decisions; the execution of ECtHR judgments finding violations of the Convention concerning actions of security forces in the Chechen Republic; restitution or compensation for properties nationalized by former communist regimes; and the development of effective domestic capacity to implement ECtHR judgments in a timely and effective way.[139] A review of the roundtables held under the HRTF programme suggests that participants are mainly government officials, civil servants, and judicial figures, with parliamentarians or parliamentary staff very rarely taking part.

The Department holds other thematic seminars which address issues common to several, or indeed all, states, in order that effective practice can be shared. Three recent multilateral seminars for which participant lists are available involved government officials, civil servants, and judicial actors, but no parliamentarians.[140] Several

[138] CM/Rec(2008)2 (n 108) para. 9. In contrast, see Brussels Declaration (n 12) para. 2.h which calls on governments to 'in particular, encourage the involvement of national parliaments in the judgment execution process, where appropriate, for instance, by transmitting to them annual or thematic reports or by holding debates with the executive authorities on the implementation of certain judgments'.

[139] 8th Annual Report of the Committee of Ministers 2014 (n 110) 22.

[140] 'The action plans and report of states for the execution of the judgments of the European Court: current practice and future perspectives' (2014); 'Excessive length of proceedings—how to solve an important systemic problem' (2012); 'Efficient domestic capacity for rapid execution of judgments of the European Court of Human Rights' (2011).

Romanian parliamentarians were, however, present at a roundtable on property restitution and compensation in Bucharest in 2011.[141] Given the Committee of Ministers' increasing acknowledgement of the necessity of involving parliaments in the execution process, engaging parliamentarians more frequently in such bilateral or multilateral initiatives would be a logical development of its working methods.

As for the Department's bilateral discussions on specific judgments, these generally take place at the invitation of the government concerned and the Department for the Execution of Judgments avoids shortcircuiting this practice by talking to parliaments (or other non-executive actors) on its own initiative.[142] Where there is an identified need for legislative action, the office responsible for co-ordinating national implementation of judgments (typically, the government agent; see 3.5.1) may seek the assistance of the Department to explain to ministries and, where relevant, parliamentarians or ombudsmen, the nature of the problem and the procedural requirements for implementation in order to expedite the process. This is especially likely where cases are technically complex; there is reluctance on the part of the executive to propose legislation or parliament to adopt legislation; there is uncertainty about what the judgment requires; or there is inertia caused by a lack of capacity at the domestic level.[143]

Christos Giakoumopoulos notes that when the Department does hold discussions with parliamentarians, they generally take place with members of the relevant parliamentary committee(s) and are largely confined to procedural issues.[144] The Department may indicate when a remedy (almost invariably proposed by the executive) is insufficient to remove the violation, but it 'does not push legislators in a specific direction in relation to substance'. Giakoumopoulos adds:

> It's a sensitive area. We leave a wide 'margin of appreciation' to legislators to determine the nature and scope of the remedy. We may say that a proposed remedy is not enough but we rarely say 'this is what you have to do'. The easier interlocutor in this respect is the government. We can say [to the government] 'please introduce this in a draft law or a regulation'. It's much more difficult to tell a parliament what to do: the Department does not have the status to do so, and the same is true for the judiciary.

Beyond matters of protocol, more fundamental questions arise about the way in which parliamentary involvement in the execution process is viewed by the Committee of Ministers. Our interviews with officials within the Committee of Ministers indicate that no inherent value is placed on the involvement of parliament in the execution process; the Committee of Ministers is, in this sense, entirely neutral about which state actor executes a judgment—the executive, parliament, or the courts—as long as it *is* implemented. In some cases, where legislative reform is

[141] Roundtable on property restitution/compensation measures to comply with the European Court's judgments, Bucharest, 17 February 2011.

[142] Interview (anonymous), 26 June 2014.

[143] Steering Committee for Human Rights, CDDH report on whether more effective measures are needed in respect of States that fail to implement Court judgments in a timely manner, CM(2013)174, 20 December 2013, para. 6.

[144] Interview, 27 June 2013.

indisputably required, there is no ambiguity about the need for parliamentary involvement. However, in many other cases, the most efficient route to execution may not be immediately apparent. It may be open to the executive either to take action itself (e.g., by means of a regulation or an executive or presidential decree), or to propose legislative reform, or to wait and see whether a remedy might be achieved via the judicial route. As one interviewee within the Department for the Execution of Judgments puts it:

> The biggest problem for government agents is to try to assess what the courts could do and what the legislature has to do [in response to a judgment]. Should a government agent immediately propose parliamentary action because that's the safest way to achieve legal certainty? But that will take a lot of time and may induce the courts not to take action. So that's an intricate relationship which it's very difficult to master.[145]

Christos Giakoumopoulos ventures that where a problem cannot be resolved via the judicial system but can be remedied by the executive without involving parliament, 'we would not object', adding that the Department would nonetheless consider it important for the parliament to be informed of the remedial measure. The Department's neutrality as to which state actors take steps to provide a remedy following an adverse judgment reflects a pragmatic approach to the often convoluted, and unavoidably political, process of implementation. In some instances, parliaments may step in to provide a remedy where executive actors have been dilatory.[146] In others, parliamentary inertia following judgments which appear to require legislative reform may prompt judicial actors to seize the initiative, resulting in action which may ultimately satisfy the Committee of Ministers.[147] Nevertheless, this pragmatic approach should not be allowed to obscure instances in which, for example, executive bodies bypass parliamentary procedure by means

[145] Interview (anonymous), 26 June 2012.

[146] See, for example, the case of *Hakkar v France*, No. 19033/91, 27 June 1995 in which the former European Commission of Human Rights (ECommHR) found multiple procedural failures under Article 6 ECHR (the right to fair trial) which had led to the life imprisonment of the applicant. The judgment required both individual measures (in the form of just satisfaction) and general measures due to the absence of any legal remedy permitting the reopening of the impugned proceedings. The French government declined to act. Following concerted pressure from PACE, and the introduction of a private member's bill, the French parliament adopted on 15 June 2000 a new law making it possible to re-examine a criminal decision following a judgment of the ECtHR. See *Hakkar v France*: Final Resolution ResDH(2001)4, 14 February 2001.

[147] For example, the Albanian Supreme Court has ordered that proceedings be reopened in several cases following findings of violations of Article 6 ECHR by the ECtHR, and in one case overturned a conviction despite the fact that neither reopening of proceedings nor review of conviction is provided for in the Albanian Code of Criminal Procedure (see *Xheraj v Albania*, No. 37959/02, 29 July 2008; Supreme Court judgment no. 01226/2011, 7 March 2012). Likewise, following the ECommHR decision finding a violation of Article 6(1) ECHR in *Dorigo v Italy*, No. 33286/96, 9 September 1998, the Italian Court of Cassation stated that judges may reopen domestic proceedings in such cases, even if parliament has not introduced a specific means to reopen the trial, 'a signal of the willingness of judges to counterbalance Parliament's inertia'; see Serena Sileoni, 'Between Political Inertia and Timid Judicial Activism: The Attempts to Overcome the Italian Implementation Failure', in Dia Anagnostou, ed., *The European Court of Human Rights: Implementing Strasbourg Judgments on Domestic Policy* (Edinburgh University Press, 2013): 49, 64–5. See also Final Resolution CM/ResDH(2007)837, 20 June 2007.

of emergency ordinances. Concern has been expressed about the overly frequent use of such emergency procedures in Romania (see 6.4.1).

Such concerns underline the need for sensitivity within the execution process to the potential role of parliaments as bodies that both initiate remedies and scrutinize executive action or inaction following adverse judgments of the Court. Moreover, they highlight the imperative for parliamentary human rights bodies to seize the opportunities available to them to become more active partners within the process of execution, including oversight of action plans and reports, and engagement where appropriate with the Department for the Execution of Judgments.

2.6 The Role of the Parliamentary Assembly of the Council of Europe

The Parliamentary Assembly plays a pivotal role within the Council of Europe. Among other functions, it elects the Secretary-General, the Commissioner for Human Rights, and judges of the Court.[148] The Assembly is composed of delegations from the national parliaments of the forty-seven member states. It currently has 324 members, with an equal number of substitute members. While in the Committee of Ministers each member state has one vote, in the Assembly the number of representatives (and consequently of votes) is roughly determined by the size of the population; the largest delegation is eighteen, the smallest, two. Delegations must reflect the balance of political forces represented in the national parliament. It is left to each member state to decide how to appoint or elect its representatives from among members of the national or federal parliament.[149] The Assembly meets four times a year in sessions lasting for about one week. The work of PACE is mainly prepared by nine specialist committees, nominations to which are in most cases proposed by national delegations and ratified by the Assembly as a whole.[150] Committee membership is reconstituted annually. Committees generally meet *in camera* but are free to admit whom they wish to their meetings.

[148] For an overview of the human rights work of the Assembly, see Andrew Drzemczewski and Julia Lowis, 'The Work of the Parliamentary Assembly of the Council of Europe', in Murray Hunt, Hayley Hooper, and Paul Yowell, eds., *Parliaments and Human Rights: Redressing the Democratic Deficit* (Oxford: Hart Publishing, 2015): 309; Philip Leach, 'The Parliamentary Assembly of the Council of Europe', in Marten Breuer and Stefanie Schmahl, eds., *The Council of Europe: Its Law and Policies* (Oxford: Oxford University Press, forthcoming in 2016).

[149] Arabella Lang, *UK Delegation to the Parliamentary Assembly of the Council of Europe*, House of Commons Library, Briefing Paper No. 7378, 16 November 2015, 13–19.

[150] These are the Committee on Political Affairs and Democracy; the Committee on Legal Affairs and Human Rights; the Committee on Social Affairs, Health, and Sustainable Development; the Committee on Migration, Refugees, and Displaced Persons; the Committee on Culture, Science, Education, and the Media; the Committee on Equality and Non-Discrimination; the Monitoring Committee; the Committee on Rules of Procedure, Immunities, and Institutional Affairs; and the Committee on the Election of Judges to the European Court of Human Rights.

2.6.1 The Committee on Legal Affairs and Human Rights

The Parliamentary Assembly has for more than a decade performed an increasingly assertive and influential role in the supervision of the enforcement of ECtHR judgments.[151] As the Assembly's former rapporteur on the execution of judgments put it in 2010,

> [W]e, the Assembly, as a statutory organ of the Council of Europe (and at the same time national parliamentarians), should not meekly accept the premise that the Committee of Ministers has 'exclusive jurisdiction' on this subject. When the Court judgments are not fully and rapidly executed, we—parliamentarians—also have a duty to help supervise the execution of the Court's judgments. The credibility and viability of our European system of human rights cannot be left solely in the hands of the executive organ of the Council of Europe (in effect, diplomatic representatives of governments).[152]

In practice, this supervisory role is carried out largely by the Committee on Legal Affairs and Human Rights ('the Legal Affairs Committee') in a process which is supplementary to that of the Committee of Ministers.[153] As a committee of PACE, its emphasis has been to take advantage of the possibilities for dialogue with national legislators, which in turn may elicit a formal response from the Committee of Ministers. The Committee has published eight reports on the implementation of judgments since 2000,[154] along with seven resolutions[155] and six recommendations[156] addressed both to member states and other Council of Europe bodies.

[151] See, for example, PACE Resolution 1226 (2000), Execution of Judgments of the European Court of Human Rights, 28 September 2000. See also Brussels Declaration (n 12) paras. C.1.c and C.3.f.

[152] PACE, Committee on Legal Affairs and Human Rights, Implementation of judgments of the European Court of Human Rights, Doc. 12455, 20 December 2010 (Rapporteur: Christos Pourgourides) ('7th Rapporteur Report') para. 213.

[153] Other PACE committees may take up the issue of the implementation of ECtHR judgments on a more ad hoc basis, notably the Monitoring Committee (Committee on the Honouring of Obligations and Commitments by Member States of the Council of Europe). See, for example, the Monitoring Committee's 2012 report on Bosnia and Herzegovina which commented on the problems with the implementation of the ECtHR judgment in *Sejdić and Finci v Bosnia and Herzegovina*, Nos. 27996/06 and 34836/06, 22 December 2009: Honouring of obligations and commitments by Bosnia and Herzegovina—Information note by the rapporteurs on their fact-finding visit to Sarajevo, Mostar and Naja Luka (3–7 June 2012), AS/Mon(2012)18 rev, 5 September 2012, paras. 10–11, 22.

[154] See 8th Rapporteur Report (n 131); 7th Rapporteur Report (n 152). See also the following reports, all under the rapporteurship of Erik Jurgens: Implementation of judgments of the European Court of Human Rights, Doc. 11020, 18 September 2006; Implementation of decisions of the European Court of Human Rights, Doc. 10351, 21 October 2004; Implementation of decisions of the European Court of Human Rights by Turkey, Doc. 10192, 1 June 2004; Implementation of decisions of the European Court of Human Rights by Turkey, Doc. 9357, 5 September 2002; Implementation of decisions of the European Court of Human Rights, Doc. 9307, 21 December 2001; Execution of judgments of the European Court of Human Rights, Doc. 8808, 12 July 2000.

[155] PACE resolutions on the execution/implementation of judgments of the European Court of Human Rights: Resolution 1787 (2011), 26 January 2011; Resolution 1516 (2006), 2 October 2006; Resolution 1411 (2004), 23 November 2004; Resolution 1381 (2004), 22 June 2004; Resolution 1297 (2002), 23 September 2002; Resolution 1268 (2002), 22 January 2002; Resolution 1226 (2000) (n 151).

[156] PACE recommendations on the execution/implementation of judgments of the European Court of Human Rights: Recommendation 1955 (2011), 26 January 2011; Recommendation 1764 (2006), 2 October 2006; Recommendation 1684 (2004), 23 November 2004; Recommendation 1576 (2002), 23 September 2002; Recommendation 1546 (2002), 23 September 2002; Recommendation 1477 (2000), 28 September 2000.

Interviewees with direct knowledge of the Committee's work, including former members, emphasized the vital role played by its secretariat (under the leadership for the past decade of Andrew Drzemczewski) whose expertise and commitment had provided continuity and momentum to the work of the Committee and had enabled members without prior legal or human rights knowledge, and/or without fluent English or French, to become actively involved. Indeed, this function of the secretariat is analogous to that played by legal advisers to national parliamentary bodies, whose expertise and political independence is vital to their effectiveness (see 3.4.3).

The Legal Affairs Committee deals with a wide range of legal and human rights topics, appointing parliamentary rapporteurs who are mandated to prepare reports based on *in situ* research, hearings, and exchanges of views with experts.[157] The Legal Affairs Committee was formerly responsible (via a sub-committee) for interviewing candidates for the posts of judges to the ECtHR, prior to their election by the Assembly. This role is now undertaken by a full Committee which began work in January 2015.[158]

There are three sub-committees of the Legal Affairs Committee: on human rights, matters related to crime and the fight against terrorism, and—newly created in 2015—the implementation of ECtHR judgments. The creation of the latter, which replaced a previous sub-committee on the rule of law, is another indication of the priority accorded to this particular function of national parliaments. Its terms of reference include addressing cases of non-implementation of judgments, especially those pointing to the existence of systemic shortcomings or requiring urgent individual measures in cases concerning serious human rights violations.[159] The sub-committee is also tasked with identifying the reasons for failure to execute judgments in co-operation with, in particular, the delegation of the state concerned in order to find solutions to outstanding problems. It is envisaged that it will draw on the expertise of representatives of parliaments, governments, and civil society.[160]

The sub-committee will work alongside the Legal Affairs Committee's rapporteur on the implementation of ECtHR judgments, a position created in 2000.[161] Among other activities, the rapporteur undertakes country visits, in order to discuss with various interlocutors, including parliamentary and government representatives, the most pressing issues relating to Strasbourg judgments which have not been fully implemented. In 2014, the rapporteur undertook fact-finding visits to Turkey,

157 PACE, Committee on Legal Affairs and Human Rights, Work of the Committee on Legal Affairs and Human Rights (AS/Jur): an overview, AS/Jur/Inf (2015) 01, 9 January 2015.

158 PACE, Committee on Legal Affairs and Human Rights, Procedure for electing judges to the European Court of Human Rights, AS/Jur/Inf (2014) 03 rev 1, 27 March 2014; Andrew Drzemczewski, 'Election of Judges to the Strasbourg Court: An Overview', *European Human Rights Law Review* 4 (2010): 377.

159 PACE, Committee on Legal Affairs and Human Rights, Work programme, AS/Jur/Inf (2015) 02 Rev, 26 February 2015, Appendix E 2.

160 8th Rapporteur Report (n 131) para. 44.

161 To date, four rapporteurs have been appointed to oversee the implementation of judgments of the Court: Erik Jurgens (2000–07), Christos Pourgourides (2007–12), Klaas de Vries (2012–15), and Pierre-Yves Le Borgn' (who was appointed in November 2015).

Italy, and Poland.[162] The report of the rapporteur published in June 2015 focuses in detail on nine states with the highest number of unenforced judgments—Italy, Turkey, Russia, Ukraine, Romania, Greece, Poland, Hungary, and Bulgaria—and deals selectively with three other states which have high numbers of cases under enhanced supervision (Moldova, Azerbaijan, and Serbia).[163]

In 2012–13, the Legal Affairs Committee held a series of innovative hearings in Strasbourg during which the heads of parliamentary delegations from the ten states which were the focus of its 2010 implementation report were asked to account for their states' failure to rectify major structural problems (Bulgaria, Greece, Italy, Republic of Moldova, Poland, Romania, the Russian Federation, Turkey, and Ukraine) or excessive delays in implementation of specific judgments (UK).[164] These hearings were, unusually, open to civil society representatives and had the aim of publicly 'naming and shaming' the states concerned.[165]

The Assembly has decided that it is entitled to summon a minister of justice (or other government minister) to attend in person to explain the failure to implement a judgment,[166] but has not done so. Given the grave problems of implementation which continue to beset the system, this would be entirely justifiable, with such ministers being, in effect, called to account by parliamentarians from across the Council of Europe. The Assembly has also advocated imposing financial sanctions on states which fail to implement ECtHR judgments, but this has not been taken up by the Committee of Ministers.[167]

At the same time as it seeks to exert leverage on recalcitrant states, the Legal Affairs Committee has sought to build the capacity of willing parliamentarians and parliamentary staff to monitor and promote human rights implementation; for example, by means of a series of seminars held since 2013 in Strasbourg and other locations.[168] This work reflects the strong emphasis placed by the Legal Affairs Committee on the importance of developing professional staff capable of providing politically independent advice on human rights law and policy to parliamentarians (see 3.4.3.1).

[162] 8th Rapporteur Report (n 131) para. 3. [163] 8th Rapporteur Report (n 131).

[164] PACE, Committee on Legal Affairs and Human Rights, Implementation of judgments of the European Court of Human Rights, extracts from the minutes of hearings, organized by the Committee, held in Strasbourg in April 2012, in June 2012, in October 2012 and in January 2013, AS/Jur (2013) 13, 28 March 2013. Alice Donald is grateful to the Legal Affairs Committee for the opportunity to observe the hearing on Russia on 28 June 2012.

[165] Drzemczewski and Lowis (n 148) 316.

[166] Resolution 1226 (2000) (n 151) para. 11.C.vi.

[167] Recommendation 1477 (2000) (n 156). See also Steering Committee for Human Rights, Memorandum on the Parliamentary Assembly's proposal to introduce a system of financial sanctions or astreintes on states who fail to implement judgments of the Strasbourg Court, GT-GDR-E(2013)002, 3 May 2013.

[168] This activity is conducted in collaboration with the Assembly's Parliamentary Project Support Division, which was created in 2012 to assist with the implementation of specific co-operation involving parliamentarians and staff of national parliaments, so as to increase the visibility and impact of PACE's work; see PACE, PPSD (2014) 07 rev. 3, The role of parliaments in implementing ECHR standards: Interparliamentary co-operation activities 2013–2014, 18 June 2014.

2.6.2 The dual mandate of Parliamentary Assembly delegates

The Legal Affairs Committee has placed considerable emphasis on the dual mandate of PACE delegates to support parliamentary involvement both at the domestic and Council of Europe levels.[169] This dual mandate is reinforced by the subsidiary nature of the Convention mechanism, according to which national authorities—including parliaments—bear the primary responsibility for guaranteeing to everyone within their jurisdiction the rights and freedoms in the Convention (see 2.1). Emphasis on the dual mandate of Assembly members raises questions about the composition and methods of selection of delegations; in particular, the extent to which there is, or should be, any overlap between membership of delegations to the Assembly and national parliamentary human rights committees. In the UK, the JCHR sees considerable merit in having such overlap, or at least co-ordination, between the two in monitoring the implementation of Convention standards and ECtHR judgments,[170] an objective which is not achieved by the UK's present system for appointing PACE delegates (see 7.3.5). The former Chair of the Assembly's Legal Affairs Committee, UK Conservative MP Christopher Chope, sees no need for overlap:

> The contribution that people like me can make [at the Parliamentary Assembly] … is to spread good practice among other countries rather than trying to bring the UK government to book because the JCHR does that perfectly well already.… There is no need for us to double up.[171]

This proposed division of responsibilities is questionable since, as noted above, the UK was one of ten states whose delegations were called to public hearings held by the Legal Affairs Committee in 2012–13 to account for (in respect of the UK) the delayed implementation of certain judgments, notably those concerning prisoners' voting rights.[172]

In other states, there is, by design, greater overlap between national parliamentary human rights bodies and the PACE delegation (including membership of the Assembly's Legal Affairs Committee); for example, in Romania (see 6.3.6) and Germany (see 9.4.3). In Greece, all seven PACE delegates are also members of the recently formed Special Permanent Committee on Monitoring the Decisions of the ECtHR (see 3.4.1.2).

Such overlap is likely to be beneficial in ensuring cross-fertilization between delegates to the Parliamentary Assembly and national parliamentary human rights bodies, and consequently the development of expertise. However, some interviewees regarded dual membership as unnecessary and unduly burdensome for individuals. Another option (which has not, to our knowledge, been explored in practice)

169 Drzemczewski and Lowis (n 148) 312–13.
170 JCHR, Fifteenth Report of Session 2009–10 (n 32) para. 196.
171 Interview, 27 June 2012.
172 PACE, Committee on Legal Affairs and Human Rights, AS/Jur (2013) 13 (n 164) 13.

would be for national parliamentary human rights bodies to send *ex officio* delegates to PACE, relieving them of the duties of full membership.

A related question is the role that Parliamentary Assembly delegates should play at the domestic level, regardless of their membership of relevant committees in the national parliament. The emphasis placed by the Assembly on the dual mandate of delegates suggests an expectation that, at a minimum, they will seek to raise awareness within their respective national parliaments about the Convention system.[173] Further, the dual mandate of Assembly members has been interpreted to mean that they 'must now play a more proactive role in [the execution of the Court's judgments]' since 'the viability of the Convention system is at issue'.[174]

Some delegates have indeed become prominent advocates for the Convention system at the domestic level, particularly when it has faced political attack as happened, for example, in France in 2015[175] and the Netherlands in 2011–12 (see 8.2.1).[176] It was former members of the Assembly who, during their membership, instigated parliamentary structures and mechanisms to monitor the implementation of judgments in Ukraine and Romania (see 5.4.1 and 6.3.4 respectively).[177] The Greek Special Permanent Committee on monitoring Court decisions was also formed at the initiative of a member of the Assembly delegation, who approached the Speaker of Parliament after gaining cross-party support for the proposal.[178]

Yet it is clear that not all delegates to the Assembly fulfil the responsibility to promote compliance with the Convention. For example, in a backbench debate in the UK Parliament in February 2011, no member of the UK delegation to the Assembly spoke in favour of implementing ECtHR judgments on the right of convicted prisoners to vote, and two, including the leader of the UK delegation, Conservative MP Robert Walter, spoke against.[179] Mr Walter subsequently told a hearing of the Legal Affairs Committee, however, that it would be 'inconceivable for the UK authorities not to implement all Strasbourg Court judgments'.[180]

The apparent contradiction between Mr Walter's statements in the House of Commons and before a hearing of the Assembly illustrate the competing pressures on elected members of parliament as they operate at the Strasbourg and domestic

[173] 8th Rapporteur Report (n 131) para. 53.

[174] European Conference of Presidents of Parliaments, Future of the European Court of Human Rights—Role of National Parliaments, Background Paper, 5 July 2012, 2.

[175] See, for example, Pierre-Yves Le Borgn', Debate on the motion for a resolution brought by Mr Pierre Lellouche, 2 April 2015 (see also 1.1.2).

[176] See, for example, motion tabled by Marie-Louise Bemelmans-Videc (CDA/Christian Democrat) on 10 May 2011: EK 32.502/32.500 V, B. on the continued commitment to human rights in accordance with the obligations arising from the ECHR (see 8.2.1). Mrs Bemelmans-Videc was a member of the Assembly from 2003 to 2011, during which period she was a member of the Legal Affairs Committee.

[177] Serhiy Holovaty, Interview, 28 June 2012; Tudor Pantiru, Interview, 26 April 2012.

[178] Konstantinos Triantafyllos, a member of the Committee on Rules of Procedure, Immunities, and Institutional Affairs of the Assembly.

[179] HC Deb, 10 February 2011, vol. 523, cols. 527–8 (Robert Walter MP) and 567–8 (Brian Binley MP). Robert Walter said the judgment was 'wrong ... illogical and unfair', but added that for the UK to withdraw from the Convention because of it would be 'counter-productive, if not dishonourable'.

[180] PACE, Committee on Legal Affairs and Human Rights, AS/Jur (2013) 13 (n 164) 11.

levels. A former Senator and head of the Dutch delegation to the Assembly, Marie-Louise Bemelmans-Videc, notes that, while in Strasbourg, MPs are able to be 'very independent of their political colour'.[181] However, Laurien Koster, President of the Netherlands Institute for Human Rights, ventures that partisanship sometimes reassertes itself in the domestic arena since it is 'far easier to be in favour of human rights on the abstract level of the Parliamentary Assembly'.[182] German MPs who were members of the Assembly appear to experience fewer tensions arising from their dual mandate, reflecting the largely consensual approach to the implementation of Strasbourg judgments in Germany (see 9.1).

Several MPs who had served as delegates to the Assembly note the considerable obstacles to sustaining active membership of the Assembly. MPs had found it difficult to attend the week-long sessions in Strasbourg, especially where alternate systems[183] do not operate reliably in the national parliament.[184] In addition, interviewees in all states suggest that membership of the Assembly was commonly viewed by parliamentarians as an esoteric activity, which is not conducive to building a high profile domestically. Members of unelected or indirectly elected upper chambers were generally viewed as being more insulated from party political pressures compared to their counterparts in lower chambers, as well as having fewer time constraints.

Commentators have been critical of the failure to integrate the Assembly's work into that of national parliaments.[185] Others have pointed to the 'varying levels of commitment' shown by some Assembly members to their Council of Europe activities,[186] and have suggested that some members are 'in the pocket' of governments,[187] and can be influenced by effective government lobbying. Our interlocutors within the Council of Europe lament the tendency for some delegations to view PACE principally as a venue within which to neutralize criticism of their respective governments (see, in respect of Ukraine, 5.5.1). An egregious example of such behaviour is the way in which the Azerbaijani delegation manoeuvred to ensure the voting down in January 2013 of a draft resolution contained in a report[188] on political prisoners in Azerbaijan presented by Christoph Strässer MP on behalf of the Legal Affairs Committee.[189] The responses by Russian delegates to questions

[181] Interview, 22 March 2012. [182] Interview, 23 March 2012.

[183] A protocol whereby MPs are paired such that those who are absent while performing other duties can count on their opposite number to abstain.

[184] Frans Timmermans, Interview, 13 June 2012.

[185] Beat Habegger, 'Democratic Accountability of International Organizations: Parliamentary Control within the Council of Europe and the OSCE and the Prospects for the United Nations', *Cooperation and Conflict* 45(2) (2010): 186, 196.

[186] Andrew MacMullen, 'Intergovernmental Functionalism? The Council of Europe in European Integration', *Journal of European Integration* 26(4) (2004): 405, 412.

[187] See, for example, Norbert Engel, 'More Transparency and Governmental Loyalty for Maintaining Professional Quality in the Election of Judges to the European Court of Human Rights', *Human Rights Law Journal* 32 (2012): 448, 453: 'It is no secret that some Governments instruct their delegation of MPs how to vote on important issues.'

[188] PACE, Committee on Legal Affairs and Human Rights, The follow-up to the issue of political prisoners in Azerbaijan, Report, Doc. 13079, 14 December 2012 (Rapporteur: Christoph Strässer).

[189] PACE, 2013 Ordinary Session (First part), Report, Sixth sitting, 23 January 2013. See also Gerald Knaus, 'Europe and Azerbaijan: The End of Shame', *Journal of Democracy* 26(3) (2015): 5.

during the hearing held by the Legal Affairs Committee in June 2012 to hold them to account for Russia's poor implementation record similarly indicated that their overriding priority was to defend their government's record.[190]

There have been suggestions that the supervisory role played by the Parliamentary Assembly should be strengthened by means of specific sanctions. In his 2010 report on implementation, former rapporteur Christos Pourgourides concluded: '[T]he Assembly ought to consider—in the future—suspending the voting rights of national delegations when their parliaments do not seriously exercise parliamentary control over the executive in cases of non-implementation of judgments of the European Court of Human Rights'.[191]

This proposal was not reiterated in the latest report by Mr Pourgourides' successor, Klaas de Vries.[192]

2.7 The Role of Other Council of Europe Bodies

Other Council of Europe agencies may also get involved in the process of ensuring the effective implementation of ECtHR judgments. For example, the Commissioner for Human Rights, an independent non-judicial institution within the Council of Europe, may meet with state officials to discuss systemic problems highlighted in ECtHR judgments. Where the implementation of judgments is problematic, the Commissioner may also meet Parliamentary Assembly delegations and/or the parliamentary committee responsible for human rights, although this does not happen routinely.[193] The state of implementation of ECtHR judgments is part of the baseline study that the Commissioner may conduct in a specific state, on the basis of which the state is encouraged to develop a national human rights action plan. The CDDH has suggested that the Commissioner could also contribute to the formal process of supervision before the Committee of Ministers.[194] The Commissioner also has the right to intervene as a third party in the proceedings of the Court, either by submitting written information or taking part in its hearings, and has done so with increasing frequency, most recently on a spate of cases concerning the situation of human rights defenders in Azerbaijan.[195]

The Venice Commission (the European Commission for Democracy through Law) is an independent consultative body, which provides states with advice—in

[190] Asked about the non-implementation of judgments arising from the Chechen conflict, Dmitry Vyatkin (a former member of the PACE Legal Affairs Committee, acting in the capacity of the Russian State Duma's expert on the execution of ECtHR judgments) stated that the judgments had 'produced negative reactions in the Russian society, due to the threats to the tranquility of the individuals having served in special units and their families. The main concern of the Russian authorities was now to maintain peace in the Chechen Republic.' See PACE, Committee on Legal Affairs and Human Rights, AS/Jur (2013) 13 (n 164) 4.

[191] 7th Rapporteur Report (n 152) para. 213.

[192] 8th Rapporteur Report (n 131).

[193] Giancarlo Cardinale, Interview, 27 June 2012.

[194] CM(2013)174 (n 143) para. 14.

[195] See the Commissioner's website at <http://www.coe.int/en/web/commissioner/third-party-interventions>.

the form of 'legal opinions'—on the compliance with international standards of either draft legislation or legislation already in force which is submitted to it for examination. Thus, the Commission may provide expert advice about legislation which is being proposed in order to comply with a judgment.[196] The Commission may supply, within its mandate, opinions upon request submitted by the Council of Europe bodies, national authorities, or international organizations participating in the Commission's work.[197] Thus either national parliaments or the Parliamentary Assembly may seize the Commission of issues, providing an additional route by which parliamentarians can take domestic issues onto the wider Council of Europe stage.

Other arms of the Council of Europe may also become involved in matters of implementation. For example, the European Commission for the Efficiency of Justice was involved in trying to resolve the problem of the excessive length of domestic court proceedings.[198] In exceptional circumstances, the Secretary-General of the Council of Europe may take up matters on enforcement.[199]

Thus, there is a range of mechanisms within the Council of Europe—legal, political, and diplomatic—which may be brought to bear on intractable problems of implementation. An illustrative example is the case of Eynulla Fatullayev, a newspaper editor who was imprisoned for more than eight years for writing articles critical of the Azerbaijani government. His case was taken up by, among others, a monitoring group reporting to the Committee of Ministers,[200] and another Council of Europe body, the European Commission against Racism and Intolerance.[201] In 2010, the ECtHR found Mr Fatullayev's conviction grossly disproportionate and, exceptionally, ordered the authorities to release him.[202] The Committee of Ministers then took up supervision of the execution of that judgment. Mr Fatullayev was released in May 2011; however, the Committee of Ministers has since issued repeated calls for the Azerbaijani authorities to ensure, among other general measures, progress (including with the provision of a timetable) in the adoption of the necessary legislative amendments aimed at reducing the possibility of imposing prison sentences in defamation cases, and in the elaboration of a larger draft law on defamation, in close co-operation with the Venice Commission.[203] In addition, the Secretary-General

196 For example, the Venice Commission provided expertise to the Azerbaijan government in relation to draft legislation on freedom of expression, in response to the *Mahmudov and Agazade* group of cases. See Committee of Ministers, *Supervision of the execution of judgments and decisions of the European Court of Human Rights: 6th Annual Report of the Committee of Ministers 2012* (2013) ('6th Annual Report of the Committee of Ministers 2012') 18.

197 Under Article 3(2) of its statute.

198 6th Annual Report of the Committee of Ministers 2012 (n 196) 15.

199 See *Loizidou v Turkey* (n 124). This case, concerning unpaid compensation to refugees displaced from northern Cyprus, was resolved following the 2003 partnership between the European Union and Turkey.

200 Committee of Ministers, Report on a visit of a delegation from the Ago Group to Armenia and Azerbaijan, 20–25 November 2009, CM (2009) 180, 4 December 2009.

201 European Commission against Racism and Intolerance, Final report on Azerbaijan adopted by ECRI at its 54th plenary meeting (Strasbourg, 23–25 March 2011), CM (2011) 54 add 1, 14 April 2011.

202 *Fatullayev v Azerbaijan* (n 50) operative para. 6.

203 See, for example, *Mahmudov and Agazade v Azerbaijan, Fatullayev v Azerbaijan*: Interim Resolution CM/ResDH(2014)183, 25 September 2014. See also Venice Commission, Opinion 692/

of the Council of Europe, Thorbjørn Jagland,[204] the Commissioner for Human Rights, Nils Muižnieks,[205] and the Parliamentary Assembly[206] have all urged the Azerbaijani authorities to reform criminal defamation laws, interventions which international NGOs have suggested are insufficient in the context of a wave of repression against human rights defenders in Azerbaijan.[207] The NGOs also argued, inter alia, that a Joint Working Group on Human Rights initiated by Mr Jagland and President Aliyev, involving MPs, government officials, and civil society representatives, was 'neither credible nor practical' in the present climate—and in October 2015, Mr Jagland announced the withdrawal of the Council's representative from the working group.[208] The fact that Azerbaijan has not (yet) reformed the impugned laws, nor produced a timetable for doing so,[209] highlights the limits of even the combined and mutually reinforcing mechanisms employed by Council of Europe bodies.

2.8 Assessing the Effectiveness of the Supervision System

As illustrated by the case of *Fatullayev*, the Council of Europe's system for supervising the execution of ECtHR judgments, centred on the Committee of Ministers' process, has had mixed results and has not infrequently been the subject of criticism from commentators.[210] The payment of just satisfaction appears to enjoy a high level of compliance: in 2014, 84 per cent of just satisfaction payments for cases in which the requisite information was available were made on time.[211] However, the caseload of the Committee of Ministers remains high, with (as noted at 1.1.1) 10,904 non-executed judgments pending before the Committee of Ministers at the end of 2014.

2012 on the draft law on protection from defamation and other legislative provisions regulating the protection from defamation in the Republic of Azerbaijan, 14 October 2013.

[204] Letter from Thorbjørn Jagland to President Aliyev, 21 March 2011.

[205] Observations by Nils Muižnieks, Council of Europe Commissioner for Human Rights, on the human rights situation in Azerbaijan: an update on freedom of expression, freedom of association, freedom of assembly, and the right to property, CommDH(2014)10, 23 April 2014.

[206] PACE Resolution 2062 (2015), The functioning of democratic institutions in Azerbaijan, 23 June 2015, para. 11.6.4.

[207] See, for example, Azerbaijan: Joint Letter to Council of Europe Secretary General Jagland, 25 September 2014.

[208] Council of Europe, 'Council of Europe Leaves Azerbaijan Human Rights Working Group', 7 October 2015.

[209] Communication from Azerbaijan concerning the Mahmudov and Agazade group of cases against Azerbaijan (Application No. 35877/04), Action plan (26/02/2014), DH-DD(2014)276, 27 February 2014.

[210] See, for example, Elisabeth Lambert Abdelgawad, 'The Court as Part of the Council of Europe: the Parliamentary Assembly and the Committee of Ministers', in Føllesdal, Peters, and Ulfstein, eds. (n 47): 263; Nicholas Sitaropoulos, 'Supervising Execution of ECtHR Judgments Concerning Minorities: The Committee of Ministers Potential and Constraints', *Annuaire International des Droits de L'Homme* No. 3 (2006): 523.

[211] 8th Annual Report of the Committee of Ministers 2014 (n 110) 10; however, the Committee of Ministers laments that in an unacceptably high number of cases (1,141 out of 2,235), information on payments had not been provided, even after the expiry of the payment deadline.

The Open Society Justice Initiative argues that the supervisory process is 'opaque and non-inclusive' for outside observers.[212] This is despite the Committee of Ministers' efforts to improve the transparency of its working methods since 2007 by publishing annual reports on supervision of the execution of Court judgments, and making states' action plans and action reports available on its website, along with press statements, resolutions, and decisions relating to states' performance. Improved transparency might be expected to assist parliamentary engagement in the supervision process; however, parliamentarians and their staff note that the availability of information on the Committee of Ministers website is no substitute for the proactive provision of information (such as action plans and reports) by executive to parliamentary bodies as part of the national system of implementation.[213]

The participation of civil society in the supervision process has increased in recent years but remains limited, in spite of changes designed to facilitate such involvement, such as publishing in advance the list of cases proposed for detailed examination at its meetings. In 2014, eighty contributions from NGOs and NHRIs were received and circulated by the Committee of Ministers (compared to eighty-one in 2013 and forty-seven in each of 2012 and 2011).[214] According to Çalı and Koch, the fact that the Committee of Ministers meets in private session 'conjures up images of deals struck behind closed doors' while the 'dense and formal language of its resolutions does not provide insight into the processes and social interactions that lead to its decisions'.[215] It has been proposed that Committee of Ministers' meetings should be made selectively open to external observers as a means of exerting leverage on resistant states and enhancing accountability in cases of persistent or flagrant non-compliance.[216] Such openness might in turn be expected to increase the potential for effective national parliamentary scrutiny of government action or inaction. Increasingly, non-governmental organizations have also sought opportunities to brief states in advance of DH meetings on complex issues arising in cases under enhanced supervision. In a pilot project funded by the Open Society Justice Initiative, eighteen cases (or groups of cases) were presented to the Committee of Ministers in 2013–14 variously by applicants and their legal representatives; national and international non-government organizations; academics; the Council of Europe Commissioner for Human Rights; and the (then) PACE rapporteur for Lesbian, Gay, Bisexual, and Transgender issues.[217]

The Council of Europe's system for supervising the execution of ECtHR judgments has become increasingly complex in respect of the plurality of actors involved. As noted at 2.3, the Court has assumed a greater role in recommending, or

[212] Open Society Justice Initiative (n 133) para. 23. [213] See 2.5.2 at n 115.

[214] 8th Annual Report of the Committee of Ministers 2014 (n 110) 43.

[215] Çalı and Koch (n 90) 311. [216] Open Society Justice Initiative (n 133) para. 25.

[217] Open Society Justice Initiative, Briefing Paper: Summary of ECtHR Judgments Presented to the Committee of Ministers, November 2014.

even prescribing, specific measures to be taken by states. The former Registrar of the Court, Erik Fribergh, ventured in 2014:

> If I look at the rather modest results of the Committee of Ministers compared to the Court, one avenue of reflection for the future is how we can move over even more of the responsibility for execution to the Court.[218]

For its part, the Parliamentary Assembly has, by its own initiative, '*de facto* and even *de jure* imposed an increasingly institutionalised right of inspection' into the supervision process.[219] Thus, the Committee of Ministers is coming under pressure from both the Court and PACE with respect to its formerly exclusive, and still dominant, role in supervising the execution of judgments. Indeed, given their traditional reticence to intrude upon the Committee of Ministers' supervision role, enshrined as it is in Article 46(2) ECHR, the increasing willingness of the two other main Council of Europe bodies to exert more influence is indicative of their frustration with the problems of implementation. A recent Parliamentary Assembly report criticizes the Committee of Ministers' failure to use all the means at its disposal to exert pressure on non-complying states; it adds that this omission 'may warrant closer examination for failing to acknowledge some weakness on its part, which indirectly weakens the action of the Court'.[220]

Nevertheless, some authors argue that the perceived ineffectiveness of the interstate peer review mechanism exemplified by the Committee of Ministers should not be overstated. Çalı and Koch address the argument that peer review of human rights compliance has 'profound structural deficiencies and is unreliable', either because states accord a low priority to this role (the problem of 'low political salience') or because they conduct such monitoring for self-interested reasons, leading to case-by-case diplomatic bargaining (the problem of 'high political salience').[221] Çalı and Koch venture that, due to the discretionary space that exists between a judgment and the specific steps that need to be taken to implement it, the Convention system is not immune from these problems. However, they conclude that the presence of a strong secretariat (the Department for the Execution of Judgments) helps to guard against these causes of unreliability because of the extent to which key post-judgment interpretive and monitoring tasks are delegated to it, thereby removing much of the supervision process from a political to a 'rule-bound' domain.[222] The delegation of tasks to the secretariat has become increasingly formalized in recent years, in part because of the expansion of the case load before the Committee of Ministers, and encompasses roles such as auditing states' action plans and reports; drafting resolutions to be considered by the Committee at DH

[218] Steering Committee for Human Rights, Committee of Experts on Reform of the Court (DH-GDR), Drafting Group 'F' on Reform of the Court (GT-GDR-F), Presentation to the 3rd meeting by the Registrar of the European Court of Human Rights, GT-GDR-F(2014)021, 24 September 2014, 9.

[219] Lambert Abdelgawad (n 210) 276.

[220] PACE, Committee on Legal Affairs and Human Rights, The effectiveness of the European Convention on Human Rights: the Brighton Declaration and beyond (Explanatory memorandum by Rapporteur, Mr Yves Pozzo di Borgo) (Provisional version), 10 December 2014, para. 62.

[221] Çalı and Koch (n 90) 302.

[222] Çalı and Koch (n 90) 314.

meetings; categorizing cases by urgency and importance under either the standard or enhanced procedures (or switching a case from one to the other); and—a powerful tool of peer review—selecting cases for an oral hearing. Within the European system, Çalı and Koch conclude, the 'double shadow' of a normative authority (the Court) and 'technocratic norm-guardians' (the Department for the Execution of Judgments) acts as 'a counter-balance against the pitfalls of politicisation and under-monitoring'.[223]

Nevertheless, calls continue to be made for reform of the supervision process of the Committee of Ministers, both to make it more transparent and to support it by means of an independent expert advisory group.[224] Such a group, it is submitted, would bring added focus, energy, and profile to efforts to facilitate resolution of the most intractable implementation issues, while their independence of state representation would bring an incisive cutting edge, which has hitherto been lacking.

In addition, the ability of the Secretariat to influence state behaviour is inherently limited by the resources at its disposal. The Department is receiving growing numbers of requests for advice from national authorities yet, in the words of its Director, '[r]egrettably ... can afford to dedicate only limited resources to this advisory and co-operation work with member states'.[225]

The advantages of the current supervision process might be enhanced further if there were greater co-ordination between the different Council of Europe bodies.[226] The Secretariat of the Parliamentary Assembly's Legal Affairs Committee sits as an observer at certain meetings of the Committee of Ministers' Steering Committee for Human Rights, the CDDH, but only sporadically due to its heavy workload.[227] Even when they are preparing reports on matters which are also on the CDDH agenda, PACE members tend not to take part in inter-governmental work which is 'often cumbersome [and] highly specialised'.[228] The CDDH has raised the possibility of holding periodic meetings between the Committee of Ministers, the Parliamentary Assembly (especially its Legal Affairs Committee), and the Commissioner for Human Rights to discuss issues relating to the execution of judgments.[229] Both the Committee of Ministers[230] and the Court[231] have suggested that there is scope for greater interaction between them. In 2014, for the first time, representatives of the Department for the Execution of Judgments met sections of the Court to discuss matters of execution, and the Court has proposed holding such meetings on a periodic basis. Certainly, complementarity and co-ordination between the various Council of Europe bodies needs to be increased from its current low base in view of the institutional and political pressures on the Strasbourg system.

223 Çalı and Koch (n 90) 322.
224 Joint NGO Response to the draft Brussels Declaration (n 132) para. 8.
225 GT-GDR-F(2014)022 (n 130) para. 20.
226 Lambert Abdelgawad (n 210) 288. See also Brussels Declaration (n 12) para. C.1.c.
227 Drzemczewski and Lowis (n 148) 317.
228 Drzemczewski and Lowis (n 148) 317.
229 CM(2013)174 (n 143) para. 10.
230 CM(2013)174 (n 143) para. 14.
231 Contribution of the Court to the Brussels Conference (n 70) para. 19.

2.9 Reform of the Convention System

As outlined at 1.1.1, for many years, the ECtHR laboured under a mountainous backlog of cases, which necessitated a series of reforms, aimed primarily at speeding up the processing of cases. In 1998, Protocol No. 11[232] to the Convention was brought into effect, abolishing the former two-tier system of the European Commission of Human Rights and the European Court of Human Rights, and creating a single full-time permanent Court. However, even such a fundamental change to the system was not sufficient to stem the tide of increasing numbers of applications to the Court caused largely by the expanding membership of the Council of Europe, especially since the late 1990s.

A further landmark in the reform process was Protocol No. 14 to the Convention, which came into force in 2010.[233] The aim of Protocol No. 14 was, in particular, to simplify and speed up the processing of individual applications including, controversially, the introduction of a new admissibility criterion according to which cases can be declared inadmissible if the applicant did not suffer a 'significant disadvantage'.[234] The changes implemented by Protocol No. 14 also permitted single judges to decide on inadmissible applications (in certain situations),[235] and a committee of three judges to decide on the admissibility and merits of an application where the underlying question in the case is already the subject of well-established case law of the Court.[236] This latter procedure is accordingly intended to speed up the processing of repetitive cases.

In 2011, the Interlaken Declaration incorporated an Action Plan for reforms up to 2019.[237] The Declaration envisaged that between 2012 and 2015 the Committee of Ministers would assess to what extent the implementation of Protocol No. 14 and the Interlaken Action Plan had improved the situation of the Court, and on the basis of that evaluation the Committee of Ministers would decide whether further action was required.

Following the Brighton Declaration of 2012, two further protocols to the Convention were adopted in 2013. Protocol No. 15 provides for a reduction in the time limit for applying to the Court from six months to four months (following the exhaustion of domestic remedies). It also introduces into the preamble to the Convention references to the principle of subsidiarity and the doctrine of the

[232] Protocol No. 11 to the Convention for the Protection of Human Rights and Fundamental Freedoms, Restructuring the Control Machinery Thereby, Council of Europe, Doc. H (94) 5.

[233] Protocol No. 14 to the Convention for the Protection of Human Rights and Fundamental Freedoms, Amending the Control System of the Convention, Council of Europe Treaty Series, No. 194, 13 May 2004.

[234] Unless respect for human rights requires an examination of the application on the merits and provided that no case may be rejected on this ground which has not been duly considered by a domestic tribunal; see Article 35(3) ECHR.

[235] Articles 26 and 27 ECHR.

[236] Article 28(1)(b) ECHR.

[237] High Level Conference on the Future of the European Court of Human Rights, Interlaken Declaration, 19 February 2010.

margin of appreciation. The ECtHR was initially sceptical about the need for the latter reform, since both principles of interpretation have been incorporated into the Court's case law for several decades. The Court sought unsuccessfully to amend the wording of Protocol No. 15 to ensure that it referred unambiguously to the principle of subsidiarity and the doctrine of the margin of appreciation 'as developed in the Court's case law'.[238] NGOs were also concerned that incorporation of these two principles of judicial interpretation, and not others of equal importance, such as the principle of proportionality and the doctrine of the Convention as a 'living instrument' (see 1.1.2), 'trespasses to an unacceptable degree on the role and autonomy of the Court in interpreting the Convention'.[239]

To understand this disquiet, it is necessary to recall the inflamed political atmosphere which surrounded the Court at the time of the Brighton conference in 2012 and, at least in the UK, has scarcely abated since. Prime Minster David Cameron had already made it clear in a speech in Strasbourg in January 2012 that the UK sought to 're-balance' states' relationship with the Court, to prevent it from becoming, as he put it, a 'small claims court' dogged by 'controversial rulings' which were having a 'corrosive effect' on popular support for human rights.[240] Then came the leaked UK proposals in the run up to the Brighton conference which would, among other things, have reduced the time limit for applications to the Strasbourg Court to as little as two months after a final domestic decision and barred the Court from accepting applications except where the national court had made an obvious error.[241] These proposals did not survive the pre-Brighton political negotiations.[242] The UK did, however, succeed in its proposal for express reference to subsidiarity and the margin of appreciation to be inserted into the preamble to the Convention.

In its own report on Protocol No. 15, the JCHR referred to the concerns of NGOs and the Equality and Human Rights Commission about the purpose and

[238] European Court of Human Rights, Opinion of the Court on Draft Protocol No. 15 to the European Convention on Human Rights, 6 February 2013, para. 4. However, to the Court's satisfaction, its desired wording was included in the Committee of Ministers' Explanatory Report to Protocol No. 15, para. 7.

[239] Joint NGO input to the ongoing negotiations on the draft Brighton Declaration on the Future of the European Court of Human Rights, 20 March 2012.

[240] David Cameron, 'Speech on the European Court of Human Rights', Strasbourg, 25 January 2012.

[241] Draft Brighton Declaration on the Future of the European Court of Human Rights, published in *The Guardian*, 25 February 2012 (see paras. 23.a and 23.c.i).

[242] The former UK Attorney General, Dominic Grieve, notes that domestic NGOs feared that 'we wished to diminish and not improve the Court's effectiveness'—a fear which he describes as 'misplaced ... [b]ut ... in the circumstances entirely understandable'. See Dominic Grieve, 'Is the European Convention Working?', Rule of Law Lecture, Faculty of Advocates, Edinburgh, 21 September 2015, 25. See also Noreen O'Meara, 'Reforming the European Court of Human Rights: The Impacts of Protocols 15 and 16 to the ECHR', in Katja S. Ziegler, Elizabeth Wicks, and Loveday Hodson, eds., *The UK and European Human Rights: A Strained Relationship?* (Oxford: Hart Publishing, 2015): 71, 73–6.

possible effects of the proposed reform.[243] In recommending ratification of Protocol No. 15, the Committee felt it necessary to draw to parliament's attention,

> the fact that subsidiarity and the margin of appreciation, properly understood in the light of the Court's case-law, are not … concerned with the primacy of national law over Convention law, or with demarcating national spheres of exclusive competence.[244]

On this basis, the JCHR welcomed Protocol No. 15 as signifying no less than 'a new era in the life of the Convention, an age of subsidiarity, in which the emphasis is on States' primary responsibility to secure the rights and freedoms set out in the Convention'.[245]

The Committee's enthusiasm for this aspect of Protocol No. 15 stands in contrast to the view of the President of the ECtHR, who described it as 'no far-reaching measure of reform, but rather a modest package'.[246] The JCHR's eagerness rests upon its view that Protocol No. 15 increases the onus on governments to conduct detailed assessments of, and justify the reasoning behind, the Convention-compatibility of their laws and policies—and on parliaments to subject executive action or inaction to conscientious and well-informed scrutiny. The Committee urges the ECtHR to accelerate and make more transparent the recent trend in its case law to pay respectful attention to such detailed and reasoned human rights assessment, in order to incentivize national authorities to 'earn' the deference of the Court. This debate is examined in greater detail at 4.5. For now, assessment of the effects of Protocol No. 15 is premature, since it will not come into force until all member states have signed and ratified it.[247]

The second major reform to flow from the Brighton Declaration, Protocol No. 16,[248] provides for the highest domestic courts and tribunals to seek an advisory opinion from the Grand Chamber of the Court on questions of principle relating to the interpretation or application of the Convention rights, with the twin aims of further reducing the ECtHR's excessive docket and enhancing dialogue between the ECtHR and higher national courts. The reform was broadly welcomed by the ECtHR.[249] However, some commentators have expressed doubt that Protocol No. 16 will achieve its laudable aims due to its optional status and the non-binding nature of the proposed advisory opinions.[250] Further, it has been

[243] JCHR, Fourth Report of Session 2014–15, *Protocol 15 to the European Convention on Human Rights*, HL Paper 71, HC 837 (2014) para. 3.3.

[244] JCHR, Fourth Report of Session 2014–15 (n 243) para. 3.11.

[245] JCHR, Fourth Report of Session 2014–15 (n 243) para. 3.17.

[246] Dean Spielmann, UCL—Current Legal Problems lecture: 'Whither the Margin of Appreciation?', University College London, 20 March 2014, 6.

[247] At the time of writing, twenty-two have done so.

[248] Protocol No. 16 was adopted on 2 October 2013 and will enter into force three months after the date on which it has been ratified by ten Council of Europe states. At the time of writing, five have done so. The Court may already give advisory opinions (at the request of the Committee of Ministers) on questions concerning the interpretation of the Convention, under Article 47 ECHR, but this procedure has rarely been used.

[249] European Court of Human Rights, Opinion of the Court on Draft Protocol No. 16 to the Convention extending its competence to give advisory opinions on the interpretation of the Convention, 6 May 2013.

[250] O'Meara (n 242) 88.

suggested that Protocol No. 16 may even undermine its objectives because of the burden that the new procedure might place on the Court's already overstretched resources, and the potential for it to undermine judicial comity should requests for advisory opinions be delayed or declined, or should a national court choose not to adjudicate in accordance with the guidance provided.[251] Once in force, Protocol No. 16 may have implications for parliaments, which will need to be alert to problems flagged by national courts, especially those of a systemic or structural nature which may imply the need for legislative reform.

2.10 Conclusion

This chapter has identified the obligations which national parliaments share with executive and judicial actors to uphold Convention rights and abide by final judgments of the ECtHR against their respective states. Despite the fact that governments are the main interlocutors of both the Court and the Committee of Ministers, there are multiple junctures at which parliaments can, and should, become involved in the implementation of judgments under the formal supervision of the Committee of Ministers and, increasingly, the de facto supervision of the Parliamentary Assembly, which has used both 'carrot' and 'stick' to increase parliamentary engagement. The Court's turn towards a more directive approach to setting out what types of action a judgment demands—including sometimes an obligation to legislate, and to do so within a specified time period—means that parliamentarians will increasingly be required to act in response to the findings of violations of the Convention.

This chapter has highlighted the importance for parliaments of developing a system for the oversight of action plans and reports. It has also identified the need for parliaments (and governments) to recognize—and act upon—the Court's interpretative authority. Further, it has identified opportunities for increased contact between national parliaments and Council of Europe institutions, including not only the Parliamentary Assembly, but also, from a presently minimal base, the Court and the Committee of Ministers (through the Department for the Execution of Judgments).

Reform to improve the effectiveness of the supervision process is of pressing concern. Measures are required to render the working methods of the Committee of Ministers more transparent and accessible to non-government actors, including parliamentarians, and to deal more robustly with recalcitrant states. Reform which will take place upon the entry into force of Protocol No. 15 holds particular significance for parliaments, with its introduction into the Convention of references to subsidiarity and the margin of appreciation. Properly understood, this reform emphasizes states' primary responsibility to secure the rights and freedoms set out in the Convention, an obligation reinforced by the Brussels Declaration of March

[251] O'Meara (n 242) 90–1.

2015. This imperative recognizes that Council of Europe bodies play a facilitative but not determinative role in the implementation of Convention standards as interpreted by the Court. The primary onus rests on national authorities, including parliaments. In the view of the Court's former Registrar, Erik Fribergh, member states should 'stop focusing on "how to reform the Court"' and instead focus on how Convention rights and judgments of the Court can be better implemented at the domestic level.[252] It is to this question of national implementation that the next chapter turns.

[252] GT-GDR-F(2014)021 (n 218) 9.

3

National Implementation and the Role of Parliaments

This chapter examines the role of national parliaments within domestic systems for the implementation of European Convention on Human Rights (ECHR) standards and European Court of Human Rights (ECtHR or 'the Court') judgments. The chapter is principally concerned with the imperative identified by the Council of Europe of improving the efficiency and effectiveness of national implementation, in accordance with the principle of subsidiarity (see 2.1). It considers both the institutional and political dimensions of the parliamentary role, since it is widely recognized that implementation requires both *capacity* and *political will*.[1] Capacity may be understood as the extent to which parliamentarians have the necessary information and expertise to conduct effective human rights oversight, combined with sufficient powers and adequately resourced structures and processes in order to enable interaction to take place at critical points in the implementation process, both with other domestic actors (such as executive bodies, the judiciary, national human rights institutions (NHRIs), and civil society) and Council of Europe bodies. A more intangible dimension of capacity is the status—formal and informal—of parliamentary human rights bodies (or, where there are no specialized bodies, of pro-compliance actors within parliament), which in turn determines the degree of influence they are capable of exerting on parliament as a whole, the executive, and other domestic actors.

Political will, too, has more than one dimension since states—and, indeed, parliaments—are not unitary actors. Political will may be understood as the motivation, or lack of motivation, that specific actors have for complying with human rights norms or judgments at particular times. It is conditioned by various factors, which may combine unpredictably. These include the extent to which human rights norms or judgments are salient[2] to politicians, and the perceived costs in terms of

[1] See, for example, Dia Anagnostou and Alina Mungiu-Pippidi, 'Domestic Implementation of Human Rights Judgments in Europe: Legal Infrastructure and Government Effectiveness Matter', *European Journal of International Law* 25(1) (2014): 205.

[2] In the context of political science, the term salience is commonly used to designate the perceived *importance* of an issue and sometimes, but not necessarily, the extent to which an issue is viewed as *problematic*, especially by voters. See Christopher Wlezien, 'On the Salience of Political Issues: The Problem with "Most Important Problem"', *Electoral Studies* 24 (2005): 555.

political capital[3] associated with either compliance or non-compliance. Political will to implement a judgment of the ECtHR is also shaped by perceptions of how far the judgment—and the Court itself—are perceived as legitimate.

This chapter proceeds as follows. First, 3.1 situates our empirical examination of the role of parliaments in the context of theories which seek to explain why states comply to varying degrees with international human rights law. In 3.2, the evidence as to how far ECtHR judgments *are*, in fact, complied with, and the methodologies used to measure compliance is examined.

The growing recognition within the Council of Europe (and beyond) of the significance of parliamentary engagement for the effective implementation of human rights norms is charted in 3.3, while 3.4 examines the structures and mechanisms adopted by parliaments in Council of Europe member states for the conduct of human rights oversight. It identifies momentum towards the establishment of such parliamentary structures and mechanisms and considers the potential advantages and disadvantages of different institutional models, as well as the principles and functions that are—or should be—common to all systems. Given the dominant role of governments as interlocutors of both the Court and Committee of Ministers, 3.5 examines the mechanisms by which executives co-ordinate implementation and report to parliaments, as well as the development in some states of national legislation designating the responsibilities of the various domestic actors—sometimes including parliaments—in this process.

The political dynamics of implementation, and the factors that affect the salience of ECtHR judgments are examined in 3.6. Taking into account the inherently political nature of the implementation process, 3.7 considers the methodologies by which the effectiveness of parliamentary human rights bodies can be identified and assessed. Finally, 3.8 concludes.

3.1 Parliaments and Theories of Compliance

Why do states create and ratify human rights (or other international) treaties?[4] And why do they subsequently comply—or fail to comply—with them?[5] The once diverse typology of compliance theories has converged around two distinct but overlapping strands, characterized as *rational choice theory*, which emphasizes sanctions and material incentives, and *constructivism*, which rests on a non-coercive,

[3] Political capital is an ill-defined term; at its broadest, it may be understood as including both a politician's personal skills and attributes and other institutional, contextual, and reputational factors, which combine to determine the levels of influence, trust, and goodwill he or she enjoys; see Mark Bennister and Ben Worthy, 'Getting It, Spending It, Losing It: Exploring Political Capital', Political Studies Association Annual Conference, Belfast, 2012.

[4] See, for example, Oona Hathaway 'Why Do Countries Commit to Human Rights Treaties?', *Journal of Conflict Resolution* 51 (2007): 588.

[5] See, for example, Harold Hongju Koh, 'Review Essay: Why Do Nations Obey International Law?', *Yale Law Journal* 106 (1997): 2599.

norm-oriented behavioural logic.[6] Parliaments, as distinct actors in the process of implementing human rights norms and judgments, have featured little in work informed by either theoretical approach. However, our focus on the role of parliaments is congruent with, and contributes to, an expanding literature which, combining both rational choice and constructivist approaches, views human rights compliance as being largely a function of domestic political bargaining and collaboration and consequently places emphasis on intra-state, rather than inter-state, relationships.[7]

The absence of parliamentary actors from rational choice explanations for compliance or non-compliance is unsurprising. Rational choice proponents understand compliance with international law instrumentally as being the result of a cost-benefit analysis performed by states on the basis of material incentives and threatened or imposed sanctions.[8] In respect of regime design, there is a consequent emphasis on inter-state bargaining and 'top down' mechanisms of coercion and enforcement as means of securing compliance. Accordingly, the state is commonly viewed as a unitary actor, leaving little scope for analysis of the capacity or motivation of particular state actors, such as parliaments.

In place of material factors, constructivists[9] argue that 'repeated interactions, argumentation, and exposure to norms characterise and construct state practice'.[10] Constructivism is diverse in respect of the breadth of explanatory accounts as to precisely *how* states come to internalize and identify with human rights (or other legal) norms.[11] Constructivist scholarship has also been eclectic in its selective integration of rational choice perspectives, while continuing to emphasize mechanisms

[6] Elizabeth Stubbins Bates, 'Sophisticated Constructivism in Human Rights Compliance Theory', *European Journal of International Law* 25(4) (2014): 1169.

[7] See, for example, Sonia Cardenas, *Conflict and Compliance: State Responses to International Human Rights Pressure* (Philadelphia, PA: University of Pennsylvania Press, 2007); Andrew P. Cortell and James W. Davis, 'How Do International Institutions Matter? The Domestic Impact of International Rules and Norms', *International Studies Quarterly* 40 (1996): 451; Courtney Hillebrecht, *Domestic Politics and International Human Rights Tribunals: The Problem of Compliance* (Cambridge: Cambridge University Press, 2014); Beth Simmons, *Mobilizing for Human Rights: International Law in Domestic Politics* (Cambridge: Cambridge University Press, 2009).

[8] See, for example, Jack L. Goldsmith and Eric A. Posner, *The Limits of International Law* (Oxford, New York: Oxford University Press, 2005); Emilie Hafner-Burton, 'Sticks and Stones: Naming and Shaming the Human Rights Enforcement Problem', *International Organization* 62(4) (2008): 689.

[9] See, for example, Jutta Brunnée and Stephen J. Toope, *Legitimacy and Legality in International Law: An Interactional Account* (Cambridge: Cambridge University Press, 2010); Abram Chayes and Antonia Handler Chayes, *The New Sovereignty: Compliance with International Regulatory Agreements* (Cambridge: Harvard University Press, 1998); Ryan Goodman and Derek Jinks, *Socializing States: Promoting Human Rights through International Law* (New York: Oxford University Press USA, 2013); Koh (n 5); Thomas Risse, Stephen C. Ropp, and Kathryn Sikkink, eds., *The Persistent Power of Human Rights: From Commitment to Compliance* (Cambridge: Cambridge University Press, 2013).

[10] Stubbins Bates (n 6) 1170.

[11] See, for example, Brunnée and Toope's 'interactional' theory, according to which the obligatory effect of international law is generated and sustained by means of shared understandings, agreed criteria of legality, and the 'embedded practice of legality'; Chayes and Chayes' 'managerialism', which assumes that states have a propensity to comply with international norms and therefore rejects enforcement in favour of the collective management of non-compliance by addressing states' bureaucratic or economic incapacity or ambiguity as to what norms require; Goodman and Jinks' theory of 'acculturation', which

of political and institutional interaction to explain compliance with human rights norms.[12]

In recent years, theories based upon the *transnational* dynamics of compliance, whether coercive or persuasive, have given way to a focus on compliance as the outcome of *domestic* political bargaining and collaboration.[13] This approach rests upon a view of the state not as a single entity, but as a collection of actors who, through their relative strengths and interactions, both collaborative and competitive, determine whether, and to what extent, compliance occurs. Thus, international human rights norms must 'creep into domestic affairs [and] be taken up by local advocates' in order to be effective,[14] while international institutions may be construed as external 'tipping point actors' to the extent that they strengthen the leverage and legitimacy of pro-compliance actors at the domestic level.[15] Explanations of compliance rooted in domestic politics are especially pertinent in the case of international human rights treaties, of which, as Simmons notes, the 'singularly unusual property' compared to other types of international treaty is that they 'are negotiated internationally but create stakeholders almost exclusively domestically'.[16]

This view of compliance with human rights norms, standards, and judgments as being driven by domestic political factors has evident implications for our examination of national parliaments as members of a domestic compliance 'community'[17] which also comprises courts, the executive, political parties, the administration, NHRIs, civil society actors, trade unions, business, the media, and indeed

traces the cognitive and social processes by which states adopt the beliefs and behaviour patterns of the prevailing 'culture' of the legal regime; Koh's 'transnational legal process' model, according to which repeated domestic interpretation of global norms causes them to become internalized and eventually become synonymous with national interests and identities; and Risse, Ropp, and Sikkink's spiral model, which explains the 'socialization' of state actors, via the influence of domestic and international civil society, from a state of repression to one of 'rule-consistent behaviour', via denial, 'tactical concessions', and 'prescriptive status', including ratification and incorporation of international human rights treaties (all n 9).

[12] Stubbins Bates (n 6) 1179. For example, Risse and Ropp identify four mechanisms that contribute to human rights compliance: coercion, incentives, persuasion/discourse, and capacity building, leading them to argue that viewing rational choice and constructivism as opposing hypotheses 'no longer makes sense': Thomas Risse and Stephen C. Ropp, 'Introduction and Overview', in Risse, Ropp, and Sikkink, eds. (n 9): 3, 12. Similarly, von Staden proposes a hybrid 'constructivist-rationalist' explanation for how liberal democratic states respond to ECtHR judgments, concluding that states display a normative sense of obligation not to disregard judgments (the constructivist hypothesis), yet generally act rationally by exploiting any remaining institutional and interpretive options to comply as minimally as possible: Andreas von Staden, 'Rational Choice within Normative Constraints: Compliance by Liberal Democracies with the Judgments of the European Court of Human Rights', SSRN eLibrary, 6 February 2012.

[13] See literature cited at n 7.

[14] Emilie Hafner-Burton, *Making Human Rights a Reality* (Princeton and Oxford: Princeton University Press, 2013) 11.

[15] Karen Alter, 'Tipping the Balance: International Courts and the Construction of International and Domestic Politics', *Cambridge Yearbook of European Legal Studies* 13 (2011): 1; Laurence R. Helfer and Erik Voeten, 'International Courts as Agents of Legal Change: Evidence from LGBT Rights in Europe', *International Organization* 68(1) (2014): 77.

[16] Simmons (n 7) 126.

[17] Andreas Føllesdal, 'The Legitimacy Deficits of the Human Rights Judiciary: Elements and Implications of a Normative Theory', *Theoretical Inquiries in Law* 14(2) (2013): 339, 342.

any domestic actor seeking to influence the state's response. As Hillebrecht ventures: 'No single domestic actor, not even the strongest executive, can satisfy all of the [international human rights] tribunals' mandates, legally or logistically.'[18]

Studies have analysed the domestic politics of compliance from various perspectives. Simmons focuses on the executive, the judiciary, and citizens and non-governmental organizations (NGOs) as the three mechanisms by which international human rights treaties exert domestic influence.[19] Other studies have highlighted the role of government advisers,[20] NHRIs,[21] courts,[22] or civil society activists.[23] Each of these actors has the potential to influence, and be influenced by, parliamentary engagement with human rights norms. Yet, as noted at the start of this section, few compliance studies have isolated and analysed the role of parliaments in the compliance process.[24] This is despite the fact that parliamentary actors are, in cases where legislative reform is required, pivotal to the success or failure of implementation, in addition to the broader effects of their oversight role. We return to the political dynamics of compliance in 3.6, having first examined the extent of compliance in the Convention system; growing recognition within the Council of Europe (and beyond) of the parliamentary role; and the current institutional capacity of both parliaments and executive bodies to fulfil their obligations under the Convention.

3.2 Identifying and Measuring Compliance in the Convention System

Assessing levels of compliance with judgments of the ECtHR is a challenging task in view of the wide margin of discretion that is generally conferred on states as they devise and execute remedies (see 2.1). The ECtHR's 'delegated' approach to redress stands in contrast to the more prescriptive 'checklist' approach of the Inter-American Court of Human Rights (IACtHR), which monitors the implementation

[18] Hillebrecht (n 7) 25. [19] Simmons (n 7) 125–47.

[20] Michael Scharf, 'International Law in Crisis: A Qualitative Empirical Contribution to the Compliance Debate', *Cardozo Law Review* 31 (2009): 35.

[21] Richard Carver, 'A New Answer to an Old Question: National Human Rights Institutions and the Domestication of International Law', *Human Rights Law Review* 10 (2010): 1; Ryan Goodman and Thomas Pegram, *Human Rights, State Compliance, and Social Change: Assessing National Human Rights Institutions* (Cambridge: Cambridge University Press, 2012).

[22] Alexandra Huneeus, 'Courts Resisting Courts: Lessons from the Inter-American Court's Struggle to Enforce Human Rights', *Cornell International Law Journal* 44 (2011): 493; Simmons (n 7) 129–35.

[23] Lucja Miara and Victoria Prais, 'The Role of Civil Society in the Execution of Judgments of the European Court of Human Rights', *European Human Rights Law Review* 5 (2012): 528; Kiyoteru Tsutsui, Claire Whitlinger, and Alwyn Lim, 'International Human Rights Law and Social Movements: States' Resistance and Civil Society's Insistence', *Annual Review of Law and Social Science* 8 (2012): 367.

[24] See, however, Anagnostou and Mungiu-Pippidi (n 1), which includes parliaments within the context of 'government effectiveness'; Druscilla Scribner and Tracy Slagter, 'Supranational Human Rights Adjudication and National Legislative Politics', Paper presented at the 2011 Annual Meeting of the International Studies Association, Montreal, Quebec.

of specific compliance orders.[25] Despite the ECtHR's shift towards a more directive approach, notably by means of the pilot judgment procedure (see 2.3), there remains significant scope for ambiguity in respect of whether states have complied with its judgments—in particular, with general measures—fully, partially, or not at all. The Committee of Ministers has shown itself to be aware of this danger by repeatedly warning states against adopting a minimalist or 'negligent' approach to implementation.[26]

The Committee of Ministers has taken steps to improve and make accessible compliance data; since 2007, it has published annual reports on the execution of judgments and more recently it has developed a database which permits a high level of case-by-case disaggregation in the tracking of compliance.[27] Using this data, Hawkins and Jacoby conclude that 'partial' compliance is the dominant outcome in the European (and also the inter-American) system, adding that:

> This cumulative picture is in tension with the older claims of the ECtHR itself—echoed by many scholars[28]—that state compliance with the ECtHR judgments was nearly universal and tracks more much closely with a growing alarm in the Court and Committee that compliance is a major and growing issue.[29]

Given that outright refusal by states to implement judgments is rare,[30] and yet the backlog of cases before the Committee of Ministers remains stubbornly at around 11,000 (see 1.1.1), the concept of partial compliance is a helpful explanatory device which transcends the cruder binary distinction between compliance and non-compliance. Hawkins and Jacoby identify four types of partial compliance.[31] These are 'split decisions', where a state complies with some but not all measures required (e.g., complying with individual but not general measures,[32] or implementing a judgment in part but not all of the state's territory[33]); 'state substitutions', where a state sidesteps particular requirement(s) of a judgment and offers a different

[25] Darren Hawkins and Wade Jacoby, 'Partial Compliance: A Comparison of the European and Inter-American Courts of Human Rights', *Journal of International Law and International Relations* 6(1) (2010): 35, 43–4. See also Hillebrecht (n 7) 41–7.

[26] Committee of Ministers, *Supervision of the Execution of Judgments and Decisions of the European Court of Human Rights: 7th Annual Report of the Committee of Ministers 2013* (2014), para. 13.

[27] The database includes the detailed case-by-case information contained in interim resolutions; communications between states and the Committee of Ministers (including action plans and reports); and decisions taken at the Committee of Ministers' quarterly DH meetings (see 2.5).

[28] See, for example, Laurence R. Helfer and Anne-Marie Slaughter, 'Toward a Theory of Effective Supranational Adjudication', *Yale Law Journal* 107 (2) (1997): 273, 276, which stated that judgments of the ECtHR were 'as effective, for the most part, as national court rulings'.

[29] Hawkins and Jacoby (n 25) 76.

[30] See, especially, the cases of *Loizidou v Turkey*, No. 15318/89, 18 December 1996 (see 2.5.2 at n 124); and *Ilaşcu and Others v Russia and Moldova*, No. 48787/99, 8 July 2004 [GC] (see Committee of Ministers Interim Resolution DH(2006)26, 10 May 2006).

[31] Hawkins and Jacoby (n 25) 77–83.

[32] See, for example, the Ukrainian authorities' response to *Oleksandr Volkov v Ukraine*, No. 21722/11, 9 January 2013 (see 5.2.1).

[33] See, for example, the UK authorities' response to *S and Marper v UK*, Nos. 30562/04 and 30566/04, 4 December 2008 [GC], which has been implemented in England and Wales, but not Northern Ireland (see 7.6.2).

response, which may or may not be deemed adequate by (in the European context) the Committee of Ministers;[34] 'slow motion' compliance, where a state takes some but not all required steps towards remedying a violation, whilst not excluding the possibility that it might do more;[35] and 'ambiguous compliance amid complexity', where the required steps are exceptionally demanding and/or political conditions are unfavourable, often leading to a stark disparity between what a judgment requires and what a state does.[36]

Hillebrecht similarly employs a disaggregated methodology to identify and measure what she terms 'à la carte' compliance in both the European and inter-American systems.[37] Based on a dataset of cases before the Committee of Ministers in 2009, different types of measures were found to enjoy widely varying compliance rates;[38] for example, financial reparations (in ECtHR parlance, just satisfaction) had a compliance rate of 82 per cent; while measures of non-repetition (general measures, involving legal, policy, or administrative reform) and accountability measures (holding perpetrators to account and reopening domestic trials) had compliance rates of 38 per cent and 31 per cent respectively, reflecting the higher political and sometimes also financial costs associated with the latter two categories.[39] On the aggregate level, the ECtHR had a compliance rate of 48 per cent, compared to 34 per cent for the IACtHR.[40]

[34] See, for example, *Modinos v Cyprus*, No. 15070/89, 22 April 1993, concerning the prohibition of male homosexual activity in violation of the right to private life under Article 8 ECHR. The Committee of Ministers found that an initial amendment to the impugned Criminal Code in 1998 did not go far enough to rectify the violation, leading to a further amendment in 2000; see Committee of Ministers Resolution ResDH(2001)152, 17 December 2001.

[35] For example, in the UK, the Voting Eligibility (Prisoners) Draft Bill satisfied the requirement in *Greens and MT v UK*, Nos. 60041/08 and 60054/08, 23 November 2010 (operative para. 6(a)) to 'bring forward ... legislative proposals' to remove the blanket ban on the rights of convicted prisoners to vote, yet legislative reform remains pending (see 7.6.1).

[36] One such example is the large group of cases relating to violations of the ECHR by the security forces in Chechnya. See, for example, Committee of Ministers Interim Resolution CM/ResDH(2011)292, Execution of the judgments of the European Court of Human Rights in 154 cases against the Russian Federation concerning actions of the security forces in the Chechen Republic of the Russian Federation, 2 December 2011.

[37] Hillebrecht (n 7) 41–2. Hillebrecht's unit of analysis is not case-level compliance but a more fine-grained distinction between the 'the discrete obligations or mandates nested within each case'. Her five-part typology of measures includes: (i) paying reparations; (ii) providing symbolic redress by acknowledging the state's responsibility and honouring the victims; (iii) holding perpetrators to account and reopening domestic trials; (iv) changing laws and practices to ensure that similar violations do not happen in future; and (v) taking individual measures aimed at providing remedy to the victim. A further measure that could be added to this typology is the provision of a system of domestic redress where the tribunal has identified that one is lacking, as, for example, in the case of *Ananyev v Russia*, Nos. 42525/07 and 60800/08, 10 April 2012, paras. 224–31.

[38] The dataset for ECtHR judgments is based on the 519 cases (involving 2,604 discrete obligations) that were on the Committee of Ministers' execution database as of 27 May 2009.

[39] Hillebrecht (n 7) 51.

[40] Hillebrecht (n 7) 48. The dataset also provides aggregate compliance rates by state. As an illustration, the five states selected for investigation in this book had compliance rates as follows: Ukraine, 41 per cent; Romania, 60 per cent; United Kingdom, 71 per cent; the Netherlands, 78 per cent; and Germany, 60 per cent. Disaggregated data in respect of Hillebrecht's five-part typology (above n 37) is not available by state.

Hillebrecht quantitatively analyses the dataset of compliance with ECtHR judgments to test her hypothesis that domestic political institutions are the 'linchpin' to compliance with the rulings of international human rights tribunals.[41] She finds that strong institutionalized constraints on the decision-making powers of executives—such as an independent judiciary and legislature, and a free media and civil society—have a positive and statistically significant effect on states' compliance with human rights judgments.[42] This is posited as being due to the dual role played by domestic institutions and actors—sometimes limiting the executive's freedom of manoeuvre and at other times providing it with willing 'compliance partners'.[43] This finding implies a role for parliaments vis-à-vis the executive which is both constraining and facilitative. This role has been increasingly acknowledged and promoted by Council of Europe institutions, in particular the Parliamentary Assembly of the Council of Europe (PACE), as we explore in the next section.

3.3 Recognition of the Parliamentary Role

In tandem with the increasing focus on national implementation of the Convention and judgments of the ECtHR demanded by the principle of subsidiarity, there has been a growing realization of the particular role that parliaments can, and should, play in this endeavour. The Parliamentary Assembly has described parliaments as being 'at the heart of human rights protection' on the basis of their role as legislators:

> Parliaments, as the representation of the people, set out the legislative framework in which societies operate. This framework must comply with national and international standards on human rights and the rule of law. Laws can serve to guarantee human rights, but they can also be sources of human rights violations. As parliaments pass the laws that are subsequently executed by the administration and interpreted by the courts, they should also control their application by the executive.[44]

The rationale for parliamentary involvement in ensuring compliance with Convention standards and ECtHR judgments was put in this way by the former Dutch Senator and PACE member, Marie-Louise Bemelmans-Videc, in 2012:

> It is the responsibility of all the state organs—the executive, the courts and the legislature—to prevent or remedy human rights violations at the national level. Governments and parliaments are principally responsible for prevention, whereas remedying violations is mainly the responsibility of the judiciary, unless the only remedy available is a change to the law. The legislature must examine whether draft legislation is compatible with the Convention and its protocols, as interpreted by the Court. Only when the domestic system fails should the Court step in. Subsequently, if and when there is an adverse finding by the Court, the emphasis shifts back to the domestic arena and the state is required to execute the judgment under the supervision of the Committee of Ministers.... At this stage, too, parliamentary

[41] Hillebrecht (n 7) 54. [42] Hillebrecht (n 7) 58. [43] Hillebrecht (n 7) 54.

[44] PACE, Committee on Legal Affairs and Human Rights, National parliaments: guarantors of human rights in Europe, Doc. 12636, 6 June 2011 (Rapporteur: Christos Pourgourides) para. 7.

involvement may be necessary. The (rapid) adoption of legislative measures is often required to ensure full compliance with Court judgments. Hence the need for parliaments, which can influence the direction and priority of legislative initiatives, to exercise effective oversight of action or inaction of the executive.[45]

It follows that parliaments are also especially well placed to *prevent* human rights violations by identifying structural problems that lead to repetitive cases and identifying workable remedies which are sensitive to the domestic context.[46]

The Parliamentary Assembly has suggested that the participation of national parliaments in the process of implementation helps to promote a 'human rights culture',[47] identified by Feldman as a process by which a parliament, in addition to its legislative role, uses its 'influence and its scrutiny powers to keep human rights standards at the forefront of the minds of ministers and departments, regulators and other public authorities'.[48]

The work of PACE aimed at invigorating the role of national parliaments reflects a wider international trend in this direction. The UN General Assembly's 2012 Declaration on the Rule of Law explicitly acknowledged 'the essential role of parliaments in the rule of law at the national level'.[49] The UN Human Rights Council has recently referred to the 'crucial role that parliaments play in, inter alia, translating international commitments into national policies and laws, and hence in contributing to the fulfilment by each State Member of the United Nations of its human rights obligations and commitments and to the strengthening of the rule of law'.[50]

Emphasis on the role of parliaments is also evident in the work of the UN treaty monitoring bodies. The UN Human Rights Committee has recognized the obligations on all arms of the state under the International Covenant on Civil and Political Rights.[51] The Committee on the Elimination of all Forms of Discrimination Against Women—which has been 'unusually far-sighted'[52] in its engagement with national

[45] PACE, Committee on Legal Affairs and Human Rights, Guaranteeing the authority and effectiveness of the European Convention on Human Rights, Doc. 12811, 3 January 2012 (Rapporteur: Marie-Louise Bemelmans-Videc) para. 56.

[46] Andrew Drzemczewski and Julia Lowis, 'The Work of the Parliamentary Assembly of the Council of Europe', in Murray Hunt, Hayley Hooper, and Paul Yowell, eds., *Parliaments and Human Rights: Redressing the Democratic Deficit* (Oxford: Hart Publishing, 2015): 309, 319.

[47] PACE, Doc. 12636 (n 44) paras. 46–50.

[48] David Feldman, 'Can and Should Parliament Protect Human Rights?', *European Public Law* 10(4) (2004): 635, 651.

[49] Declaration of the High-Level Meeting of the General Assembly on the Rule of Law at the National and International Levels, UN General Assembly Resolution A/67/L.1, 19 September 2012, para. 34.

[50] UN Human Rights Council, Contribution of parliaments to the work of the Human Rights Council and its universal periodic review, A/HRC/30/L.23, 29 September 2015.

[51] UN Human Rights Committee, General Comment No. 31, The Nature of the General Legal Obligation Imposed on States Parties to the Covenant, UN Doc. CCPR/C/21/Rev.1/Add. 13, 26 May 2004, paras. 3–4. Para. 4 states, inter alia: 'All branches of government (executive, legislative, and judicial), and other public or governmental authorities, at whatever level—national, regional or local—are in a position to engage the responsibility of the State Party.'

[52] Murray Hunt, 'Enhancing Parliaments' Role in the Protection and Realisation of Human Rights', in Hunt, Hooper, and Yowell, eds. (n 46): 469, 476.

parliaments—has since 2008 included a prominent paragraph in its concluding observations on state reports highlighting the importance of involving parliaments in the reporting and implementation process.[53]

For its part, the Inter-Parliamentary Union has devoted significant attention since the early 1990s towards building the capacity and competence of parliaments in relation to both regional and international human rights mechanisms.[54]

Council of Europe governments have been much slower to recognize the parliamentary dimension of subsidiarity, the Brussels Declaration of 2015 being the first high-level declaration to specify in detail what governments should do to facilitate parliamentary engagement.[55]

As the spotlight shifted on to national parliaments from around 2000 onwards, it became clear that relatively few within Europe had adequate—or any—structures or mechanisms to enable them to conduct systematic monitoring of the implementation of Convention standards and ECtHR judgments.[56] A study of nine Council of Europe states published in 2009 concluded that in seven of them, parliaments did not have 'an active or decisive role' in the implementation of Court judgments.[57] Such findings reflect the fact that institutional arrangements for implementation 'predominantly rely on the executive and in most countries ... are characterised by a strong degree of centralisation'.[58] In 2011, the Parliamentary Assembly called on parliaments across Europe to implement a series of 'basic principles for parliamentary supervision of international human rights standards' requiring , among other things, that appropriate parliamentary structures should be established and that governments should report regularly to parliaments about the implementation of ECtHR judgments.[59] This exhortation highlights a weakness at the heart of the Convention system which, guided by the principle of subsidiarity, relies on national institutions to implement human rights norms and judgments—institutions which in many states are embryonic, ineffective, or non-existent. As discussed in the next section, however, there is now gathering impetus in this direction in respect of the parliamentary dimension of implementation.

[53] Ingeborg Schwarz, 'The Work of the Inter-Parliamentary Union', in Hunt, Hooper, and Yowell, eds. (n 46): 329, 335.

[54] Inter-Parliamentary Union and Office of the United Nations High Commissioner for Human Rights, *Human Rights Handbook for Parliamentarians* (IPU and OHCHR: Geneva, 2005); Schwarz (n 53).

[55] See 1.1.3 at n 79.

[56] Drzemczewski and Lowis (n 46) 312.

[57] Dia Anagnostou and Alina Mungiu-Pippidi, *Why Do States Implement Differently the European Court of Human Rights Judgments? The Case Law on Civil Liberties and the Rights of Minorities*, JURISTRAS Project (2009) 23. The states found lacking were Austria, Italy, France, Romania, Greece, Bulgaria, and Turkey. The exceptions were Germany and the UK.

[58] Dia Anagnostou, 'Introduction: Untangling the Domestic Implementation of the European Court of Human Rights' Judgments', in Dia Anagnostou, ed., *The European Court of Human Rights: Implementing Strasbourg's Judgments on Domestic Policy* (Edinburgh: Edinburgh University Press, 2013): 1, 12.

[59] PACE Resolution 1823 (2011), National parliaments: guarantors of human rights in Europe, 23 June 2011 (Appendix 1: Basic principles for parliamentary supervision of international human rights standards, para. 2).

3.4 Parliamentary Structures and Mechanisms for Human Rights Oversight

Some parliaments in the Council of Europe have developed—or begun to develop—structures and mechanisms for conducting human rights oversight; typically, establishing parliamentary committees or sub-committees with a specific human rights remit or adding this remit to an existing committee. Starting from a very low base, the number of parliaments taking such action is growing. Whatever their precise form, the aim of these initiatives is to ensure that parliamentarians develop a 'structural interest'[60] in human rights rather than confining their engagement to reactive, incidental, or opportunistic interventions.

This section considers the variety of institutional models adopted (3.4.1);[61] their respective advantages and disadvantages (3.4.2); and the principles underpinning this area of parliamentary work in respect of the status, remit, powers, functions, and resources of parliamentary human rights committees (3.4.3).

3.4.1 Institutional models

Previous surveys of parliamentary human rights committees—European or international—have proposed a two-part typology of the structures adopted: cross-cutting (or 'mainstreamed') and specialized.[62] We refine this approach by suggesting a three-part typology which characterizes the various institutional models as either cross-cutting,[63] specialized, or hybrid.[64] In cross-cutting systems, no single

[60] Jasper Krommendijk, 'Parliaments in the Reporting Procedures under UN Human Rights Treaties', paper presented to MultiRights workshop on 'The International Human Rights Judiciary and National Parliaments', University of Oslo, 12–13 March 2015 (on file).

[61] We confine our review to standing (permanent) parliamentary committees and sub-committees since they 'operate on a continuing basis from one parliamentary term to the next, [and] carry out the bulk of parliamentary business', including undertaking legislative and oversight functions, preparing the work of the plenary, scrutinizing proposed legislative texts, and submitting recommendations (PACE Doc. 12636 (n 44) para. 7). Other parliamentary formations which are not considered systematically include: temporary committees created to inquire into a specific matter; committees (standing or ad hoc) which are concerned with specific aspects of human rights, for example, children's or women's rights; Ombudsmen, whose function is typically to ensure fairness and legality in public administration, which may include government compliance with human rights obligations; and informal party groups or caucuses which may have an identified interest in human rights. See also Hironori Yamamoto, *Tools for Parliamentary Oversight: A Comparative Study of 88 National Parliaments* (Inter-Parliamentary Union, 2007).

[62] National Democratic Institute for International Affairs, *Parliamentary Human Rights Committees* (Rule of Law Series Paper, 2004) 9–10; PACE Doc. 12636 (n 44) paras. 26–30.

[63] In previous publications, we have used the term 'mainstreamed'; see, for example, Alice Donald and Philip Leach, 'The Role of Parliaments Following Judgments of the European Court of Human Rights', in Hunt, Hooper, and Yowell, eds. (n 46): 59. However, we opt here for the term 'cross-cutting' as a more appropriate generic description of arrangements in which no committee has an identified human rights remit, since 'mainstreamed' implies that human rights oversight is, in practice, embedded in the work of all committees, which is not the case in all parliaments that have a cross-cutting committee structure. In that sense, mainstreaming may be understood in many parliaments as more of an aspiration than a description of actual practice.

[64] The labels cross-cutting, specialized, and hybrid are purely descriptive in relation to structure and remit and are not intended to capture the constitutional role of parliamentary bodies; for example,

committee has a remit covering human rights matters, which are instead dealt with by different committees as they arise within their respective mandates (often including, but not limited to, committees with broader remits covering justice, legal affairs, and/or the constitution). In the specialized model, a single standing committee exists with a remit which is mainly or exclusively concerned with human rights. The committee's remit may expressly include, or be able to be interpreted to include, functions such as the vetting of legislation for compliance with domestic, regional, or international commitments, and oversight of the implementation of human rights judgments. In hybrid systems, more than one committee exists which has an identified interest in human rights and/or a specialized human rights subcommittee is established within an otherwise hybrid system.[65]

The categories are not intended to be rigid; for example, the existence of a specialized committee does not—and should not—preclude consideration of human rights matters by other committees. Rather, the typology captures the range of models that have been developed by parliaments, from a single focal body to a partly or wholly decentralized approach.

We do not attempt in this section to assess the impact or effectiveness of parliamentary structures in particular states. Indeed, it is difficult in many cases even to identify the precise remit and activity of parliamentary committees, due to the paucity of information that many of them make publicly available. In particular, it is rarely stated by parliamentary committees on their websites whether they have any role in monitoring the implementation of ECtHR judgments. Our modest aim in this section, then, is to provide a descriptive account of existing institutional approaches as the basis for a discussion (at 3.4.2) of their potential advantages and disadvantages.

3.4.1.1 Cross-cutting models

The cross-cutting approach is adopted by the bicameral Dutch parliament (the *Staten-Generaal*); no single committee in either the lower house (the House of Representatives) or the upper house (the Senate) is tasked to deal with human rights matters—arrangements which are examined in detail at 8.3. Switzerland's bicameral Federal Assembly likewise has no dedicated human rights committee.[66] In Spain's bicameral parliament, the *Cortes Generales*, human rights matters are

Kavanagh argues that the JCHR, although a specialized committee in terms of its structure and remit, performs a 'hybrid' role constitutionally, by virtue of being a joint committee which operates in a relatively non-partisan way and by combining the dual roles of legislative scrutiny and executive oversight; Aileen Kavanagh, 'The Joint Committee on Human Rights: A Hybrid Breed of Constitutional Watchdog', in Hunt, Hooper, and Yowell, eds. (n 46): 115, 118–19.

[65] Previous typologies have included hybrid structures within the 'specialized' category; however, we consider it preferable to classify hybrid models separately because of the potential issues that such arrangements create in respect of, for example, lack of clarity as to different committees' remits, and variation in the relative status and powers (formal and informal) of different human rights-related committees in the same parliament.

[66] PACE Doc. 12636 (n 44) para. 28.

generally, but not exclusively, considered by the Constitutional Committees of the lower house (the Congress of Deputies) and the upper house (the Senate).[67]

In the unicameral parliament of Estonia, the *Riigikogu*, several standing committees such as the Constitutional Committee or the Legal Affairs Committee may deal with human rights issues.[68] A number of the unicameral parliaments in the Nordic states also adopt a cross-cutting approach. In the Swedish parliament, the *Riksdag*, legislative proposals are first examined by a commission of inquiry comprised of MPs from all parties represented in parliament, as well as experts from governmental agencies and sometimes also judicial figures or academics.[69] Commission reports are then opened up to public consultation. If the proposal is taken forward, the draft bill is submitted to parliament for scrutiny by the permanent select committee responsible for the relevant subject matter. Permanent select committees mirror the structure of government departments, meaning that none has a specialized human rights remit.[70] The *Riksdag* has no specific mechanism for monitoring the implementation of ECtHR judgments, and becomes involved only if the government considers that legislation is necessary to remedy a violation and introduces a bill via a commission of inquiry; parliamentary questions could also be asked about what action the executive was taking in response to a judgment.[71] The Norwegian parliament, the *Storting*, operates in a broadly similar way to that of the *Riksdag* in respect of human rights oversight.[72] In the Danish parliament, the *Folketing*, each committee deals with human rights within its respective sphere of competence. The Legal Affairs Committee maintains contact with, and discusses the annual reports of, the Danish Institute for Human Rights and the Ombudsman.[73] The *Folketing* has no formal procedures for monitoring the implementation of ECtHR judgments and there is no system of executive reporting to Parliament on implementation. The same is true of the Icelandic parliament, the *Althing*.[74]

In Russia, the lower house, or State Duma, has thirty committees, none of which deals specifically with human rights matters. According to various interlocutors

[67] PACE Doc. 12636 (n 44) para. 28. There is also a Joint Committee on Relations with the Ombudsman.

[68] PACE Doc. 12636 (n 44) para. 28.

[69] Thomas Bull and Iain Cameron, 'Legislative Review for Human Rights Compatibility: A View from Sweden', in Hunt, Hooper, and Yowell, eds. (n 46): 279.

[70] Bull and Cameron (n 69) 281–4. Draft legislation will also have been reviewed before submission to Parliament by the Law Council, an advisory body comprised of sitting or former members of the Supreme Courts. In the event that a bill submitted to Parliament raises constitutional issues (including institutional or individual rights), it will be reviewed by the Constitutional Committee of Parliament.

[71] Email correspondence with Iain Cameron, Professor in Public International Law at Uppsala University, 7 April 2015.

[72] In addition, in April 2015, the *Storting* passed the legislation and orders for Norway's new national human rights institution, which operates under the auspices of the *Storting*, but will have an independent and autonomous position in line with the Paris Principles for NHRIs. The NHRI will 'promote and protect human rights as laid down in the Constitution, the Human Rights Act and other applicable legislation, international treaties and international law in general'. See *Storting* news release, 'Candidates for the National Human Rights Institution', 7 May 2015.

[73] PACE Doc. 12636 (n 44) para. 28.

[74] Email correspondence with Vilborg Ása Guðjónsdóttir, Adviser on International Affairs at the *Althing*, 24 September 2015.

within the Council of Europe, questions relating to Convention compliance and ECtHR judgments fall primarily, though not exclusively, within the remit of three Committees covering: Civil, Criminal, Arbitration and Procedural Legislation; Constitutional Legislation and State Building; and Foreign Affairs.[75] There is no institutionalized parliamentary mechanism to monitor the implementation of judgments. Since 2011, in accordance with a presidential decree,[76] annual reports are prepared by the Ministry of Justice for the attention of the president, which include, among other things, a list of the laws which have had to be adopted or repealed by the State Duma in order to comply with judgments of the ECtHR.[77]

3.4.1.2 Specialized models

The specialized model is exemplified by the UK Joint Committee on Human Rights (JCHR), established in 2001 as a joint parliamentary select committee composed of members of both the House of Commons and House of Lords. The JCHR's wide remit to 'examine matters relating to human rights' within the UK has been interpreted by the Committee to include monitoring of the implementation of human rights judgments, both those delivered by UK courts and the ECtHR, as explained at 7.3.

The Finnish parliament, the *Eduskunta*, has a Constitutional Law Committee whose principal function is to issue statements on bills (or other matters) sent to it for consideration regarding their constitutionality and their bearing on international human rights instruments, including the European Convention.[78] Once a legislative proposal has been submitted, the Constitutional Law Committee elicits the views of civil servants and external experts at a formal hearing, before adopting a reasoned opinion or report. If incompatibilities are identified, the Committee proposes amendments to eliminate the problem. Opinions of the Committee are, as a matter of constitutional custom, treated as formally binding on parliament. According to the former chair of the Committee, Kimmo Sasi, it frequently refers to judgments of the ECtHR.[79] The Foreign Ministry sends all ECtHR decisions against Finland to the secretariat of the Committee for information; they are not circulated unless requested. The Parliamentary Ombudsman submits an annual

[75] Email correspondence with: Olga Chernishova, Registry of the ECtHR, 21 July 2015; Nikita Ivanov, Registry of the ECtHR, 21 July 2015; and Nikita Kolomiets, Department for the Execution of Judgments, 4 August 2015.

[76] Presidential Decree on monitoring the application of law in the Russian Federation, No. 657, 20 May 2011.

[77] In 2013, the Ministry of Justice noted that legislative reform was required in respect of nine judgments and three groups of cases; in six of them the draft laws were prepared and pending before Duma, while in others the Ministry of Justice was preparing the drafts or asking other state bodies to do so. We are grateful to Nikolay Mikhailov, Deputy Head of the Office of the Russian Federation at the ECtHR, for providing a copy in Russian of the 2013 report.

[78] Maartje de Visser, *Constitutional Review in Europe: A Comparative Analysis*, 1st edn. (Oxford: Hart Publishing, 2013) 26–8.

[79] Email correspondence with Kimmo Sasi, Chair of the Constitutional Law Committee (2003–11), member (2011–15), 21 July 2015.

report to the parliament which includes a section on all relevant cases decided in relation to Finland, new cases, and figures for compensation. The report is scrutinized by the Constitutional Law Committee; however, Kimmo Sasi notes that the Committee has never taken a position on that section of the report.

Specialized committees are also found in several other unicameral parliaments. The Hungarian National Assembly confers responsibility for human rights oversight onto the Committee on Justice, which receives an annual report by the government agent on judgments against Hungary and their state of execution.[80] The Turkish Grand National Assembly, too, has adopted the specialized model: the Human Rights Inquiry Committee handles human rights matters relating both to domestic and international affairs and in 2015 added oversight of the implementation of ECtHR judgments to its remit.[81] Within the National Assembly of Montenegro, the Committee on Human Rights and Freedoms deals with human rights issues, and has instigated the production of information reports on proceedings against Montenegro before the ECtHR with proposals for follow up.[82] The Slovenian National Assembly has a Commission for Petitions, Human Rights, and Equal Opportunities which, inter alia, 'monitors the realisation of the international obligations of the Republic of Slovenia which pertain to human rights'.[83] In the Croatian parliament (the *Sabor*), the Standing Committee on Human and National Minority Rights is responsible for, among other areas, 'the implementation of ratified international human rights treaties'.[84] In late 2013, the Greek Parliament established a Special Permanent Committee on Monitoring the Decisions of the ECtHR. The Committee's remit is to vet legislation for Convention compliance and conduct oversight of the execution of ECtHR judgments. The Committee had not begun its work as of October 2014, but was reported to be meeting regularly in the parliament elected in January 2015.[85] In Albania, the Committee on Legal Issues, Public Administration, and Human Rights (which also has a Sub-committee on Human Rights) within the parliament (or *Kuvendi*) performs a legislative vetting role; however, it has no specific mechanism for monitoring the execution of ECtHR judgments, which is purely an executive matter.[86]

[80] There were formerly two committees with human rights responsibilities: the Constitutional, Judicial, and Standing Orders Committee and the Committee on Human Rights, Minorities, Civil, and Religious Affairs. The latter had the primary responsibility to ensure compliance with Hungary's international human rights obligations. The two committees combined to form the Justice Committee in 2014.

[81] Email correspondence with Kenan Altaş, former Legislative Expert to the Human Rights Inquiry Committee, 22 January, 1 April, and 6 July 2015. As of July 2015, the monitoring function had not yet begun in earnest as the Committee had not yet been re-established following elections in June 2015.

[82] PACE, Parliamentary Project Support Division, The role of parliaments in implementing ECHR Standards: Interparliamentary co-operation activities 2013–2014, PPSD (2014) 07 rev. 31, 8 June 2014, 2.

[83] See website of the National Assembly at <http://www.dz-rs.si/wps/portal/en/Home/ODrzavnemZboru/KdoJeKdo/DelovnoTelo?idDT=DT006>.

[84] See website of the *Sabor* at <http://www.sabor.hr/Default.aspx?sec=5260>.

[85] Email correspondence with Voula Syrigos, Head of the Directorate for International Relations and Organizations of the Greek Parliament, 2 July 2015.

[86] Information provided at Parliamentary Assembly of the Council of Europe capacity-building seminar on the ECHR (execution of judgments), Strasbourg, 4–5 September 2014 (on file).

Other unicameral parliaments with specialized human rights committees include the Latvian parliament, the *Saeima*, whose Human Rights and Public Affairs Committee is formally responsible for monitoring the implementation of international human rights norms. The deputy chair of the Committee reports that in practice other aspects of the Committee's remit, including media law and regulation, occupy much more space on its agenda than human rights-related issues.[87] There are no institutional arrangements for monitoring the implementation of ECtHR judgments. However, approximately once a year the Latvian government agent reports to the Committee about the state of execution. The Committee may question the government agent but no decisions or legislative initiatives have been produced on the basis of the reports. The Legal Affairs Committee has also held periodic meetings with the government agent. Legislative scrutiny for human rights compliance is a cross-cutting activity.[88]

A variant of the specialized model is where a specialized sub-committee is formed under a single committee with a broader mandate. For example, in December 2014, the Justice, Defence, and Equality Committee, a joint committee of the two houses of the Irish parliament (the Houses of the *Oireachtas*), established a Sub-committee on Human Rights Relative to Justice and Equality Matters.[89] Specialized sub-committees may also exist within hybrid systems, as discussed below.

3.4.1.3 Hybrid models

In other parliaments—both bicameral and unicameral—a hybrid approach is taken, in which more than one parliamentary committee has human rights within its remit, which may or may not be specified to include monitoring of the implementation of ECtHR judgments.

In the *Bundestag*, the lower house of the bicameral German parliament, the Committee on Legal Affairs and Consumer Protection leads on all matters relating to the Ministry of Justice, including legislative reform necessitated by judgments of the ECtHR, while the Committee on Human Rights and Humanitarian Aid discusses human rights issues from a broader perspective, both on an international basis and in relation to Germany (see 9.4.1).

87 Email correspondence with Boriss Cilevics, Vice-Chair of the Committee on Human Rights and Public Affairs, 29 July 2015.

88 Correspondence between Inese Lībiņa-Egnere, Chair of the Latvian delegation to PACE, and Anne Brasseur, President of PACE, 2 September 2015 (on file).

89 The orders of reference of the sub-committee are to 'examine issues, themes and proposals, legislative or otherwise, in regard to compliance with the human rights of persons within the State'. They do not expressly include monitoring the implementation of human rights judgments. See Sub-Committee on Human Rights Relative to Justice and Equality Matters, Orders of Reference (undated). In respect of legislative scrutiny for human rights compliance, Senator Katherine Zappone had previously reported that such scrutiny was 'ad hoc and ... *there are no shared methods of analysis in applying a human rights-based approach to the scrutiny of legislation*' (emphasis in original); see 'How Can Parliaments Become (Effective) Human Rights Actors?', Presentation to workshop on 'Effective Parliamentary Oversight of Human Rights', King's College London, 13–14 November 2013 (on file).

In the bicameral Italian parliament, both the Chamber of Deputies and the Senate have Constitutional Affairs Committees, while the Senate also has an Extraordinary Commission for the Protection and Promotion of Human Rights.[90] These three committees examine judgments of the ECtHR with the aim of evaluating and adopting necessary legislative reforms. As noted at 3.5.2, these committees also receive an annual report on judgments from the Prime Minister's office. They are not, however, responsible for legislative vetting for compliance with the ECHR, which is a cross-cutting activity.[91]

Several unicameral parliaments also have hybrid systems. In the House of Representatives in Cyprus, two committees—the Standing Committee on Human Rights and Equal Opportunities for Men and Women and the Committee on Legal Affairs—may each become involved in both legislative vetting and follow up of ECtHR judgments. Both committees were involved, for example, in monitoring the implementation of the judgment in *Rantsev v Cyprus and Russia*,[92] concerning (on the part of Cyprus) failures to protect a victim of human trafficking, Oxana Rantseva, and (on the part of both states) a failure adequately to investigate her death.[93] The Parliament of Macedonia also has two parliamentary committees with a human rights-related remit: the Committee on Political System and Inter-Ethnic Relations and the Standing Inquiry Committee on Protection of Civil Freedoms and Rights. As noted at 3.5.2, the latter receives an annual report from an inter-departmental commission comprising senior government and judicial officials. The Serbian National Assembly has (at least) three committees to which human rights are relevant: the Committee for Human and Minority Rights and Gender Equality, the Committee on Constitutional and Legislative Issues, and the Committee on the Rights of the Child.[94]

In Slovakia, the National Council has established a Committee on Human Rights and Minorities and a Committee on Constitutional and Legal Affairs. The latter vets all bills for compliance with international treaties and other standards; however, neither Committee has a specific mechanism for monitoring the implementation of ECtHR judgments, nor is there any procedure for executive reporting on implementation.[95]

The Lithuanian parliament, the *Seimas*, also has two committees which may handle human rights matters, the Committee on Legal Affairs and the Committee on Human Rights. The Statute of the *Seimas* establishes that the Committee on Legal Affairs exercises oversight over law enforcement agencies (except courts) while the Committee on Human Rights conducts oversight of institutions dealing with 'ensuring human and civil rights'.[96] Neither Committee has the function of

90 See website of the Senate at <https://www.senato.it/3723?shadow_organo=1170075>.

91 PACE Doc. 12636 (n 44) para. 29.

92 No. 25965/04, 7 January 2010.

93 Email correspondence with Eleni Georgiou, International Relations Officer of the House of Representatives of the Republic of Cyprus, 3 July 2015.

94 See the website of the National Assembly at <http://www.parlament.gov.rs/national-assembly/organisation-and-support-service/national-assembly-working-bodies-.2179.html>.

95 Email correspondence with Martina Okruhlicova, clerk to the Constitutional and Legal Affairs Committee of the Slovak National Council, 31 August 2015.

96 Statute, Seimas of the Republic of Lithuania, 17 February 1994, No. I–399, Vilnius (as last amended on 16 December 2014, No. XII–1440), Articles 67, 70.

monitoring the implementation of ECtHR judgments as part of its stated remit. Since 2010 the government agent has presented an annual report to the Committee on Legal Affairs on cases against Lithuania and the status of execution; however, parliamentary consideration and approval of the report appears to be a largely formalistic process.[97] In the Moldovan parliament, the Committee for Human Rights and Inter-ethnic Relations has the task of 'monitoring and assessing the implementation of human rights norms' generally,[98] while the Committee on Legal Affairs, Nominations, and Immunities is responsible for monitoring the execution of ECtHR judgments.[99] This Committee also receives an annual report on the execution of judgments from the executive. At the time of writing, a legislative initiative is pending to create a Sub-committee on the execution of Strasbourg judgments.[100]

Several other former Soviet states have hybrid systems which assign human rights responsibility to more than one committee but do not include any institutionalized mechanism for monitoring ECtHR judgments. The Ukrainian parliament (the *Verkhovna Rada*) has several committees whose remit could include human rights, including the Committee on Human Rights, National Minorities, and Interethnic Relations ('the Human Rights Committee') and the Committee on Legal Policy and Justice ('the Justice Committee') although none is in fact routinely involved in the implementation of ECtHR judgments—as discussed at 5.4.1. In the Georgian parliament, the Human Rights and Civil Integration Committee ('Human Rights Committee') has 'broad powers to monitor and evaluate the human rights situation in the country and the government's compliance with and respect for national laws and international agreements affecting human rights'.[101] The Legal Issues Committee may also become involved occasionally when a draft law is required in response to a judgment, usually relating to criminal justice. There is, however, no system of monitoring the implementation of judgments, nor any obligation on the government to report regularly to parliament on the matter. The Action Plan for 2015–16 developed by the Human Rights Committee makes no reference either to the Convention or judgments of the ECtHR.[102] A member of the Human Rights Committee reports that the Committee rarely uses its power to hold hearings or submit questions to ministers about specific judgments, and when it does

[97] We are grateful to Ramute Remezaite, legal consultant to the European Human Rights Advocacy Centre, for providing unofficial translations of the 2013 annual report of the government agent and sessional reports of the Committee on Legal Affairs and the Committee on Human Rights, 2013 and 2014.

[98] See website of the Parliament at <http://www.parlament.md/StructuraParlamentului/Comisiipermanente/tabid/84/CommissionId/6/language/en-US/Default.aspx>.

[99] See website of the Parliament at <http://www.parlament.md/StructuraParlamentului/Comisiipermanente/tabid/84/CommissionId/9/language/en-US/Default.aspx>.

[100] Information supplied by Raisa Apolschii, Chair of Committee on Legal Affairs, Nominations, and Immunities, to seminar organized by the PACE Parliamentary Project Support Division in cooperation with the Committee on Legal Affairs and Human Rights, Tbilisi, 21–22 September 2015 (on file).

[101] See website of the Parliament at <http://www.parliament.ge/en/saparlamento-saqmianoba/komitetebi/adamianis-uflebata-dacvisa-da-samoqalaqo-integraciis-komiteti/komitetis-shesaxeb>.

[102] Committee on Human Rights and Civil Integration of the Parliament of Georgia, *Action Plan 2015–2016* (2014).

so, responses from the government are generally vague and non-case-specific.[103] Within the National Assembly of Armenia, the Committee on Human Rights and Public Affairs and the Committee on State and Legal Affairs each has human rights within its sphere of competence, although legislative vetting is a cross-cutting activity.[104] Again, neither presently has a mechanism for monitoring the implementation of ECtHR judgments and there is no requirement on government to report regularly to parliament.

Hybrid systems may contain within them specialized sub-committees with a remit that is specifically concerned with Convention standards and ECtHR judgments. In the bicameral Romanian parliament, the upper house (the Senate) and the lower house (the Chamber of Deputies) each has two committees which variously handle human rights matters—the Committees on Legal Matters, Discipline, and Immunities ('Legal Committees') and the Committees on Human Rights, Cults, and National Minorities ('Human Rights Committees'). In 2009, the Legal Committee in the Chamber of Deputies established a Sub-committee to monitor the execution of ECtHR judgments, whose work is examined at 6.3.4.

In Poland, the Committee on Justice and Human Rights in the lower house (or *Sejm*) of the bicameral parliament also has a Sub-committee on the execution of ECtHR judgments.[105] The Sub-committee was established in 2014 at the joint initiative of the Committee on Justice and Human Rights and a committee in the upper house (the Senate)—the Human Rights, Rule of Law, and Petitions Committee. The Sub-committee prepares draft desiderata or opinions on the execution of ECtHR judgments for two *Sejm* committees—the Committee on Justice and Human Rights and the Foreign Affairs Committee. Thus, the Sub-committee is the product of, and reports to, a hybrid committee system.

In the bicameral Czech parliament, the Constitutional and Legal Committee in the lower house, the Chamber of Deputies, has established a Sub-committee on legislative initiatives of the Ombudsman[106] and the European Court of Human Rights.[107] In addition, the Committee on Petitions has a Sub-committee on Human Rights.[108] The sub-committees are effectively working groups of their parent committee, and meet in private. The Sub-committee on legislative initiatives of the Ombudsman and the ECtHR discusses the annual report prepared by the government agent on judgments against the Czech Republic and their state of execution. The Constitutional and Legal Committee and Committee on Petitions

[103] Interview (anonymous), 6 August 2015.

[104] Email correspondence with Arpine Hovhannisyan, member of the Committee of State and Legal Affairs, 7 August 2015.

[105] Ministry of Foreign Affairs of the Republic of Poland, 'Parliamentary Subcommittee on Execution of European Court of Human Rights' Judgments Established', 6 February 2014. See also 'Parliaments and the European Court of Human Rights', report of conference organized by Middlesex University and the Helsinki Foundation for Human Rights at the Senate, Warsaw, 12 May 2015 ('Warsaw Conference Report').

[106] The Ombudsman, also known as the Public Defender of Rights, mediates between complainants and public bodies.

[107] See website of the Chamber of Deputies at <http://www.psp.cz/en/sqw/hp.sqw?k=4024>.

[108] See website of the Chamber of Deputies at <http://www.psp.cz/sqw/hp.sqw?k=3920>.

play the leading role in vetting the conformity of government and non-government bills with international human rights treaties, including the Convention.[109]

In summary, we have identified a range of models adopted by parliaments that have taken any initiative to conducting vetting of legislation for Convention compliance, and sometimes also monitoring of ECtHR judgments, in addition to other functions. Aside from the cross-cutting approach in the unicameral parliaments of several Nordic states, there is no distinctive pattern in the models adopted elsewhere in the Council of Europe. Each of the approaches—cross-cutting, specialized, and hybrid—is found in unicameral and bicameral parliaments; systems which are (at least formally) monist or dualist; presidential, semi-presidential, and parliamentary systems; and older and newer Convention member states. The resulting patchwork of parliamentary approaches to conducting human rights oversight reflects in part the incremental and ad hoc nature of their development, which has frequently been reliant on the initiative of individual parliamentarians (see 2.6.2).

A striking feature of the structures and mechanisms outlined in this section is that many have been developed relatively recently, spurred in several instances by interventions of the Parliamentary Assembly.[110] Moreover, there may be a considerable time lag between the formal creation of a parliamentary structure and the point at which it starts to meet regularly and achieve clarity as to its remit and working methods (or between the addition of human rights to the remit of an existing committee and the point at which that expanded remit becomes embedded within the committee's day-to-day business). As an illustration, the specialized Sub-committee in the Romanian Chamber of Deputies was formed in 2009. Our interviews in 2012 suggested that it was inactive and hardly known outside the parliament; however, interviews in 2013 and 2015 suggested that the Sub-committee's work was slowly gaining in momentum (see 6.3.4). The embryonic nature of many of the structures described in this section, and the paucity of information that is generally publicly available about their work, precludes detailed assessment of their impact or effectiveness (see, however, chapters 5–9 for assessment of the impact of parliamentary bodies in Ukraine, Romania, the UK, the Netherlands, and Germany; and 3.7 for discussion about how effectiveness can be assessed). In the next section, we consider the potential advantages or disadvantages of different institutional approaches.

3.4.2 Advantages and disadvantages of different models

The Parliamentary Assembly has declined to endorse any single model for institutionalizing parliamentary human rights work, recognizing that different approaches suit different national contexts. Its Legal Affairs Committee has urged parliaments

[109] Email correspondence with Ota Hlinomaz of the Office of the Government Agent and Martin Kavěna of the Parliamentary Institute, 11 August 2015.

[110] See, for example, presentation by Adam Bodnar, Warsaw Conference Report (n 105). Tracing the development of the Polish Sub-committee on the execution of judgments, Bodnar highlights the instrumental role played by the Parliamentary Assembly, especially Resolution 1787 (2011) and the work of the Council of Europe office in Warsaw.

to create 'dedicated human rights committees *or appropriate analogous structures*, whose remits shall be clearly defined and enshrined in law'(emphasis added).[111] A similar approach has been recommended by the UN High Commissioner for Human Rights.[112] While these approaches are not prescriptive, they do indicate a preference for either specialized or hybrid over cross-cutting systems, at least for parliaments that are instigating human rights oversight for the first time. The former Parliamentary Assembly rapporteur, Christos Pourgourides, argues that the specialized committee model has 'clear advantages' since it 'pools competences and provides direction'.[113]

An obvious risk of having a cross-cutting approach to human rights oversight is that it becomes a euphemism for sporadic (or, indeed, non-existent) human rights oversight—that 'everyone's responsibility is no-one's responsibility'. The French National Assembly and Senate, for example, have no mechanism in place to carry out regular monitoring of ECtHR case law, and a draft constitutional law has been proposed to create such a mechanism.[114] As noted at 3.4.1.1, Russia's cross-cutting system has no systematic mechanism for monitoring implementation of ECtHR judgments.

Interviews conducted with MPs and others in the Netherlands yielded contrasting opinions about the effectiveness of the cross-cutting structure of the Dutch parliament (see 8.3.2). Some favoured introducing a greater degree of specialization as a way of concentrating expertise and encouraging 'ownership' of domestic human rights among MPs. Others expressed concern that a specialized committee would lack political influence and might be used by other committees as a venue to offload responsibility for contentious issues.

The Open Society Justice Initiative (OSJI) ventures that in weak parliamentary systems, characterized by strong party discipline and dominance by a single party, 'mainstreaming human rights might have little effect'.[115] Especially in states where (unlike in the Netherlands) the execution of judgments and the verification of legislation for human rights compatibility is poorly co-ordinated within the executive, there are considerable advantages to having a specialized human rights committee or sub-committee, which can, over time, develop both systematic oversight mechanisms and human rights expertise among its members and staff. A dedicated human rights institution within parliament creates an interlocutor with the executive and a body which can perform specialized functions such as 'real time' scrutiny of action plans and action reports (see 2.5.2) and consideration of reports by the executive on ECtHR judgments and their state of execution (see 3.5.2). A further

[111] PACE Resolution 1823 (2011) (Appendix 1) (n 59) para. 1.

[112] Navanethem Pillay, *Strengthening the United Nations Human Rights Treaty Body System. A Report by the United Nations High Commissioner for Human Rights*, June 2012, 85 ('[w]ithin parliaments, appropriate standing committees or similar bodies should be established and involved in monitoring and assessing the level of domestic implementation of the recommendations, particularly those related to legislative reform').

[113] PACE Doc. 12636 (n 44) para. 30.

[114] See 3.5.3 at n 186.

[115] Open Society Justice Initiative, *From Rights to Remedies: Structures and Strategies for Implementing International Human Rights Decisions* (New York: Open Society Foundations, 2013) 68.

advantage to having a focal human rights body within parliament is the potential for it to develop understanding of, and independent contact with, the Court (see 2.4), the Committee of Ministers (see 2.5.5), and the Parliamentary Assembly (see 2.6.2). Further, a specialized committee or sub-committee is more able than a cross-cutting model to oversee and recommend improvements to the executive *system* of implementation (as, e.g., the JCHR has done in the UK; see 7.3.1). With effective co-ordination, hybrid systems can in principle yield the same benefits. However, as OSJI observes, 'tacking human rights on to the mandates of other standing committees runs the risk of thin commitment to, and insufficient time and resources for, implementation'.[116]

Our interviews in the UK suggest that, if the decision is taken to establish a specialized human rights committee within a bicameral parliament, there are advantages in making it a joint committee of both chambers in order to combine the political muscle of the lower house and the capacity for dispassionate reflection and detailed scrutiny in the upper house. Inspired in part by the example of the JCHR, discussion has begun in Romania on the creation of a joint parliamentary standing committee to replace the current hybrid arrangement (see 6.3.4).[117] In the absence of a joint structure, co-ordination between committees in the lower and upper chambers of bicameral parliaments is essential in order to maximize the contributions of each.[118]

Despite the undoubted advantages of having specialized parliamentary human rights bodies, it is important not to fetishize structures. Committees that bear the label 'human rights' may create the illusion of activity where none exists. The Azerbaijani parliament (the *Milli Mejlis*), for example, has a standing Committee on Human Rights yet we have found no evidence of activity on its part in relation to Convention standards or ECtHR judgments.[119] Further, concentrating human rights scrutiny and expertise within a specialized body creates the concomitant risk of discouraging the integration of human rights and related rule of law issues across the entire range of a parliament's functions and structures, including both committees and legal and research services. Murray Hunt, legal adviser to the JCHR since 2004, ventures that specialization and 'mainstreaming' should not be viewed as mutually exclusive options; rather, a dedicated human rights committee should aspire to be an 'engine' of mainstreaming (see also 7.3.2).[120] In the UK context, Hunt argues that:

> While a specialised human rights committee undoubtedly remains an essential part of the constitutional arrangements for human rights protection, the time may well be drawing near

[116] OSJI (n 115) 68. [117] Daniel Florea, Interview, 13 May 2015.

[118] On the respective roles of committees in the Polish *Sejm* and Senate, see presentation by Adam Bodnar, Warsaw Conference Report (n 105).

[119] Information provided by members of the Human Rights Legislation Division of the *Milli Mejlis* to the Parliamentary Assembly's Parliamentary Project Support Division (on file) suggests that proposals on amending or revoking existing legislation or adopting new legal provisions in response to ECtHR judgments are submitted directly to the Head of the Parliament Office, thereby appearing to bypass the Committee on Human Rights.

[120] Interview, 10 September 2012.

when there will be more general recognition that leaving the task of human rights scrutiny to a single committee is not sufficient.[121]

If specialized committees are to act as a catalyst for human rights oversight to become more integrated into the work of committees across parliament, the first step is likely to be taking a cross-cutting approach to the provision of human rights legal advice and information provided by legal and research services. In respect of the UK Parliament, Hunt suggests that parliamentary staff should make a 'concerted effort ... to anticipate and identify more proactively and effectively any rule of law and human rights dimensions of any work Parliament is carrying out'.[122]

A degree of realism is also required as to what can be achieved by a single committee or sub-committee, which may have only a few members—for example, a maximum of seven in the case of the Romanian Sub-committee on the execution of judgments (see 6.3.4)—and which may therefore lack time, expertise, and political clout. Another problematic issue raised repeatedly by interviewees was the status and credibility of human rights-related committees, as reflected both in their formal powers and informal standing. In Ukraine, interviewees emphasized that the Justice Committee (which has, at the time of writing, thirty-three members) is regarded as particularly influential, partly because it is involved in politically sensitive areas such as the appointment of judges, while the Human Rights Committee (which presently has nine members) has a lower profile and status due to its lack of budgetary powers and a history of ineffective leadership (see 5.4.1).[123] In Romania, too, membership of the Human Rights Committees in both houses of the bicameral parliament is prized less than membership of the more powerful Legal Committees (see 6.3.3). The Human Rights Committee in the lower house was regarded by interviewees as lacking in credibility, in part because its chairperson since 2000, Nicolae Păun, has a record of introducing legislative proposals which would risk violating human rights, such as measures to criminalize begging, fortune-telling, and 'witchcraft'. This observation demonstrates the particular vulnerability of specialized structures to leadership which is either weak or obstructive. As one Ukrainian government official ventured, '[t]he crucial role is played by the head of a committee, who can either promote a draft law or block it'.[124]

3.4.3 Principles underpinning the parliamentary role

There is no internationally agreed set of principles and guidelines on the role of parliaments in the protection and realization of human rights and the rule of law, akin to the Paris Principles which, since their adoption in 1993, have set international

[121] Murray Hunt, 'The Joint Committee on Human Rights', in Alexander Horne, Gavin Drewry, and Dawn Oliver, eds., *Parliament and the Law* (Oxford: Hart Publishing, 2013): 223, 247.

[122] Hunt (n 121) 247.

[123] See website of the *Verkhovna Rada* at <http://gapp.rada.gov.ua/radatransl/Home/Committees/en>.

[124] Interview (anonymous), 22 May 2012.

standards for the status, powers, and functioning of NHRIs.[125] This is a striking omission in view of the growing recognition of the parliamentary role by both regional and human rights bodies charted in 3.3. However, a significant step has been taken with the proposal of a set of Draft Principles and Guidelines on the Role of Parliaments in the Protection and Realisation of the Rule of Law and Human Rights, initiated by the JCHR's legal adviser, Murray Hunt.[126] The Draft Principles and Guidelines emphasize that as an organ of the state, parliaments share with the executive and judiciary the 'primary responsibility for securing in national law the rights and freedoms recognised in international treaties, and for ensuring the availability at national level of an effective remedy if those rights or freedoms are violated'.[127] They reflect many of the recommendations made in reports and resolutions of the Parliamentary Assembly[128] and the Inter-Parliamentary Union.[129] Endorsement of a set of Guidelines and Principles by national, regional, and international parliamentary bodies and by international organizations (such as the UN, Council of Europe, and Inter-Parliamentary Union) would be a welcome confirmation of the parliamentary role in relation to the protection and realization of the rule of law and human rights.[130] Moreover, their adoption would clearly signal to *executive* bodies the necessity of ensuring that parliamentarians are able to fulfil this function.

The Draft Principles and Guidelines recommend that parliaments either establish a committee solely dedicated to human rights, or identify or establish a committee which has human rights as part of its remit (either being referred to as a 'human rights committee').[131] This approach accords with the flexible approach of the Parliamentary Assembly in not prescribing a particular institutional model. In addition, the Draft Principles and Guidelines recommend that parliaments should take active steps to mainstream human rights and the rule of law across the entire range of parliamentary activities and functions, including making legal and other expert advice available to all parliamentary committees and officials (see 3.4.3.1).[132] It is further recommended that a human rights committee should have a permanent status and a remit that is clearly defined and enshrined in the parliament's standing orders (or equivalent).[133] The remit should be sufficiently broad so

[125] Principles relating to the Status of National Institutions (The Paris Principles), adopted by General Assembly resolution 48/134 of 20 December 1993.

[126] Hunt, Hooper, and Yowell, eds. (n 46) 485–95 (Appendix: Draft Principles and Guidelines on the Role of Parliaments in the Protection and Realisation of the Rule of Law and Human Rights) ('Draft Principles and Guidelines').

[127] Draft Principles and Guidelines (n 126) 485.

[128] See, especially, PACE Resolution 1823 (2011) (Appendix 1) (n 59).

[129] Inter-Parliamentary Union and Office of the United Nations High Commissioner for Human Rights (n 54).

[130] The Draft Principles and Guidelines were debated at a conference on 'The Role of Parliaments in the Protection and Realisation of the Rule and Human Rights' held at Portcullis House, Westminster, 7 September 2015.

[131] Draft Principles and Guidelines (n 126) section I A.

[132] Draft Principles and Guidelines (n 126) section I B.

[133] Draft Principles and Guidelines (n 126) section II A.

as to reflect the imperative for parliament both to protect and realize human rights in the state concerned and to take into account all relevant sources of human rights standards in both national and international law.[134] This recommendation reflects the importance for the work of human rights committees of developing an intellectually coherent view of human rights in the domestic setting, particularly in the case of committees whose remit also covers human rights in relation to matters such as foreign policy or humanitarian aid (as in Germany; see 9.4.1). Further, an expansive conception of human rights, drawing on rights under any treaty which binds the state in international law, maximizes the parliament's opportunity to scrutinize the government in matters of both domestic and foreign policy and, as Feldman suggests, 'reinforces the parliament's armoury in its constant battle with the government for control over information and relative authority'.[135]

The Draft Principles and Guidelines also recommend that the method of appointment of the committee should be transparent and should ensure that it is independent of both the government and non-state actors and that its membership reflects the principles of political pluralism and gender balance.[136] The committee should have subpoena powers over witnesses and documents and the power to initiate inquiries; hold oral evidence hearings; conduct visits at home or abroad; access places of detention without notice; report to parliament; and make recommendations to government.[137] Where possible, its powers could also include initiating parliamentary debates on its reports or other subjects, proposing legislative amendments, or introducing bills into parliament on matters within its remit.

Various 'core functions' of a human rights committee are proposed in the Draft Principles and Guidelines.[138] These include: legislative scrutiny (including systematic scrutiny of all government bills for their compatibility with human rights, facilitated where possible by executive human rights memoranda attached to every bill); scrutiny of the executive response to human rights judgments of domestic and international courts, facilitated by (at least) annual reporting by the executive on its response to human rights judgments;[139] and monitoring of compliance with international human rights treaties, including scrutiny of state reports to UN treaty bodies and the executive's response to the concluding observations of those bodies, together with scrutiny of international treaties prior to ratification and of subsequent decisions to sign or ratify treaties. Other proposed core functions are inquiries into topical human rights issues; and monitoring the adequacy of national mechanisms for the protection and realization of human rights.

134 Draft Principles and Guidelines (n 126) section II B.

135 David Feldman, 'Democracy, Law and Human Rights: Politics as Challenge and Opportunity', in Hunt, Hooper, and Yowell, eds. (n 46): 95, 105.

136 Draft Principles and Guidelines (n 126) section II C.

137 Draft Principles and Guidelines (n 126) section II D.

138 Draft Principles and Guidelines (n 126) section III A.

139 It is also suggested that the human rights committee could monitor developments in human rights case law, including judgments of international courts against other states, with a view to identifying possible implications for national law, policy, or practice; see, however, 2.1.1, on the considerable obstacles to such activity being conducted systematically by parliamentary bodies.

The Draft Principles and Guidelines propose various working methods for human rights committees, including publication of a prioritized work programme; the creation of opportunities for civil society to have direct input into parliamentary consideration of human rights issues; and regular reporting to parliament on its activities.[140] Transparency is also posited as an important principle, requiring the maintenance of an up-to-date website containing, for example, correspondence and transcripts or recordings of evidence sessions. Decision-making by consensus is also recommended, so far as it is possible to do so. This principle reflects the fact that membership of committees may reflect different political and philosophical conceptions of human rights; for example, in relation to the balance to be struck between monitoring state obligations of, one the one hand, civil and political rights and, on the other hand, economic, social, and cultural rights. A human rights committee may have to debate and negotiate these differences in deciding its overall priorities and in its response to specific judgments and decisions of international human rights bodies (see, for example, the discussion of the work of the JCHR at 7.6.4).

It is further recommended that human rights committees develop consistent and effective working relationships with key external interlocutors, including the executive, courts, national human rights institutions,[141] civil society groups; other parts of the national and international human rights machinery;[142] other parliamentary committees; the media; academics; and the legal profession.[143] Further, it is suggested that parliamentarians should be given appropriate induction training on human rights and the rule of law.[144] Such training is not routinely provided in any of the parliaments in our five case-study states, highlighting the importance of the capacity-building work of the Parliamentary Assembly, the Inter-Parliamentary Union,[145] initiatives such as the Westminster Consortium for Parliaments and Democracy,[146] and briefings provided by NGOs.[147] Human rights committees are also encouraged to develop methodologies for assessing their effectiveness,[148] a point considered further at 3.7.

[140] Draft Principles and Guidelines (n 126) section IV A–F.

[141] See also the Belgrade Principles on the Relationship between National Human Rights Institutions and Parliaments, February 2012.

[142] The Draft Principles and Guidelines do not cover the role of delegates to international or regional parliamentary assemblies such as PACE. Such guidance would be useful in view of the problems identified at 2.6.2 in respect of PACE delegations, including the lack of integration in the work of national parliaments, and the conduct of delegates who use the Assembly principally as a venue within which to neutralize criticism of their respective states. It should be recalled, however, that delegates to PACE are not necessarily also members of human rights committees in national parliaments.

[143] Draft Principles and Guidelines (n 126) section V A–J.

[144] Draft Principles and Guidelines (n 126) section VI A and B.

[145] Schwarz (n 53).

[146] George Kunnath and Angela Patrick, 'The Work of the Westminster Foundation for Democracy', in Hunt, Hooper, and Yowell, eds. (n 46): 338.

[147] See, for example, JUSTICE, *Law for Lawmakers: A JUSTICE Guide to the Law* (2015) Chapter 5.

[148] Draft Principles and Guidelines (n 126) section VII.

3.4.3.1 Provision of independent legal advice

In addition, the Draft Principles and Guidelines reflect the imperative for human rights committees to be supported by expert staff capable of providing politically independent advice on human rights law and policy, meaning that they should not be on secondment from government or NGOs.[149] The importance of access to independent advice on human rights has been repeatedly stressed by the Parliamentary Assembly,[150] whose capacity-building programme reflects this priority in its attention to training parliamentary staff as well as MPs (see 2.6.1).[151] It was frequently reiterated in our research interviews that the development of a professional parliamentary staff provides continuity between parliaments and ensures the creation of an institutional memory attached to the work of parliamentary committees, both in relation to substantive issues and working methods, including the relationship with executive actors and international human rights bodies. The provision of such advice was widely viewed as facilitative, rather than constraining, of the work of parliamentary committees; advisers can provide political cover for parliamentarians in matters that are contentious, ensuring that they are briefed as to the range of Convention-compliant options available to them. As Kavanagh notes in respect of the JCHR, once legal expertise is presented in an accessible style in reports to parliament, it can '*serve* legislative deliberation across the board and strengthen the ability of parliamentarians to probe legislation in a meaningful and effective way' (emphasis in original).[152] This observation is borne out by empirical research in the Australian federal parliament, which reveals the importance of access to legal expertise for the productivity and effectiveness of parliamentary committees.[153] In this sense, parliamentary advisers may be as viewed as 'mediators' between national parliamentarians and international human rights bodies, facilitating mutual understanding and exchange of information within a shared normative framework.[154] Access to politically neutral advice also helps to ensure both the independence—and the *appearance* of independence—of human rights committees. This benefit is much less likely to occur where advisers are transient appointees of either individual MPs or party groups.

3.5 Executive Structures and Mechanisms

Domestic institutional arrangements for implementation of ECtHR judgments rely to a large extent on the executive. It is the executive that represents the state

[149] Draft Principles and Guidelines (n 126) section II E.
[150] PACE Resolution 1823 (2011) (Appendix 1) (n 59) para. 2.
[151] PACE, PPSD (2014) 07 rev. 31 (n 82).
[152] Kavanagh (n 64) 129. See also Feldman (n 135) 112.
[153] Carolyn Evans and Simon Evans, 'Messages from the Front Line: Parliamentarians' Perspectives on Rights protection', in Tom Campbell, Keith Ewing, and Adam Tomkins, eds., *The Legal Protection of Human Rights: Sceptical Essays* (Oxford: Oxford University Press, 2011): 329, 338.
[154] We are grateful to Murray Hunt for this insight.

before the Court and the Committee of Ministers and that possesses both the information and law- and policy-making apparatus to formulate the state's response to adverse judgments (in the first instance, by means of the action plan or action report and later, where necessary, by proposing legislative reform). Therefore, even the most conscientious and well-resourced of parliamentary human rights committees cannot ensure smooth implementation of Court judgments in the absence of executive co-ordination and information sharing. This observation implies that an important role for parliaments is to conduct oversight not only of the government's response to specific judgments, or particular legislative proposals, but also the domestic *system* of implementation, including the extent to which it is responsive to, and facilitative of, the role of parliament itself. Indeed, many of the improvements made to executive systems of implementation have demonstrably resulted from parliamentary pressure.

This section covers executive structures and mechanisms for co-ordinating implementation (3.5.1), and arrangements for transmitting to parliamentarians the information they need to conduct human rights-based scrutiny (3.5.2). In addition, it considers a further option adopted by a few states: the development of national legislation which enshrines the role of different domestic actors in the implementation process (3.5.3).

3.5.1 Executive co-ordination of implementation

The Committee of Ministers has recommended that all Convention states designate a co-ordinator for the execution of judgments at the national level, a function which in most states is carried out by the office of the government agent.[155] Co-ordination of implementation at the executive level is frequently a complex and demanding task, particularly where action is required by multiple agencies.

The role and status of the government agent is not mentioned in the Convention and is defined only vaguely in the Court's rules of procedure.[156] Some government agents have called for standardized regulations to be drawn up within the Council of Europe defining the powers, duties, and professional requirements of the role,[157] while others doubt that such standardization is possible given the variation between constitutional and legal systems.[158] It has also been proposed that government agents should be appointed by a transparent and formalized nomination process similar to that for appointing senior members of the judiciary in order that the agent 'would enjoy both a close relationship with democratic institutions and

[155] Recommendation CM/Rec(2008)2 of the Committee of Ministers to member states on efficient domestic capacity for rapid execution of judgments of the European Court of Human Rights, 6 February 2008, Recommendation 1.

[156] Rule 35 of the Rules of Court (1 June 2015) states only: 'The Contracting Parties shall be represented by Agents, who may have the assistance of advocates or advisers.'

[157] 'The Role of Government Agents in Ensuring Effective Human Rights Protection', Seminar organized under the Slovak Chairmanship of the Committee of Ministers of the Council of Europe (Bratislava, 3–4 April 2008) ('ECtHR Agents' Report') 33, 67.

[158] ECtHR Agents' Report (n 157) 39.

civil society and a degree of independence, as well as authority of their own not derived from their operational attachment to a ministry or executive organ'.[159] In the absence of such standardization, an important function of parliamentary human rights bodies is to scrutinize the adequacy of executive arrangements for responding to ECtHR judgments and to propose reforms where necessary.

The majority of government agents or their equivalents are located within their respective justice ministries, as in Ukraine and Germany.[160] Many are alternatively located within foreign affairs ministries (as in Romania) or, exceptionally, the presidential administration or prosecutor's office. There is evidence that agents who are situated within foreign affairs ministries, and do not have strong connections to a counterpart in the justice ministry, are comparatively poorly placed to co-ordinate implementation, given that the majority of Strasbourg cases implicate the activities of the ministries of justice or home (interior) affairs.[161] Several interviewees in Romania ventured that the transfer of the government agent from the Ministry of Justice to the Ministry of Foreign Affairs in 2003 was an unwelcome development which had led some holders of the post to see their principal role as being to 'defend the state to the last' (see 6.4).[162] A further challenge is presented by the dual—and sometimes multiple—roles of government agents, who commonly act both as advocates for the state before the ECtHR and co-ordinators of implementation in the event of an adverse judgment. As Deniz Akçay, former co-agent of the Turkish government, notes:

> The execution phase is extremely sensitive, in that the finding of a violation comes between the agent and the authorities.... In this new scenario, the agent has to convince the authorities to take measures at odds with their position, which in some cases he or she may even have argued as the government's agent before the Court.[163]

Such arrangements are not ubiquitous, however. For example, in the UK, the agent is part of the Foreign and Commonwealth Office, while the Ministry of Justice has since 2010 had lead responsibility for the receipt and co-ordination of ECtHR judgments (see 7.4). In the Netherlands, the government agent is formally part of the Ministry of Foreign Affairs, but works closely with the legislation directorate of the Ministry of Security and Justice, which often takes responsibility for implementation at the policy level given that many ECtHR judgments implicate the justice system (see 8.4).

The political rank and status of government agents is critical to their ability to communicate with disparate executive actors and convince them of the need to respond to judgments of the ECtHR.[164] The Committee of Ministers recommends

159 ECtHR Agents' Report (n 157) 84–5.

160 Round-table on Recommendation 2008(2) of the Committee of Ministers to Member States on efficient domestic capacity for rapid execution of judgments of the European Court of Human Rights, 15–16 December 2011, Tirana, Albania, 'Synthesis of the replies by member states to the questionnaire on the domestic mechanisms for rapid execution of the Court's judgments', 3–4.

161 OSJI (n 115) 37–8.

162 Monica Macovei, Interview, 12 June 2012.

163 ECtHR Agents' Report (n 157) 69.

164 Philip Leach, Helen Hardman, Svetlana Stephenson, and Brad Blitz, *Responding to Systemic Human Rights Violations—An Analysis of Pilot Judgments of the European Court of Human Rights and Their Impact at National Level* (Antwerp-Oxford-Portland: Intersentia, 2010) 179.

that the co-ordinating body should have the necessary power and authority to acquire relevant information; liaise with those responsible at the national level for deciding on the measures required to execute a judgment; and, if required, take necessary measures to accelerate the execution process.[165] Problems may arise where the office of the government agent is under-resourced, where there is a rapid turnover of government agents who consequently lack experience, or where the government agent is an appointee whose office is dependent on maintaining political favour. Speaking in 2012, interviewees in Romania—including former government agents—suggested that each of these problems had arisen in recent years in respect of the executive system for co-ordinating implementation (see 6.4). Interviewees in Ukraine also report persistent problems relating to the status, authority, and capacity of the government agent (see 5.3.2).

Some executives have developed systematized methods for co-ordinating execution, such as, in the UK, an implementation form, which the Ministry of Justice sends to lead policy teams within the relevant government departments to elicit within a set time frame what action they intend to take in response to an adverse judgment (see 7.4).[166] Similarly, in Poland, the Ministry of Justice has prepared a special instruction that describes to government agencies the different steps required to execute Court judgments.[167]

Another approach to executive co-ordination of the implementation process, recommended by the Open Society Justice Initiative, is the creation of a standing inter-ministerial committee, in addition to the government agent.[168] Such committees exist, for example, in Macedonia[169] and Poland.[170] Inter-ministerial committees, OSJI notes, can minimize the risk of miscommunication and duplication and serve as the natural interlocutor for other political branches, including parliament and the judiciary.[171] Inter-ministerial working groups have also been established on an ad hoc basis to co-ordinate the implementation of specific judgments which involve multiple state actors, including parliaments.[172] In addition, to support the work of the government agent, the Council of Europe recommends the appointment, at the national and regional level (in federal states), of human rights liaison officers in all ministries.[173] It also recommends that the government agent maintains both formal and informal links with judicial authorities, and promotes

[165] Recommendation CM/Rec(2008)2 (n 155) Recommendation 1.

[166] Ministry of Justice, *Responding to Human Rights Judgments: Report to the Joint Committee on Human Rights on the Government's Response to Human Rights Judgments 2010–11*, CM 1862 (2011) 27. See also 7.4.1.

[167] Adam Bodnar and Renata Uitz, *Efficient Enforcement of Judgments of the European Court of Human Rights in Poland and in Hungary*, Ernst & Young 'Better Government' Programme (2011).

[168] OSJI (n 115) 51. [169] See 3.5.3 at n 184.

[170] OSJI (n 115) 46–7; see also Justyna Chrzanowska, Warsaw Conference Report (n 105) 9.

[171] OSJI (n 115) 52.

[172] In Romania, an inter-departmental working group was established in December 2010 to resolve the systemic problem arising from the nationalization of property during the communist era, following the ECtHR's application of the pilot judgment procedure in *Maria Atanasiu and Others v Romania*, Nos. 30767/05 and 33800/06, 12 October 2010 (see 6.6.3).

[173] Council of Europe, Round table: Efficient Domestic Capacity for Rapid Execution of the European Court's Judgments, 15–16 December 2011, Conclusions of the Chairperson at 2.

involvement in the execution process by national human rights institutions, ombudsmen, and civil society actors.

3.5.2 Reporting mechanisms

Where systematic reporting on human rights by the executive to parliament takes place, this usually consists of an annual report on the governmental response to ECtHR judgments prepared either by the responsible ministry or by the government agent. The first state to adopt this practice was the Netherlands (in 1996) followed by Germany (in 2004) (see, respectively, 8.4 and 9.5). Subsequent adopters include Bulgaria, Croatia, the Czech Republic, Greece, Hungary, Italy (see 3.4.1.3), Latvia, Lithuania, Macedonia, Moldova, Poland, Switzerland, and the UK (see 7.4.1).[174] The Netherlands and Germany also provide or commission analysis of judgments against other states that might have implications for their respective legal orders. Since 2010, the Dutch annual report has also contained information about reasoned inadmissibility decisions of the ECtHR and an analysis of the areas of law and policy implicated in pending cases against the Netherlands.

It is difficult to identify tangible impacts resulting from annual reports in relation to the implementation of specific judgments, especially where parliament has access to timelier sources of information such as the government's action plans or external sources. As OSJI notes, there is a risk that such reports are 'more ceremonial than substantive', especially where—as is common—they are not systematically followed up or debated in parliament.[175] However, such reporting mechanisms offer several potential advantages. First, the *anticipation* of scrutiny may itself have a galvanizing effect on executive bodies. Regular reporting mechanisms can prompt governments to systematize and streamline co-ordination within the executive branch, thereby increasing the efficiency of the implementation process. Such a process can also highlight problems that occur where, for example, the government agent lacks the political status required to influence or obtain information from other arms of the executive. In the longer term, regular reporting to parliament by the executive may have the beneficial effect of normalizing the implementation process and preventing it from becoming unduly politicized. Annual reports also provide a cumulative public record of a state's compliance performance which may be used by parliamentarians and civil society actors. These factors are considered further in 3.7 in relation to assessment of the effectiveness of parliamentary human rights bodies.

[174] PACE, Parliamentary Project Support Division, The Role of Parliaments in Implementing ECHR Standards: Overview of Existing Structures and Mechanisms: Background Memorandum, PPSD (2014) 22 rev, 8 September 2015, para. 2.1. On Greece and Bulgaria, see also Committee of Ministers, *Supervision of the Execution of Judgments and Decisions of the European Court of Human Rights: 8th Annual Report of the Committee of Ministers 2014* (2015) ('8th Annual Report of the Committee of Ministers 2014') 206.

[175] OSJI (n 115) 70.

Another important aspect of information sharing is the provision to the relevant parliamentary bodies of action plans or reports at the same time as they are transmitted to the Committee of Ministers. As noted at 2.3.2, although the Committee of Ministers has since 2011 published action plans or action reports on its website, this does not always happen immediately or in a way that makes them easily accessible. Regular monitoring by parliamentary human rights committees of action plans and reports would not only facilitate 'real time' monitoring of executive action or inaction but would also have the additional advantage of galvanizing executives to improve the quality and timeliness of action plans and reports from the outset. In practice, this is likely to mean that parliamentary staff review action plans and reports and selectively draw MPs' attention to those which merit scrutiny.

Another key aspect of information sharing is the translation, publication, and dissemination of ECtHR judgments. The publication and dissemination of judgments is frequently a requirement of general measures.[176] In Ukraine, there is a legal requirement on the government agent to provide a summary of judgments against Ukraine for publication in two official newspapers, and to provide full translations of judgments to the Ombudsman (Parliamentary Commissioner for Human Rights), state bodies, and other people directly affected (see 5.3.1). In Romania, judgments concerning structural problems, possibly requiring legislative change, are translated and published in an official journal (see 6.5). The Supreme Council of Magistracy also translates selected judgments, as does the European Institute of Romania under a protocol with the government agent. Similar arrangements exist in Poland.[177] NGO representatives in Romania interviewed in 2012 suggested that official arrangements for ensuring translation of all judgments concerning Romania were, in practice, haphazard. As discussed at 2.1.1, respect for the interpretative authority of the ECtHR also implies that governments should selectively translate judgments against *other* states which have implications for their own legal orders. However, it is far from certain that most states do so systematically, if at all.

3.5.3 National implementation legislation

In a few European states, parliament has legislated to provide a national legislative framework for the implementation of judgments. Such legislation enshrines the authorities and duties of domestic actors with jurisdiction over implementation—the executive, parliament, and the judiciary—with respect to deadlines, information sharing, and other matters. Such legislation may also clarify how regional and international human rights conventions should be applied within the domestic legal order.

Ukraine introduced a law in 2006 imposing detailed, time-bound obligations on state actors after a judgment of the ECtHR against Ukraine becomes final, yet (as discussed at 5.3.1) its practical effect has been disappointing.[178] In 2006,

[176] See, for example, 2.5.1 at n 103.

[177] Chrzanowska (n 170) 9.

[178] Law on the Enforcement of Judgments and the Application of the Case-Law of the European Court of Human Rights Judgments 2006, Law No. 3477–IV of 23 February 2006. For an unofficial English translation of this law (prior to its amendment in 2010), see OSJI (n 115) 171–9.

Italy passed the 'Azzolini law', which transferred responsibility for implementation of ECtHR judgments from the Ministry of Foreign Affairs to the office of the prime minister; specified the prime minister's powers and duties relating to the enforcement of Court's judgments; and defined the relationship between the main domestic actors involved in the implementation of ECtHR judgments, including enumerating the duties of the Prime Minister for communicating judgments in a timely fashion to parliament and reporting annually to parliament on the state of implementation of judgments against Italy.[179] Sileoni notes that the Azzolini law enables parliament 'to rapidly adopt legislative measures as they become necessary' and has 'above all, a strong symbolic meaning' by signalling the priority attached to the implementation of ECtHR judgments.[180] However, other authors note that the practical effect of the law has been mixed and that 'insufficient measures have been taken as a result',[181] as evidenced by the backlog of unimplemented judgments against Italy (2,622 at the latest count).[182]

In Romania, too, a law exists stipulating the obligation of verifying the compatibility of bills, legislative proposals, and other normative acts and procedures with the standards enshrined in the Convention and ECtHR jurisprudence (see 6.3.1).[183] The law also requires the government to submit to parliament within three months of an adverse ECtHR judgment against Romania a draft law for amending and supplementing or repealing the offending provision. In Macedonia, a law on enforcement of ECtHR judgments was adopted in 2009 (which was amended in 2014).[184] This followed a review which had revealed that the state lacked a defined process for executing judgments. Under the law, an Inter-Departmental Commission was established. It comprises senior officials from the ministries of Justice, the Interior, Foreign Affairs, and Finance.[185] The Commission drafts analyses of ECtHR judgments; recommends individual and general measures to remedy violations; proposes legislative reform; and monitors the enforcement of the ECtHR's judgments, in line with various deadlines set out in the Law on Execution. As noted at 3.4.1.3, the Commission reports annually to the Standing Inquiry Committee on Civil Freedoms and Rights, one of two parliamentary committees with a human rights-related remit.

[179] Law No. 12/2006 (Italian Official Bulletin No. 15, 10 January 2006) on 'Provisions regarding the execution of judgments by the European Court of Human Rights'. For an unofficial English translation of the 2006 law, see OSJI (n 115) 180.

[180] Serena Sileoni, 'Between Political Inertia and Timid Judicial Activism: The Attempts to Overcome the Italian Implementation Failure', in Anagnostou, ed. (n 58): 49, 61.

[181] Leach, Hardman, Stephenson, and Blitz (n 164) 128–9.

[182] 8th Annual Report of the Committee of Ministers 2014 (n 174) 36.

[183] Law No. 29/2011 which amends and supplements Law No. 24/2000 on legislative technique.

[184] Law on Execution of the Decisions of the European Court of Human Rights, No. 07–2328/1, 21 May 2009. We are grateful to Ivan Petrushevski of the International Cooperation Department of the Assembly of the Republic of Macedonia for providing the text of the law and to the Parliamentary Project Support Division of PACE for providing an unofficial English translation.

[185] Ex officio members include the presidents of the Judicial Council, the Supreme Court, the Constitutional Court, and the Higher Administrative Court; the Public Prosecutors' Council; the Ombudsman; and the government agent, as well as the presidents of the Appeal Courts in Skopje and three other cities.

In June 2015, a member of the French National Assembly proposed a draft constitutional law to improve parliamentary monitoring of ECtHR decisions and facilitate compliance of domestic law with the Convention.[186] The author of the draft constitutional law, Pierre-Yves Le Borgn', argues that the law is necessary because (as noted at 3.4.2) there is currently no mechanism in place for the National Assembly to conduct regular monitoring of ECtHR judgments or for the executive to report regularly to the National Assembly or the Senate.[187] To rectify this omission, the draft law proposes that the government should transmit new judgments concerning France immediately to the National Assembly and Senate, and report annually to parliament on measures taken to execute judgments against France, justifying any delay in execution of more than six months. Parliament would in turn be entitled to adopt resolutions on the follow up to these decisions. The draft constitutional law would also require the government to report on cases concerning other states that are likely to have a direct impact on France.

As the statistics attest, the mere existence of a legislative framework does not guarantee smooth implementation of Strasbourg judgments (Ukraine, Italy, and Romania accounting for almost 40% of the caseload of the Committee of Ministers).[188] Nevertheless, providing a legal basis for the implementation process may be beneficial since it insulates institutional arrangements from being 'undone by executive fiat'.[189] Moreover, such laws may provide a foundation for more effective state practice; for example, by increasing the status of the government agent within the executive apparatus; stipulating time frames within which judgments are to be implemented and information provided to parliament; or simplifying complex or contradictory administrative procedures. It was also noted in Ukraine that such legislation may encourage the implementation of ECHR norms by making them appear closer to national law. However, neither the Parliamentary Assembly nor the Committee of Ministers has made it a priority to recommend that states should enact legislation setting out how judgments are to be implemented, suggesting that it is deemed neither a necessary nor sufficient condition for strengthening implementation in practice.[190]

Indeed, the mere existence of either laws or structures is no guarantee of effective implementation. Laws may be ignored or bypassed and structures may atrophy due to neglect, misuse, under-resourcing, or political enfeeblement. Thus, we return to the matter of political will and the motivations that parliamentarians have for advancing or resisting compliance with Convention standards and judgments of the ECtHR.

[186] See Pierre-Yves Le Borgn', Proposition de Loi Constitutionnelle visant à permettre au Parlement d'assurer un suivi optimal des arrêts de la Cour européenne des droits de l'homme (Proposal for a constitutional law to permit Parliament to ensure optimum monitoring of the judgments of the European Court of Human Rights), 17 June 2015. In November 2015, Mr Le Borgn' was appointed as the PACE rapporteur on the implementation of judgments of the ECtHR (see 2.6.1).

[187] Email correspondence with Pierre-Yves Le Borgn', Deputy, National Assembly, 21 July 2015.

[188] 8th Annual Report of the Committee of Ministers 2014 (n 174) 167.

[189] OSJI (n 115) 61.

[190] For example, PACE Resolution 1787 (2011) recommends (para. 10.2) that parliaments create effective domestic mechanisms for the implementation of ECtHR judgments 'either by legislation or otherwise'.

3.6 Parliaments and the Domestic Politics of Compliance

Given the discretion inherent in the Council of Europe's supervision mechanism, the process of implementing a judgment of the ECtHR is not merely a legalistic or technocratic process, but also, as the JCHR observes, an 'unavoidably political' one.[191] As noted at the start of this chapter, compliance is dependent not only upon the *capacity* of parliamentarians to participate in this elaborate legal and political process, but also their *will* to do so. Political will is far from being a monolithic concept, given the plurality of actors involved in the domestic implementation process. Within parliaments, there may be many 'political wills', given the potential for political fault lines both within and between parties, committees, and other formations.

Hillebrecht identifies three distinct causal mechanisms for domestic compliance with international human rights norms, which she associates principally with executive actors as the 'gatekeepers' of the implementation process.[192] First, governments comply with human rights judgments in order to signal their commitment to human rights norms in response to pro-compliance pressure from both domestic and international constituencies.[193] Secondly, judgments are invoked by executives in order to provide impetus and political legitimacy to domestic reform.[194] Thirdly, governments, especially in established democracies, comply grudgingly, resenting the ruling but 'arguing that their hands are tied by … longstanding commitment to international law, human rights and democracy'.[195]

While they are mainly addressed to executive actors, these causal mechanisms also imply subtly different incentives for parliamentary and, indeed, other non-executive actors to become involved in the compliance process. First, parliamentarians may signal their own commitment to human rights norms by applying pressure on the executive to comply. Secondly, they may seize selectively on human rights judgments to instigate or advance their preferred domestic reform agenda and to lend it legitimacy. Thirdly, as Hillebrecht notes, parliamentary bodies may provide a useful 'scapegoat' for governments torn between meeting their international legal obligations and the political fallout of contentious judgments, at the same time as '[raising] the stakes of non-compliance'.[196] The paradox we identify at 7.2.2 between the UK's strong record of implementing ECtHR judgments and rising political opprobrium directed at the Court suggests that grudging compliance is, as Hillebrecht identifies, an important mechanism. While the ECtHR or domestic courts provide *judicial* scapegoats for unpopular measures, pro-compliance actors

[191] Joint Committee on Human Rights, Fifteenth Report of Session 2009–10, *Enhancing Parliament's Role in Relation to Human Rights Judgments*, HL Paper 85, HC 455 (2010) para. 15.

[192] Hillebrecht (n 7) 29. [193] Hillebrecht (n 7) 25–9.

[194] Hillebrecht (n 7) 29–31.

[195] Hillebrecht (n 7) 31–3. See also Başak Çalı and Alice Wyss, *Why Do Democracies Comply with Human Rights Judgments? A Comparative Analysis of the UK, Ireland and Germany*, SSRN eLibrary, 26 August 2009.

[196] Hillebrecht (n 7) 102.

in parliament provide convenient *political* cover in the face of public disquiet about a judgment. The behaviour of successive UK governments in response to ECtHR judgments concerning the treatment of suspected terrorists provides paradigmatic instances of grudging compliance; for example, the saga of the deportation of the terrorist suspect known as Abu Qatada to Jordan, in which the UK government railed against the Court's decision but nonetheless went to considerable lengths to obtain the necessary assurances from Jordan that Abu Qatada would not face trial on the basis of evidence obtained by torture.[197]

As the case of *Hirst*[198] on prisoner voting rights illustrates, however, grudging compliance is not a reliable mechanism, and the majority opinion in parliament may become a scapegoat for *non*-compliance when a government is called to account for its inaction either by Council of Europe bodies,[199] or by a parliamentary human rights body.[200] Parliamentarians may be divided politically about judgments, or have other disincentives to comply, or be unaware of or indifferent to them, as discussed in the next section.

3.6.1 Factors affecting the salience of judgments

At the risk of over-generalization, our research suggests that ECtHR judgments per se tend to be of low salience for parliamentarians. Repeated reference was made by parliamentarians and their advisers in all five states under review to the numerous competing demands on MPs' time and attention, and to the generally low levels of awareness and expertise among parliamentarians about human rights. Interest in ECtHR judgments in the domestic context was generally viewed as a niche interest, cultivated by individual MPs or members of upper chambers, especially those who were also members of the Parliamentary Assembly. Members of upper chambers who are either unelected or indirectly elected were commonly viewed as having more potential to develop human rights expertise, in view of their greater capacity for detailed legislative scrutiny and dispassionate reflection on contentious matters. For most parliamentarians, however, engagement with Strasbourg judgments tends to be reactive and incidental.

However, at certain moments, judgments of the Court can become highly salient. This might be positive if high salience converts into political impetus towards

[197] 'Theresa May Criticises Human Rights Convention after Abu Qatada Affair', *The Guardian*, 8 July 2013, referring to *Othman (Abu Qatada) v UK*, No. 8139/09, 17 January 2012.

[198] *Hirst v UK (No. 2)*, No. 74025/01, 6 October 2005 [GC].

[199] See, for example, Communication from the authorities (06/08/2015) concerning the Hirst No. 2 and Greens & MT cases against the United Kingdom (Applications No. 74025/01 and 60041/08), DH-DD(2015)782. In a letter to the Department for the Execution of Judgments, the Deputy Permanent Representative of the UK delegation to the Council of Europe stated: '[I]t is clear following the result of the General Election in the UK that there remains widespread hostility in Parliament to giving prisoners the vote; you will be aware that UK Government Ministers continue to believe that this issue is ultimately a matter for elected representatives in national parliaments to decide.'

[200] See, for example, evidence by the (then) Justice Secretary, Chris Grayling, to the JCHR: 'The vote in the House of Commons on prisoner voting ... is an indication that Parliament itself is not happy about this.' (JCHR Uncorrected Transcript of Oral Evidence on the Government's Human Rights Policy, 18 December 2013, 29.)

implementation. Alternatively, high salience might be negative, if it means that the judgment becomes the object of political bargaining or contestation in ways that frustrate its implementation. Identifying the factors that cause particular judgments to be of high or low salience—with either positive or negative consequences—is an empirical task that can be achieved qualitatively by observing the dynamics at play in specific instances or quantitatively by, for example, identifying the case characteristics that are associated with slower or faster implementation.[201] This section has the more modest aim of hypothesizing various factors that affect the salience of judgments, and providing illustrative examples. We identify, first, inherent factors linked to the characteristics of the judgment itself and, secondly, contextual factors.

3.6.1.1 Inherent factors

Where an area of law or policy is of high salience—such as, in many states, national security, crime, or immigration—judgments that implicate that area of law or policy might be presumed to be more likely than usual also to be of high salience. In many such instances, the nature of the applicant or wider beneficiary group may make a case salient in a negative sense. During parliamentary debate on the prisoner voting issue in the UK in February 2011, for example, the perception of prisoners as unpopular and undeserving loomed large, with many MPs arguing that their principal reason for defying the judgment was that their constituents were appalled at the idea of enfranchising prisoners and that it was their duty to represent public sentiment (see 7.6.1).[202] High salience linked to the beneficiary group does not necessarily denote resistance, however, as illustrated by the generally more favourable political response in Germany to the cases of *M*[203] (concerning preventive detention of individuals considered to be dangerous to the public) and *Gäfgen*[204] (concerning ill-treatment of suspects for the purpose of obtaining information) (see 9.3).

The substance of the right(s) and obligation(s) involved in a judgment may also affect political responses to it. Grewal and Voeten venture that violations of Article 2 ECHR (the right to life) and Article 3 ECHR (prohibition of torture and inhuman or degrading treatment) 'almost by definition strike at the heart of executive control over a society, and thereby are likely to elicit executive resistance'.[205] However,

[201] See, especially, Sharanbir Grewal and Erik Voeten, 'Are New Democracies Better Human Rights Compliers?', *International Organization* 69(2) (2015): 497; Erik Voeten, 'Domestic Implementation of European Court of Human Rights Judgments: Legal Infrastructure and Government Effectiveness Matter: A Reply to Dia Anagnostou and Alina Mungiu-Pippidi', *European Journal of International Law* 25(1) (2014): 229. It should be noted, however, that the speed of implementation may be linked to the complexity, as well as the contentiousness, of a judgment.

[202] Aruna Sathanapally, *Beyond Disagreement: Open Remedies in Human Rights Adjudication* (Oxford: Oxford University Press, 2012) 218.

[203] No. 19359/04, 17 December 2009.

[204] No. 22978/05, 1 June 2010.

[205] Grewal and Voeten (n 201). Analysing a dataset of lead cases for all Articles and all states issued by 31 December 2006, Voeten ((n 201) 234) notes that judgments that involved Articles 2 or 3 ECHR were slower to be implemented than judgments concerning other violations.

such generalizations are perilous as a guide to the salience of particular judgments in particular contexts. Political responses to particular judgments may also be conditioned by the competing political and philosophical conceptions of rights espoused by parliamentarians, including members of human rights committees. In respect of the UK, Angela Patrick, a former assistant adviser to the JCHR, states that '[t]he most problematic cases tend to be those where there is an element of positivity—where the state has to start doing something [rather than refrain from doing something] and there are different perspectives about what the right requires'.[206]

The potential for dissensus may be accentuated where judgments concerning the appropriate balance to be struck in cases in which sensitive social or moral questions engage qualified rights. Patrick recalls that the judgment in *A v UK*, concerning children's right to effective legal protection from parental corporal punishment, was highly contentious both within the JCHR and in Parliament at large because of its perceived intrusion into the private sphere, and took six years to implement.[207] A decision by the European Committee of Social Rights (which monitors states' conformity with the European Social Charter) that French law and case law on corporal punishment in the family, schools, and other settings are not 'sufficiently clear, binding and precise' has proved similarly controversial.[208] Judgments concerning restrictions on the wearing or displaying of religious symbols or dress (e.g., *Lautsi v Italy*,[209] *Eweida and Others v UK*,[210] and *SAS v France*[211]) have also proved highly salient, both in the respondent states and beyond. Judgments relating to the electoral system may also be hypothesized as being likely to be of high political salience (see 7.6.1 in relation to prisoner voting rights).

Judgments involving multiple violations of an Article of the Convention, or of more than one Article, might also be presumed to be more likely to be of high salience, as might the requirement for general measures (executive, legislative, and/or judicial) as opposed to only individual measures—unless the individual happens to be high profile. Judgments requiring measures that have significant financial implications for the state may also be of greater salience than those which do not; for example, cases concerning restitution of or compensation for nationalized property monopolized the attention of the Romanian parliamentary sub-committee on the execution of ECtHR judgments in its early years (see 6.3.4 and 6.6.3).

[206] Interview, 8 March 2012.

[207] No. 25599/94, 23 September 1998, implemented in England and Wales by means of the Children Act 2004.

[208] *Association for the Protection of All Children (APPROACH) v France* Complaint No. 92/2013, adopted 12 September 2014, para. 37. See 'France to Ignore Call to Introduce Full Ban on Smacking Children', *The Telegraph*, 4 March 2015.

[209] No. 30814/06, 3 November 2009, which was overturned by the Grand Chamber judgment of 18 March 2011.

[210] Nos. 48420/10, 59842/10, 51671/10, and 36516/10, 15 January 2013. As one measure of the contentiousness of this case, the former president of the ECtHR, Sir Nicolas Bratza, notes that the Court was 'flooded by an exceptional number' of third-party requests to intervene in four UK cases brought by Christian claimants. See Nicolas Bratza, 'The "Precious Asset": Freedom of Religion under the European Convention on Human Rights', *Ecclesiastical Law Journal* 14(2) (2012): 270.

[211] No. 43835/11, 1 July 2014.

The extent to which a judgment is directive in the proposed remedy, whether on matters of substance or timing, in particular through the application of the pilot judgment procedure, might also be expected to propel it up or down the political agenda. As discussed at 2.3.1, greater directiveness on the part of the ECtHR might engender either positive or negative political responses, depending on whether the prescription is seen as providing certainty and urgency about what a judgment requires or as an unwarranted intrusion in domestic decision-making.[212] In practice, the impact of pilot judgments is uneven. The pilot judgment against Germany in the case of *Rumpf*[213] (concerning overly lengthy domestic legal proceedings) had a galvanizing effect after several years of foot-dragging in the *Bundestag* since the earlier judgment in *Sürmeli*[214] (see 9.3). The pilot judgment in *Maria Atanasiu*[215] likewise impelled more concerted action from the Romanian authorities to resolve the problem of restitution of nationalized properties or compensation in lieu (see 6.6.3). No such effect was achieved by the pilot judgment in *Greens and MT*[216] concerning prisoner voting rights in the UK: MPs taking part in the backbench debate three months later appeared unmoved by the significance of the Court's decision to use the pilot judgment procedure and none (including the few pro-compliance voices) referred to the six-month deadline stipulated in *Greens* or suggested that the judgment required parliament to accelerate its response.[217] In Ukraine, the pilot judgment in *Ivanov*,[218] concerning non-enforcement of domestic judgments, also failed to impel MPs to act (see 5.2). Leach et al. observe that a common feature of pilot judgments and 'quasi-pilot' judgments is an a priori recognition by the state's constitutional court (or other higher court) that the existing law or practice in question violates the Convention, and that there has been a failure on the part of the executive or the legislature to respond adequately.[219] In this sense, the ECtHR may use the pilot judgment process to exert leverage on recalcitrant executive and/or parliamentary actors by aligning itself to other domestic 'forces in favour'.

Other inherent factors that might be hypothesized to affect the salience of a judgments concern the nature of the ECtHR's reasoning. Relevant factors that might provide a motivation for political engagement include whether or not it comes from the Grand Chamber (indicating that it concerns an important question affecting the interpretation or application of the Convention or a serious issue of general importance); the existence or otherwise of dissenting opinions, and the strength of dissent both in respect of numbers and tone; and the quality of the

212 Philip Leach, 'No Longer Offering Fine Mantras to a Parched Child? The European Court's Developing Approach to Remedies', in Andreas Føllesdal, Birgit Peters, and Geir Ulfstein, eds., *Constituting Europe: The European Court of Human Rights in a National, European and Global Context* (Cambridge: Cambridge University Press, 2013).

213 *Rumpf v Germany*, No. 46344/06, 2 September 2010.

214 *Sürmeli v Germany*, No. 75529/01, 8 June 2006 [GC].

215 *Maria Atanasiu and Others v Romania* (n 172).

216 Nos. 60041/08 and 60054/08, 23 November 2010.

217 HC Deb, 10 February 2011, vol. 523, cols. 493–584.

218 *Yuriy Nikolayevich Ivanov v Ukraine*, No. 40450/04, 15 October 2009.

219 Leach, Hardman, Stephenson, and Blitz (n 164) 177–8.

judgment in terms of the clarity, consistency, and/or expansiveness of its reasoning. Another factor of increasing interest is the extent to which the Court makes explicit reference to the quality—or paucity—of parliamentary engagement as a factor contributing to its determination of the margin of appreciation (see 4.5 for a detailed examination of this aspect of the ECtHR's case law).

However, our interviews with parliamentarians and parliamentary staff suggest that these many of the factors are likely to condition political responses at most indirectly, given MPs' strong reliance on legal advisers or external sources to summarize and analyse judgments, whether against their own or another state. It cannot be safely assumed that parliamentarians will engage with the provenance of a judgment or its detailed content—or accurately grasp its legal and policy implications. This observation underlines the importance of providing parliamentary committees with independent and expert legal advisers, whose screening function in drawing judgments selectively to MPs' attention is likely to be highly influential in determining the committee's priorities and informing its debate and conclusions (see 3.4.3.1).

3.6.1.2 Contextual factors

It is not only the characteristics of a particular judgment, and the rights, obligations, and beneficiaries involved, that are pertinent to our discussion, but also the wider context in which it is issued. Simmons refers to the 'agenda setting'[220] effect of the judgments of international human rights courts, which in certain contexts increase the salience of hitherto latent or marginalized reform agendas. In a study of the impact of judgments concerning lesbian, gay, bisexual, and transgender rights, Helfer and Voeten argue that, in both respondent and non-respondent states, legislators may refrain from acting until a judgment of an international court 'catapults the issue to the top of the legislative agenda'.[221] This effect is greatest, they observe, in contexts where politicians are (at least) not averse to reform but public support is low, in which case 'the increased issue salience and declaration of illegality that results from an [international court] ruling may tip the balance in favour of reforms'.[222]

Incidental factors may also come into play. In particular, timing can be crucial. A judgment issued in advance of an election may, depending on the result, benefit from a greater willingness by incoming ministers to remedy violations that occurred under their predecessors. This appears to have been the case in the (partial) implementation shortly after elections in 2014 of *Volkov v Ukraine*,[223] which required, among other measures, both judicial and parliamentary action to reinstate a sacked Supreme Court judge (see 5.2.1).

An ever-present contextual factor affecting political receptiveness towards judgments is the prevailing attitude within a state towards the idea of

[220] Simmons (n 7) 127. [221] Helfer and Voeten (n 15) 82–3.
[222] Helfer and Voeten (n 15) 83. [223] See 3.2 at n 32.

international protection of individual rights in general and the ECtHR in particular. Receptiveness—or not—to pressure from other Council of Europe bodies (such as decisions and resolutions of the Committee of Ministers and Parliamentary Assembly) may also affect the fate of a judgment in the implementation phase. The contrasting political responses noted above to *Hirst* and *Greens* in the UK and *M* in Germany are illustrative: while MPs in the UK have, in the face of successive ECtHR judgments and mounting pressure from other Council of Europe bodies, continued to debate *whether* to implement the judgments, their German counterparts largely confined their discussion to *how* implementation should proceed, against a background presumption of respect for the authority and legitimacy of the Court (see 7.6.1 and 9.3).[224] However, this background condition of respect or lack of respect for the authority and legitimacy of the Court is not determinative of the outcome of any particular judgment. As noted above, the delay in resolving the systemic problem of overly lengthy domestic proceedings in Germany was partly due to the procrastination of parliamentarians who were reluctant to accept a judgment (*Sürmeli*) that impugned the workings of the domestic judiciary.

Inherent and contextual factors may combine in sometimes unforeseeable ways. An illustrative case is *S and Marper v UK*,[225] concerning the policy of retaining indefinitely DNA profiles and samples of everyone arrested for a recordable offence, which the ECtHR held to be a disproportionate interference with the applicants' right to respect for private life under Article 8 ECHR (see 7.6.2). Timing appears to have been a determinative factor in the implementation of *Marper* soon after the 2010 general election by an incoming Conservative-led government for which the judgment was a symbolic opportunity to distance itself from its Labour predecessor. Inherent factors may also have played a role in the Conservatives' eagerness to implement the judgment despite their simultaneous anti-Strasbourg rhetoric in respect of *Hirst*. *Marper* may have benefited from British MPs being, as noted above, more accepting of judicial determinations that restrain the state from interfering in civil liberties than those that involve positive obligations or that interpret the Convention dynamically so as to extend human rights protection in ways that are socially contentious. The nature of the applicants—innocent individuals, one of them a child—may also have forestalled potential Conservative resistance to the judgment, despite the fact that, unlike *Hirst*, it had material implications for public policy to tackle crime.

3.6.2 Scepticism about the reliability of parliaments as compliance partners

In the course of conducting our research, we have encountered scepticism from various quarters in some states about both the feasibility and likely effectiveness of fostering a greater role for parliaments in the implementation of ECtHR

[224] See also Çalı and Wyss (n 195). [225] Above n 33.

judgments, at least under current conditions. This response was based on a perception, especially among some civil society actors, that parliamentarians in their states lack human rights expertise, that their interest in ECtHR judgments is shallow or contingent, or that they are opportunistically prone to manipulate the issues raised in ECtHR judgments. Interviewees from civil society organizations in Ukraine and Romania cited various factors that in recent years had made them regard parliaments as an unproductive venue in which to apply pressure for implementation: corruption; the relative weakness of parliament vis-à-vis the executive; strong party discipline; and a political culture perceived to be affected by 'short-termism' and populism (see 5.1.2 and 6.3.7). The tendency in these states for the executive to bypass parliament by using decrees or ordinances as a means of responding to adverse Court judgments had also led civil society groups to view parliament as a secondary venue for applying pro-compliance pressure, compared to, for example, the powerful presidential administration in Ukraine or the general secretariat of the government in Romania.

As is evident from the examples cited in 3.6.1, it certainly cannot be assumed that parliamentarians will invariably urge the executive towards full or swift compliance with Court judgments; sometimes, the opposite is the case. For example, the protracted delay in legislating to implement the pilot judgment in *Ivanov*, concerning unenforced domestic judgments, is attributable partly to the fact that some members of parliament had a direct financial interest in maintaining the status quo (see 5.2).

A question that arises, then, is whether systematizing parliamentary engagement with human rights judgments increases the likelihood that the implementation process will become unduly politicized in ways that frustrate its effectiveness. This was certainly the view of some (serving or former) government officials in some states, who expressed reluctance to involve parliamentarians in the implementation process any more than was strictly necessary, preferring to view it as a technocratic exercise in international law compliance to be kept as far away as possible from the political fray. Non-governmental observers, too, advocated a depoliticized approach to implementation led by civil servants rather than parliamentarians (see 5.4.1 in respect of Ukraine).

We suggest, however, that this is a mistaken basis on which to proceed. First, it is not supported by evidence. While the recent and still evolving development of parliamentary human rights committees (among other factors) makes it hard to make a comprehensive assessment of their impact (see 3.7), experience to date does not substantiate the view that 'more' parliamentary engagement leads to 'less' implementation—as, for example, the UK experience shows.[226] Secondly, it places an excessive amount of trust in executive structures and processes for implementation and the political will upon which their effectiveness depends. While implementation is necessarily an executive-*led* process, a system that marginalizes parliamentary involvement in the interests of simplification or depoliticization will—even in

[226] See also Anagnostou and Mungiu-Pippidi (n 1).

established democracies—remain vulnerable to changes between administrations, or in the broader political climate surrounding human rights, or to personnel, such as the departure of conscientious officials and their replacement by officers who are dilatory or inexperienced. Thirdly, such an approach appears unduly pessimistic about the potential for parliamentarians to strengthen compliance, even—or perhaps especially—in the many states in which they are starting from a low base in relation to both capacity and political will.

Christos Giakoumopoulos, Director of Human Rights in the Council of Europe's Directorate General Human Rights and Rule of Law, captures the dilemmas inherent in increasing political engagement with the Court's judgments:

> Regular parliamentary discussion [of judgments] is important so that not only conflictual aspects reach parliament's attention but also matters of common interest, where the parliament can show its power and that it is taking the lead ... Parliaments will by their very nature politicise the tricky questions. This risk can only be reduced if you give parliaments the opportunity to be involved also in cases which are not so sensitive. Parliaments should be made aware that not all judgments of the Court touch on conflictual issues. In most cases they just make things easier for citizens, the government, and parliament itself.[227]

Frans Timmermans (a former Dutch Labour Party MP and Minister for Foreign Affairs, who became Vice-President of the European Commission in November 2014), expresses a similar sentiment. Speaking in 2012, at a time of highly politicized national debate about the Court in the Netherlands, he comments:

> In the past two years [in the Netherlands], increased parliamentary involvement has not necessarily been very positive because many things have been put into question which before would have been accepted. However, I'm deeply convinced that we should keep parliaments much more involved. In the long run, if you keep parliamentarians active in Strasbourg, keep them informed about human rights issues, I think [they] want to do the right thing. It's not that they're mischievous, but they're badly informed.[228]

From one perspective, the *Hirst* saga in the UK appears to confirm the worst fears of those who believe that exposing contentious issues to parliamentary debate can magnify or entrench political and philosophical differences about human rights, thereby limiting the scope for executive action and delaying implementation. Yet an alternative and, we suggest, preferable reading of these events is the desirability of requiring parliament *at the earliest possible stage* to engage with specific legislative proposals and reasoned, justificatory arguments about the meaning and scope of rights and the necessity and proportionality of restrictions upon them. As Friederycke Haijer, President of the Dutch Section of the International Commission of Jurists, ventures in relation to the Dutch lower house: 'One problem is the lack of ownership [of human rights] by parliamentarians ... There's a sense in parliament that [the Convention] is not their treaty. They can shoot at it without shooting themselves. If they had been more involved, they wouldn't be so critical.'[229]

[227] Interview, 27 June 2013.
[228] Interview, 13 June 2012.
[229] Interview, 22 March 2012.

Indeed, debate among both scholars and practitioners now centres on the institutional machinery required to enable parliaments to 'engage with human rights in their day-to-day business',[230] in order to meet the dual imperatives identified in Chapter 1 of both effective implementation and legitimation of human rights norms.

3.7 Assessing the Effectiveness of Parliamentary Bodies

We noted at 3.4.3 that parliamentary human rights bodies have been encouraged to develop methodologies for assessing their effectiveness. In the context of the implementation of Convention standards and ECtHR judgments, how might such effectiveness be identified and assessed? Evaluation of the effectiveness of parliaments has generated an expanding literature in respect of the policy impact of parliaments in general,[231] or their legislative[232] or scrutiny[233] functions. Attention has also been paid to the impact of parliaments' human rights-related functions specifically.[234] The impact of the UK Joint Committee on Human Rights, with its combined functions of legislative scrutiny and executive oversight, has been analysed in particular detail. Studies have examined both quantitatively and qualitatively the JCHR's impact on legislative deliberation,[235] executive decision-making,[236] the use of its materials in judicial review,[237] or a combination of these.[238] The JCHR's working methods have also, at its own instigation, been assessed in terms of how best to strike a balance 'between its legislative scrutiny work, other scrutiny work such as that related to international treaties, and more thematic, policy-orientated work'.[239]

[230] Murray Hunt, 'Introduction', in Hunt, Hooper, and Yowell, eds. (n 46): 1, 12.

[231] For a useful survey of literature, see Meg Russell and Meghan Benton, 'Assessing the Policy Impact of Parliament: Methodological Challenges and Possible Future Approaches', Paper for PSA Legislative Studies Specialist Group Conference, 24 June 2009.

[232] David Arter, 'Comparing the Legislative Performances of Legislatures', *The Journal of Legislative Studies* 12(3–4) (2006): 245.

[233] Meg Russell and Meghan Benton, *Selective Influence: The Policy Impact of House of Commons Select Committees* (The Constitution Unit, University College London, 2011).

[234] Simon Evans and Carolyn Evans, 'Evaluating the Human Rights Performance of Legislatures', *Human Rights Law Review* 6(3) (2006): 545; Philippa Webb and Kirsten Roberts, 'Effective Parliamentary Oversight of Human Rights: A Framework for Designing and Determining Effectiveness' (King's College London, 2014).

[235] Paul Yowell, 'The Impact of the Joint Committee on Human Rights on Legislative Deliberation', in Hunt, Hooper, and Yowell, eds. (n 46): 141.

[236] Janet Hiebert, 'Governing under the Human Rights Act. The Limitations of Wishful Thinking', *Public Law* 1 (2012): 27.

[237] Hayley J. Hooper, 'The Use of Parliamentary Materials in Proportionality Judgments', in Hunt, Hooper, and Yowell, eds. (n 46): 363.

[238] Francesca Klug and Helen Wildbore, 'Breaking New Ground: The Joint Committee on Human Rights and the Role of Parliament in Human Rights Compliance', *European Human Rights Review* 3 (2007): 231; Michael C. Tolley, 'Parliamentary Scrutiny of Rights in the United Kingdom: Assessing the Work of the Joint Committee on Human Rights', *Australian Journal of Political Science* 44(1) (2009): 41.

[239] JCHR, Twenty-Third Report of Session 2005–06, *The Committee's Future Working Practices*, HL Paper 239, HC 1575 (2006), para. 7.

A central insight to emerge from this literature is the methodological difficulties that bedevil any attempt systematically to assess the impact of parliamentary activity. As Russell and Benton observe of the UK Parliament, much parliamentary influence is 'subtle, largely invisible, and frequently even immeasurable'.[240] The impact of parliamentary work has been likened to an iceberg, with a visible tip and a large, hidden base.[241] At the tip are quantifiable impacts such as legislative amendments secured or recommendations acted upon by the executive. Also in the public domain are documents that might permit contextualized assessment of impact, such as committee reports, evidence obtained by committees in hearings and consultations, correspondence with ministers, and government responses to all of these.

In respect of ECtHR judgments, visible impacts might include direct influence upon the executive response to specific judgments; for example, by securing revisions to action plans or legislative amendments. Another indicator relevant to judgments is the time taken to implement them; pro-compliance pressure in parliament might be expected to hasten implementation and this might therefore be an indicator of effectiveness. However, while the average duration of the execution process might provide an overall indicator of the effectiveness of domestic systems of implementation, it is an imperfect indicator of success in every case, since the response to a judgment may be unavoidably protracted if it is to be workable and command consensus and thus delay may not necessarily denote procrastination or resistance on the part either of parliament or the executive.[242] At a more general level, a parliamentary human rights committee might achieve impact by securing changes to the executive *system* of implementation, including mechanisms and deadlines for reporting to and sharing information with parliament. In respect of all of these visible impacts, in order for effectiveness to be assessed, causality needs to be established, especially where influence might be simultaneously exerted by actors external to parliament, such as 'watchdog' bodies or public campaigns.[243]

At the base of the iceberg, impact may be invisible (or at least less easily measurable) for several reasons. For example, it may result from informal, often undocumented activity, such as contact between parliamentarians and/or their legal advisers and civil servants, which may take place in the corridors rather than committee rooms or chambers of parliament.[244] Jean Corston, a former chair of the JCHR (2001–05), recalls:

> I found Secretaries of State coming up to me outside the Committee and asking about, for example, relevant judgments or the human rights implications of planned legislation. So what developed were formal processes in Committee, open to the public through our

[240] Russell and Benton (n 231) 1. [241] Webb and Roberts (n 234) 4.

[242] For example, the judgment in *Christine Goodwin v UK*, No. 28957/95, 11 July 2002 [GC], on the legal recognition of transsexuals took two years to implement (by means of the Gender Recognition Act 2004) due to the administrative complexity involved and the 'careful and reflective legislative process'; see Sathanapally (n 202) 168.

[243] Russell and Benton (n 231) 5; Klug and Wildbore (n 238) 241.

[244] Evans and Evans (n 153) 338.

reports, but also a quite sophisticated informal network whereby [the then JCHR legal adviser] David Feldman … became a de facto legal adviser to government departments.

Russell and Benton identify several non-quantifiable forms of influence in respect of select committees in the House of Commons: 'contributing to debate, drawing together evidence, spotlighting issues, brokering between actors in government, improving the quality of government decision-making through accountability, exposing failures, and perhaps most importantly "generating fear"'.[245] The latter might be termed the anticipatory influence of parliamentary oversight, which Russell and Benton suggest is 'the most important of all, but also the least measurable', since it may become so ingrained that it is 'largely subconscious'. Jean Corston observed of the JCHR that 'it is the threat of parliamentary scrutiny, and an adverse opinion from [the Committee], that is the key factor' in affecting legislative outcomes,[246] a preventive influence corroborated in other accounts of the JCHR's work.[247] Hiebert adds that the JCHR's scrutiny also draws attention to issues that may have been overlooked in the pre-introduction evaluation of bills, and increases pressure on government departments to provide substantive explanations to support a claim that a bill is compatible with Convention rights.[248]

Ultimately, assessment of the effectiveness of a parliamentary body depends upon what it seeks to achieve within its available powers and resources. Thus, a prerequisite of self-evaluation by a parliamentary human rights committee is to determine both its overarching goals and specific objectives. Those goals and objectives should, moreover, be transparent, as should the work of the committee by means of periodic reporting to parliament, public hearings, maintenance of up-to-date websites, and other methods. We suggest that the goals of such a committee should include strengthening the state's compliance with human rights norms and judgments in accordance with the principle of subsidiarity. A human rights committee can further this goal by making concrete the abstract norms and standards to which a state has subscribed and by identifying the measures required by human rights judgments as a basis for its oversight of executive action or inaction. Another strategic goal of a human rights committee, we suggest, should be the legitimation of human rights norms and standards, an outcome that can be achieved in part by requiring parliamentarians to engage with reasoned arguments about the scope and meaning of human rights in the domestic context. This obligation of open, public reasoning within a 'culture of justification'[249] extends to all branches of the state, including parliaments, as we explore further in Chapter 4.

[245] Russell and Benton (n 233) 8.

[246] Memorandum by Rt Hon Jean Corston, MP, Chair, Joint Committee on Human Rights, to the Lords Constitution Committee, Session 2003–04, 13 October 2004.

[247] Hiebert (n 236) 39. [248] Hiebert (n 236) 39.

[249] Murray Hunt, 'Reshaping Constitutionalism', in John Morison, Kieran McEvoy, and Gordon Anthony, eds., *Judges, Transition and Human Rights* (Oxford: Oxford University Press, 2007): 467, 469.

3.8 Conclusion

The Convention system, guided by the principle of subsidiarity, relies upon national institutions to ensure the implementation of human rights norms and judgments, institutions which in many states are embryonic or ineffective, lacking in both capacity and political will. This chapter has charted the growing recognition of the functions and obligations of parliaments in respect of human rights implementation, at both a theoretical and empirical level. We have identified gathering impetus towards the establishment of parliamentary structures and processes geared towards the implementation of Convention standards and ECtHR judgments, albeit from a very low starting point in many states. Parliaments have adopted a variety of institutional models for the conduct of human rights oversight: some are wholly decentralized (the cross-cutting model), while others have allocated the role to a single committee (the specialized model) or to more than one committee (the hybrid model). Some domestic systems of implementation have a basis in national legislation, although the mere presence of such legislation is no guarantee of effectiveness in the absence of political commitment. Whatever their precise form, the aim of such initiatives is to ensure that parliamentarians develop systematic interest in human rights, rather than confining their engagement to purely reactive or opportunistic interventions.

The chapter has emphasized the overriding importance of having independent, expert legal advice available to parliamentary human rights committees, as well as systematic and timely reporting by the executive to parliament on its proposed response to adverse judgments. These are among the imperatives proposed in the Draft Principles and Guidelines on the Role of Parliaments in the Protection and Realisation of the Rule of Law and Human Rights (examined at 3.4.3), initiated by the legal adviser to the UK Joint Committee on Human Rights, the adoption of which would, we propose, fill a significant gap by establishing international standards in this area.

Implementation of human rights norms is an unavoidably political and sometimes messy and protracted process. Parliamentarians may be divided about human rights judgments, or have political or material disincentives to comply, or be simply unaware of or apathetic towards them. It is unsurprising, then, that in some states the idea of increased parliamentary monitoring of human rights norms is met with scepticism. However, we have argued that to marginalize parliamentary involvement in the interests of 'depoliticization' places undue faith in executive bodies and, moreover, is unduly pessimistic about the longer-term advantages of developing structures and processes that require parliamentarians to engage with reasoned, justificatory arguments about the meaning and scope of rights and their application in the domestic context. Structures which embed parliamentary consideration of ECtHR judgments and promotion of Convention standards, rather than relying on reactive or intermittent responses, may in the longer term help both to strengthen implementation and pre-empt opportunistic attacks on the Strasbourg system. Moreover, parliamentary engagement is increasingly viewed as *conferring* legitimacy on human rights norms and discourse. Thus, as Hunt observes, legitimacy may be viewed as both a precondition and a result of effectiveness,[250] a normative dimension to human rights implementation that is explored in the next chapter.

[250] Hunt (n 230) 14.

4

Human Rights, Democracy, and Legitimacy in the Convention System

This chapter is concerned with the relationship between human rights, democratic governance, and legitimate authority. It draws on arguments about the legitimacy of international human rights regimes[1] and discusses these within the context of the system established by the European Convention on Human Rights (ECHR or 'the Convention') and, in particular, its relationship with national parliaments.[2]

The purported 'democratic deficit' of judicial review to protect human rights has long been contentious with respect to the appropriate allocation of powers at the domestic level. As Hunt observes, '"human rights" are frequently experienced by democratically elected politicians as a disempowering discourse which only constrains and prohibits what democratic governments and parliaments can do'.[3] This perception connects to the long-standing normative divide between legal and political constitutionalism, within which legal constitutionalists champion the judicial model of rights protection lest the rights of individuals or minorities are placed at the mercy of transient and potentially irrational or unjust legislative majorities or executive diktat;[4] while political constitutionalists doubt the legitimacy of judicial review because it removes from the sphere of democratic contestation matters, such as the meaning and scope of rights, which are inescapably disputable and, it is argued, hands them over to unaccountable judges.[5] As noted in the introduction to

[1] See, generally, Andreas Føllesdal, Johan Karlsson Schaffer, and Geir Ulfstein, eds., *The Legitimacy of International Human Rights Regimes: Legal, Political and Philosophical Perspectives* (Cambridge: Cambridge University Press, 2013).

[2] See, generally, Murray Hunt, Hayley Hooper, and Paul Yowell, eds., *Parliaments and Human Rights: Redressing the Democratic Deficit* (Oxford: Hart Publishing, 2015).

[3] Murray Hunt, 'Introduction', in Hunt, Hooper, and Yowell, eds. (n 2): 1, 11.

[4] See, for example, T.R.S. Allan, *Law, Liberty and Justice: The Legal Foundations of British Constitutionalism* (Oxford: Clarendon Press, 1994); Vernon Bogdanor, *The New British Constitution* (Oxford: Hart Publishing, 2009) Chapter 3; Ronald Dworkin, *Taking Rights Seriously* (London: Duckworth, 1996); Tom Hickman, 'In Defence of the Legal Constitution', *University of Toronto Law Journal* 55(4) (2005): 981; Jeffrey Jowell, 'Beyond the Rule of Law: Towards Constitutional Judicial Review', *Public Law* Winter (2000): 671.

[5] See, for example, Richard Bellamy, *Political Constitutionalism: A Republican Defence of the Constitutionalism of Democracy* (Cambridge: Cambridge University Press, 2007); Tom Campbell, Keith D. Ewing, and Adam Tomkins, *The Legal Protection of Human Rights: Sceptical Essays* (Oxford: Oxford University Press, 2010); Mark Tushnet, *Taking the Constitution Away from the Courts* (Princeton: Princeton University Press, 1999); Jeremy Waldron, 'The Core of the Case against Judicial

Chapter 1, this dichotomous understanding has increasingly given way to arguments for an 'overarching coherent vision of democratic constitutionalism',[6] in which all branches of the state—the executive, parliament, and the courts—are partners in the shared endeavour of protecting and fulfilling human rights, rather than 'adversaries in a perpetual quest for supremacy'.[7] From this perspective, the perceived democratic deficit afflicting human rights stems less from a surfeit of judicial interference than from the inadequacy—or at least uneven development—of political structures and processes to 'domesticate' human rights, both in respect of executive decision-making and the legislative and oversight functions of parliament.[8]

Yet the evolving consensus around a dialogic model of constitutionalism is not unanimous,[9] and, so far as it exists, is built on unstable foundations. In respect of the UK, Hunt observes that constitutional discourse is prone to lurch between democratic positivism and liberal constitutionalism, each being invoked—sometimes by the same judge or commentator—to justify a particular decision at a particular moment.[10] Moreover, in recent years, debate about the democratic legitimacy of judicial review has extended to address the role of human rights institutions beyond the state. From one perspective, if domestic judicial review to protect human rights is viewed as lacking legitimacy, '[b]y extension, *international* courts and tribunals ... are even less subject to democratic accountability, hence even more suspect' (emphasis in original).[11] These concerns may be heightened by other factors, such as international courts' or treaty bodies' dynamic interpretation of human rights treaties, and perceptions that officials or judges in such institutions are 'less familiar with national culture, constitutional traditions and the legitimate expectations of citizenry' than their domestic counterparts.[12]

This chapter proceeds as follows. First, 4.1 asks whether, in fact, international human rights regimes (and the European Court of Human Rights (ECtHR or 'the Court') in particular) have a problem in respect of their legitimacy, and if so, what the nature of this problem might be. Different conceptions of legitimacy are examined in 4.2, noting, in particular, the distinction—and inter-relationship—between its normative, legal, and social dimensions, and the institutional and

Review', *Yale Law Journal* 115 (2009): 1346; Grégoire Webber, *The Negotiable Constitution: On the Limitation of Rights* (Cambridge: Cambridge University Press, 2009).

[6] Murray Hunt, 'Reshaping Constitutionalism', in John Morison, Kieran McEvoy, and Gordon Anthony, eds., *Judges, Transition and Human Rights* (Oxford: Oxford University Press, 2007): 467, 469.

[7] Liora Lazarus and Natasha Simonsen, 'Judicial Review and Parliamentary Debate: Enriching the Doctrine of Due Deference', in Hunt, Hooper, and Yowell, eds. (n 2): 385, 386.

[8] See, for example, Hunt (n 3) 10–15. See also David Kinley, 'Finding and Filling the Democratic Deficit in Human Rights', in Hunt, Hooper, and Yowell, eds. (n 2): 29.

[9] See, for example, Keith Ewing, 'Doughty Defenders of the Human Rights Act', in Nicolas Kang-Riou, Jo Milner, and Suryia Nayak, eds., *Confronting the Human Rights Act: Contemporary Themes and Perspectives* (Abingdon: Routledge, 2012): 119.

[10] Hunt (n 6) 469.

[11] Andreas Føllesdal, 'The Legitimacy Deficits of the Human Rights Judiciary: Elements and Implications of a Normative Theory', *Theoretical Inquiries in Law* 14 (2013): 339, 344.

[12] Andreas Føllesdal, 'Much Ado about Nothing? International Judicial Review of Human Rights in Well-Functioning Democracies', in Føllesdal, Schaffer, and Ulfstein, eds. (n 1): 272, 277.

procedural factors which may enhance or undermine them. In 4.3 the focus is on the notion of *democratic* legitimacy, in respect of both institutional and procedural factors and the allocation of power between the international human rights judiciary and domestic democratic decision-making. In the Council of Europe context, we are concerned with the democratic legitimacy of the Convention system as a whole; accordingly, 4.3 examines not only the legitimacy of the ECtHR but also the (potentially) legitimacy-enhancing role of the Parliamentary Assembly of the Council of Europe (PACE).

The relationship between the ECtHR and national parliaments is discussed in 4.4–4.6. In 4.4, it is argued that parliaments have strong reasons to defer to the interpretive authority of the Court and respect the finality of its adjudicatory authority since, among other reasons, engagement with the Strasbourg system enhances, rather than undermines, the democratic credentials of institutions at the domestic level. Moreover, it does so in ways that cannot be achieved by even well-functioning democratic institutions acting alone within the boundaries of the nation state. The following section, 4.5, discusses the ways in which the Court might facilitate or incentivize parliamentary engagement in the implementation of its judgments and of Convention standards, by making assessment of the *quality* of parliamentary processes a systematic feature of its adjudications. Discussion proceeds to the risks and opportunities inherent in such an approach, and the likelihood of parliamentarians 'hearing' the signals sent by the Court. Next, 4.6 explores what happens when apparently insoluble differences arise between the interpretations of the Court and national parliaments; specifically, arguments for 'democratic override' of judgments to which a majority of parliamentarians are opposed are considered—and rejected. Finally, 4.7 concludes.

4.1 Is There a Problem of Legitimacy?

As discussed at 1.1.2, human rights regimes have been subject to 'multifarious criticism, scepticism and resistance', prompting fears of an existential crisis.[13] The purported illegitimacy of the ECtHR has become part of mainstream public discourse in the UK, a trend exemplified by the assertion made by the former UK Justice Secretary, Chris Grayling, that the binding nature of Court judgments under Article 46(1) ECHR—which requires respondent states to abide by the final judgment of the Court—is 'wrong in principle' and has created a 'crisis of democratic legitimacy'.[14] Antipathy towards the Court has surfaced elsewhere in Europe; however, as discussed at 1.1.2, it has tended to be sporadic, confined to the political margins, and/or expressed in response to specific judgments rather than challenging the underlying legitimacy or authority of the Court.

[13] Johan Karlsson Schaffer, Andreas Føllesdal, and Geir Ulfstein, 'International Human Rights and the Challenge of Legitimacy', in Føllesdal, Schaffer, and Ulfstein, eds. (n 1): 1, 12.

[14] Joint Committee on Human Rights, Uncorrected Transcript of Oral Evidence on the Government's Human Rights Policy, 18 December 2013, 15.

Some authors contest the validity or utility of applying the concept of legitimacy to international law, politics, or morality. Carol Harlow views legitimacy as a '"portmanteau word", empty of hard content, fluid, capable of bearing variant meanings, both contingent and contestable'.[15] For Martti Koskenniemi, legitimacy is an ideological concept characterized by its 'elusiveness'.[16] Legitimacy is not, he argues, 'a standard external to power, against which power might be assessed, but a vocabulary produced and reproduced by power itself through its institutionalised mechanisms of self-validation'.[17]

Koskenniemi's scepticism about the (potentially) self-serving purposes of 'legitimacy talk' reminds us that the mere fact of resistance to international human rights regimes from some quarters does not necessarily denote an underlying crisis of legitimacy. Nor, we suggest, should stridently critical voices among the political elite or mass media in the UK—or indeed any other state—be assumed to be a proxy for public opinion. In the European context, both political and scholarly debate about the legitimacy of the Court is generally conducted at a high level of abstraction, at several removes from the experience of individual applicants, litigators, or civil society actors. The volume of individual applications to the Court—around 60–70,000 annually—provides one, albeit crude, measure of the public trust placed in it.[18] There are no comparative surveys of public attitudes towards the Strasbourg Court across the Council of Europe.[19] Opinion polls in the UK appear to show a fall in public support for the Court in the past twenty years, although the data are inconsistent.[20] There have also been peaks of public opposition to specific judgments.[21] Survey data need to be understood in the context of the large volume of critical, and not always well-substantiated, press commentary about the ECtHR and the confusion that exists between the Strasbourg Court and the Court of Justice of the European Union and their respective parent bodies (see 1.1.2). Nevertheless, negative polling figures in the UK demonstrate

[15] Carol Harlow, *The Concepts and Methods of Reasoning of the New Public Law: Legitimacy*, LSE Law, Society and Economy Working Papers 19/2010, 11.

[16] Martti Koskenniemi, 'Legitimacy, Rights, and Ideology: Notes towards a Critique of the New Moral Internationalism', *Associations* 7 (2003): 349, 373.

[17] Koskenniemi (n 16) 373.

[18] See 1.1.1 at n 21.

[19] Erik Voeten, 'Public Opinion and the Legitimacy of International Courts', *Theoretical Inquiries in Law* 14 (2013): 411, 423. See, however, Åse B. Grødeland, 'Public and Elite Perceptions of Supranational Courts: The European Perspective', *Review of Central and East European Law* 39 (2014): 41, which investigates the perceptions of 'legal insiders' (those working professionally with law) and 'legal outsiders' (those affected by law) of European supranational courts in general, and the ECtHR in particular. Drawing on qualitative and quantitative data collected in Bulgaria, Norway, Poland, Ukraine, and the UK, Grødeland argues (at 91) that the ECtHR enjoys 'considerable support among ordinary citizens across Europe', while support among legal insiders is also considerable—although weaker.

[20] Voeten (n 19 at 418) cites a Polling the Nations survey showing that in 1996, 70 per cent of the British public were in favour of the ECtHR. A YouGov poll in July 2014 suggested that 41 per cent of the British population favoured leaving the Convention; see William Jordan, 'Scepticism About Human Rights As Well As the ECHR', YouGov, 20 July 2014. Grødeland (n 19) found (at 65) that 74 per cent of 'legal outsiders' who participated in quantitative surveys in England between 2008 and 2012 considered that the existence of the ECtHR to which people can appeal if they feel that their own authorities have treated them badly is 'a good thing'.

[21] Voeten (n 19) 419.

the vulnerability of the Court's 'stock of legitimacy' to the repercussions of unpopular judgments and decisions.[22]

Empirical evidence of 'elite'[23] opinion is also scant, save for a study undertaken in 2008–11, which found that the ECtHR enjoys 'a high level of legitimacy-credit' among politicians, judges, and lawyers in five Council of Europe states (Bulgaria, Germany, Ireland, Turkey, and the UK), with 'strong constitutive support for a human rights court above and beyond the state in actively intervening in states' domestic decisions in rights protections'.[24] Moreover, elected politicians across the five states supported the idea of the Court as an 'external corrective' more strongly than lawyers and judges did.[25] Interviews conducted for this book, while they did not examine as closely the matter of the Court's (perceived) legitimacy among specific audiences, do not contradict these findings. No interviewee expressed the view that the Court lacks constitutive legitimacy, or considered that view to be widely held in their respective states either by particular constituencies or the public at large.

As noted at 9.1, interviewees in Germany, including current and former parliamentarians, unanimously endorsed the Court's legitimacy—and believed that view to be widely shared, even in the face of judgments on potentially sensitive issues such as the preventive detention of violent criminals. In Ukraine and Romania, too, interviewees viewed the Court as enjoying high levels of perceived legitimacy among the public. Criticisms of the Court related to its performance (especially length of proceedings) or a view that it was not interventionist enough (e.g., in respect of property-related cases in Romania; see 6.6.3). Other criticisms related less to the Court than to the process of supervision of implementation under the Committee of Ministers and the apparent unenforceability of certain judgments (such as *Ivanov*[26] in Ukraine, concerning the structural problem of the failure to comply with domestic court judgments). In Ukraine and Romania, judicial attitudes towards the Court were identified as being equivocal, with some resistance to applying its case law, especially among the older generation of judges (see 5.2.1 and 6.2.2).

Political attitudes, too, are complex. For example, it was noted in Romania that MPs who politicized the implementation of particular judgments for opportunistic ends nevertheless sought to portray the Court's judgments as vindicating their position, even to the point of misrepresenting what judgments had actually said.[27] While such practices are problematic from the perspective of effective implementation,

[22] Voeten (n 19) 415.

[23] Defined as 'domestic actors whose views carry a special weight in understanding the perceptions of the Court's legitimacy and who are in a unique position to make assessments because their sphere of action and choice is affected by the Court's judgments'. Başak Çalı, Anne Koch, and Nicola Bruch, *The Legitimacy of the European Court of Human Rights: The View from the Ground* (Department of Political Science, University College London, 2011) 6.

[24] Çalı, Koch, and Bruch (n 23) 35. Constitutive legitimacy refers (at 8) to 'whether there are good reasons for an institution to exist in the first place, and whether those reasons demand deference to that institution's decisions in the future'.

[25] Çalı, Koch, and Bruch (n 23) 36.

[26] *Yuriy Nikolayevich Ivanov v Ukraine*, No. 40450/04, 15 October 2009.

[27] See 6.2.2 at n 68.

they indicate that politicians in Romania view the Court as having positive currency in respect of its legitimacy. In the UK and the Netherlands, legitimacy-related problems that were expressed or reported by interviewees were not held by them to undermine the constitutive legitimacy of the Court, notwithstanding the persistent criticisms from some politicians, judicial figures, and newspapers.

Schaffer, Føllesdal, and Ulfstein venture that the *absence* of resistance could be equally indicative of illegitimacy, since international human rights institutions should always be 'potentially disputable, disruptive and provoking' to (among others) governments, whose acquiescence could indicate that the institutions are powerless or 'politically irrelevant'.[28] The questions we might ask about the legitimacy of international human rights regimes are also conditioned by how powerful they are perceived to be vis-à-vis states and the various costs they are thought to exact in terms of loss of sovereignty, finances, reputational damage, and domestic political capital. For Moravcsik, the distinctiveness of international human rights regimes lies in the way in which they regulate states' conduct towards those *within* their jurisdiction, in contrast to the majority of international institutions which regulate *inter*-state relations.[29] The particular intrusiveness of human rights regimes, Moravcsik argues, give rise to the paradox of why any state, democratic or dictatorial, would 'favour establishing an effective independent international authority, the sole purpose of which is to constrain its domestic sovereignty in such an unprecedentedly invasive and overtly nonmajoritarian manner'.[30]

This framing of the apparent paradox is questionable on two grounds. First, as we argue at 4.4.2, international human rights systems should be regarded as constitutive rather than constraining of democracy, both in their purposes and effects. Secondly, a more nuanced appraisal of the influence of such systems is required. As argued at 3.1, the role of the international courts in bringing about compliance with human rights norms is facilitative rather than determinative, treaties being largely dependent for their impact on *domestic* political structures and dynamics. On this account, criticism of the alleged intrusiveness of international human rights norms into democratic decision-making within states appears exaggerated. Rather, 'empirical research may … lead us to ask new, qualified questions about how to normatively evaluate the soft, subtle and conditioned influence international legal norms do have when they interact with domestic institutions of rule of law and political democracy'.[31]

Whatever their basis, the deleterious effects of legitimacy-based critiques of the Convention system have galvanized some parliamentary bodies to reflect on their own role in framing and reinforcing the legitimacy of human rights norms, standards, and judgments. In doing so, they have articulated why parliamentary involvement in the implementation of Convention standards and judgments of the Court can be considered normatively desirable, over and above the requirements of

[28] Schaffer, Føllesdal, and Ulfstein (n 13) 13.

[29] Andrew Moravcsik, 'The Origins of Human Rights Regimes: Democratic Delegation in Postwar Europe', *International Organization* (2000) 54: 217. See also Føllesdal (n 11) 344.

[30] Moravcsik (n 29) 219.

[31] Schaffer, Føllesdal, and Ulfstein (n 13) 16.

efficiency and effectiveness—and, indeed, even if parliaments sometimes complicate or delay implementation. The Joint Committee on Human Rights (JCHR) in the UK parliament argues that:

> [P]arliamentary scrutiny facilitates democratic input into legal changes following court judgments and so helps to counter the perception that the legal protection of human rights tends to marginalise the role of democratic institutions.[32]

Enhancing the role of national parliaments in the Convention system, the Committee adds, 'is the key to addressing concerns and anxieties about the democratic legitimacy of the Convention and the Court and thereby ensuring their long term survival'.[33] The Parliamentary Assembly is also mindful of the legitimacy-boosting potential of national parliamentary engagement. As Drzemczewski and Lowis observe,

> The work of the Assembly directed at increasing the role of parliaments in relation to human rights ... has two distinct, but mutually supportive goals: first, ensuring the rapid and full execution of judgments of the Strasbourg Court; and, second, increasing human rights discourse at the national level, which in turn helps to enhance the democratic legitimacy of human rights.[34]

These statements are concerned, explicitly or implicitly, with the need to address *perceptions* that the Court and the wider Convention system lack democratic legitimacy. Such concerns may co-exist with a view that the system *is*, in fact, democratically legitimate or that it enjoys legitimacy of other kinds, since legitimacy is not a singular or absolute concept, as the next section explores.

4.2 What is Legitimacy?

Accounts of the legitimacy of international human rights bodies (and other types of global law or governance institutions) commonly distinguish between its normative, legal, and social dimensions.[35] Normative legitimacy concerns the normative 'pull' or non-coercive 'compliance-eliciting force' of the judgments, decisions, or recommendations of such bodies.[36] Following Hart[37] and Raz,[38] this is expressed as meaning that legitimate institutions generate 'content-independent' reasons for

[32] JCHR, Seventh Report of Session 2014–15, *Human Rights Judgments*, HL Paper 130, HC 1088 (2015), para. 1.1.

[33] JCHR, Seventh Report of Session 2014–15 (n 32) para. 5.3.

[34] Andrew Drzemczewski and Julia Lowis, 'The Work of the Parliamentary Assembly of the Council of Europe', in Hunt, Hooper, and Yowell, eds. (n 2): 309, 311.

[35] Çalı, Koch, and Bruch (n 23) 8–10; Føllesdal (n 11) 345. Note that Çalı, Koch, and Bruch's concept of 'constitutive' legitimacy encompasses both normative and legal legitimacy.

[36] Føllesdal (n 11) 345; Thomas M. Franck, *The Power of Legitimacy among Nations* (Oxford, New York: Oxford University Press, 1990) 24.

[37] H.L.A. Hart, *Essays on Bentham* (Oxford: Oxford University Press, 1982) 254–5.

[38] Joseph Raz, *Ethics in the Public Domain: Essays in the Morality of Law and Politics* (Oxford: Oxford University Press, 1995); Joseph Raz, 'The Problem of Authority: Revisiting the Service Conception', *Minnesota Law Review* 90 (2006): 1003.

those within their domain—including parliaments—to support, or at least not interfere with, their functioning and to comply with the duties they impose, regardless of whether the specific content of the duties is regarded as good or useful.[39]

Legal legitimacy is concerned with whether international human rights bodies have the legal authority they claim and whether their decisions accord with the principles of legality.[40] It is commonly invoked in respect of whether a human rights body is deemed to have interpreted a treaty unduly creatively or expansively.[41]

Social legitimacy addresses the question: does the international human rights judiciary 'command general public belief that it has *rightful authority* or secure general *compliance*?' (emphasis in original).[42] The relationship between, on the one hand, the social dimension of legitimacy and, on the other hand, its normative and legal dimensions, is contested.[43] Some authors regard the two as conceptually distinct: thus, social legitimacy reflects the fluctuating views that *are* held towards an institution (which are susceptible to empirical measurement, expressed either through compliant behaviour or levels of 'diffuse support' captured in representative surveys), while normative legitimacy reflects the views that *should* be held (based on independently derived criteria for justifiability).[44] An alternative perspective posits a closer relationship between the social and normative legitimacy of an institution. Çalı, Koch, and Bruch, following Beetham,[45] venture that 'social analysis should be concerned with capturing what normative expectations actors have of an institution and how actors assess whether such expectations are met'.[46] This approach eschews, on the one hand, conceptions of legitimacy that are purely normative in the sense of being abstract, based upon ideal conditions, and divorced from social-historical context and, on the other hand, notions that are purely socially derived and consequently '[reduce] the legitimacy of power to people's belief in its legitimacy'.[47] Instead, Beetham proposes a social-scientific concept of 'legitimacy-in-context, assessed against the relevant norms, principles and criteria for consent pertaining in the given society'.[48] This approach is sensitive to the *reasons* why different actors believe an institution to be legitimate, and the

[39] Allen Buchanan and Robert O. Keohane, 'The Legitimacy of Global Governance Institutions', *Ethics and International Affairs* 20(4) (2006): 405, 411.

[40] Føllesdal (n 11) 345.

[41] Laurence R. Helfer and Karen J. Alter, 'Legitimacy and Lawmaking: A Tale of Three International Courts', *Theoretical Inquiries in Law* 14(2) (2013): 479; George Letsas, 'The ECHR as a Living Instrument: Its Meaning and Legitimacy', in Andreas Føllesdal, Birgit Peters, and Geir Ulfstein, eds., *Constituting Europe: The European Court of Human Rights in a National, European and Global Context* (Cambridge: Cambridge University Press, 2013): 106.

[42] Føllesdal (n 11) 345.

[43] Başak Çalı, Anne Koch, and Nicola Bruch, ' The Social Legitimacy of Human Rights Courts: A Grounded Interpretivist Theory of the Elite Accounts of the Legitimacy of the European Court of Human Rights', *Human Rights Quarterly* 35(3) (2013): 955, 959.

[44] Voeten (n 19) 414–15.

[45] David Beetham, *The Legitimation of Power* (Prometheus Books, 1990).

[46] Çalı, Koch, and Bruch (n 43) 960.

[47] David Beetham, *The Legitimation of Power*, 2nd edn. (Palgrave Macmillan, 2013) 37–8.

[48] Beetham (n 47) 38.

extent to which independently derived normative standards of legitimacy are 'socially embedded or appropriated'.[49]

This multi-dimensional understanding of legitimacy has several advantages. It permits an account of the legitimacy of an institution that takes into consideration the multiple and sometimes contradictory accounts of legitimacy proposed by different actors. Accordingly, it demands awareness of whose view of legitimacy is heard—and whose is missing—in public debate about human rights. This is significant in view of the fact that comparative surveys of public attitudes towards international courts are rare[50]—especially in the case of the ECtHR (see 4.1)—and that a narrow range of voices may come to dominate or manipulate public discourse. The 'legitimacy-in-context' approach is also sensitive to the contextual and comparative nature of legitimacy. It recognizes that legitimacy may be assessed differently in relation to the different functions of human rights bodies; for example, their interpretive or adjudicatory functions or their role in dispensing remedies.[51] Thus, legitimacy emerges 'in the interplay between international human rights institutions, the domestic institutions of states, and individuals and groups', each of which may make competing and credible claims to legitimacy.[52] This insight frames our discussion in this chapter of legitimacy within the Convention system: it precludes absolute or 'hard-edged' claims to legitimacy by *either* courts (domestic or supranational) *or* parliaments in favour of claims which acknowledge the multiple grounds of legitimacy within a pluralist, 'heterarchical' system,[53] and the need for contextualization when legitimacy is invoked by any particular actor. Further, the 'legitimacy-in-context' approach implies that the legitimacy of any single actor should be assessed in relation to the legitimacy of the system as a whole.

4.2.1 Institutional and procedural factors affecting legitimacy

A host of institutional and procedural features are generally considered to affect the normative, legal, and/or social legitimacy of international human rights bodies.[54]

[49] Çalı, Koch, and Bruch (n 43) 960.

[50] The exception being the Eurobarometer surveys of trust in the Court of Justice of the European Union conducted by the European Commission; see Voeten (n 19) 423–6.

[51] Başak Çalı, 'The Legitimacy of International Interpretive Authorities for Human Rights Treaties: An Indirect-Instrumentalist Defence' in Føllesdal, Schaffer, and Ulfstein, eds. (n 1): 141.

[52] Schaffer, Føllesdal, and Ulfstein (n 13) 11. See also Lynn Dobson, 'Legitimacy, Institutional Power, and International Human Rights Institutions: A Conceptual Enquiry', in Føllesdal, Schaffer, and Ulfstein, eds. (n 1): 190.

[53] Nico Krisch, 'The Open Architecture of European Human Rights Law', *Modern Law Review* 71(2) (2008): 183.

[54] See, for example, Tom Barkhuysen and Michiel van Emmerik, 'Legitimacy of European Court of Human Rights: Procedural Aspects', in Nick Huls, Maurice Adams, and Jacco Bomhoff, eds., *The Legitimacy of Highest Courts' Rulings: Judicial Deliberation and Beyond* (The Hague: TMC Asser Press, 2009): 437; Jean-Paul Costa, 'On the Legitimacy of the European Court of Human Rights' Judgments', *European Constitutional Law Review* 7 (2011): 173; Andreas Føllesdal, 'The Legitimacy of International Human Rights Review: The Case of the European Court of Human Rights', *Journal of Social Philosophy* 40(4) Winter (2009): 595; Nienke Grossman, 'Legitimacy and International Adjudicative Bodies', *The George Washington International Law Review* 41 (2010): 47; Tulio Treves, 'Aspects of Legitimacy

Essential requirements are commonly deemed to include independence, an absence of bias, transparency, and openness to the participation of civil society. Also of relevance is the robustness of vetting procedures by which judges are selected or (as is the case with ECtHR judges) elected; their professional standing; and their diversity in respect of the various legal traditions present within the regime and other variables such as gender and ethnicity. Attention is also paid to the quality of judicial deliberation, including the clarity and consistency of judgments,[55] and the extent to which they are informed both by expert opinion and the rules of systematic treaty interpretation laid down in the Vienna Convention on the Law of Treaties.[56] In addition, performance-related aspects such as efficiency and cost-effectiveness may affect international courts' legitimacy.

In respect of the ECtHR, much debate has centred on the composition and quality of the judiciary. Çalı notes that the 'one country, one judge' principle ensures the widest possible representation of legal traditions, an essential feature of an international interpretative body.[57] Judges of the ECtHR have previously been criticized for lacking the requisite qualifications and experience, or for lacking diversity in respect of gender,[58] or for being nominated by states on the basis of 'an opaque mix of nepotism and diplomatic strategy'[59]—all factors that might be viewed as undermining the Court's legitimacy. Such concerns, expressed by NGOs among others,[60] prompted the Parliamentary Assembly to increase the robustness and transparency of its vetting of judicial candidates prior to their election,[61] and the Committee of Ministers to strengthen its mechanisms for advising states on the selection of candidates for election as judges to the Court.[62]

of Decisions of International Courts and Tribunals', in Rüdiger Wolfrum and Volker Röben, eds., *Legitimacy in International Law* (Berlin: Springer, 2008).

[55] Barkhuysen and van Emmerik (n 54); Janneke Gerards, 'Judicial Deliberations in the European Court of Human Rights', in Huls, Adams, and Bomhoff, eds. (n 54): 407.

[56] Vienna Convention on the Law of Treaties, Articles 31–33.

[57] Çalı (n 51) 160.

[58] To ensure gender balance on the ECtHR, states are required to nominate at least one person of the 'the under-represented sex' (meaning the sex comprising less than 40 per cent of the existing judges) unless exceptional circumstances prevent this. See PACE, Committee on Legal Affairs and Human Rights, Procedure for electing judges to the European Court of Human Rights, AS/Jur/Inf (2014)03 rev 1, 27 March 2014, para. 8. As of June 2015, around one-third of judges of the ECtHR were women (fourteen out of forty-five, two spaces being vacant). Across the history of the Court, only one-fifth of judges have been women (thirty-five out of 175). See GQUAL (Campaign for gender parity in international representation), *The Current Composition of International Tribunals and Monitoring Bodies* (2015).

[59] Føllesdal (n 12) 287.

[60] Jutta Limbach, Pedro Cruz Villalón, Roger Errera, Anthony Lester, Tamara Morshchakova, Stephen Sedley, and Andrzej Zoll, *Judicial Independence: Law and Practice of Appointments to the European Court of Human Rights* (Interights, 2003).

[61] PACE Resolution 2002 (2014) Evaluation of the implementation of the reform of the Parliamentary Assembly, 24 June 2014, paras. 9–10. In 2015, the Committee on the Election of Judges to the ECtHR began work within the Assembly; previously, this function had been undertaken by a sub-committee of the Committee on Legal Affairs and Human Rights (see 2.6.1).

[62] See Guidelines of the Committee of Ministers on the selection of candidates for the post of judge at the European Court of Human Rights, CM(2012)40 final, 29 March 2012; Steering Committee on Human Rights, CDDH report on the review of the functioning of the Advisory Panel of experts on candidates for election as judge to the European Court of Human Rights, CDDH(2013)R79 Addendum II, 29 November 2013.

In respect of the Court's effectiveness, concerns persist about the backlog of pending applications; however, the dramatic downward trend in the backlog in recent years, and the renewed focus on failures in national implementation as a cause of the backlog, suggest that, to the extent that this is a source of (perceived) illegitimacy, it is one of diminishing proportions (see 1.1.1).

In respect of the Court's legal legitimacy, attention focuses on its dynamic interpretation of the Convention as a 'living instrument', which has attracted much critical commentary.[63] Yet this aspect of the Court's jurisprudence has been defended,[64] including by the authors,[65] on the grounds that such practice is not unique to the ECtHR, but is common to many other treaties and domestic legal systems; that it is in accordance with the Vienna Convention on the Law of Treaties Article 31(1), which permits interpretation 'in light of a treaty's object and purpose'; and that the object and purpose of the ECHR *requires* a dynamic approach in order that the Court may respond effectively to new or previously neglected threats to human rights. In their study of the Court's legitimacy in several Council of Europe states, Çalı, Koch, and Bruch observe that the living instrument doctrine was raised as a 'legitimacy issue' by only one in five respondents.[66]

4.3 What is Democratic Legitimacy?

Some of the institutional and procedural aspects already identified are hypothesized to affect the *democratic* legitimacy of international human rights bodies, which has both normative and social dimensions.[67] These include the extent to which parliamentarians are involved in electing judges,[68] and the opportunities for the participation of civil society actors (such as third-party interventions and *amicus curiae* briefs;[69] see 2.2), which enhance the democratic legitimacy of international courts by connecting judicial decision-making to a broad range of opinions and experience among civil society groups and individuals who are not parties to the

[63] See 1.1.2 at n 37.

[64] Føllesdal (n 12) 285–7; Dominic Grieve, 'Is the European Convention Working?', Rule of Law Lecture, Faculty of Advocates, Edinburgh, 21 September 2015, 7–8; Letsas (n 41).

[65] Alice Donald, Jane Gordon, and Philip Leach, *The UK and the European Court of Human Rights*, Research Report 83 (Manchester; Equality and Human Rights Commission, 2012) Chapter 6.

[66] Çalı, Koch, and Bruch (n 23) 12.

[67] Armin von Bogdandy and Ingo Venzke, 'In Whose Name? An Investigation of International Courts' Public Authority and Its Democratic Justification', *European Journal of International Law* 23(1) (2012): 7; Jamie Mayerfeld, 'The Democratic Legitimacy of International Human Rights Law', *Indiana International and Comparative Law Review* 19(1) (2009): 49; Andreas von Staden, 'The Democratic Legitimacy of Judicial Review beyond the State: Normative Subsidiarity and Judicial Standards of Review', *International Journal of Constitutional Law* 10(4) (2012): 1023.

[68] Von Bogdandy and Venzke (n 67) 32–5.

[69] See, especially, Nicole Bürli, 'Amicus Curiae as a Means to Reinforce the Legitimacy of the European Court of Human Rights', in Janneke Gerards and Joseph Fleuren, eds., *Implementation of the European Convention on Human Rights and of the Judgments of the ECtHR in National Case Law: A Comparative Analysis* (Antwerp: Intersentia, 2014): 135.

case but might potentially be affected by its outcome.[70] Allied to this imperative is the requirement for judicial proceedings and decisions to be well-publicized and accessible to actors beyond the executive, including parliaments and civil society. In this regard, the ECtHR may claim considerable credit for its efforts to make its judgments, decisions, and other documents available on the Hudoc database, in multiple languages (see 2.1.1) and in the form of accessible summaries.[71]

A further consideration is the accessibility of the Court to individual applicants. The procedure for lodging applications has traditionally been very open; for example, there is no requirement for applicants to pay a fee or (at the application stage) to obtain legal representation, such reforms having been rejected by states. However, procedural reforms prompted by the Court's once mountainous backlog have introduced stricter conditions for applicants; for example, the 'significant disadvantage' admissibility criterion introduced under Protocol No. 14 to the Convention (see 2.9); the mandatory application form and requirements for documentation introduced by the Court in January 2014;[72] and the significant change to the admissibility criteria under Protocol No. 15 which would reduce the time limit for making applications from six to four months after the final domestic decision.[73] Academic and NGO commentators have expressed alarm about the cumulative effect of such procedural reforms on access to justice, arguing that the Court's caseload would be more effectively tackled by, among other measures, making the supervision process of the Committee of Ministers more transparent and robust (see 2.8).[74]

Such institutional and procedural features do not, however, exhaust accounts of the *democratic* legitimacy of international human rights bodies. Von Bogdandy and Venzke venture that *all* international courts, as autonomous actors wielding public authority, 'require a genuine mode of justification that lives up to basic tenets of democratic theory'.[75] For von Staden, this justification must extend beyond the type of institutional and procedural factors outlined above to embrace the concept of 'normative subsidiarity'; that is, the 'normatively sensitive separation of powers between judicial review by an international court and democratic decision-making

[70] Von Bogdandy and Venzke (n 67) 25–30.

[71] See, for example, the thematic factsheets produced by the Court at <http://www.echr.coe.int/Pages/home.aspx?p=press/factsheets>.

[72] Rule 47 of the Rules of the Court.

[73] Article 4 of Protocol No. 15. NGOs have expressed concern that this reform will impede access to justice, especially for individuals who live in geographically remote areas, lack access to communications technology, have complicated cases, or are represented by lawyers who are not adequately experienced in lodging claims before the Court. See Joint NGO statement, 'Protocol 15 to the European Convention on Human Rights Must Not Result in a Weakening of Human Rights Protection', 20 June 2013.

[74] Philip Leach, 'On Reform of the European Court of Human Rights', *European Human Rights Law Review* 6 (2009): 725.

[75] Von Bogdandy and Venzke (n 67) 8. On the legitimacy of international courts and governance institutions generally, see, for example, Buchanan and Keohane (n 39); Andrea Ribeiro Hoffmann and Anna van der Vleuten, *Closing or Widening the Gap? Legitimacy and Democracy in Regional Integration Organizations* (Farnham: Ashgate, 2007); Andrew Moravcsik, 'Is there a 'Democratic Deficit' in World Politics? A Framework for Analysis', *Government and Opposition* 39(2) (2004): 336; Steven Wheatley, *The Democratic Legitimacy of International Law* (Oxford: Hart Publishing, 2010).

at the national level'.[76] Von Staden locates the ECtHR's democratic legitimacy principally in its doctrine of the margin of appreciation (see 2.1.1 and 2.9), which he identifies as 'the most elaborate ... standard of review reflecting a normatively sensitive separation of powers between judicial review by an international court and democratic decision-making at the national level'.[77] Similarly, Harlow describes the margin of appreciation as a doctrine that 'defuse[s] issues of clashing legitimacies', and ventures that disagreement over individual cases does not imperil the 'clear legitimacy' of the Court.[78] To this legitimacy-enhancing feature of the Convention system might be added the Court's exercise of a 'weak' form of international judicial review, meaning that, while its judgments are binding (under Article 46(1) ECHR; see 2.1), they do not directly invalidate domestic legislation that has been held to be incompatible with the ECHR. As noted at 2.3, a considerable degree of discretion is generally conferred on states in the post-judgment phase, during which national authorities determine the specific steps by which they intend to remedy a violation. The modus operandi of the Committee of Ministers, in which government representatives meet privately on a peer-to-peer basis, may also be viewed as highly responsive to the legitimacy-based concerns of states.

Yet, in the view of some authors, such features cannot shoulder the entire legitimatory burden created by international judicial review. This is because the public authority of the international judiciary, in contrast to that of the domestic judiciary, is not 'embedded in a responsive political system' characterized by the separation of powers between the legislative and judicial functions.[79] As a result, it is argued, international courts 'long for politico-legislative counterparts'.[80] Føllesdal similarly observes that 'there are no identifiable legislative or executive bodies that serve to check and balance the international judiciary'.[81] For Bellamy, the creation of 'global or regional democratic legislatures' in parallel with the creation of supranational courts is some way from being realized, 'with the partial exception of the European Parliament'.[82]

4.3.1 The legitimacy-enhancing role of the Parliamentary Assembly

In the context of the Convention system, the analyses outlined above appear to neglect the role played by the Parliamentary Assembly, not only in relation to the Court—electing its judges and pressing for the implementation of its judgments—but also in respect of the ways in which the Assembly seeks to ensure greater transparency and accountability of Council of Europe processes and institutions.[83]

[76] Von Staden (n 67) 1039.
[77] Von Staden (n 67) 1039–42.
[78] Harlow (n 15) 32.
[79] Von Bogdandy and Venzke (n 67) 19.
[80] Von Bogdandy and Venzke (n 67) 30.
[81] Føllesdal (n 11) 344.
[82] Richard Bellamy, 'The Democratic Legitimacy of International Human Rights Conventions: Political Constitutionalism and the Hirst Case', in Føllesdal, Schaffer, and Ulfstein, eds. (n 1): 243, 261.
[83] See, for example, Beat Habegger, 'Democratic Accountability of International Organizations: Parliamentary Control within the Council of Europe and the OSCE and the Prospects for the United

Kraft-Kassack observes that parliamentary assemblies in general are 'remarkably under-researched'.[84] This is despite the fact that, as politically pluralistic bodies, they may 'improve participation in comparison with intergovernmental forums as they provide for more direct and—as opposition MPs participate—fuller representation'.[85]

As noted at 2.6.2, the basis of the Assembly's legitimacy is the dual mandate enjoyed by delegates as members both of the Assembly and national parliaments. Beat Habegger ventures that:

> Owing to their 'double mandate' of serving both at the national and international level, all elected parliamentarians represent the interests, ideas and values of their constituents not only in the national parliament, but also in the parliamentary assembly, and are particularly suited to forging effective links between the different levels of governance.[86]

Habegger argues that, although PACE is formally a consultative body,[87] it has 'managed to expand its competencies significantly from those of a purely consultative body to those of a decision-making organ'.[88] In addition to its role in electing the senior representatives of Council of Europe bodies, it has exercised influence in deciding upon the accession of new member states, and in the processes of treaty-making[89] and policy formation.[90] The Assembly's ability to question heads of state and government, and executive bodies, 'makes it possible to bring into the public spotlight issues on which the intergovernmental decision-makers are willing neither to divulge information nor to engage in debate, and thus contributes to more transparent governance'.[91] However, the democratic credentials of PACE, and its ability effectively to constrain governmental decision-making within the Council of Europe, should not be overstated; as noted at 2.6.2, some PACE members are highly susceptible to government lobbying and/or display weak commitment to the dual mandate conferred by their membership of the Assembly.

Nevertheless, the legitimacy-enhancing potential of PACE is, we suggest, an important and under-explored feature of the Convention system. Von Bogdandy and Venzke describe the Assembly's role in, for example, judicial elections as being 'truly forward-looking from the point of view of democratic theory',[92] a point insisted on

Nations', *Cooperation and Conflict* 45(2) (2010): 186; Philip Leach, 'The Parliamentary Assembly of the Council of Europe', in Marten Breuer and Stefanie Schmahl, eds., *The Council of Europe: Its Law and Policies* (Oxford: Oxford University Press, forthcoming 2016).

[84] Christiane Kraft-Kasack, 'Transnational Parliamentary Assemblies: A Remedy for the Democratic Deficit of International Governance?', *West European Politics* 31 (2008): 534, 535.

[85] Kraft-Kassack (n 84) 537.

[86] Habegger (n 83) 190–1.

[87] Statute of the Council of Europe, 5 May 1949, ETS 1, Articles 22 and 23.

[88] Habegger (n 83) 191.

[89] Empirical studies suggest that around one-third of Council of Europe conventions (international law treaties) have been initiated by PACE; see Habegger (n 83) 193.

[90] About one-fifth of the recommendations adopted by the Committee of Ministers, and subsequently addressed to the member states, refer to recommendations initially adopted by PACE; see Habegger (n 83) 193.

[91] Habegger (n 83) 196.

[92] Von Bogdandy and Venzke (n 67) 36.

by the Assembly itself when, for example, it notes on its website that that the election of judges '[provides] them with democratic legitimacy'.[93]

4.4 The Democratic Legitimacy of the European Court of Human Rights

The preceding section considered some of the institutional and procedural factors which mitigate the legitimacy-related concerns of states in respect of their obligations under the ECHR. These include the degree of discretion conferred on states in both the pre- and post-judgment phases, and the role of the Parliamentary Assembly in electing ECtHR judges and in standard-setting, policy formation, and ensuring a measure of transparency and accountability of Council of Europe institutions and processes. We noted, however, residual concerns about the perceived tensions between international human rights regimes and domestic democratic governance. Given these concerns, why can international human rights bodies claim to be normatively legitimate and why, in particular, should 'generally human rights-compliant, well-functioning *democratic* states bind themselves thus?' (emphasis in original).[94] In this section, we consider the reasons that national parliaments have to engage with international human rights bodies (for the purposes of our discussion, the ECtHR) and to adopt, as Çalı terms it, a 'presumption of deference'[95] towards their interpretative authority and to respect the finality of their adjudicatory authority. We argue that strong reasons exist for national parliaments to adopt such a position, based on three overlapping sets of arguments. These derive from, first, the authority and legitimacy that the Court derives from the freely given consent of states to be bound by its judgments (4.4.1); secondly, the various ways in which international human rights regimes enhance, rather than undermine, democratic authority and legitimacy at the domestic level (4.4.2); and, thirdly, the distinct contribution made by *international* human rights regimes that even the most conscientious domestic regimes cannot achieve by acting alone (4.4.3).

4.4.1 Legitimacy derived from consent

It is often argued that international human rights regimes enjoy at least a measure of democratic legitimacy by virtue of the fact that states' decisions to create, and subsequently ratify, treaties generally follows a process of democratic debate and procedure which is similar to that for adopting national legislation.[96] On this account, such regimes enjoy a form of delegated democratic authority based on states' freely given consent.

[93] See website of the Parliamentary Assembly at <http://website-pace.net/web/as-cdh/main>.

[94] Føllesdal (n 11) 352.

[95] Çalı (n 51) 147.

[96] Steven Wheatley, 'On the Legitimate Authority of International Human Rights Bodies', in Føllesdal, Schaffer, and Ulfstein, eds. (n 1): 84, 109.

Von Staden argues, however, that the democratic legitimacy of the allocation of competences between international courts and national authorities 'is not exhausted by the initial act of ratification of the underlying agreement' but 'needs to be complemented with democratically informed standards that guide their exercise in practice'.[97] Thus, consent-based arguments for deference to an international human rights regime remain vulnerable to subsequent decisions by states to withdraw their consent to be bound by human rights judgments—or to seek to modify the system or denounce it altogether—on the basis that conditions or practices within that system have (in the states' view) changed unacceptably, or that other, domestically derived imperatives should take precedence over international obligations.

Von Bogdandy and Venzke add that the democratic justification created by the initial act of ratification is diminished where, for example, the process is driven by elite negotiation hidden from popular or parliamentary view, or where the financial, reputational, or other costs of exiting a regime are prohibitively high.[98] In respect of the Convention, the UK experience suggests that concerns about the minimal involvement of parliaments in the ratification of both the original treaty and subsequent additional protocols are well-founded. Bates notes that the UK government's decision to ratify the Convention in 1950 was taken without a debate in parliament.[99] Parliamentary scrutiny of international treaties prior to ratification was only placed on a statutory footing in the UK as a result of the Constitutional Reform and Governance Act 2010, prior to which 'for many years there was very little opportunity for any meaningful parliamentary scrutiny or participation before ratification'.[100] The JCHR has given priority to this function of national parliaments; for example, in its report recommending ratification of Protocol No. 15 to the Convention (see 2.9), it called on the government to ensure that it 'should be debated in both Houses in order to raise awareness, within Parliament and beyond, of the significance of the Protocol'.[101]

In view of the caveats outlined above, we suggest that voluntary consent is a necessary, but not sufficient, requirement of democratic legitimacy for the European Court.

4.4.2 Enhancing the legitimacy of domestic democratic institutions

If the act of ratification is an insufficient normative basis for establishing the Court's legitimacy, what justifications, then, might provide such a basis? In this section, we

[97] Von Staden (n 67) 1033. [98] Von Bogdandy and Venzke (n 67) 21.

[99] Ed Bates, *The Evolution of the European Convention on Human Rights: From Its Inception to the Creation of a Permanent Court of Human Rights* (Oxford: Oxford University Press, 2010) 101, text at n 144.

[100] JCHR, Seventh Report of Session 2014–15 (n 32) para. 1.7.

[101] JCHR, Seventh Report of Session 2014–15 (n 32) para. 1.16. Ministers agreed to extend the statutory scrutiny period to allow members of both houses to consider the JCHR's report; however, it was for the JCHR to propose a motion to take note of its report and to secure time for a debate in either or both houses of parliament. In the event, no debate was held.

consider arguments based on the way in which international human rights regimes enrich, rather than diminish, the democratic process at national level—and enhance, rather than undermine, the democratic credentials of domestic decision-makers.

A widely acknowledged justification for international human rights bodies is the need to provide an external safety mechanism given the inevitability that even well-functioning majoritarian democracies may make mistakes.[102] Even strong advocates of political constitutionalism concede that, as Bellamy puts it, 'no democratic process is perfect'[103] and that judicial review provides an external corrective to, rather than a substitute for, domestic democratic deliberation. Wheatley terms this idea 'epistemic humility', which he views as 'inherent in the practice of democracy'.[104] It requires political and legal institutions to acknowledge the uncertainty of their claims that they 'know better' and to 'remain open to the possibility that they have failed to regulate in accordance with the interests and perspective of subjects' and thereby caused injustice. The position of minorities or other vulnerable groups within majoritarian systems is of primary concern. As Føllesdal, observes, '[t]he majority may exploit its powers, intentionally and knowingly or not, in ways that unduly harm those that happen to find themselves in the minority'.[105] Such undue harm may arise for groups who are in a permanent minority and who cannot therefore rely on the standard mechanisms that ensure responsiveness of politicians to the electorate, or who need special arrangements to protect their way of life.

We should recall here, too, that the external corrective provided by international human rights regimes is not dependent for its effects on external *enforcement*; rather, as noted at 3.1, the decisions of supranational courts exert influence largely through the outcome of *domestic* political competition and collaboration. Thus, parliaments may invoke judgments to instigate or advance domestic reform and to lend it greater legitimacy, as may other domestic actors. This empirically grounded insight adds nuance to the arguments about the legitimacy of supranational courts such as the ECtHR, given that they act as a catalyst for, rather than a determinant of, domestic reform.

A second, and closely related, advantage of membership of international human rights regimes even for relatively well-functioning democracies is the way in which such regimes enhance the normative and social legitimacy of democratic institutions at the domestic level.[106] As Føllesdal argues, external human rights review 'may provide citizens much-needed reassurance about others' compliance—including that of their government.... It may thus help bestow legitimacy on states by providing assurance *when appropriate* that these [domestic] actors are providing normatively

[102] See, for example, Allen Buchanan, 'Why *International Legal* Human Rights?', in Rowan Cruft, S. Matthew Liao, and Massimo Renzo, eds., *Philosophical Foundations of Human Rights* (Oxford: Oxford University Press, 2015): 244, 251.

[103] Richard Bellamy, 'The Democratic Legitimacy of International Human Rights Conventions: Political Constitutionalism and the European Convention on Human Rights', *European Journal of International Law* 25(4): 1019, 1033. See also Waldron (n 5) 1370.

[104] Wheatley (n 96) 111–12.

[105] Føllesdal (n 12) 282.

[106] Buchanan (n 102) 252; Çalı, Koch, and Bruch (n 23) 8–9; Føllesdal (n 11) 357–8.

just policies' (emphasis in original).[107] This analysis requires us to look at the entire functioning and output of international human rights bodies, and not only adverse judgments or decisions. For example, the large proportion of applications against the UK that the Court decides are inadmissible and the very small percentage that eventually result in an adverse judgment, combined with the UK's relatively strong record of implementing judgments, 'serves to assure the citizens that this particular government generally merits compliance'.[108] This observation underlines the importance of parliamentarians being made aware of the full context of their respective states' relationship with the ECtHR, for example by means of executive reporting mechanisms which highlight not only adverse judgments but also judgments finding no violation and reasoned inadmissibility decisions (as—uniquely—the Dutch government's annual report does; see 8.4).

The ECtHR's extensive jurisprudence on the promotion of democracy provides a further reason for parliaments to view it as being constitutive, rather than undermining, of domestic democratic arrangements—with its emphasis on pluralism, protection of minorities, state accountability, and the substantive and procedural dimensions of democratic self-governance. Jurisprudence on the rights to freedom of expression, freedom of assembly and association, and free elections may all be seen as enhancing the capacities of states to better protect and uphold democratic standards, notwithstanding the possibility of contestation between national authorities and the Court over specific judgments in which these rights are engaged.[109]

Combined with the role of supranational human rights courts as a safeguard that prevents or corrects state failures to uphold rights, Çalı, Koch, and Bruch summarize the instrumental role of such courts as being that of 'legitimising the functions and performances of ... states themselves. Supranational human rights courts do not act against states, they help them be better states'.[110] Further, since states are not unitary actors, we might equally say (following Çalı et al.) that the international human rights judiciary does not 'act against' parliaments, but helps them be 'better' parliaments, whether by correcting the mistakes or injustices of majoritarian rule, or boosting public trust and confidence that the parliament is pursuing normatively just laws and policies.

4.4.3 The value of a supranational court

A third set of justifications for the normative legitimacy of the Court vis-à-vis domestic democratic bodies—which intersects closely with the second—is the benefits that accrue from the supranational model of adjudication entrenched in the Convention system that cannot be achieved by democratic states acting alone within their national jurisdiction. As we have argued elsewhere, one of the

[107] Føllesdal (n 11) 357. [108] Føllesdal (n 11) 358. See also the discussion at 7.2.2.
[109] See, for example, Alastair Mowbray, 'Contemporary Aspects of the Promotion of Democracy by the European Court of Human Rights', *European Public Law* 20(3) (2014): 469.
[110] Çalı, Koch, and Bruch (n 23) 8–9.

major strengths of the supranational authority of the ECtHR is the development of a normative system of common standards across multiple jurisdictions.[111] The Strasbourg Court is uniquely well placed to examine evidence, data, and national practices across the forty-seven Council of Europe states in order to identify any emerging convergence of domestic laws or legal practice.

Çalı argues that 'isolationist' accounts of legitimacy developed in the context of a single sovereign state cannot simply be transposed to the international context.[112] First, such a test is unfair, since 'no international interpretive [human rights] authority in a world of sovereign states can meet the legitimacy standards developed for liberal democratic states'.[113] Secondly, it is the wrong test because it is developed in the context of a single political community rather than from 'the circumstances of an association of states as representatives of individuals on the international plane'.[114]

The idea of 'citizenship' beyond the boundaries of the nation state opens up new avenues of democratic justification for international human rights courts. This characterization connects to the idea of 'transnational' or 'cosmopolitan' citizenship, in which the individual is the 'ultimate reference point in the justification of public authority' and is endowed with both a national and a cosmopolitan identity.[115] As Allen Buchanan argues,

> The further we depart from the picture of international laws as being created solely by states and as dealing solely with the relations of states to one another—and the more seriously we take the idea that human beings, not states, are the ultimate objects of moral concern—the clearer it becomes that a satisfactory account of the legitimacy of international law must include more than an explanation of why States ought to regard the international institutions through which law is made as having the right to rule.[116]

Kumm likewise rejects the conventional 'statist' paradigm of constitutionalism in favour of a 'cosmopolitan' paradigm which is a 'conceptually more refined, morally more attuned, and empirically more informed account of national and international public law practice' and the connections between them.[117]

The notion of cosmopolitan constitutionalism is instantiated in Article 1 ECHR, which imposes an obligation on member states to secure to 'everyone within their jurisdiction' the rights and freedoms it enshrines (see 2.1). Member states are

[111] Donald, Gordon, and Leach (n 65) 167.

[112] Çalı (n 51) 152–3. Çalı's account (143) is focused on the interpretive authority of international human rights bodies; that is, their authority to 'specify, clarify and infer specific standards of policy and action from the general international human rights law clauses enshrined in international human rights law treaties'.

[113] Çalı (n 51) 154. [114] Çalı (n 51) 153.

[115] Von Bogdandy and Venzke (n 67) 35. See also Samantha Besson, 'The Authority of International Law—Lifting the State Veil', *Sydney Law Review* 31(3) (2009): 343.

[116] Allen Buchanan, 'The Legitimacy of International Law', in Samantha Besson and John Tasioulas, eds., *The Philosophy of International Law* (Oxford: Oxford University Press, 2010): 79, 88.

[117] Mathias Kumm, 'The Cosmopolitan Turn in Constitutionalism: On the Relationship Between Constitutionalism in and Beyond the State', in Jeffrey L. Dunoff and Joel. P. Trachtman, eds., *Ruling The World? Constitutionalism, International Law, and Global Governance* (Cambridge: Cambridge University Press, 2009): 315, 323.

accordingly required to uphold those rights and freedoms, regardless of an individual's residence, nationality, citizenship, or any other characteristic. The value of this feature of the Convention system is particularly evident in cases concerning cross-border issues. Only a supranational body such as the ECtHR could, for example, have provided redress to the father of Oxana Rantseva, who died after she was trafficked from Russia to Cyprus for the purpose of sexual exploitation.[118] Among other cross-border issues, the Court has also had to consider the human rights issues arising from the application of European Union asylum law,[119] and criminal justice matters such as international child abduction.[120] In view of its interpretative authority (see 2.1.1), the Court also frequently provides guidance in its judgments on human rights issues of immediate relevance to states other than the respondent state; take, for example, the case of *Salduz v Turkey*,[121] concerning the right of access to a lawyer prior to being interviewed by the police, which prompted legislative reform in several states.

Føllesdal suggests that the acknowledged fallibility of majoritarian democracy (referred to at 4.4.2) creates a further justification for the 'added value' of the international human rights judiciary, since the domestic judiciary may be an unreliable guarantor of minority rights if, say, it is mainly drawn from the majority culture and consequently blind to the deleterious effects of majority rule.[122] By contrast, international human rights bodies may be considered more impartial, being more diverse in their composition and having no parochial allegiances, and may therefore sometimes be better placed than their domestic counterparts to 'identify mistaken assumptions that particular national "local" rights-violating practices are "necessary" to secure certain objectives'.[123] Judgments of the European Court concerning, for example, the rights of Roma people[124] exemplify this potential for supranational courts to act as an 'external corrective to domestic biases, protecting disempowered individuals before the domestic polity'.[125] Further, it is not only the spatial remove of Strasbourg judges from domestic decision-making that may in some instances be viewed as beneficial, but also their temporal remove. Judgments of the Court against the UK have, for example, identified violations of the Convention arising from anti-terrorism provisions which, as Gearty observes, are frequently rushed through parliament in a 'frenetic political climate'.[126]

Assessment of the value of international human rights regimes to well-functioning democracies must, in addition, take into account their impact in less democratic states whose populations have much to gain from external judicial oversight. This

[118] *Rantsev v Cyprus and Russia*, No. 25965/04, 7 January 2010.

[119] See, for example, *M.S.S. v Belgium and Greece*, No. 30696/09, 21 January 2011 [GC].

[120] European Court of Human Rights, *Factsheet: International Child Abductions*, July 2015.

[121] No. 36391/02, 27 November 2008 [GC].

[122] Føllesdal (n 11) 355–6.

[123] Føllesdal (n 12) 289.

[124] European Court of Human Rights, *Factsheet: Roma and Travellers*, July 2015.

[125] Çalı, Koch, and Bruch (n 23) 8.

[126] Conor Gearty, *Can Human Rights Survive? The Hamlyn Lectures 2005* (Cambridge: Cambridge University Press, 2006) 105. See, for example, *Gillan and Quinton v UK*, No. 4158/05, 12 January 2010, concerning police powers under sections 44–47 of the Terrorism Act 2000, to stop and search individuals without reasonable suspicion of wrongdoing.

argument appears to be compatible with the political constitutionalist position. As Bellamy argues, '[m]ature democracies may doubt the utility or legitimacy of such arrangements for themselves but regard them as helpful for less established democracies'.[127] Ronald Dworkin goes further by arguing that the 'true moral basis' of international law is the requirement for states to accept 'feasible and shared constraints' on their own power, since 'the general obligation of each state to improve its political legitimacy includes an obligation to try to improve the overall international system', the legitimacy of states and the system as a whole being construed as interdependent.[128]

Çalı ventures that the distinct moral contribution of international human regimes extends beyond the domestic benefits they confer (such as assurances to minorities) and encompasses their ability to advance the instrumental goal of promoting 'a human rights respecting culture globally'.[129] Accordingly, she offers an instrumentalist account of the legitimacy of international human rights treaties and institutions which emphasizes that 'the role [they] play internationally in encouraging orientation and structured debate about common standards, and in fostering the understanding that all individuals have entitlements to human rights, regardless of which sovereign state they live in'.[130] On this account, international human rights regimes further the goal of promoting a rights respecting culture globally in a way which even well-motivated democratic domestic authorities with similar expertise cannot achieve by acting autonomously.

The foregoing analysis has significant implications for our understanding of the relationship between national parliaments and the ECtHR. First, the benefit of legitimizing and building trust in domestic democratic authorities provide legislatures with strong incentives to constrain their authority by engaging with the Strasbourg Court. Secondly, as Çalı argues, the distinct moral contribution of international interpretative human rights bodies such as the ECtHR 'justifies an attitude of conditional deference towards the interpretive authority by domestic interpreters of all kinds'.[131] The international interpretative process, Çalı observes, 'facilitates a constructive dialogue about the best interpretation of human rights treaties, both through deference and rebuttal'.[132]

The following sections examine these themes of deference and rebuttal in respect of the relationship between the ECtHR and national parliaments. In 4.5 this relationship is examined from the perspective of the ECtHR, which is making increasingly explicit in its case law the potential for parliaments to 'earn' deference from Strasbourg by virtue of the quality of their deliberative and participatory processes. The way in which parliaments should approach situations of interpretive deadlock with the Court is discussed in 4.6. Finally, 4.7 examines—and rejects as both normatively undesirable and unworkable—proposals for either a de facto or de jure

[127] Bellamy (n 103) 1032.

[128] Ronald Dworkin, 'A New Philosophy for International Law', *Philosophy and Public Affairs* 41(2) (2013): 2, 17.

[129] Çalı (n 51) 143.

[130] Çalı (n 51) 155.

[131] Çalı (n 51) 162.

[132] Çalı (n 51) 162.

mechanism for 'democratic override' of judgments or decisions which do not command the support of national parliaments.

4.5 The Court's Engagement with the Parliamentary Process: Deference and Subsidiarity

Within the Convention system, executives are the principal domestic interlocutors of the ECtHR. Yet, increasingly, attention is being paid to the ways in which the Court might facilitate, incentivize, or even stipulate parliamentary engagement in the implementation of its judgments and of Convention standards.[133] This emerging area of research and debate is highly relevant to our discussion about democratic legitimacy in human rights adjudication, as well as to the place of national parliaments in the domestic compliance community on which international human rights law depends for its impact. This section examines the 'Strasbourg dimension' of the concept of due deference that operates between courts and parliaments in the national context (4.5.1). It goes on to discuss the Court's motivations for, and approach towards, making assessment of the quality of parliamentary processes a more prominent and systematic feature of its adjudications (4.5.2), and the potential effects, both advantageous and disadvantageous, of such an approach (4.5.3).

4.5.1 The doctrine of due deference: the Strasbourg dimension

We noted in the introduction to this chapter the emergence of a form of modern democratic constitutionalism which eschews doctrines of either legislative or judicial supremacy in favour of a dialogic model in which all branches of the state share responsibility for protecting human rights. As Lazarus and Simonsen argue, such an approach 'calls on the one hand to strengthen democratic oversight of human rights and on the other hand to find creative ways for courts to complement these participatory processes'.[134] This partnership is configured around the notion of judicial deference to the elected branches of government.[135] A common element of this approach is that judges should take an expansive view of what is appropriate for judicial resolution, rather than regarding some areas of policy, such as national security or resource allocation, as inherently inappropriate for adjudication. From this perspective, human rights are relevant to any or all areas of

[133] See Chapter 2 for a discussion of inter-institutional contact between national parliaments and the Court (2.4), the Committee of Ministers (2.5.5), and the Parliamentary Assembly (2.6.2).

[134] Liora Lazarus and Natasha Simonsen, 'Judicial Review and Parliamentary Debate: Enriching the Doctrine of Due Deference', in Hunt, Hooper, and Yowell, eds. (n 2): 385, 386.

[135] Aileen Kavanagh, 'Defending Deference in Public Law and Constitutional Theory', *Law Quarterly Review* 126 (2010): 222; Jeff King, *Judging Social Rights* (Cambridge: Cambridge University Press, 2012) Part II; Murray Hunt, 'Sovereignty's Blight: Why Contemporary Public Law Needs the Concept of "Due Deference"', in Nicholas Bamforth and Peter Leyland, eds., *Public Law in a Multi-Layered Constitution* (Oxford: Hart Publishing, 2003); Alison Young, 'In Defence of Due Deference', *Modern Law Review* 72 (2009): 554.

decision-making, and there are no hard boundaries between legal and political redress. Another dimension of this approach is that judges should assign weight, and sometimes considerable weight, to the views of elected parliamentarians and decision-makers in public institutions to whom legislators have delegated policy-making and interpretative roles.

Some,[136] but not all,[137] advocates of the practice of judicial deference have gone further to elaborate a doctrine of judicial restraint structured around certain explicit principles. Notably, Kavanagh distinguishes between 'minimal' and 'substantial' judicial deference.[138] Minimal deference is always due and simply requires that judges 'cannot make light of, or be sceptical about, attempts by Parliament to solve a social problem in legislation'. Substantial deference has to be 'earned' by the elected branches and is justified only where a court considers itself to suffer from particular institutional shortcomings with regard to the matter at hand. These are cases in which a court judges parliament or the executive to have more institutional competence; more expertise, and/or greater legitimacy to assess a particular issue.

While debate about judicial deference has commonly been addressed to constitutional arrangements within a state, it is also relevant to supranational courts such as the ECtHR. Indeed, the arguments for judicial deference are commonly held to apply with *greater* force to supranational than national courts.[139] In respect of the ECHR, this is because of the principle of subsidiarity, which reinforces the primary duty of states to secure the human rights set out in the Convention, and the margin of appreciation which follows from that principle (see 2.9). For Lazarus and Simonsen, '[i]n the Strasbourg context, assessing the quality of legislative debate in deciding whether a particular measure falls within the margin of appreciation allows the principle of subsidiarity to operate to its fullest effect'.[140]

How, then, has the Court approached the development of a fuller concept of subsidiarity?

4.5.2 The Court's approach: deepening the concept of subsidiarity?

Judge Robert Spano identifies a trend in the ECtHR's case law towards 'a more foreseeable and rational application of the margin of appreciation in line with a more robust concept of subsidiarity' inspired by the Brighton Declaration of

[136] See, for example, Young (n 135); King (n 135) Part II.

[137] See, for example, T.R.S. Allan, 'Deference, Defiance, and Doctrine: Defining the Limits of Judicial Review', *University of Toronto Law Journal* 60(1) (2010): 41; Tom Hickman, *Public Law after the Human Rights Act* (Oxford: Hart Publishing, 2012).

[138] Aileen Kavanagh, *Constitutional Review under the Human Rights Act* (Cambridge: Cambridge University Press, 2009) 181–2.

[139] Aileen Kavanagh, 'Proportionality and Parliamentary Debates: Exploring Some Forbidden Territory', *Oxford Journal of Legal Studies* 34(3) (2014): 443, 478; Janneke Gerards, 'Pluralism, Deference and the Margin of Appreciation', *European Law Journal* 17(1) (2011): 80, 118–20.

[140] Lazarus and Simonsen (n 134) 390.

2012.[141] This case law, he explains, has three elements: first, the 'democratic element' according to which '[t]he Court acknowledges that national authorities have "direct democratic legitimation"'; secondly, the element of domestic expertise and knowledge, which recognizes that the national authorities are 'better placed than an international court to evaluate local needs and conditions'; and, thirdly, the policy element, manifested in the role of the domestic policy-maker to which the Strasbourg Court gives special weight.

Saul notes that the ECtHR's standard approach to deference is based on the assumption that domestic institutions and decision-making processes are working optimally.[142] What is distinctive within a strengthened concept of subsidiarity is that this assumption is probed using qualitative assessments of the parliamentary process under review. The Court hinted at this development in its submission to the Brussels High-Level Conference in March 2015, when it highlighted case law showing that,

> [T]he fact that the parliamentary record indicates that there was *in-depth consideration* of the human rights implications of an enactment can be of significance in certain types of case, i.e. in which the margin of appreciation arises (emphasis added).[143]

A recent prominent case of this type is *Animal Defenders International v UK*, in which the Grand Chamber upheld by a narrow majority (9–8) the UK's ban on political advertising on television and radio as a necessary interference with the right to free expression.[144] The majority held that, when assessing the compatibility of a general measure with the Convention, '[t]he quality of the parliamentary and judicial review of the necessity of the measure is of particular importance in this respect, including to the operation of the relevant margin of appreciation'.[145]

These considerations are not entirely novel features of the Court's case law; Judge Spano draws attention to cases going back more than a decade that are 'classic example[s] of the appropriate way of constructing and applying a meaningful level of deference afforded by the Court in accordance with the principle of subsidiarity'.[146] Yet in Judge Spano's view, *Animal Defenders International* and a line of similar recent cases,[147]

[141] Robert Spano, 'The European Court of Human Rights: Anti-Democratic or Guardian of Fundamental Values?', UK Human Rights blog, 19 November 2014.

[142] Matthew Saul, 'The ECtHR's Margin of Appreciation and the Process of National Parliaments', *Human Rights Law Review* 15 (2015): 745, 751.

[143] European Court of Human Rights, Contribution of the Court to the Brussels Conference, 26 January 2015, para. 14.

[144] *Animal Defenders International v UK*, No. 48876/08, 22 April 2013 [GC]. The decision was a departure from previous case law in *VgT Verein gegen Tierfabrik v Switzerland*, No. 32772/02, 30 June 2009, in which the authorities' refusal to broadcast a commercial concerning animal welfare was found to be a violation of Article 10.

[145] *Animal Defenders International v UK* (n 144) para. 108.

[146] Robert Spano, 'Universality or Diversity of Human Rights? Strasbourg in the Age of Subsidiarity', *Human Rights Law Review* 14 (2014): 487. See, for example, *Hatton and Others v UK*, No. 36022/97, 8 July 2003 [GC], paras. 128–9.

[147] See, for example, *Murphy v Ireland*, No. 44179/98, 10 July 2003, para. 73; *Maurice v France*, No. 11810/03, 6 October 2005 [GC], para. 121; *Ždanoka v Latvia*, No. 58278/00, 16 March 2006

demonstrate that the Strasbourg Court is currently in the process of reformulating the substantive and procedural criteria that regulate the appropriate level of deference to be afforded to Member States so as to implement a more robust and coherent concept of subsidiarity in conformity with [the Brighton Declaration] and Protocol 15 [of the Convention].[148]

These judgments, he adds,

stand for the important proposition that when examining whether and to what extent the Court should grant a Member State a margin of appreciation, as to the latter's assessment of the necessity and proportionality of a restriction on human rights, the quality of decision-making, both at the legislative stage and before the courts, is crucial *and may ultimately be decisive in borderline cases* (emphasis added).[149]

At the same time, Judge Spano ventures, the Court's refinement of the principle of subsidiarity 'addresses to some extent' the alleged democratic deficit in respect of the Court's relationship with domestic democratic institutions.[150] Not all of his fellow judges are in agreement with what he terms this 'qualitative and democracy-enhancing approach' to the Court's application of the principle of subsidiarity and the margin of appreciation.[151] This much is evident from the narrow margin in *Animal Defenders International*, in which the dissenters argued that 'excessive weight' had been attached to the quality of the parliamentary process in the case.[152] Academic commentary, too, has been divided on the judgment.[153] Saul ventures that, although the Court is sometimes divided and frequently implicit or ambiguous[154] about the extent to which it has connected the quality of parliamentary process and its determination of the margin of appreciation, there is a growing body of case law that 'supports the thesis of deeper subsidiarity in relation

[GC], para. 134; *Evans v UK*, No. 6339/05, 10 April 2007 [GC], para. 86; *A, B and C v Ireland*, No. 25579/05, 10 December 2010 [GC], para. 239; *SH v Austria*, No. 57813/00, 3 November 2011 [GC], para. 114; *Shindler v UK*, No. 19840/09, 22 April 2013, para. 117; *National Union of Rail, Maritime and Transport Workers v UK*, No. 31045/10, 8 April 2014, para. 89. Other pertinent judgments issued since the publication of Judge Spano's article include: *Lambert and Others v France*, No. 46043/14, 5 June 2015 [GC], para. 181; *Parrillo v Italy*, No. 46470/11, 27 August 2015 [GC], paras. 183–8.

148 Spano (n 146) 498. For discussion of Protocol No. 15 of the ECHR, see 2.9.

149 Spano (n 146) 498. 150 Spano (n 146) 499. 151 Spano (n 146) 497.

152 Joint dissenting opinion of Judges Ziemele, Sajó, Kalaydjieva, Vučinić, and de Gaetano, para. 9. Contrast this view with the Concurring opinion of Judge Bratza, para. 12.

153 Contrast, for example, Tom Wyn Lewis, 'Animal Defenders International v United Kingdom: Sensible Dialogue or a Bad Case of Strasbourg Jitters?', *Modern Law Review* 77(3) (2014): 460 and Jeff King, 'Deference, Dialogue and Animal Defenders International', UK Constitutional Law Association blog, 25 April 2013.

154 See, for example, *Lindheim v Norway*, Nos. 13221/08 and 2139/10, 12 June 2012, in which the applicant (para. 85) and the government (para. 118) gave conflicting opinions as to the quality of parliamentary process that led to reform of the law on ground lease agreements. The Court held that rent controls were disproportionate given the excessive burden on the lessors under the lease conditions imposed by the state, and referred (para. 128) to the fact that no specific assessment had been made of whether the law 'achieved a "fair balance" between the interests of the lessors, on the one hand, and those of the lessees, on the other hand'. The Court did not, however, expressly relate the quality of the decision-making process to its decision to apply a narrow margin of appreciation.

to parliaments'.[155] Detailed reviews of case law conducted separately by Saul and Kavanagh[156] identify several features of this case law.

First, there has been a preponderance of 'positive inference' cases, in which the Court has given weight to the fact that legislation was the product of meaningful parliamentary engagement with the rights issue, over 'negative inference' cases, in which judges have highlighted the absence of such engagement.[157] Both positive and negative inference cases have concerned general measures affecting rights that 'expressly, or at least by strong implication'[158] allow for restrictions by states, commonly involving either the allocation of resources or the need to strike a fair balance between competing interests. This observation underlines the importance for the Court of ensuring that its developing approach to deference is not applied in inappropriate contexts, such as in relation to absolute rights that are not capable of justified limitation.

Animal Defenders International is the stand-out example of a positive inference case. The Court noted that the ban on political advertising was 'the culmination of an exceptional examination by parliamentary bodies of the cultural, political and legal aspects of the prohibition'.[159] It was this particular competence of parliament—and the extensive pre-legislative consultation on the Convention compatibility of the prohibition (including by the JCHR; see 7.6.3)—which explained the degree of deference shown by the domestic courts to parliament's decision to adopt the ban.[160] For its part, the ECtHR attached 'considerable weight to these exacting and pertinent reviews, by both parliamentary and judicial bodies'.[161]

Another UK case, *Hirst* on prisoner voting rights, is the most prominent example of a negative inference case, in which the Court narrowed the margin of appreciation on the basis that 'there is no evidence that Parliament has ever sought to weigh the competing interests or to assess the proportionality of a blanket ban on the right of a convicted prisoner to vote' (see 7.6.1).[162] The weight attached to the absence of parliamentary engagement, although it was not determinative in this case,[163] excited controversy among the five dissenting judges, who argued that it was 'not for the Court to prescribe the way in which national legislatures carry out their legislative functions'.[164]

[155] Saul (n 142) 772. [156] Kavanagh (n 139) 472–8.

[157] Kavanagh (n 139) 456–7, 473–4. [158] Spano (n 146) 499.

[159] *Animal Defenders International v UK* (n 144) para. 114.

[160] *Animal Defenders International v UK* (n 144) para. 115.

[161] *Animal Defenders International v UK* (n 144) para. 116.

[162] *Hirst v UK (No.2)*, No. 74025/01, 6 October 2005 [GC], para. 79. See also *Greens and MT v UK*, Nos. 60041/08 and 60054/08, 23 November 2010, para. 31, which cites the 'overriding disappointment' expressed by the Joint Committee on Human Rights at the lack of progress on implementing *Hirst*. For other negative inference cases, see *Christine Goodwin v UK*, No. 28957/95, 11 July 2002 [GC], paras. 92–3; *Dickson v UK*, No. 44362/04, 4 December 2007, para. 83.

[163] Kavanagh (n 139) 476–7.

[164] Joint dissenting opinion of Judges Wildhaber, Costa, Lorenzen, Kovler, and Jebens, para. 7. This concern was echoed in the joint concurring opinion of Judges Tulkens and Zagrebelsky: 'This is an area in which two sources of legitimacy meet, the Court on the one hand and the national parliament on the other. This is a difficult and slippery terrain for the Court in view of the nature of its role, especially when it itself accepts that a wide margin of appreciation must be allowed to the Contracting States.'

The second notable feature of the case law under review is the type of parliamentary processes that have been assessed by the Court. As noted at 1.2.3, parliamentary human rights activity, whether for legislative or general oversight purposes, is diverse. It may take place in a plenary formation or in committees or sub-committees. It may involve correspondence with ministers, or the gathering of oral or written evidence; and it may be supplemented by commissions or consultations that are external to parliament but influence its decisions. It may or may not involve a vote. Saul concludes that all these formations and activities have fallen within the scope of the Court's concept of parliamentary process.[165] For committee work, he observes, the Court has been particularly interested in consultations and reports; while for plenary sessions it has attached value to debates and votes. In some cases, the ECtHR gave a positive inference to the presence of all of these,[166] as well as, in the case of *Animal Defenders International*, correspondence with ministers and the recommendations of an advisory committee (the Committee on Standards in Public Life created by the government).[167]

A third characteristic of the case law under review is its tendency to 'focus on the decision-making quality and its democratic pedigree, rather than assessing the merits of the individual arguments advanced in support of the policy'.[168] For example, the Court has variously deferred to parliamentary consideration that was 'meticulous';[169] 'careful and cautious';[170] 'comprehensive' in taking account of legal, ethical and social considerations;[171] or 'exceptionally detailed' and 'the fruit of much reflection, consultation and debate'.[172] In so doing, the Court has generally opted for a less exacting form of scrutiny of parliamentary conduct than would be involved in evaluating the sufficiency of the reasons and justification for a rights-restricting measure.[173]

A fourth and related feature of the case law is that, while the quality of debate and decision-making may be an influential factor in some cases, it is not necessarily determinative, since 'there will be some issues where no amount of debate will save an otherwise rights-violating measure'.[174] The Court has itself stated that even where a legislature debates an issue repeatedly, this does not mean that the conclusion arrived at by legislators will necessarily be Convention compliant: 'It simply means that that review is taken into consideration by the Court for the purpose of deciding whether a fair balance has been struck between competing interests.'[175]

165 Saul (n 142) 760–2.

166 See, for example, *Evans v UK* (n 147) paras. 33, 36; *SAS v France*, No. 43835/11, 1 July 2014 [GC], paras. 15–17, 26–7, 141, 148–9; *Shindler v UK* (n 147) para. 117.

167 *Animal Defenders International v UK* (n 144) paras. 44–6, 53, 56, 114.

168 Kavanagh (n 139) 476.

169 *Lambert and Others v France* (n 147) para. 181.

170 *SH v Austria* (n 147) para. 114.

171 *Maurice v France* (n 147) para. 121.

172 *Evans v UK* (n 147) para. 86.

173 See, however, *Animal Defenders International v UK* (n 144), Dissenting opinion of Judge Tulkens, joined by Judges Spielmann and Laffranque, paras. 16–20; *Parrillo v Italy* (n 147), Dissenting opinion of Judge Sajó, paras. 12–13.

174 Kavanagh (n 139) 477.

175 *Shindler v UK* (n 147) para. 117.

The fifth area of interest is the extent to which the Court sets out the criteria it uses to assess the quality of parliamentary process. Saul notes that while the Court has not always been explicit or detailed in this regard, it does appear to be 'developing a framework of considerations for the assessment of parliamentary processes'.[176] This framework, he suggests, is informed by the Court's understanding of the three main grounds for its subsidiary role identified above by Judge Spano: democracy, domestic expertise, and the nature and context of the domestic decision-maker. Thus, for example, the Court has valued the participatory quality of committee-led consultations;[177] and the representative quality of debates, especially those that take place within elected chambers.[178] In relation to domestic expertise, the Court has referred approvingly to the use by parliament of expert evidence providing different perspectives on the legal, social, political, cultural, or ethical aspects of a legislative proposal.[179] In attaching weight to the views of domestic decision-makers, Saul observes, the Court has referred to the extent to which human rights questions were kept under review over a long time period,[180] or were reviewed simultaneously by a range of parliamentary, judicial, and independent bodies.[181] The degree of cross-party consensus for a legislative measure is sometimes also referred to, but does not appear to be a determinative factor.[182]

In summary, reviews of ECtHR case law reveal a prevalence of positive inference over negative inference cases. The Court has taken into account a variety of parliamentary formations and activities and has principally focused on assessing the quality of the decision-making process rather than the outcome of that process, without regarding that assessment as necessarily determinative. As Saul notes, the Court has not been explicit about the criteria it uses for assessing the quality of parliamentary process, but a number of recurring features indicate aspects of process that the Court 'can be construed as valuing', each of which connects to the well-established articulation of the basis of its subsidiary role.[183]

4.5.3 Risks and opportunities

The Court's developing approach to subsidiarity outlined above is a matter of uncertainty and contention, both as to its significance and future development. The various features of the parliamentary process referred to by the Court do not appear

[176] Saul (n 142) 767. [177] See, for example, *Evans v UK* (n 147) paras. 31, 87.
[178] See, for example, *Maurice v France* (n 147) para. 121.
[179] See, for example, *Parrillo v Italy* (n 147) para. 184.
[180] See, for example, *SH v Austria* (n 147) para. 118; *Shindler v UK* (n 147) para. 117.
[181] See, for example, *SAS v France* (n 166) para. 26; *Lambert and Others v France* (n 147) para. 181.
[182] Contrast, for example, two judgments in which the state was afforded a wide margin of appreciation even though the political context in each case differed sharply: *Animal Defenders International v UK* (n 144) para. 114, which refers to the unanimous cross-party support for the legislation concerned, and *National Union of Rail, Maritime and Transport Workers v UK* (n 147) para. 89, which notes that the statutory ban on secondary strikes at issue in the case was 'sharply contested' by the opposition in parliament.
[183] Saul (n 142) 767.

to exist in any clear relationship or hierarchy in its jurisprudence.[184] The question remains as to how far, and on what basis, the Court should attach weight to each of the features—especially where some, but not all, are present.[185] The Court's sometimes ambiguous, indeterminate, or inconsistent references to the quality of parliamentary process, and the strength of judicial dissent on the matter in some cases, suggest that it is unlikely to proceed swiftly towards a more explicit articulation of, as Judge Spano puts it, a more 'robust and coherent' concept of subsidiarity.

For Judge Spano, the Court's willingness to defer to the reasoned assessment by national authorities of their Convention obligations 'does not introduce, in essence, any novel feature into Strasbourg jurisprudence, but constitutes rather a further refinement or reformulation of pre-existing doctrines'.[186] Saul adds that the Court is likely to be alive to the risk that 'deepening its framework beyond what is already in place will run the risk of the Court assuming a primary rather than secondary role in the determination of what parliamentary process should look like'.[187] In this sense, the underlying logic of subsidiarity appears to place inherent limits to the strength of the 'signal' that the Court may wish to send to states about the promotion of procedural justice or standards of political democracy.

Such caution may disappoint commentators like Lazarus and Simonsen, who, while welcoming the Strasbourg Court's approach to evaluating the quality of parliamentary deliberation in *Animal Defenders International*, suggest that it is in 'urgent need of further substantiation' by both domestic and supranational courts in order to 'deepen the rigour' with which deference is exercised towards political bodies on democratic grounds.[188] At the same time, they acknowledge that explicit criteria might be resisted on the grounds that they might increase the length or complexity of legal proceedings; or that they are insensitive both to the limited capacity and expertise of parliamentarians with regards to human rights and institutional constraints such as the crowded parliamentary agenda.[189] Other authors have expressed

[184] See, for example, the questions concerning the Court's qualitative assessment of parliamentary process posed by the Human Rights Centre at Ghent University in the case of *Fouzia Dakir v Belgium*, Application No. 4619/12, concerning the ban in Belgium on covering the face in public. We are grateful to Matthew Saul at the University of Oslo for drawing this submission to our attention.

[185] See, for example, the dissenting opinion of Judge Sajó in *Parrillo v Italy* (n 147) at para. 12, which implies that cross-party support should be a weighty factor in any determination by the ECtHR to defer to the quality of the parliamentary process in its application of the margin of appreciation. Judge Sajó departed from the majority on the Grand Chamber, which had found that a 2004 Italian law prohibiting experiments on human embryos, including for the purposes of scientific research, fell within the margin of appreciation, even though it had been enacted without cross-party support and amid 'serious disagreement' in society, as expressed in an (inquorate) referendum on the issue. The majority judgment does not refer to the extent of cross-party support for the measure; rather, it emphasizes (para. 184) the fact that the legislative debate had 'taken account of the different scientific and ethical opinions and questions' on the matter.

[186] Spano (n 146) 491. [187] Saul (n 142) 773.

[188] Lazarus and Simonsen (n 134) 402. Lazarus and Simonsen (403) propose general criteria that should be used as the basis for a prior assessment of the quality of democratic deliberation, including the representative conditions of democratic debate and the extent to which parliament meaningfully engaged with the views and interests of minority rights bearers.

[189] Lazarus and Simonsen (n 134) 392. See also Carolyn Evans and Simon Evans, 'Legislative Scrutiny Committees and Parliamentary Conceptions of Human Rights', *Public Law* Winter (2006): 785, 786.

concern about the potential 'chilling' effect of judicial scrutiny on parliamentary speech.[190] At the European level, there is a possibility that more systematic scrutiny of parliamentary conduct, especially in negative inference cases, might engender resistance rather than providing a motivation for enhanced deliberation. In this sense, the Court's developing approach to deference is by no means risk free.

Further, developing a consistent approach in respect of the deference paid to parliamentary deliberation poses particular challenges for a supranational court such as the ECtHR—challenges which are not discernible from analysis of any single judgment. The Court might potentially need to assess the quality of the process in any of the forty-seven parliaments rooted in different legal and political systems across the Council of Europe. Moreover, its appraisal of the process in any particular case needs to be informed by an underlying assessment of the democratic credentials of the parliamentary body in question, a task complicated by the close overlap between different constitutional organs in systems where there is strong executive control of parliament.

While the Court has, as Saul's review illustrates, cast the net wide in respect of the types of activity and parliamentary formation it has included in its qualitative assessments, it is dependent on the submissions of both applicants and governments in order to ensure that such assessments are well informed and comprehensive. Even then, important aspects of parliamentary process may be inaccessible, such as preparatory materials, unpublished correspondence with ministers, or simply discussion that takes place in the corridors, rather than the debating chamber or committee rooms, of parliaments. Further, the Court may also need to understand the workings of the legislative agenda and the competing priorities facing parliament as a whole and individual parliamentarians as part of their democratic mandate. Consequently,

> [C]aution must be exercised by courts, especially supra-national courts from which there is no appeal, in their approach to judging the activities of parliaments for conformity with external standards on issues to which there can reasonably be a plurality of views.[191]

Equally, the Court must be alive to the risk that executives or parliaments may orchestrate proceedings or engage in shallow 'rights talk' in order to create the appearance of democratic deliberation about a human rights matter in an attempt to earn deference which is not, in fact, warranted.[192] Conversely, the Court may

[190] Hayley J. Hooper, 'The Use of Parliamentary Materials in Proportionality Judgments', in Hunt, Hooper, and Yowell, eds. (n 2): 363, 365.

[191] Hooper (n 190) 384. Hooper argues (383) that, in *Hirst*, the ECtHR 'based its consideration to refuse the benefit of the margin of appreciation on an extremely limited understanding of the legislative agenda, and in turn overlooked in many respects what Parliament does in a wider constitutional sense'.

[192] This difficulty is illustrated by the contrasting appraisals of the quality of the backbench debate in the UK Parliament on prisoner voting rights. In its intervention in the case of *Scoppola v Italy (No. 3)*, No. 126/05, 22 May 2012 (para. 79), the UK government based its argument that *Hirst* should be overturned in part on the fact that the compatibility of the impugned legislation with the guidelines established in *Hirst* had been debated in the House of Commons and that MPs had voted by 234 to twenty-two against legislative reform. However, as discussed at 7.6.1, several authors have questioned the quality of the debate, suggesting that it failed substantively to reassess the justification for the legislation.

need to recognize the presence of pertinent democratic debate on a matter of law or policy implicating human rights even when the language of rights is not explicitly used.[193]

These pragmatic considerations should guide the ECtHR's developing approach to deference but do not, in our view, invalidate the larger goal of strengthening democratic dialogue between parliaments and the Court. Such an approach accords with the parliamentary conception of rights envisaged by Evans and Evans, which aims not to 'second guess judges or apply legal standards in a rote manner' but to bring political values and experience into play, moving away from legal notions when this best fits parliament's conception of 'community understandings of rights'.[194] Overall, the concerns outlined above vindicate the Court's developing practice of attaching no *automatic* or *determinative* weight to legislative deliberation, but demonstrating clearly and consistently in its judgments when it has examined parliamentary proceedings and found reason to defer to the arguments advanced therein.

The nuanced or equivocal signal that might thereby be transmitted to political bodies raises the important question of how far the Court's assessment of parliamentary process will, in fact, act as a 'catalyst for enhanced democratic deliberation'.[195] Put another way, if the Court seeks to send a signal to domestic actors, how likely are they to hear it? In theory, both positive and negative inference cases should incentivize parliaments to take human rights standards and judgments into account and deliberate about them in transparent and reasoned manner during the legislative process. Such influence is evident in instances where a parliament debates legislative change pursuant to a judgment of the Court, with the clear intention of ensuring that the resulting reform should not similarly be found in breach of the Convention.[196] In such cases, Lazarus and Simonsen note, by prompting reconsideration of rights-restricting legislation, a court 'enriches the deliberative process'.[197]

A further question to be confronted is how, in practice, members of parliament in Council of Europe states will be made more aware of the possibility of 'earning' deference from the Court, since this is likely to appear an abstract issue to many of them. Parliamentarians' often sporadic approach to the monitoring of judgments, and almost invariable reliance on summarized reports of judgments, implies a vital role for intermediaries in highlighting this development in the Court's case law and its implications for parliaments. Such intermediaries include parliamentary and government legal advisers, Council of Europe bodies, national human rights institutions, and civil society actors.

[193] Lazarus and Simonsen (n 134) 398.

[194] Evans and Evans (n 189) 806.

[195] Kavanagh (n 139) 466.

[196] As happened, for example, following the case of *Christine Goodwin v UK* (n 162) and the ensuing legislative debate leading to the Gender Recognition Act 2004. See Aruna Sathanapally, *Beyond Disagreement: Open Remedies in Human Rights Adjudication* (Oxford: Oxford University Press, 2012) 166–72.

[197] Lazarus and Simonsen (n 134) 400.

Applicants and their legal representatives also have every incentive to alert the Court to deficiencies in the parliamentary process. Third-party interveners also have a role to play in informing the Court's assessment of the quality of parliamentary process, both in respect of specific cases and at a more general level.[198] Moreover, governments should be incentivized to include in their submissions to the Court detail of parliamentary consideration of the issues at stake.

Indeed, another effect of encouraging democratic institutions to earn deference from the ECtHR is that it may prompt *executives* to assign greater priority to ensuring that legislative deliberation occurs; for example, by inviting scrutiny of draft legislation at an early stage or ensuring that parliaments are fully informed about the executive's proposed response to an adverse judgment.[199] Given that governments are the main interlocutors of the Court, it may be within the executive that the signal sent by judicial scrutiny of democratic deliberation is heard first and loudest. The Court could encourage such behaviour to become institutionalized by routinely requiring governments to provide it with all relevant evidence of parliamentary consideration of the human rights compatibility of laws which are the subject of applications, along with, for example, evidence of ECHR impact assessment in policy-making and reasoned statements of compatibility accompanying legislation—and, in turn, by routinely including within judgments 'a more explicit explanation of the role played by that parliamentary consideration (or lack of it)' in its application of the margin of appreciation.[200]

4.6 Resolving Disagreements about Rights

If the deepening of subsidiarity creates opportunities for a dialogic relationship between the ECtHR and political actors at the domestic level, an issue still to be confronted is what happens when apparently irresolvable disagreements arise between them.[201] Among other cases, the *Hirst* judgment on prisoner voting rights, which remains unresolved after a decade, has given rise to unprecedented tension between the UK and the ECtHR—leading, as noted at 1.1.2, proposals to make the Court's judgments merely advisory in respect of the UK.[202] In February 2011, backbench MPs debated a motion introduced by Labour MP Jack Straw and David Davis of

[198] See, for example, Human Rights Centre, Ghent University (n 184).

[199] The UK government showed itself to be aware of this factor when, in the course of its response to the ECtHR judgment on retention of biometric data (*S and Marper*, Nos. 30562/04 and 30566/04, 4 December 2008 [GC]) it suggested that 'where a complex issue has been subjected to Parliamentary scrutiny, there is an argument that a wide margin of appreciation should be applied' (see 7.6.2). See Home Office Memorandum on the Protection of Freedoms Bill, February 2011, para. 13.

[200] Murray Hunt, 'Enhancing Parliaments' Role in the Protection and Realisation of Human Rights', in Hunt, Hooper, and Yowell, eds. (n 2): 469, 474.

[201] We are grateful to Dr Ed Bates of the University of Leicester for helpful comments on a draft of this section.

[202] Ed Bates, 'Analysing the Prisoner Voting Saga and the British Challenge to Strasbourg', *Human Rights Law Review* 14 (2014): 503. See also the discussion at 7.6.1.

the Conservatives that 'legislative decisions of this nature should be a matter for democratically-elected lawmakers' (see 7.6.1). Straw ventured that the ECtHR was 'setting itself up as a Supreme Court for Europe, with an ever-widening remit' and so 'should be subject to some form of democratic override'.[203] In *Hirst*, he argued, the UK parliament was 'faced with a court judgment following which, without warrant from the treaties to which we signed up, we as elected MPs are expected to do the opposite of that in which we believe'. For his part, Davis stated that MPs needed to have 'the right of recall, the right of review and the right of challenge'.[204]

The idea of a democratic override of ECtHR decisions also surfaced in the Commission on a Bill of Rights, which was formed in 2011 to examine options for reform of UK human rights law.[205] Several proposals were made, none of which commanded the support of the full Commission: for example, that the Parliamentary Assembly or the Committee of Ministers, or both, might be given the authority to override a Court decision, or that the Committee of Ministers might not enforce a judgment if the state's 'most senior democratic institution' clearly opposed it.

Some senior judicial figures in the UK, too, have promoted this idea. Notably, in the view of the former Lord Chief Justice, Lord Judge, the UK parliament is not bound 'to enact laws which will bring the decisions of the Strasbourg Court into effect'.[206]

While this debate has thus far surfaced most visibly in the UK, Føllesdal ventures that criticism of the ECtHR by member states '*may* give rise to a new phenomenon: principled non-compliance by a State as an accountability mechanism and ultimate correction device' (emphasis in original), akin to an act of civil disobedience in the domestic setting.[207] The idea of 'principled non-compliance' surfaced in inter-governmental discussion of reform of the Convention system, but was rejected since it would 'involve problems of incompatibility with the principle of the rule of law'.[208] However, in view of proposals to legislate to make ECtHR judgments merely advisory in respect of the UK (see 1.1.2), it seems inevitable that the binding authority of the Court's judgments will continue to face political

[203] HC Deb, 10 February 2011, vol. 523, col. 503. See also Jack Straw, *Aspects of Law Reform: An Insider's Perspective* (Cambridge: Cambridge University Press, 2013) 26; The Rt Hon. Lord Judge, 'Constitutional Change: Unfinished Business', University College London, 4 December 2013, para. 47.

[204] HC Deb, 10 February 2011, vol. 523, col. 498.

[205] Side letter on Reform of the European Court of Human Rights from Sir Leigh Lewis KCB, Chair of the Commission on a Bill of Rights, to Deputy Prime Minster, Nick Clegg MP, and Secretary of State for Justice, Kenneth Clarke MP, 28 July 2011, 4–5.

[206] Lord Judge, 'A View from London', *Counsel*, October 2014.

[207] Andreas Føllesdal, 'Accountability and Authority' in Proceedings of the MultiRights Annual Conference on 'The Long-Term Future of the European Court of Human Rights', organized by PluriCourts under the auspices of the Council of Europe, Holmenkollen Park Hotel, Oslo, Norway, 7–8 April 2014, 84.

[208] Steering Committee for Human Rights, Drafting Group 'F' on Reform of the Court (GT-GDR-F), Draft text on preserving and reinforcing the current system, GT-GDR-F(2015)002, 2 February 2015, para. 42.

challenge. Indeed, senior figures in the Court have begun to respond to this challenge. The President of the ECtHR, Dean Spielmann, ventured in 2014 that, there is 'a natural tension between fundamental rights and democracy. The strength of the Convention lies in recognising that democracy cannot be meaningful unless it operates within the rule of law'.[209] Consequently, 'in some situations the rule of law trumps the majority view, even if expressed through a democratic process'. Spielmann added: 'That is why the idea of any "democratic override" … is inimical to the effective protection of human rights and would undermine the whole system set up by the Convention.'

In the rest of this section, we examine justifications that have been advanced in political and scholarly debate for 'democratic override' of ECtHR judgments (or indeed, the judgments or decisions of any international human rights body). We focus in particular on the proposed mechanisms for democratic override in the European Convention context in order to address what we consider to be a lacuna in the debate thus far—namely, how such arrangements would work in practice. We argue that the justifications and proposed mechanisms are misconceived and unworkable, and we propose an alternative and, in our view, preferable approach to resolving disagreements between national parliaments and the Court.

The argument for ultimate authority to rest with domestic political institutions connects to the discussion at 4.4 about the extent to which the decisions of international human rights courts are capable of democratic justification. For Bellamy, 'it remains important for the democratic legitimacy of … judicial opinions that the final word lies with the legislature'.

> [G]iven that courts may be as mistaken as legislators, the possibility for a democratic override of an [international human rights court] judgment must … exist, with such decisions resting with a consensus among the representatives of the democratic governments, who should be ultimately charged with monitoring state compliance with the Court's rulings.[210]

On this account, the binding nature of final judgments of the ECtHR under Article 46(1) is problematic in respect of the Court's democratic legitimacy, notwithstanding the fact that its decisions do not automatically invalidate domestic legislation but leave considerable discretion to domestic authorities about how to comply. Bellamy proposes that the present arrangement be replaced by a system in which the Committee of Ministers becomes 'the final court of appeal',[211] in order that democratic states which challenge decisions of the Court would ultimately be judged by their peers.[212]

Several immediate objections may be made to the notion of democratic override thereby envisaged. First, it is not clear what it entails. Bellamy's argument is inconsistent in that he first suggests a *legislative* override, only to propose that *governments* (via peer review within the Committee of Ministers) should have the final word as to whether a judgment of the ECtHR should be able to be ignored.

[209] Dean Spielmann, 'A View from Strasbourg', *Counsel*, April 2014.
[210] Bellamy (n 103) 1034.
[211] Bellamy (n 103) 1037.
[212] Bellamy (n 103) 1034.

The latter option would appear to make the ultimate assessment of whether ECtHR judgments should be implemented subject to negotiations behind closed doors between government representatives (in practice, diplomats and legal advisers) and an unelected secretariat. As noted at 2.8, the present system of supervision under the Committee of Ministers is far from immune to the perils of over-politicization and diplomatic bargaining between states. Arguably, then, Bellamy's proposed system of executive override would be *less* democratically accountable than the present arrangements in which, although inter-governmental meetings are private, domestic constituencies, including parliaments, are able to hold governments publicly to account for their action or inaction in respect of legally binding judgments of the ECtHR. Indeed, greater democratic accountability would more easily be achieved by reforming the current system, in which the Committee of Ministers' meetings are closed, to one in which they are at least sometimes opened to external observers, and by giving further impetus to the role in the supervision process of the Parliamentary Assembly (see 2.6 and 2.8).

Moreover, *either* legislative *or* executive override would be likely to give rise to the problem of non-rights-respecting states with weak or compliant parliaments evading their obligations under the Convention. Bellamy elsewhere clarifies that his proposed scheme rests on the assumption that signatories to an international human rights court are 'at least credibly democratising', since they would,

> appreciate the need to attune rights to domestic situations and the adverse reaction an [international human rights court] decision perceived as insensitive to such considerations and in error might arouse. Yet, that need not mean they would tolerate almost any objection to a ruling that proved inconvenient for the government concerned—quite the contrary. For they would also be fully alive to the dangers of allowing states to renege on their solidaristic obligations and of undermining the Court's authority through frivolous or self-serving challenges—particularly with regard to democratizing states.[213]

Bellamy acknowledges that many problems stand in the way of realizing such a scheme, and that he is merely seeking to establish its 'normative and institutional underpinnings'.[214] Nevertheless, he argues that 'the plausibility of this approach can be gauged by the significant degree to which the [ECtHR] can be assimilated to it'.[215] The fact that signatories must meet certain democratic standards; the governance structure provided by the Committee of Ministers and the Parliamentary Assembly; the Court's application of the margin of appreciation; and the principle of subsidiarity under which the primary duty for the implementation of Convention rights rests with domestic legal and political organs—all these, in Bellamy's view, contribute to making the Convention system one which might be regarded as realizing political constitutionalism at a regional level.[216] From this perspective, the point where the Convention system 'falls down' is in the binding force of final judgments of the ECtHR.[217]

213 Bellamy (n 103) 1034.
214 Bellamy (n 103) 1035.
215 Bellamy (n 103) 1035.
216 Bellamy (n 103) 1035–7.
217 Bellamy (n 103) 1037.

It appears, then, that Bellamy's proposal for democratic override is intended to apply to the ECtHR *under current conditions* and not in a future or idealized scheme. If so, his faith in the sincerity of states' motives is highly contestable. For example, it is indisputable that at least some of the criticism of the ECtHR from political actors in the UK is 'frivolous or self-serving' in the sense that it is frequently expressed in populist terms and appears at times to have opportunistic motives.[218] It might be counter-argued that such challenges would be made only in exceptional circumstances and would not, therefore, unduly disturb the authority of the Court or the system of supervision under the Committee of Ministers. It might also be suggested that representatives of democratic governments, working through the Committee of Ministers, would be able to spot bad faith challenges to a judgment of the Court and refuse to override it, thereby preserving the integrity of the system. However, neither of these outcomes could be guaranteed. On the first point, once the principle is admitted that a state can ignore a judgment and seek other states' approval for its stance, there is no inherent limit to how often, or in what circumstances, it might be invoked, nor any certainty that it would not prompt a contagion in this direction. On the contrary, once formalized as proposed by Bellamy, a system of override could prove irresistible; one need only recall the judgments in the Court's history that were highly contentious at the time, even though the principles they enshrined later gained wide acceptance.[219] On the second point, there is ample evidence of governments, operating through the Committee of Ministers, responding in a slow or lenient fashion to egregious violations by a member state.[220] Bellamy himself recognizes that, where conditions are not ideal, there is a risk of 'asymmetric bargaining between richer and more powerful states and poorer and weaker states'.[221]

Further practical questions remain which have not, to our knowledge, been addressed by proponents of democratic override. If (say) the Committee of Ministers was empowered to authorize override in exceptional cases, what majority would be required? Would the whole judgment be revoked or merely the specific provision(s) deemed unreasonable or unworkable by the respondent state? What would happen if judgments finding similar violations on the basis of similar reasoning had already been issued against other states? If such judgments were still in the process of being implemented, would those states, too, be permitted to override them? If so, what would be the implications for the interpretative authority of the Court, which requires that non-respondent states consider the implications

[218] The populism of much political debate was exemplified by David Cameron's comment that complying with the ECtHR judgments on prisoner voting rights made him feel 'physically ill' (see 1.1.2 at n 39).

[219] See, for example, *Marckx v Belgium*, No. 6833/74, 13 June 1979, which ended state discrimination against children on the grounds of their illegitimacy; *Tyrer v UK*, No. 5856/72, 25 April 1978, which led to the discontinuation of judicially sanctioned corporal punishment. See also Grieve (n 64).

[220] For example, the Committee of Ministers' refusal to denounce the Russian Federation, or consider suspending its membership of the Council of Europe, over its conduct during the Second Chechen War which began in 1999; see Committee of Ministers, Conflict in the Chechen Republic: Implementation by the Russian Federation of Recommendation 1444, Reply from the Committee of Ministers to Recommendation 1456 (200), Doc. 8783, 27 June 2000.

[221] Bellamy (n 103) 1035.

of judgments for their own legal order? Note, for example, that while successive UK governments have failed to implement *Hirst*, the judgment led to legislative reform in Ireland, Latvia, and Cyprus, each of which removed partial or blanket bans and introduced full enfranchisement for prisoners.[222] A further question as yet unanswered is whether any de facto or de jure override mechanism would be limited to certain rights. Would it, for example, exclude judgments in which absolute rights are engaged? Or might there be instances in which those judgments, too, might permissibly be rejected by states?[223]

Proponents of the view that decisions about the effect of international norms or judicial decisions should be made on the basis of the municipal legal and constitutional order when the two conflict acknowledge that this possibility may need to be restricted to liberal democracies.[224] Statements by UK ministers have implicitly adopted similar reasoning; for example, in evidence to the JCHR in which he advocated the possibility of democratic override in order to preserve the sovereignty of the UK parliament, the former Justice Secretary, Chris Grayling, referred repeatedly to the fact that the UK had been described by an official of the ECtHR as 'best in class'. This might be taken to suggest that states with superior human rights records should be entrusted with more leeway than weak compliers to disregard judgments that they consider to be unreasonable.[225] However, the opposite can equally be argued: that states with strong human rights records have a duty to promote rights-respecting structures and practices in states where they do not exist or where they are weak.[226] Hafner-Burton refers to such states as 'steward states', whose governments are (or should be) 'engines of international human rights promotion'.[227] As Bellamy acknowledges, a compelling reason for the UK to comply with *Hirst*, regardless of the correctness of the judgment or the strength of parliamentary opposition, is 'so as not to weaken the authority of the Court vis-à-vis democratising states'.[228] This observation connects to the argument proposed at 4.4.3 as to the

[222] Alexander Horne and Isobel White, *Prisoners' Voting Rights*, House of Commons Library: SN/PC/01764, 11 February 2015, 9, 57–8.

[223] Consider, for example, the judgment in *Bouyid v Belgium*, No. 23380/09, 28 September 2015 [GC], in which the Grand Chamber overruled a unanimous Chamber judgment in deciding by 14–3 that slaps inflicted once each on a juvenile and an adult in police custody constituted degrading treatment in violation of Article 3 ECHR. In their partly dissenting opinion, Judges De Gaetano, Lemmens, and Mahoney stated (para. 7): 'We fear that the judgment may impose an unrealistic standard by rendering meaningless the requirement of a minimum level of severity for acts of violence by law-enforcement officers.' The dissenters also questioned (at n 2) whether Article 3 would henceforth 'stand in the way of the extradition or deportation of an alien to a country where he or she is at risk of being slapped (once)'. It is not inconceivable that these grounds for judicial dissent might in turn be invoked by states seeking to limit the impact of the judgment.

[224] Von Bogdandy and Venzke (n 67) 39.

[225] Oral evidence to the Joint Committee on Human Rights (n 14) 10, 13, 14. Mr Grayling added (15): 'If the United Kingdom is saying "Enough is enough", and if we are an important part of that structure in Strasbourg, they have to take that seriously.... We are in a position where the [Court] can effectively tell us what to do, and there is no democratic override.'

[226] Føllesdal (n 11) 357.

[227] Emilie M. Hafner-Burton, *Making Human Rights a Reality* (Princeton: Princeton University Press, 2013) 5.

[228] Bellamy (n 82) 268.

distinct moral value of supranational human rights regimes and the consequent obligation on states to constrain their own power in the interests of strengthening the system overall, since the legitimacy of domestic political institutions, severally and collectively, depends upon that outcome. This is a consideration to which some proponents of democratic override have been remarkably insouciant.[229]

If democratic override was to be limited to liberal democratic states, a further difficulty is how such a distinction would be made within a human rights system comprising forty-seven states at various uneven stages of democratization. If no such distinction is to be made, then any option of override granted to the UK parliament (or government) must, as a matter of principle within a collective system of equal control, be open to, say, the Russian Duma (or Kremlin)—an option which recent developments suggest the Russian authorities may be ready to seize.[230] Further complexity is added when we consider that the nature of democratically derived authority, and therefore the locus of the state's highest democratic authority, varies between states with different political, legal and constitutional traditions—and might not always be the legislature.[231] Given these complexities, parochially developed notions of democratic override become immediately unworkable at the international level.

As for 'principled' non-compliance, it was established in 3.1 that states are not unitary actors in respect of compliance with international human rights norms; rather, compliance is to a significant degree determined by domestic structures and political bargaining, as well as contingent factors of timing. In this sense, it is arguable that states, as such, are incapable of reaching a stable, principled view of whether a judgment is unreasonable or unworkable to the extent that it should be abrogated. To take *Hirst* as the example, while a backbench parliamentary vote rejected the ECtHR's decision, and successive UK governments have failed to implement it, a majority of members of a cross-party parliamentary committee formed to scrutinize the draft legislative response to the judgment advocated compliance, and proposed a specific remedy (see 7.6.1). The JCHR has also repeatedly called for *Hirst* to be implemented, as have, for example, a range of penal reform organizations, Her Majesty's Inspectorate of Prisons, the Prison Governors' Association, and the Catholic Bishops' Conference of England and Wales.[232] In such instances, in

[229] See, for example, Michael Pinto-Duschinsky, *Bring Rights Back Home: Making Human Rights Compatible with Parliamentary Democracy in the UK* (London: Policy Exchange, 2011) 65: 'When the issue at stake is the welfare and integrity of the UK's system of justice and democracy, it may be argued that this must be the predominant consideration. If the existence of an international court ... undermines our constitution, then that is something too important and too intimate to be sacrificed for the supposed but unproven advantage of other peoples.' The Conservative Party's consultation document on the future of UK human rights law and the UK's relationship with Strasbourg issued in October 2014 was silent on this question in its section entitled 'The international implications for our plan'; see Conservative Party, *Protecting Human Rights in the UK: the Conservatives' Proposals for Changing Britain's Human Rights Laws* (2014) 8.

[230] See 1.1.2 at n 36.

[231] For example, popular will in some states—such as Switzerland and Ireland—is expressed through periodic referenda.

[232] Joint Committee on the draft Voting Eligibility (Prisoners) Bill, Oral and Written Evidence.

which the domestic forces ranged against compliance have thus far prevailed over pro-compliance actors, but are not monolithic, can the protracted failure to implement a judgment be labelled as 'principled' non-compliance, as opposed to simply the outcome of political competition at a particular point in time?

Other objections are foreseen by those who propose (or reluctantly acknowledge the possibility of) override of ECtHR judgments at the national level. For von Bogdandy and Venzke, given the high stakes involved, non-compliance triggers 'argumentative burdens' on states seeking to disapply a judgment of an international court: 'Domestic organs should consider the consequences of their decisions for the international legal order. Non-compliance may indeed damage broader processes of legalization and could place stress on constitutional principles such as the rule of law and a general openness towards international law.'[233]

How, then, are these burdens to be discharged? Çalı argues that the burden of proof for identifying a 'bad interpretation' of an international interpretative authority rests with the domestic authority: 'That is, the domestic authority must show through reasoned argument why an interpretation is unreasonable for *any* domestic authority' (emphasis in original).[234] This explanation is aimed both at the international interpretative authority and the 'global audience that the treaty serves'.[235] Following Rawls, Çalı adds that domestic interpreters should be barred from using 'comprehensive doctrines' as the sole grounds for declaring interpretations to be 'bad', such as their own history, culture or laws.[236] Rather, 'they should appeal to reasons that can be understood and recognised by anyone engaged in human rights interpretation'. Arguments based on the 'original intent' of the drafters are suspect, since 'a purposive reading of international human treaties is required by the very nature of these treaties by all interpreters, domestic and international alike'.[237] A further requirement is for states that consider a particular interpretation to be unworkable 'to provide normative reasons that advise against [it] and to offer solutions to interpretive deadlock'.[238]

Føllesdal argues that, in order to distinguish principled non-compliance from 'ordinary' law breaking, a Council of Europe member state must show that it is 'involved in a judicial dialogue of sorts, that it seeks to *voice loyalty* to the Convention—possibly to avoid *exit* as a last resort ... [and] the State must state reasons for non-compliance, including a preferred alternative interpretation of the ECHR' (emphases in original).[239] 'Exit' could occur in two ways: expulsion or withdrawal. Given that expulsion from the Council of Europe is highly unlikely to be imposed on a state, in view of the Committee of Ministers' marked reluctance to use even lesser sanctions in the face of egregious examples of non-compliance (see 2.5.3), the idea that it is either necessary or desirable to *formalize* a mechanism of non-compliance as a safety valve to avoid that outcome can, we suggest, be discounted. Moreover, given the potential effects of such a mechanism in undermining

[233] Von Bogdandy and Venzke (n 67) 40. [234] Çalı (n 51) 157.
[235] Çalı (n 51) 158. [236] Çalı (n 51) 157. [237] Çalı (n 51) 158.
[238] Çalı (n 51) 158. [239] Føllesdal (n 207) 84.

the Convention system, we suggest that its introduction as a means of pre-empting *voluntary* withdrawal would be a disproportionate response to the problems created by specific contentious judgments.

The procrastination of successive UK governments in responding to *Hirst*, Føllesdal ventures, does not meet the criteria he proposes.[240] The argumentative burdens proposed by both Çalı and Føllesdal are, however, at least partially fulfilled in another example from the UK—the framing of the Communications Bill (leading to the Communications Act 2003), which reformed the regulation of electronic and broadcast media in England and Wales. As discussed at 7.6.3, at issue was the maintenance of a blanket ban on political advertising in the broadcast media, which the JCHR considered likely, if challenged, to be found incompatible with Article 10 ECHR (the right to freedom of expression), a risk also acknowledged by the government.[241] In its report on the bill, the JCHR proposed to the government certain criteria which should be met if it wished to legislate in ways which it knew to be potentially incompatible with Convention rights. These included that the legislation should not evince a lack of respect for human rights standards; and that the reasons for risking incompatibility should be sufficiently compelling and consistent with general aim of maintaining respect for rights.[242] As noted at 4.5.2, the UK's stance was subsequently vindicated by the Grand Chamber in its judgment in *Animal Defenders International*, which placed particular weight on the detailed scrutiny and consultation that had taken place in its conclusion that the UK's ban on political advertising on radio and television was a necessary interference with the right to free expression.

The conduct of the UK government and parliament in this instance provide an example of the way in which national authorities may meet the obligation of open, public reasoning within a 'culture of justification', defined by Hunt as requiring that, 'all exercises of powers which impinge upon fundamental rights, interests or values require public justification by reference to reasons, that is, rational explanations for why a particular action or decision has been taken, or why there has been an omission to act'.[243] For Hiebert, the requirement of justification covers both the pre-legislative process and the post-judicial phase of considering remedial legislation.[244] In cases of profound inter-institutional disagreement, as in the case of *Hirst*, 'it is incumbent upon Parliament to find a way to critically assess and distinguish when its dissenting judgment is justified as a reasonable response to legitimate rights-based concerns, from when Parliament's dissenting opinion can only be explained as an assertion of political and constitutional power'.[245]

240 Føllesdal (n 207) 84.

241 In view of the judgment in *VgT Verein Gegen Tierfabriken v Switzerland* (n 144).

242 JCHR, First Report of Session 2002–03, *Scrutiny of Bills: Progress Report*, HL Paper 24, HC 191 (2002) para. 11.

243 Hunt (n 6) 470.

244 Janet Hiebert, 'The Human Rights Act: Ambiguity about Parliamentary Sovereignty', *German Law Journal* 14(12) (2013): 2253.

245 Hiebert (n 244) 2255.

This requirement for reasoned justification is consistent with a political constitutionalist position since it rejects the idea that 'courts alone are capable of, or have legitimacy for, judgments about rights'.[246] Rather, it is predicated on the idea that parliaments are capable of developing their own interpretations of rights, but must defend those interpretations—whether against the executive or an international interpreting body—in a way that is consistent with the protection of fundamental rights and does not trivialize the matter or '[portray] the obligation to enact remedies as both optional and unimportant'.[247] In this sense, national parliaments and the ECtHR can be construed as existing not in a hierarchical relationship,[248] but in a partnership whose purpose is the shared endeavour of realizing human rights internationally. From the perspective of national parliaments, this partnership is not only an *obligation*, but also an *opportunity*; parliaments can, by developing their own interpretation of human rights, influence the interpretations of other domestic actors, other states, and the Strasbourg Court. We have established, however, intractable practical and normative objections to the notion of 'democratic override' of contested judgments. Such propositions are unworkable, being parochially conceived and reliant upon idealized conditions, and risk fatally undermining the shared 'aspiration of equal respect and concern for each individual globally'.[249]

4.7 Conclusion

Political debate about the legitimacy of the European Court of Human Rights has tended to be conducted in abstract—and, in the UK, predominantly negative—terms, with scant connection to the experience of individual applicants, litigators, or civil society actors. This chapter has advanced several broad propositions which, we suggest, constitute a set of ground rules for debate about the legitimacy of the Court. It has taken as its starting point a contextualized understanding of legitimacy which recognizes that diverse, and sometimes contradictory, accounts of the legitimacy of human rights institutions may be proposed by different actors—and that certain voices may be silenced or marginalized within that discussion. Certainly, accounts of legitimacy proposed by powerful actors in any state—whether political, judicial, commercial, media, or other types of actors—should not be assumed to be proxies for public opinion, particularly in the absence of robust representative surveys. Moreover, opprobrium directed at the Court does not necessarily denote a fundamental crisis of legitimacy; on the contrary, political resistance may equally be a sign of the efficacy of the Convention system at holding national authorities to account for their actions, or inaction, in fulfilling their human rights obligations. We suggest, too, that legitimacy-based critiques of the ECtHR have taken insufficient account of the ways in which both the Court and the wider Convention system are

246 Hiebert (n 244) 2255.
247 Hiebert (n 244) 2274.
248 Krisch (n 53) 185.
249 Çalı (n 51) 149.

responsive to the democratic concerns of states, including by means of the under-explored role of the Parliamentary Assembly.

The elected branches of the state have good reasons to adopt, as Çalı puts it, a 'presumption of deference' towards the Court's interpretative authority and to respect the finality of its adjudicatory authority. These reasons relate partly to the domestic effects of human rights norms, which act as an external corrective to the mistakes and injustices that even well-functioning majoritarian democracies may perpetrate, and consequently bolster, rather than undermine confidence in the democratic credentials of national decision-makers. Yet public discourse about the Court's legitimacy should not be purely parochial, since an inward-looking assessment neglects the distinctive value of international human rights bodies which, as Wheatley ventures,

> lies in their capacity to give expression to the ... overlapping consensus on 'human rights' ... reflecting a commitment by the democratic States parties to uncover together a collective understanding of a morally worthy political culture, and the inherent limits of legitimate political authority in democratic States.[250]

Against this background, proposals to allow domestic legislative override of unpopular ECtHR judgments are, we suggest, undesirable and, indeed, unworkable within a community of forty-seven states at varying levels of democratic development. Rather, the imperative is to strengthen political structures and processes to embed human rights within both executive decision-making and the legislative and oversight functions of parliament. Such conduct may mean that laws and policies have a greater chance of surviving scrutiny by judges in Strasbourg, who are increasingly attuned to the relevance of domestic democratic deliberation to their own determinations.

[250] Wheatley (n 96) 113.

PART II

5

Ukraine

5.1 The Constitutional, Legal, and Political Landscape

Following the dissolution of the Soviet Union, Ukraine attained independence in August 1991, as a republic with a semi-presidential system, comprising twenty-four provinces (*oblasts*) and one autonomous republic (Crimea). The president is the formal head of state, and is directly elected for a five-year term. The parliament (known as the *Verkhovna Rada*) is unicameral and has 450 deputies who are elected for four-year terms (on a system of proportional representation with a party representation minimum threshold of 5% of the national vote). In accordance with the 1996 Constitution, the powers of the *Verkhovna Rada* include the ability to exercise control of the activities of the cabinet of ministers, to grant consent to the appointment by the president of the prime minister and procurator general, and to elect judges (including one-third of Constitutional Court judges).

The Constitutional Court has the power to abrogate laws, acts of the cabinet of ministers, and presidential decrees, should they be found to violate the Constitution. The judicial system also encompasses courts of general jurisdiction (at the head of which is the Supreme Court) and specialized courts (the *Arbitrazh* courts, military courts, and administrative courts). As regards the implementation of international law, Ukraine is a monist state—in accordance with Article 9 of the Constitution, ratified international treaties become part of domestic law.

Although the last decade in Ukraine has represented a period of significant political instability, the tumultuous upheavals of 2013–14 were unprecedented. From November 2013 to February 2014 there were large-scale street protests in Kiev (focused on Independence Square—the *Maidan*), initially caused by President Viktor Yanukovych's decision to reject an association agreement with the European Union, which resulted in the use of lethal force by the authorities and the deaths of up to 100 protesters in early 2014.[1] These events led to the downfall of the government, the departure of President Yanukovych (to Russia), and the installation of an

[1] See, for example, Parliamentary Assembly of the Council of Europe, Resolution 1988 (2014), Recent developments in Ukraine: threats to the functioning of democratic institutions, 9 April 2014; United Nations, General Assembly, Report of the United Nations High Commissioner for Human Rights on the situation of human rights in Ukraine, A/HRC/27/75, 19 September 2014; Council of Europe, Report of the International Advisory Panel on its review of the Maidan Investigations, 31 March 2015.

interim government at the end of February. In March 2014, unidentified soldiers and paramilitary groups (widely believed to be from, or controlled by, Russia) took control of the Autonomous Republic of Crimea, resulting in reports of cases of disappearance, violations of the human rights of the Crimean Tatar community, and the repression of the media,[2] and leading to Russia's purported annexation of the region. The conflict escalated further in April, with armed gangs taking control of public buildings across the Donetsk and Luhansk regions, in eastern Ukraine, where 'people's republics' were then self-proclaimed. Hostilities intensified, leading to the deaths of thousands of civilians: by September 2014 the United Nations High Commissioner for Human Rights reported that at least 2,905 civilians had been killed. The UN Human Rights Monitoring Mission reported that in Donetsk and Luhansk 'the rule of law was replaced by the rule of violence':

> [T]he regional governments ceased to function effectively, as did the police and judiciary. Banks were robbed, coal mines were attacked, with many forced to close. Railways were blown up and salaries, pensions and other social welfare payments were stopped in places under the control of the armed groups.[3]

A new President, Petro Poroshenko, was elected in May 2014 and at the end of June he signed a trade agreement with the European Union, completing the association process. In August he called a parliamentary election which was held in October 2014. The Petro Poroshenko Bloc gained most seats (132), ahead of the People's Front led by Prime Minister Arseniy Yatsenyuk (eighty-two seats), and the new parliament began to function at the end of November 2014. The Party of Regions, which had had the highest number of seats following the 2012 elections (185), did not participate in the election, although a number of its former members stood for the Opposition Bloc (which won twenty-nine seats). Elections were not held in fifteen constituencies in Donetsk and Luhansk, or in twelve constituencies in Crimea and Sevastopol. For the first time in Ukraine's history, the Communist Party does not have any parliamentary seats. A large number of the deputies have not had previous experience in parliament. Of the 420 deputies elected, forty-nine were women (about 12%).[4]

As the Parliamentary Assembly of the Council of Europe (PACE) noted in April 2014, the events in Ukraine created potential opportunities for positive democratic change, including broader representation within the *Verkhovna Rada*, constitutional and judicial reform, the strengthening of local and regional authorities, and the decentralization of government: 'The Assembly considers that the new political environment following the events on Maidan ... and the resulting change of power, has opened a window of opportunity for Ukraine's democratic development.'[5]

[2] See, for example, Commissioner for Human Rights of the Council of Europe, Report by Nils Muižnieks following his mission in Kyiv, Moscow and Crimea from 7 to 12 September 2014, CommDH(2014)19, 27 October 2014.

[3] United Nations, General Assembly, A/HRC/27/75 (n 1) para. 13.

[4] See the Inter-Parliamentary Union's Parline Database at <http://www.ipu.org/parline-e/reports/2331_E.htm>.

[5] PACE Resolution 1988 (2014) (n 1) para. 4.

Following the October 2014 parliamentary elections, Hryhoriy Nemyria (deputy leader of the All Ukrainian Union 'Fatherland' party, and a former Deputy Prime Minister under Yulia Tymoshenko) was elected as chair of the Committee on Human Rights, National Minorities and Interethnic Relations of the *Verkhovna Rada* ('Human Rights Committee') (see 5.4.1). As to the question of parliament's role in the implementation of European Court of Human Rights (ECtHR or 'the Court') judgments concerning Ukraine, Hryhoriy Nemyria, is optimistic of being able to expand the committee's remit to include the scrutiny of implementation issues (as discussed further at 5.4 below).

5.1.1 Political climate

The last decade in Ukraine has represented a period of 'systemic political crisis', according to the Monitoring Committee of the Parliamentary Assembly.[6] Following fraudulent presidential elections in 2004, mass peaceful protests marked the Orange Revolution, leading in January 2005 to the ascendancy as President of Viktor Yushchenko, who was succeeded by Viktor Yanukovych in 2010. In the period following the Orange Revolution and prior to President Yanukovych leaving power in 2014, Ukraine's transition to a fully democratic state respecting the rule of law was hindered by endemic obstacles within the body politic, including widespread corruption, acrimonious political in-fighting, a parliament dominated by oligarchs and businessmen, and regional divisions. Substantial reform of domestic political institutions has also been hampered by the concentration of power within the presidential administration and a narrow ruling elite, to which the legislature and judiciary have tended to be subservient.

The period has witnessed a protracted and flawed process of constitutional reform, frequently ignoring the advice of the Venice Commission (see 2.7) which has called for parliamentary powers to be strengthened since 2003. Changes implemented in 2004, to introduce a mixed presidential-parliamentary system, were subsequently declared unconstitutional by the Constitutional Court in October 2010. Reporting in 2010, the Venice Commission concluded that '[t]he fundamental problems with Ukraine have been dysfunctional institutions, lack of checks and balances especially with respect to the president and constant clashes between the state organs'.[7] The Venice Commission accordingly called for comprehensive constitutional reform in order to 'strengthen the stability, independence and effectiveness of state institutions through a clear division of competencies and effective checks and balances', and advocated the introduction of further mechanisms of parliamentary control over the executive.[8]

[6] Committee on the Honouring of Obligations and Commitments by Member States of the Council of Europe (Monitoring Committee), The functioning of democratic institutions in Ukraine, Report, Doc. 12357, 20 September 2010, para. 1.

[7] Venice Commission, Opinion on the constitutional situation in Ukraine, Opinion No. 599/2010, CDL-AD(2010)044, 20 December 2010, para. 64.

[8] Venice Commission, Opinion No. 599/2010 (n 7) para. 66.

The international community remains seriously concerned by the lack of independence of the judiciary (including the roles played by the president, the High Council of Justice and the *Verkhovna Rada* in the appointment of judges)[9] and a poorly funded justice system. Reforms to tackle the politicization of law enforcement bodies—notably the over-bearing authority and influence of the *Prokuratura* (combining the functions of pre-trial investigation, criminal prosecution, and oversight over other inquiry bodies)[10]—have not been effectively implemented, and Ukraine's Security Service (SBU) has become increasingly influential within domestic politics.

More recently, apparently politically motivated prosecutions have been brought against former government ministers and officials,[11] for alleged abuses of power, a number of which have led to the defendants successfully bringing cases before the European Court, including former Minister of the Interior, Yuriy Lutsenko.[12] The most high profile of these cases was the prosecution of former Prime Minister Yuliya Tymoshenko for abuse of office and misuse of state funds.[13]

[9] See, for example, Venice Commission, Joint opinion on the draft law on the judicial system and the status of judges of Ukraine, Opinion No. 550/2009, CDL-AD(2010)003, 16 March 2010; Venice Commission, Joint opinion on the law amending certain legislative acts of Ukraine in relation to the prevention of abuse of the right of appeal, Opinion No. 588/2010, CDL-AD(2010)029, 18 October 2010; OECD Anti-Corruption Network for Eastern Europe and Central Asia, Istanbul Anti-Corruption Action Plan, Second Round of Monitoring—Ukraine Monitoring Report, 8 December 2010; Report by Thomas Hammarberg, Commissioner for Human Rights of the Council of Europe, following his visit to Ukraine from 19 to 26 November 2011, CommDH(2012)10, 23 February 2012. Writing in 2011, Freedom House suggested that 'the strong perception among many observers is that the judicial system does not serve as a check or balance against the executive branch': David J. Kramer et al., *Sounding the Alarm: Protecting Democracy in Ukraine: A Freedom House Report on the State of Democracy and Human Rights in Ukraine*, Freedom House, April 2011, 11. European Court judgments concerning the lack of independence of the courts in Ukraine include *Sovtransavto Holding v Ukraine*, No. 48553/99, 25 July 2002 and *Agrokompleks v Ukraine*, No. 23465/03, 6 October 2011 (finding, inter alia, that state authorities intervened in judicial proceedings and that judicial superiors exercised undue influence over other judges).

[10] The Venice Commission has described the *Prokuratura* as 'a very powerful institution whose functions considerably exceed the scope of functions by a prosecutor in a democratic, law abiding state': Opinion on the draft law of Ukraine on the office of the public prosecutor, Opinion No. 539/2009, CDL-AD(2009)048, 27 October 2009. It was described by PACE in 2012 as 'an excessively centralised institution with excessive powers': PACE Resolution 1862 (2012), The functioning of democratic institutions in Ukraine, para. 9. One senior government official told us that former prosecutors form a powerful bloc within parliament, which resists the implementation of changes to the laws regulating the role of prosecutors (Government Official, Interview, 22 May 2012).

[11] See, for example, PACE Resolution 1862 (2012) (n 10); Committee on the Honouring of Obligations and Commitments by Member States of the Council of Europe (Monitoring Committee), Honouring of obligations and commitments by Ukraine—Information note by the co-rapporteurs on the fact-finding visit to Kyiv (26–30 March 2012) and to Kyiv and Kharkiv (14–18 May 2012), AS/Mon(2012)13 rev, 27 June 2012. On 12 April 2012 the former Minister of Defence, Valeriy Ivashchenko, was sentenced to five years' imprisonment for 'abuse of power'.

[12] See *Lutsenko v Ukraine*, No. 6492/11, 3 July 2012 in which the ECtHR found violations of the right to liberty under Articles 5(1), 5(2), 5(3) and 5(4) ECHR, as well as a violation of Article 18 ECHR taken together with Article 5 on the basis that the prosecuting authorities had attempted 'to punish the applicant for publicly disagreeing with accusations against him and for asserting his innocence' (para. 109).

[13] See, for example, European Parliament Resolution, Ukraine: the cases of Yulia Tymoshenko and other members of the former government, 9 June 2011; Committee on the Honouring of Obligations and Commitments by Member States of the Council of Europe (Monitoring Committee),

In the 2000s, Ukraine slid down the ranks of Transparency International's Corruption Perceptions Index, from a rank of 107 in 2005 to 142 in 2014 (out of 175).[14] Between 2005 and 2013, Ukraine was described each year in Freedom House's *Freedom of the Press Index* as being 'Partly Free'; however, in 2014 it was downgraded to 'Not Free'.[15]

5.1.2 The role and status of parliament

The 'top down' nature of the political system in Ukraine, dominated as it has been by the presidential administration, has had the effect of sidelining parliament, which has not in practice had a decisive role in developing appropriate legal frameworks, ensuring the proper execution of ECtHR judgments, or otherwise promoting the observance of human rights standards. In 2005, PACE noted the absence or weakness of parliamentary opposition, resulting in a lack of parliamentary oversight which accordingly offered little impetus to ensure the accountability and transparency of public administration.[16] This view was confirmed by Olena Petsun, of the Office of the Commissioner for Human Rights of the Council of Europe, who describes the reactive role played by the parliament, explaining (during the period of the Yanukovych presidency) that '[l]aws that need to be adopted by parliament in relation to the Council of Europe have been introduced by the president himself'.[17]

PACE has reiterated its call for fundamental reform of the electoral system.[18] Freedom House reported a prevailing view within civil society in 2011 that the *Verkhovna Rada* had 'deteriorated into a rubber stamp for the government'.[19]

The level of public trust in MPs has clearly been very low. Speaking in 2012, Dmytro Groysman, the former Executive Director of the Vinnytsya Human Rights group (VHRG) explained the reasons for this:

> Parliamentarians are not at all close to the ordinary people. They have a big number of privileges—separate medical and transport facilities. They are totally dependent on their big

The functioning of democratic institutions in Ukraine, Report, Doc. 12814, 9 January 2012. Ms Tymoshenko was convicted in October 2011 and sentenced, inter alia, to seven years' imprisonment and was banned from holding official office for three years. In its judgment in the case of *Tymoshenko v Ukraine*, No. 49872/11, 30 April 2013, the ECtHR found violations of Articles 5(1), 5(4), 5(5) ECHR, and Article 18 ECHR taken together with Article 5, after several sets of criminal proceedings had been brought against her in 2010–11.

[14] See the Transparency International Corruption Perceptions Index: <http://www.transparency.org/cpi2014/results>.

[15] See Freedom House, Freedom of the Press 2014: Ukraine at <https://freedomhouse.org/report/freedom-press/2014/ukraine#.VLzqM9KsW-k>.

[16] Committee on the Honouring of Obligations and Commitments by Member States of the Council of Europe (Monitoring Committee), Honouring of obligations and commitments by Ukraine, Report, Doc. 10676, 19 September 2005, paras. 79–82.

[17] Interview, 27 June 2012.

[18] PACE Resolution 1755(2010), The functioning of democratic institutions in Ukraine, 5 October 2010.

[19] Kramer et al. (n 9) 5.

political bosses, so they have no reason to think about human rights. It is not to their benefit, it will not help them get re-elected.... If they represent the governmental fraction, they must always advocate the majority stance that the position is not bad. If they are in opposition, they can criticise, but in the current context, everyone knows that they were recently in power and doing the same things.... Plus most have big businesses and concentrate on that—they use their mandate for the development and protection of their own businesses.[20]

Under the Yanukovych regime, it had become a common practice for MPs to vote in parliament electronically on behalf of other, absent MPs, a practice which breaches the Ukrainian Constitution.[21] Speaking in 2012, Stanislav Shevchuk, Professor of Law at the National University 'Kyiv–Mohyla Academy', suggested that this was indicative of a parliamentary crisis in Ukraine: 'The culture is "push the button, get the result", with no debate, no influence from parliamentary committees.'[22] Myroslava Antonovych, Head of the International Law Department at the National University 'Kyiv–Mohyla Academy', has subsequently commented that 'such cases are now rather the exception, although the practice has not been entirely ruled out'.[23]

5.2 Ukraine and the Convention System

Ukraine acceded to the Council of Europe in 1995, just four years after it attained independence in 1991. The process of accession has been described by Angelika Nußberger as being very difficult and marked by controversy (including issues arising from Ukraine's bilateral relations with Russia concerning the Black Sea Fleet and access to naval facilities in Sevastopol).[24] The admission process necessitated a series of visits by members of three Parliamentary Assembly committees, legal experts, and the Assembly President and the drafting of various reports and opinions on domestic Ukrainian legislation and its systems of human rights protection, during a period of three years.[25] Bruno Haller has suggested that there was political sympathy within the Parliamentary Assembly for Ukraine, and that it was eager to have such a major eastern European state within the Council of Europe. Accession

[20] Interview, 22 May 2012. Very sadly, Dmytro Groysman died in August 2013. He has been described by Halya Coynash (of the Kharkiv Human Rights Protection Group) as 'one of Ukraine's most prominent human rights activists'.

[21] For example, in the case of *Oleksandr Volkov v Ukraine*, No. 41722/11, 9 January 2013, which concerned the dismissal of a Supreme Court judge (a decision which was 'ratified' by the plenary parliament), the ECtHR found that 'the MPs present deliberately and unlawfully cast multiple votes belonging to their absent peers' (para. 145).

[22] Interview, 21 May 2012. See also Kharkiv Human Rights Protection Group, 'Unconvincing Assurances over Enforcement of Crucial ECHR Judgment', 10 June 2013.

[23] Email correspondence with Myroslava Antonovych, 20 July 2015.

[24] Angelika Nußberger, 'The Reception Process in Russia and Ukraine', in Helen Keller and Alec Stone Sweet, eds., *A Europe of Rights: The Impact of the ECHR on National Legal Systems* (Oxford: Oxford University Press, 2008) 603, 610.

[25] Bruno Haller, 'The Admission of Ukraine to the Council of Europe: the Role of the Parliamentary Assembly', *Human Rights Law Review* 27(9–12) (2006): 341.

led to the imposition of a detailed list of obligations which then became the focus of the monitoring process, including a new constitution, revised criminal and civil codes, and laws on elections and political parties, as well as changes to the role of the Prosecutor's Office, measures to ensure the independence of the judiciary, and the establishment of a professional Bar Association.[26] From 1995, these and other commitments, were subject to Council of Europe monitoring procedures, but the legislative process was ponderous, and the political will to reform so limited, that just over three years later the Assembly threatened Ukraine with suspension under Article 8 of the Charter of the Council of Europe.[27] The Assembly deplored the fact that

> ... in the transitional phase between a totalitarian and a democratic state, Ukraine has not achieved a clear separation between the judicial, legislative and executive powers. There is continuing control by the executive and a determination to seek and hold political power, sometimes illegally.[28]

Another issue of particular concern for the Council of Europe was Ukraine's retention of the death penalty. In 1997 the Assembly expressed its anguish at the eighty-nine executions that had taken place in the first half of 1996, describing the situation as a 'flagrant violation of [Ukraine's] commitments and obligations'. The executions were 'shrouded in secrecy'—the victims were buried in unmarked graves and not even their families were informed.[29] The death penalty was subsequently abolished in Ukraine in 2000.[30] By September 2001, PACE was satisfied that significant further progress as to Ukraine's commitments had been made, so that further measures were not needed.[31]

Ukraine ratified the European Convention on Human Rights (ECHR or 'the Convention') in 1997,[32] whereupon it became part of domestic law,[33] taking precedence over domestic legislation.[34] As regards numbers of pending applications at the ECtHR, in recent years Ukraine has consistently remained at or near the top of the 'league table of states': for example, as at December 2014, 19 per cent

[26] PACE, Opinion No. 190 (1995) on the application by Ukraine for membership of the Council of Europe, 26 September 1995.

[27] Nußberger (n 24) 611.

[28] PACE Resolution 1179 (1999) Honouring of obligations and commitments by Ukraine, 27 January 1999.

[29] PACE Resolution 1112 (1997) Honouring of the commitment entered into by Ukraine upon accession to the Council of Europe to put into place a moratorium on executions, 29 January 1997. See also Renate Wohlwend, 'The Role of the Council of Europe's Parliamentary Assembly', in Council of Europe, *The Death Penalty Beyond Abolition* (Council of Europe, 2004): 65, 69–75.

[30] Ukraine ratified Protocol No. 6 to the ECHR on 4 April 2000 and Protocol No. 13 to the ECHR on 11 March 2003.

[31] PACE, Honouring of obligations and commitments by Ukraine, Report, Doc. 10676, 19 September 2005.

[32] The ECHR and Protocols 1–5, 8, and 11 entered into force on 11 September 1997. Protocol 7 entered into force on 1 December 1997 and Protocol 11 on 1 November 1998. Protocol 6 (abolishing the death penalty in peacetime) entered into force on 1 May 2000 and Protocol 13 (abolishing the death penalty in all circumstances) entered into force on 1 July 2003.

[33] In accordance with Article 9 of the Constitution.

[34] In accordance with Article 19(2) of the Law on International Treaties of 29 June 2004.

of pending cases at the Court (13,635) concerned Ukraine.[35] Such a high level of applications may signify a certain level of popular trust in the Strasbourg Court, but a high proportion of the cases is likely to be unsustainable. For example, in the course of 2014, the Court dealt with 13,084 Ukrainian cases, of which 12,731 were declared inadmissible or struck out.[36]

The first judgment of the Court relating to Ukraine was published in 2001,[37] and since then there have been a number of significant issues which have led to findings of Convention violations. The poor treatment of prisoners in Ukraine has repeatedly been the subject of the Court's judgments.[38] The case of *Aliev v Ukraine*[39] concerned the conditions of the applicant's detention on death row (prior to the abolition of the death penalty in Ukraine in 2000).[40] The notorious state of Ukrainian prisons led the Court to take the highly unusual step in *Aliev* of despatching a delegation of its judges to Simferopol Prison in order to take evidence directly from witnesses.[41] Another grave concern for the Council of Europe has been the intimidation of journalists in Ukraine.[42] The exceptionally high profile case of *Gongadze v Ukraine*[43] related to the disappearance and murder of political journalist Georgiy

[35] See Table 1.1 at 1.2.2.

[36] ECtHR, Press Country Profile: Ukraine (last updated October 2015).

[37] *Kaysin and Others v Ukraine*, No. 46144/99, 3 May 2001.

[38] See, for example, *Yuriy Illarionovich Shchokin v Ukraine*, No. 4299/03, 3 October 2013.

[39] No. 41220/98, 29 April 2003. Another example is *Yakovenko v Ukraine*, No. 15825/06, 25 October 2007 (the failure to provide adequate medical care to the applicant detainee who was suffering from HIV and tuberculosis infections).

[40] In its judgment No. 11pn/99 (29 December 1999) the Ukrainian Constitutional Court held that the provisions of the Criminal Code concerning the death penalty were contrary to the Constitution, and accordingly the death penalty was abolished and replaced by life imprisonment (by Act no. 1483-III, 22 February 2000). A de facto moratorium on the death penalty had been in place since 1997. However, the fact that more than 200 people had been executed in Ukraine *after* it had joined the Council of Europe in 1995 meant that this had been the Council's priority issue as regards its relations with Ukraine in the mid-to-late 1990s. See: PACE Resolution 1097 (1996) on the abolition of the death penalty in Europe; Resolution 1112 (1997) on the honouring of the commitment entered into by Ukraine upon accession to the Council of Europe to put into place a moratorium on executions; Resolution 1179 (1999) and Recommendation 1395 (1999) on the honouring of obligations and commitments by Ukraine.

[41] On the Court's fact-finding missions, see: Philip Leach, Costas Paraskeva, and Gordana Uzelac, *International Human Rights and Fact-Finding: An Analysis of the Fact-Finding Missions Conducted by the European Commission and Court of Human Rights*, Human Rights and Social Justice Research Institute, London Metropolitan University, February 2009; Michael O'Boyle and Natalia Brady, 'Investigatory Powers of the European Court of Human Rights', *European Human Rights Law Review* 4 (2013): 378. The Court also undertook fact-finding missions in the cases of *Dankevich v Ukraine*, No. 40679/98, 29 April 2003; *Khokhlich v Ukraine*, No. 41707/98, 29 April 2003; *Kuznetsov v Ukraine*, No. 39042/97, 29 April 2003; *Nazarenko v Ukraine*, No. 39483/98, 29 April 2003; *Poltoratskiy v Ukraine*, No. 38812/97, 29 April 2003; *Davydov and Others v Ukraine*, Nos 17674/02 and 39081/02, 1 July 2010.

[42] See, for example, PACE Resolution 1239 (2001); PACE Recommendation 1497 (2001) of 25 January 2001; PACE Resolution 1244 (2001) and Recommendation 1513 (2001) of 26 April 2001; and PACE Resolution 1262 (2001) of 27 September 2001.

[43] No. 34056/02, 8 November 2005. The case remains unresolved and is still subject to the supervision of the Committee of Ministers: Committee of Ministers, *Supervision of the Execution of Judgments and Decisions of the European Court of Human Rights: 7th Annual Report of the Committee of Ministers 2013* (2014) ('7th Annual Report of the Committee of Ministers 2013'): 85–6. See also the linked case of *Melnychenko v Ukraine*, No. 17707/02, 19 October 2004.

Gongadze in 2000 at a time when he was editor-in-chief of the online newspaper *Ukrayinska Pravda*, and when he was involved in investigating corruption at a high level in Ukraine. The ad hoc Ukrainian parliamentary committee established to investigate the case found in 2005 that the kidnapping and murder of Mr Gongadze had been organized by the former President of Ukraine, Leonid Kuchma, together with the former Minister of the Interior, Yuriy Kravchenko, and that the Parliamentary Speaker, Volodymyr Lytvyn and another MP, Leonid Derkach, had also been involved in the crimes.[44]

Other cases have highlighted the dysfunctionality of the judicial and legal systems,[45] the lack of independence and impartiality of the courts,[46] and the ill-treatment of detainees held in police custody.[47] Furthermore, the domestic laws applicable to detention for the purposes of extradition,[48] and on defamation,[49] have been found wanting. The budgetary implications of Convention violations by Ukraine rose significantly in 2013, during which year the total amount of damages awarded by the European Court against Ukraine was nearly €33 million (compared with €1,699,753 in 2012 and €7,684,574 in 2014).[50]

The events of 2013–14 in Ukraine resulted in a series of applications to the European Court relating to both the anti-government protests,[51] as well as developments in eastern Ukraine. The Ukrainian government introduced four inter-state cases against Russia in 2014 and 2015 relating to eastern Ukraine and Crimea.[52] In addition, by October 2015, more than 1,400 individual applications arising from events in those regions had been lodged at the ECtHR against Russia and/or Ukraine, and interim measures (see 2.2) had been applied in more than 150 cases. In relation to the first inter-state case, the Court invoked its interim measures jurisdiction (under Rule 39) in order to call on both the Russian and Ukrainian governments to refrain from taking action which might lead to violations of the Convention rights of the civilian population, in particular Article 2 ECHR (right to life) and Article 3 ECHR (prohibition of torture and inhuman or degrading treatment). In June 2015, the Ukrainian government registered a derogation to the

[44] *Gongadze v Ukraine* (n 43) para. 146.

[45] *Sovtransavto Holding v Ukraine* (n 9), a judgment in which the ECtHR expressed its surprise at the conflicting approaches taken by the Ukrainian courts in applying the domestic law, and noted that the Ukrainian authorities—'acting at the highest level'—had intervened in the domestic legal proceedings, which it found to be incompatible with the Convention (paras. 79–80, 97).

[46] *Salov v Ukraine*, No. 65518/01, 6 September 2005.

[47] *Afanasyev v Ukraine*, No. 38722/02, 5 April 2005.

[48] *Soldatenko v Ukraine*, No. 2440/07, 23 October 2008.

[49] *Ukrainian Media Group v Ukraine*, No. 72713/01, 29 March 2005.

[50] 7th Annual Report of the Committee of Ministers 2013 (n 43) 57; Committee of Ministers, *Supervision of the Execution of Judgments and Decisions of the European Court of Human Rights: 8th Annual Report of the Committee of Ministers 2014* (2015): 58.

[51] See, for example, *Sirenko v Ukraine*, No. 9078/14 (communicated in January 2014) and *Derevyanko v Ukraine*, No. 7684/14 (communicated in February 2014).

[52] *Ukraine v Russia (I)* (No. 20958/14), *Ukraine v Russia (II)* (No. 43800/14), *Ukraine v Russia (III)* (No. 49537/14), and *Ukraine v Russia (IV)* (No. 42410/15).

Convention (pursuant to Article 15 ECHR) in relation to Articles 5, 6, 8, and 13 ECHR, in respect of the Donetsk and Luhansk regions.[53]

In a number of situations, ECtHR judgments against Ukraine have led to legislative changes. For example, in the case of *Soldatenko v Ukraine*[54] in 2008 the Court found that there were no specific provisions in Ukrainian law which provided for detention pending extradition. In response to that decision, amendments were introduced to the Code of Criminal Procedure on 17 June 2010 which established a procedure for arrest and detention pending extradition, together with an appeal process. Another example is the first judgment in *Gurepka v Ukraine*[55] which led to legislative changes to enable a challenge to be made to an order of administrative detention. However, Judge Ganna Yudkivska has suggested that as the Ukrainian authorities failed to give full consideration to the applicability of Article 6 ECHR to administrative offences, the Code of Administrative Offences will need to be amended again in the light of the subsequent judgment in *Kornev and Karpenko v Ukraine*.[56]

Of even greater significance, however, is that fact that a number of structural or systemic violations of the Convention in Ukraine have been identified by the Court in recent years,[57] such as the excessive length of criminal and civil proceedings,[58] the malfunctioning of the judicial system,[59] and problems in both legislation and practice as regards freedom of assembly.[60] Furthermore, the recurrence of cases of ill-treatment in police custody was highlighted in *Kaverzin v Ukraine* in 2002.[61] The Court has also identified and adjudicated on a variety of structural problems concerning arrest and pre-trial detention, resulting in Ukraine being urged by the Court in 2011 to introduce reforms to both domestic legislation and administrative practice, in order to ensure its compliance with Article 5 ECHR.[62]

[53] ECtHR Press Release, Interim measure granted in inter-state case brought by Ukraine against Russia, 13 March 2014; ECtHR Press Release, European Court of Human Rights communicates to Russia new inter-State case concerning events in Crimea and Eastern Ukraine, 1 October 2015. See also: Philip Leach, 'Ukraine, Russia and Crimea and the European Court of Human Rights', European Journal of International Law blog, 19 March 2014.

[54] See above n 48.

[55] No. 61406/00, 6 September 2005.

[56] No. 17444/04, 21 October 2010. Interview, 27 June 2012.

[57] See further: PACE, Committee on Legal Affairs and Human Rights, Implementation of judgments of the European Court of Human Rights, Doc. 12455, 20 December 2010 (Rapporteur: Christos Pourgourides) ('7th Rapporteur Report'); PACE, Committee on Legal Affairs and Human Rights, Implementation of judgments of the European Court of Human Rights, Doc. 13864, 9 September 2015 (Rapporteur: Klaas de Vries) ('8th Rapporteur Report').

[58] See, for example, *Svetlana Naumenko and Others v Ukraine*, No. 41984/98, 9 November 2004 and *Merit v Ukraine*, No. 66561/01, 30 March 2004. The issues have still not been resolved and remain subject to the supervision of the Committee of Ministers; see 7th Annual Report of the Committee of Ministers 2013 (n 43) 52.

[59] *Oleksandr Volkov v Ukraine* (n 21).

[60] *Vyerentsov v Ukraine*, No. 20372/11, 11 July 2013.

[61] No. 23893/03, 15 May 2002. Although, in response to such decisions, amendments to the Law on the Militia were introduced in January 2005, a PACE report in 2010 (7th Rapporteur Report (n 57) para. 169) concluded that 'the deliberate physical ill-treatment of detainees by police officers remains widespread in Ukraine, in particular during initial questioning in district police stations with a view to securing confessions relating to unsolved crimes. Eradicating this practice requires comprehensive measures at all levels'.

[62] *Kharchenko v Ukraine*, No. 40107/02, 10 May 2011; *Balitskiy v Ukraine*, No. 12793/03, 3 November 2011. See also *Doronin v Ukraine*, No. 16505/02, 19 February 2009.

The most serious structural deficiency in Ukraine is the failure to comply with domestic court judgments, which was first highlighted by the Court in 2004,[63] and which led to the pilot judgment in the case of *Yuriy Nikolayevich Ivanov v Ukraine* in 2009.[64] The majority of such cases relate to unenforced domestic judgments requiring the state to pay salary debts, disability allowances, and compensation (for pecuniary and non-pecuniary damages). The principal reasons for the non-enforcement of these decisions have been the lack of sufficient funds (in state or local budgets) and the application of a series of laws preventing enforcement in particular circumstances. These have included, notably, a moratorium on the forced sale of assets of companies in which the state holds at least 25 per cent of the shares, the inability to enforce judgments against fuel and energy companies (listed in a register held by the Ministry of Fuel and Energy), and a moratorium on the forced sale of satisfying creditors' claims in bankruptcy proceedings.[65]

Even prior to the *Ivanov* judgment, the issue had been firmly on the radar of the Committee of Ministers,[66] and in 2009, after more than 300 judgments on the issue, it deplored the fact that 'despite the urgency of the situation ... the Ukrainian authorities have continuously failed to give priority to finding effective solutions to the important problem of non-enforcement of domestic courts' decisions'.[67] The Committee of Ministers reiterated its call to the Ukrainian authorities 'at the highest level' to comply with their political commitment to resolving the problem. However, even the pilot judgment, which necessitated the introduction of a suitable remedy within a year, has not had the desired effect.[68] In February 2012, as a result of the failure of the Ukrainian authorities to resolve the issue, the Court resumed its consideration of the similar pending cases which had been frozen since the *Ivanov* judgment had been issued.[69] This was the first time that the Court had had to take such action as a result of a state's non-compliance with a pilot judgment.

The extent of systemic Convention violations in Ukraine has also resulted in scrutiny by the Parliamentary Assembly (see the further discussion about the role of PACE at 5.5.1 below). When members of the Assembly's Committee on Legal Affairs and Human Rights ('Legal Affairs Committee') started to carry out fact-finding visits in-country, in 2006, in order to investigate the non-implementation of judgments of the European Court, Ukraine was one of the first target states (along with Italy, Russia, Turkey, and the UK) and when, in 2012, the Legal Affairs Committee instigated a programme of hearings in Strasbourg, the Ukrainian delegation was one of those asked to attend to discuss questions of implementation.

[63] *Zhovner v Ukraine*, No. 56948/00, 29 September 2004.

[64] No. 40450/04, 15 October 2009.

[65] See, for example, Committee of Ministers, Case of Yuriy Nikolayevich Ivanov against Ukraine, and Group of cases of Zhovner against Ukraine, CM/Inf/DH(2012)29, 19 September 2012.

[66] Interim Resolution CM/ResDH(2008)1, 6 March 2008.

[67] Interim Resolution CM/ResDH(2009)159, 3 December 2009.

[68] Interim Resolution CM/ResDH(2010)222, 30 November 2010; Interim Resolution CM/ResDH(2011)184, 14 September 2011.

[69] ECtHR Press Release, 29 February 2012. On that date there were about 2,500 similar pending cases. See *Kharuk and Others v Ukraine*, No. 703/05, 26 July 2012.

As noted at 2.6.2, the Assembly will consider suspending the voting rights of a national delegation where its national parliament is not deemed to exercise sufficient parliamentary control over the executive in cases which are not implemented.[70]

The former Deputy Minister of Justice, Dmytro Kotliar, explains that at one stage the government introduced into the draft law relating to the enforcement of judgments various proposals which would have had the effect of reducing the state's liability for social benefits.[71] The government was thought to be trying to get such amendments through quietly under the guise of ECHR implementation. However, in the end the proposals were withdrawn as the ruling party MPs were opposed to cutting benefits before an election.[72]

Another particular reason for the excessive delay in securing an effective remedy in respect of the non-enforcement of domestic judgments has been the absence of political will to enforce judgments against bodies that were partly state-owned and partly privately owned. It was proposed to cancel a moratorium which had been in place since 2001 on the sale of the property of an enterprise of which 25 per cent or more of the shares were owned by the state, and also to ensure court rulings could be enforced in respect of enterprises in the fuel and energy sector (as discussed earlier).[73] However, many members of parliament have had personal stakes in such entities (or were driven by other political interests), which accordingly explains why the requisite legislative reforms were not forthcoming.[74]

It was only in January 2013 that a law was finally introduced with the aim of resolving the problem of the non-enforcement of judgments.[75] However, the new remedy has no retroactive application, as it only applies to domestic judgments delivered after January 2013, and therefore will not resolve the problem of the older, repetitive applications pending before the Court, a fact that was met with 'deep regret' by the Committee of Ministers.[76]

[70] PACE, Committee on Legal Affairs and Human Rights, Progress report: Implementation of judgments of the European Court of Human Rights, AS/Jur (2009) 36, 31 August 2009 (Rapporteur: Mr Christos Pourgourides) para. 23. See also the discussion of PACE's role and powers at 2.6.

[71] Interview, 21 May 2012. See also PACE, Committee on Legal Affairs and Human Rights, Implementation of judgments of the European Court of Human Rights—Extracts from the minutes of hearings, organized by the Committee, held in Strasbourg in April 2012, in June 2012, in October 2012, and in January 2013, AS/Jur (2013) 13, 28 March 2013, 2–3.

[72] Government Official, Interview, 22 May 2012. As to public protest in Ukraine about the proposed abolition of social benefits, see, for example, Kharkiv Human Rights Protection Group, 'Former Chornobyl Clean-Up Workers Outraged Over Trick with New Law', 7 June 2012.

[73] See, further, Maxim Shcherbatyuk and Volodymyr Yavorsky (Ukrainian Helsinki Human Rights Union), 'New Draft Bill on Enforcement of Court Rulings, Same Old Problems', 24 September 2011.

[74] Government Official, Interview, 22 May 2012. Pavlo Pushkar, Interview, 26 June 2012.

[75] On 5 June 2012, a new law 'On State guarantees concerning execution of judicial decisions' was adopted by parliament, and was signed by the president on 22 June 2012. It entered into force on 1 January 2013. The law introduced a new procedure for the execution of domestic judicial decisions against the state, according to which debts are paid by the State Treasury if the other debtor body fails to do so. Compensation is automatically due if payments under the new procedure are delayed.

[76] Committee of Ministers, *Supervision of the Execution of the Judgments and Decisions of the European Court of Human Rights: 6th Annual Report of the Committee of Ministers 2012* (2013) 17. See also: 7th Annual Report of the Committee of Ministers 2013 (n 43) 126–7.

The failure of the pilot judgment procedure to resolve the situation (at least for several years after the *Ivanov* judgment) is illustrative of the fact that the Court needs a certain level of active co-operation from the state, at the highest levels, in order for the process to achieve its aims of systemic reform.[77] It is, to a certain extent, a consensual process.

A Ukrainian senior lawyer at the Registry of the European Court, Pavlo Pushkar, is critical of what he describes as 'quasi-legislative attempts' by the government to implement Strasbourg decisions. By way of example, he cites the government's response to the judgment in *Sovtransavto Holding v Ukraine*, in which the Court was highly critical of the Ukrainian president's interference in the domestic judicial proceedings, as the president had 'urged the President of the Higher Arbitration Court to protect the State's interests' in the course of the judicial examination of the case.[78] There, the government sought to suggest that it had complied with the judgment because the president of Ukraine had instructed the prime minister and the General Prosecutor's Office to prevent any interference with the independence of the judiciary.[79]

5.2.1 Attitudes towards the Convention system

As noted above, the high numbers of applications submitted against Ukraine, may indicate a degree of popular faith in the Strasbourg Court, in contrast to the domestic courts. However, such attitudes are not necessarily reflected within the ruling political elite. During the Yanukovych years, it was undoubtedly the case that, in order to ensure compliance with ECHR standards in Ukraine, the stance taken by the President was all-important.[80] For example, Oksana Klymovych of the Westminster Foundation for Democracy–Ukraine told us in mid-2012: 'Now everything depends on the president—if he says implement, it will be implemented.'[81]

One (former) senior government official told us that the problems with implementation in Ukraine arise because most state bodies have a very weak understanding of the Convention and the practice of the ECtHR, and that ministry lawyers do not have sufficient expertise to assess the compliance of domestic legal provisions with the Convention. This is a result of the education process in Ukraine—the ECHR and the practice of the ECtHR are taught as being quite separate from national legislation.[82] According to Oksana Klymovych, for judges there remain serious questions about the inter-relationship between the ECtHR and the national law: 'Ukraine has never been at the point where all Strasbourg decisions were taken seriously as a source of law.'[83] Stanislav Shevchuk, Professor of Law at the

[77] Philip Leach, Helen Hardman, Svetlana Stephenson, and Brad Blitz, *Responding to Systemic Human Rights Violations—An Analysis of Pilot Judgments of the European Court of Human Rights and Their Impact at National Level* (Antwerp-Oxford-Portland: Intersentia, 2010) 34–9.

[78] See 5.1.1 at n 9.

[79] *Sovtransavto Holding v Ukraine*: Interim Resolution ResDH(2004)14, 11 February 2004.

[80] This was the view, for example, of former Ukrainian MP Elina Shyshkina; Interview, 5 July 2012.

[81] Interview, 22 May 2012.

[82] Government Official, Interview, 22 May 2012.

[83] Interview, 22 May 2012.

National University 'Kyiv–Mohyla Academy', refers to the 'long-standing Soviet tradition in Ukraine ... that if something is decided on the international level, it somehow doesn't apply to us on the domestic level'.[84] Yuriy Zaitsev, the former Ukrainian government agent, believes there are fundamentally different legal approaches at play:

> We love provisions to be spelled out; we love to have them in writing. While [in Strasbourg] you have a legal system based on precedent.... Legal positions ... are formed on the basis of a specific judgment ... by the European Court of Human Rights. So, it is a completely different philosophy of law.[85]

Zaitsev also believes that there is an inadequate level of parliamentary scrutiny of draft legislation in order to ensure compliance with the Convention.

Valentyna Telychenko, a lawyer who has represented Yuliya Tymoshenko and the family of Georgiy Gongadze, would welcome Strasbourg adopting a clearer and more direct approach as to the appropriate remedy in its judgments, as, in her view, it would then be more likely that the Ukrainian authorities would implement the decision.[86] Although the ECtHR's pilot judgment in the *Ivanov* case has not led to its successful implementation, some commentators argue that the pilot judgment procedure can in fact be useful in assisting governments:

> Sometimes issues are complex or controversial and you do need to do awareness-raising, training of relevant institutions, with involvement of civil society, before a new law becomes [politically feasible].... This approach also means that when a law is passed it has more chance of being implemented because the ground has been prepared.[87]

According to one (former) government official, where there are significant financial implications of implementing a particular judgment, this is a considerable impediment in Ukraine: it is generally much easier to get changes through which only require amendments to administrative practice or legislation, without there being further financial costs.[88] However, other interviewees are sceptical about claims of state coffers being empty, stressing instead the overriding importance of political will.[89]

Nevertheless, in spite of such difficulties, all of our interviewees indicated that there is a high level of respect for the European Convention system in Ukraine.[90] Speaking in 2012, Dmytro Kotliar, the former Deputy Minister of Justice, highlights the public backing for Ukraine's role within Europe: 'European integration

[84] Interview, 21 May 2012. A similar view was expressed by Valentyna Telychenko; Interview, 18 June 2012.

[85] Interview, 23 July 2012.

[86] Interview, 18 June 2012. See also the discussion at 2.3 on the clarity and prescriptiveness of ECtHR judgments.

[87] Olena Petsun, Interview, 27 June 2012.

[88] Government Official, Interview, 22 May 2012. This was also the view of Irene Fedorovych, of the Social Action Centre/No Borders Project; Interview, 21 May 2012.

[89] Arkadiy Bushchenko, Interview, 21 May 2012; Stanislav Shevchuk, Interview, 21 May 2012.

[90] This was confirmed, for example, by Hryhoriy Nemyria, the current Chair of the Human Rights Committee; Interview, 17 February 2015.

is the only idea which is widely supported by the whole population. If someone says a measure is required to satisfy our obligations to the Council of Europe or the European Union, it has more chance of being adopted.'[91]

Of course, popular support for greater European orientation (and opposition to a Russian-led Eurasian regional union) was at the heart of the protests against Viktor Yanukovych in 2013–14, leading to the conflict in eastern Ukraine.[92] Kotliar emphasizes the perception amongst Ukrainian politicians of the greater importance of the European Union over the Council of Europe, which 'is seen as being of less relevance, but they are still worried about what it says because its statements are picked up by the EU and others'.

Valentyna Telychenko considers that public confidence in the Strasbourg Court is high 'because they don't trust the Ukrainian court system, they have only one institut[ion] that would be for justice ... the European Court'.[93]

European Court Registry lawyer Pavlo Pushkar concurs that there is generally a high level of respect for the Strasbourg Court, although he argues that the problem of judgments becoming apparently unenforceable, for various reasons, as has been the case in relation to *Ivanov*, reduces its perceived legitimacy.[94] Have prevailing political attitudes towards the European Court changed since President Yanukovych left office in February 2014? One indicator may be the responses to the Court's judgment in *Oleksandr Volkov v Ukraine*, which concerned political control over the appointment and dismissal of judges. Supreme Court judge Oleksandr Volkov was dismissed in 2010 at the instigation of the High Council of Justice, a body dominated by politicians (as provided by the Ukrainian Constitution), and confirmed by the *Verkhovna Rada* acting in plenary.[95] Having found four separate violations of the right to a fair trial (Article 6 ECHR) the Court ordered Volkov's reinstatement 'at the earliest possible date'—the first time that such an order had been made by the Court.[96] In spite of the Court's stipulation, successive parliamentary votes in 2013 and 2014 failed to overturn the decision to dismiss judge Volkov.[97] Interestingly, in justifying the opposition to reinstatement, former Ukrainian Minister of Justice Aleksandr Lavrinovich even cited negative British political attitudes towards the

[91] Interview, 21 May 2012.

[92] See, for example, Roy Allison, 'Russian "Deniable" Intervention in Ukraine: How and Why Russia Broke the Rules', *International Affairs* 90: 6 (2014): 1255, 1256–7. Allison argues (1272) that 'Russian action in Crimea only made the new Ukrainian President, Petro Poroshenko, more determined to consolidate Ukraine's orientation towards the EU'.

[93] Interview, 18 June 2012.

[94] Interview, 26 June 2012. See also the discussion of the question of legitimacy in chapter 4.

[95] At the time, Serhiy Kivalov (see also 5.4.1 and 5.5.1) was Chairman of the Parliamentary Committee on the Judiciary and was also a member of the High Council of Justice. The European Court judgments notes that it was Mr Kivalov (referred to in the judgment as 'S.K.') and two other members of the Parliamentary Committee on the Judiciary who lodged requests with the High Council of Justice, asking it to carry out preliminary inquiries into possible professional misconduct by Mr Volkov. He subsequently took part in both bodies' consideration of Mr Volkov's case, as well as a plenary meeting of parliament which also deliberated on the case. See, in particular, paragraphs 14, 16, 23, 26–27, 116, 119, and 121 of the judgment.

[96] *Oleksandr Volkov v Ukraine* (n 21).

[97] *Volkov v Ukraine*: Interim Resolution, CM/ResDH(2014)275, 4 December 2014.

ECtHR.[98] However, the position in Ukraine changed in late 2014, after the parliamentary elections held in October 2014, in which the Petro Poroshenko Bloc received the highest number of seats. Volkov was then reinstated as a Supreme Court judge on 30 January 2015, following a decision by the president of the court.[99]

Serhiy Holovaty, a former Minister of Justice, a former deputy of the *Verkhovna Rada*, and a former member of PACE, argues that although Ukrainian MPs are not very interested in human rights, it is positive that they do not have a hostile attitude to the ECtHR. Instead, they are receptive and recognize the authority of the Court. Speaking during the time of the Yanukovych presidency, he suggested that 'even the ruling majority do not see it as an institution which interferes in domestic affairs and [do not view] national affairs as sovereign in that way'.[100] Dmytro Kotliar agrees that resistance is not on the agenda—but that amongst MPs there is a general lack of understanding of, or interest in, human rights.[101] Oksana Klymovych, of the Westminster Foundation for Democracy–Ukraine, considers that respect for Strasbourg has increased since the introduction of the 2006 Law on Implementation of Judgments, after which Strasbourg judgments were considered to be 'closer to' national legislation, and it became obligatory for the national authorities to implement judgments against Ukraine (including both individual and general measures).[102] Yuriy Zaitsev argues that the very adoption of the 2006 Law was an indication of how seriously MPs were taking the decisions of the ECtHR.[103] Hryhoriy Nemyria, who was elected as chair of the Human Rights Committee of the *Verkhovna Rada* following the October 2014 elections, suggests that awareness of the European Court in Ukraine was at its height in 2012–13 as a result of the *Lutsenko* and *Tymoshenko* judgments, and that 'this helped to focus parliament's attention on the issue—because of the high social importance and [because] the public was very much interested [in] and aware of these issues'.[104]

5.3 Implementation of ECtHR Judgments: The Current System in Ukraine

In this section we examine the current system in Ukraine for the implementation of European Court judgments, which is based on a specific piece of legislation which

[98] This position was then picked up by politicians involved in the domestic debates in the UK about its future engagement with the ECtHR. See: 'Khan Attacks Cameron's stance on European Court of Human Rights', *Observer*, 28 December 2013.

[99] See: Committee of Ministers, 1230 meeting, 9–11 June 2015, Decision case No. 27—Oleksandr Volkov against Ukraine, CM/Del/Dec(2015)1230/27, 12 June 2015. However, as regards general measures concerning legislation regulating the appointment and dismissal of judges, the position at the time of writing remained unresolved. The ministers' deputies emphasized that 'the reform of the Constitution is essential to a full execution of the present judgment in order to restructure the institutional basis of the system of judicial discipline, as called for by the Court's judgment'.

[100] Interview, 28 June 2012.

[101] Interview, 21 May 2012.

[102] Interview, 22 May 2012.

[103] Interview, 23 July 2012.

[104] Interview, 17 February 2015.

came into force in 2006. We primarily consider the respective functions of various government actors, as well as the roles played by the Ombudsman (or Parliament Commissioner for Human Rights), civil society organizations, and the media. The next section discusses the position of parliament, including the potential for it to be involved more centrally in the matter of implementation.

5.3.1 The 2006 Law on the implementation of judgments

Unique within European states at the time it was introduced in 2006, there is a Ukrainian law which specifically addresses the implementation of ECtHR judgments by imposing concrete obligations on various state actors once a judgment has become final (the '2006 Law' or the 'Law on the Implementation of Judgments') (see 3.5.3).[105] According to the 2006 Law, within three days of a Strasbourg Court judgment, the government agent is required to provide a summary of the judgment for publication in the *Uriadovyi Kurier* and *Golos Ukrayiny* newspapers.[106] The full text of the judgment must be translated and the government agent is required to send the judgment to the Ombudsman and to state bodies and officials and other people directly affected.[107] The 2006 Law requires the government agent and the State Bailiff's Office (and other state bodies) to take various steps to ensure compliance with the individual measures required by the judgment.[108]

The state authorities are also required by the 2006 Law to implement general measures, in order to eliminate any underlying systemic problems.[109] To that end, the government agent must, within one month of the final judgment, send a 'motion on general measures' to the cabinet of ministers.[110] The motion should contain, inter alia, information about the cause of the violation and proposals for legislative amendments and changes to administrative practice, and any other general measures required. Briefings must also be sent to the Supreme Court and the Secretariat of the *Verkhovna Rada*. The 2006 Law requires general measures to be adopted and relevant draft laws to be submitted by the cabinet of ministers to the *Verkhovna Rada*, within three months of the prime minister's instruction.[111]

On its face, the 2006 Law is to be welcomed because it imposes clear, time-limited obligations on the government in relation to the implementation of Strasbourg judgments. However, two fundamental questions arise when commentators discuss the 2006 Law: does it work, and is it necessary? These questions are asked in the context of a system in which political will is all-important. Indeed, one (former) senior government official told us that the processes required by the 2006 Law are complied with, but there is little or no response from the cabinet of

[105] Law on the Enforcement of Judgments and the Application of the Case-Law of the European Court of Human Rights Judgments 2006, Law No. 3477-IV of 23 February 2006. Various, largely technical amendments were made to the 2006 Law under Law No. 3135-VI (2011). See also the discussion about national implementation legislation at 3.5.3.

[106] Article 4 of the 2006 Law.

[107] Articles 5 and 6 of the 2006 Law.

[108] Articles 7–12 of the 2006 Law.

[109] Article 13 of the 2006 Law.

[110] Article 14 of the 2006 Law.

[111] Article 15 of the 2006 Law.

ministers, which means that the initiative to get things moving lies with the office of the government agent. Subsequently, many proposals put forward by the government agent are then blocked by the cabinet of ministers, for want of sufficient political will to instigate the requisite changes.[112] The former MP Serhiy Holovaty argues that the problems of non-compliance with European standards in Ukraine are not the result of the inefficiency of particular structures or systems, but, more fundamentally, result from the prevailing political and legal culture, and the absence of political will to bring about the requisite changes.[113] In spite of the unusual specificity of the 2006 Law, commentators have argued that the law is not in fact effectively applied[114] or only partially so,[115] or that there are sometimes substantial delays.[116] It is also suggested that there is insufficient time or technical expertise for adequate translations of judgments to be produced, as required by the 2006 Law.[117]

There is also a good deal of scepticism about the need for a specific law on implementation. One senior government official suggests that the 2006 Law had been introduced because of the lack of understanding within state bodies about the ECtHR, and in particular why its judgments should be executed.[118] However, for Pavlo Pushkar, the Ukrainian Court Registry lawyer, the introduction of the law was not an important necessity, but was rather emblematic of Ukraine's overly positivistic legal culture: 'When things are not functioning there is an idea that a new law will surely help—but it is not the law itself that is the problem, it's mostly the way it is implemented in practice.'[119]

The government agent's practice is not to publish the motions regarding the implementation of judgments that are sent to the cabinet[120] (so that they are available for scrutiny by, e.g., MPs and civil society),[121] although they are not formally confidential. Dmytro Kotliar believes it would be useful to require the government agent to report on this and publish the motion itself, although as it only comprises initial proposals to the government, he questions how worthwhile it would be in practice to make it public, as the government may well reject such proposals.

Attempts by Serhiy Holovaty, the former deputy of the *Verkhovna Rada* and former member of PACE, to amend the 2006 Law in order to develop the extent of parliamentary oversight of the implementation of Strasbourg judgments are discussed at 5.4.3.

[112] Government Official, Interview, 22 May 2012.

[113] Interview, 28 June 2012. We heard a similar view from Valentyna Telychenko; Interview, 18 June 2012.

[114] Myroslava Antonovych, Interview, 21 May 2012; Serhiy Holovaty, Interview, 28 June 2012; Elina Shyshkina, Interview, 5 July 2012. See also Leach et al. (n 77) 149–50.

[115] Arkadiy Bushchenko, Executive Director of the Ukrainian Helsinki Human Rights Union, considers that the 2006 Law works well in relation to issues of just satisfaction, but otherwise there are many problems with it; Interview, 21 May 2012.

[116] Stanislav Shevchuk, Interview, 21 May 2012; Written Answers to Questionnaire, Alexander Galkin, 21 May 2012.

[117] Pavlo Pushkar, Interview, 26 June 2012.

[118] Government Official, Interview, 22 May 2012.

[119] Interview, 26 June 2012.

[120] Stanislav Shevchuk, Interview, 21 May 2012.

[121] Arkadiy Bushchenko confirms that the motions are never discussed with civil society; Interview, 21 May 2012.

Despite the ineffectiveness of the Ukrainian law (at least in relation to general measures), and the still uncertain impact of similar laws elsewhere, some commentators argue that providing a legal basis for the implementation of decisions of international courts is inherently beneficial, for reasons discussed at 3.5.3. Such arguments reflect aspects of the 'managerialist' approach, or even of acculturation (both of which we discuss at 3.1). National implementation legislation should not, however, be viewed as a panacea. As we argue at 3.5.3, and as the experience of Ukraine demonstrates, the mere *existence* of such legislation is neither a necessary nor sufficient condition for effective implementation.

5.3.2 The government agent

The role played by the Ukrainian government agent (who represents the government in its dealings with the European Court) in respect of the implementation of Court judgments has been enshrined in law since 2006 (as discussed at 3.5.1). In Ukraine, the government agent is appointed by the Cabinet of Ministers and is de facto subordinate to the Minister of Justice. The government agent's office is in practice a vital source of information about Court judgments within the government.[122]

Commentators have pointed to the significance of the 'clout' enjoyed by government agents for getting things done—both in terms of their formal status and their personal ability to engage effectively with senior politicians (see 3.5.1).[123] One government official expresses clear frustration at the impotence of the government agent in Ukraine: 'In practice, there is no reaction [to the information disseminated by the government agent], even from the cabinet of ministers.'[124] European Court Registry lawyer Pavlo Pushkar observes that some of the proposals for legislative changes in response to the judgments of the Court put forward by the government agent in the past were changed and eventually 'weakened', after their review and amendment by the Ministry of Justice and the cabinet of ministers.[125] Dmytro Kotliar suggests that 'it all depends on the personal profile of the individual who holds the office'.[126] The government agent corresponds with ministries and seeks information from them, but according to Kotliar, the post does not have sufficient status to push through particular general measures, unless there is support from the Minister of Justice, or otherwise from the government.[127] This view is echoed by the Director of the Ukrainian Helsinki Human Rights Union, Arkadiy Bushchenko, who also suggests that the government agent's office has insufficient influence over parliament or the judicial system.[128]

According to Kotliar, a further problem is that the office of the government agent has insufficient capacity to handle the large volume of cases against Ukraine

[122] Pavlo Pushkar, Interview, 26 June 2012.

[123] See, for example, Leach et al. (n 77) 72–3 (Poland), 140–1 (Russia).

[124] Government Official, Interview, 22 May 2012.

[125] Interview, 26 June 2012.

[126] Interview, 21 May 2012.

[127] Interview, 21 May 2012.

[128] Interview, 21 May 2012.

(including interim measures (Rule 39) applications),[129] as well as deal with the implementation of judgments.[130] For that reason, Judge Ganna Yudkivska advocates having one person taking responsibility for the pending cases and another handling the implementation process.[131] This is a proposal supported by Arkadiy Bushchenko who sees a conflict of interest in the current arrangements.[132] However, Serhiy Holovaty argues that there is no need to strengthen the power or capacity of the office of the government agent: 'to a great extent the efficiency of these institutions depends on the political will of the individuals who hold these positions'.[133]

5.4 Implementation of ECtHR Judgments: The Role of Parliament

This section examines to what extent the *Verkhovna Rada* is involved in the consideration of the appropriate response to ECtHR judgments against Ukraine, and how it might be further developed.

5.4.1 Parliamentary committees

Within the *Verkhovna Rada* there are various parliamentary committees which do not have formal or permanent legal status as their remits are defined by parliamentary resolution (during each new parliament). The membership of parliamentary committees is decided in proportion to parties' representation in parliament.

In recent years, there have been several committees whose remits could be relevant to the question of human rights implementation, notably the Committee on Legal Policy and Justice ('the Justice Committee') and the Committee on Human Rights, National Minorities and Interethnic Relations ('the Human Rights Committee') (and possibly also the Committee on European Integration or the Committee on Legislative Support of Law Enforcement). To date, however, none has in fact been routinely involved in examining the enforcement of European Court judgments. According to the Ukrainian lawyer Pavlo Pushkar, the parliament evidently does not always in its practice effectively analyse draft legislation for compliance with the Convention and the case law of the Court, even though in theory it has the full technical capacity to do so.[134] The former Deputy Minister of Justice, Dmytro Kotliar, argues that the monitoring of implementation is not being carried out because there is no formal requirement to do so: 'Ukraine is a very positivistic country, so if it is not written down somewhere, in some instruction or law, no one will do it.'[135]

129 See the discussion of interim measures at 2.2.
130 Interview, 21 May 2012.
131 Interview, 27 June 2012.
132 Interview, 21 May 2012.
133 Interview, 28 June 2012.
134 Interview, 26 June 2012.
135 Interview, 21 May 2012.

Oksana Klymovych, of the Westminster Foundation for Democracy–Ukraine, agrees that it seems in practice to be problematic for MPs to monitor how the executive is responding to a judgment; however, she explains: 'We encourage parliament all the time to make requests. We remind [parliamentary] staff during our training that they are not only responsible for the drafting of legislation, but also for monitoring its implementation.'[136]

One of the most influential committees has been the Justice Committee, in part because it has been involved in the appointment of judges, and in reviewing the law on the judiciary, which have been politically highly contentious areas in Ukraine.[137] It was formerly chaired by Serhiy Kivalov (Party of Regions) who exercised powerful political influence. In 2011, the former MP Serhiy Holovaty proposed that the scope of the Justice Committee should be expanded to include control over the execution of Court decisions, however, it was not passed as it did not have sufficient support (as we discuss further at 5.4.3).

The Human Rights Committee has had a lower profile and status than the Justice Committee (see 3.4.2). Dmytro Kotliar argues that there are two principal reasons for this—under the Yanukovych regime the question of human rights was not high on the political agenda and the Human Rights Committee did not have budgetary responsibility. It was formerly chaired by Oleg Zarubinsky, a representative of the Lytvyn Bloc (People's Party, Labour Party of Ukraine) which had a relatively small number of deputies.

Aside from the question of appropriate structures, Oksana Klymovych argues that inculcating a human rights culture across parliament is critical. In her view, many members of parliamentary committees often deal with human rights issues in their everyday work without realizing that these *are* human rights related issues:

> The question ... is how the judgments of the ECHR are embedded into the work of parliament. If somebody brings a judgment to the attention of the staff, then it might be reflected in the discussion ... but if this doesn't happen at the right moment, then it's not incorporated.[138]

Natalia Pogrebnyak, of the Ukrainian Centre for Parliamentary Studies, emphasizes the primary importance of the role which parliament has in realizing human rights, but she is at the same time frustrated by the limited influence of the parliamentary committees in the legislative process.[139]

Pavlo Pushkar, the European Court Registry lawyer, argues in favour of a specialist parliamentary committee dealing, inter alia, with the enforcement of judgments, which would liaise directly with the existing Council of Europe structures, including the Registry of the Court, and the government agent's office (and the parliament's expert department—see 5.4.2), and which would review draft legislation for compliance with the ECHR and provide expert advice (in the light of both Ukrainian and non-Ukrainian cases).[140] Halnya Shevchuk and Oksana Klymovych

[136] Interview, 22 May 2012. [137] See 5.1.1 at n 9. [138] Interview, 22 May 2012.

[139] Natalia Pogrebnyak, *Human Beings and their Rights: How is the Parliament Ensuring Those?* Ukrainian Centre for Parliamentary Studies, 7 February 2001.

[140] Interview, 26 June 2012.

(of the Westminster Foundation for Democracy–Ukraine) are also in favour of the establishment of a permanent body within parliament dedicated to the implementation of judgments. However, they suggest that it should be established within the permanent staff of the parliament, and accordingly at arm's length from the political parties.[141] Arguably, this could be a useful transitional model in states where parliamentary controls have proved weak, and are still in development, but we would suggest that to 'depoliticize' the process would neither be feasible nor desirable.

5.4.2 Provision of legal advice

As noted at 5.2.1, our interviewees confirm that MPs in Ukraine have a low level of knowledge about the Convention and the ECtHR. Serhiy Holovaty considers that most MPs are not interested in the ECHR, and, speaking in 2012 during the period of the Yanukovych regime, he argued that even the Human Rights Committee was 'completely ignorant'.[142] A senior government official describes the level of MPs' knowledge about the Convention as being very poor.[143] Stanislav Shevchuk, Professor of Law at the National University 'Kyiv–Mohyla Academy', suggests that MPs' interest is focused on the overtly political cases, such as the Lutsenko or Tymoshenko decisions.[144]

Elina Shyshkina, a former MP from the *Verkhovna Rada* (BYuT faction) suggests that language skills are an important factor (see also 5.3.1 as to the need to translate ECtHR judgments): 'There is no specific place for MPs to become informed about new decisions of the ECtHR. It's a matter of who is interested already and who can read English or French.'[145] She also argues that MPs do not understand the importance of the Court and its case law and that the Council of Europe is not regarded as important: 'The first thing that needs to be changed is [their] attitude and mentality.'

Pavlo Pushkar considers that MPs have a basic awareness about the ECHR, but emphasizes that few have had a legal education, and few have competence in international law or legislative drafting or any in-depth knowledge of the case law—they have a tendency to focus on current problems arising in particular cases, rather than considering issues that may prove to be problematic in the future or they are involved in drafting legislation in response to an immediate situation, rather than looking into strategic, long-term goals. He also suggests that MPs' conception of human rights is more concerned with economic and social rights (reflecting the classic Soviet

[141] Interviews, 22 May 2012.

[142] Interview, 28 June 2012. A similar view about MPs' ignorance of the ECHR and/or ECtHR was expressed to us by NGOs and lawyers: Interview with various NGO representatives, 21 May 2012; Dmytro Groysman, Interview, 22 May 2012; Alexander Galkin (written questionnaire), 21 May 2012; Valentyna Telychenko, Interview, 18 June 2012.

[143] Interview (anonymous), 22 May 2012.

[144] Interview, 21 May 2012. See 5.1.1 at nn 12 and 13 as to the cases.

[145] Interview, 5 July 2012. This point was also made by Yuriy Zaitsev, the former Ukrainian government agent; Interview, 23 July 2012.

tradition) rather than with fundamental civil and political rights (which he considers is also a reflection of the general societal attitude to human rights).[146]

The Westminster Foundation for Democracy–Ukraine works with parliamentary committee staff in developing their knowledge of the ECtHR and its case law, but according to Oksana Klymovych (from the Foundation) they have a limited knowledge of the ECtHR's case law.[147] Klymovych believes that it is vital that there is independent human rights expertise within parliament, responsible for the analysis of all draft laws, especially those submitted to the parliament by the cabinet of ministers, and for scrutinizing compliance with the standards developed in the case law of the ECtHR.

Within parliament MPs are able to draw on the resources of the legal department and a separate scientific expert department. The latter prepares opinions on all draft laws submitted to parliament. There is no strict definition of the scope of its remit, but in essence the department analyses draft laws for compliance with existing legislation and the Constitution. It will occasionally make reference to human rights, but there is no formal system for the department to verify compliance with the Convention. Pavlo Pushkar believes that the scientific expert department is competent to scrutinize compliance of draft laws with the Convention, but that its views are not always taken into account.[148] The former Deputy Minister of Justice, Dmytro Kotliar, agrees that the opinions of the scientific expert department have authority, but believes its views may be ignored simply because of political will in favour of or against a particular proposed measure.[149] Hryhoriy Nemyria, who chairs the Human Rights Committee of the *Verkhovna Rada*, considers that external civil society support for MPs is essential: 'The support [from the secretariat] is absolutely not sufficient, so it's necessary to reach out to professional bodies and NGOs in analysing the practices of the European Court of Human Rights.'[150]

Serhiy Holovaty has proposed the establishment of a screening unit within the parliamentary legal department with the role of preparing opinions on draft legislation and its compliance with the ECHR. However, his 2011 proposal to this effect did not muster sufficient support (see 5.4.3). Nevertheless, because of its potential, he considers it would be worthwhile to set up such a body, working on a professional, legal basis, even in the absence of political interest (see our comments at 5.4.1 on such 'depoliticization').[151]

5.4.3 Proposals to strengthen the role of parliament in implementation

Serhiy Holovaty, during his time as a deputy of the *Verkhovna Rada* and member of the Parliamentary Assembly, campaigned in favour of parliamentary oversight of the implementation of Strasbourg judgments. As he considered that the 2006 Law

146 Interview, 26 June 2012.
147 Interview, 22 May 2012.
148 Interview, 26 June 2012.
149 Interview, 21 May 2012.
150 Interview, 17 February 2015.
151 Interview, 28 June 2012.

was not operative or effective in practice,[152] in November 2011 he tabled a resolution in the *Verkhovna Rada* which was aimed at amending the 2006 Law to this effect.[153] The amendments would have required the government agent to submit the motion on general measures to parliament at the same time as it is sent to the cabinet of ministers (Article 14(4)). The Holovaty proposals would also have added a new Article 20 to the 2006 Law, requiring the *Verkhovna Rada* to 'carry out parliamentary control in the area of implementation of judgments and application of the case law' of the ECtHR and establishing a duty on the government agent to submit to the *Verkhovna Rada* an annual report about the implementation of judgments and the application of ECtHR case law, including legislative amendments in relation to cases requiring 'general measures'. Holovaty also tabled a draft parliamentary resolution proposing the following innovations in the parliamentary process:[154]

- the Parliamentary Secretariat should prepare proposals on the resources required for the verification of draft legislation for Convention compliance;
- the Justice Committee should regularly review and analyse the implementation of judgments against Ukraine and against other states where cases may have implications for Ukraine;
- there should be six-monthly Justice Committee hearings on the implementation situation, with the involvement of relevant government officials, parliamentarians, NGOs, and experts; and
- there should be annual parliamentary hearings on the implementation situation, with relevant government officials, NGOs, and experts.

The explanatory note to the resolution recalled that the 2006 Law placed the responsibility for implementation on the executive, but that the Parliamentary Assembly also expected a parliamentary dimension to it. Holovaty recalls that PACE had threatened Ukraine with the removal of its delegation's credentials if the national parliament did not become involved.[155] In October 2006, PACE had passed a resolution on the implementation of Strasbourg judgments which underlined the importance of parliamentary monitoring at the national level, and which also reserved the right to challenge the credentials of a national delegation where the state in question failed to take the requisite measures to implement a judgment or where the national parliament failed to exert the necessary pressure on the government to achieve effective implementation.[156] Further pressure had been exerted by PACE in 2009, when, following a visit to Kiev, Christos Pourgourides, the PACE rapporteur

[152] Serhiy Holovaty, Interview, 28 June 2012.

[153] We are grateful to Dmytro Kotliar for providing an unofficial translation of these proposed amendments.

[154] Draft resolution 'On the Parliamentary Control of Implementation of the European Court of Human Rights Judgments', Mr Holovaty, 2011 (unofficial translation provided by Dmytro Kotliar).

[155] Interview, 28 June 2012.

[156] PACE Resolution 1516 (2006), Implementation of judgments of the European Court of Human Rights, 2 October 2006, para. 22.7.

on the implementation of judgments of the European Court, called for greater levels of supervision of the implementation of judgments by the *Verkhovna Rada* (see 5.5.1).

The Holovaty proposals were passed on first reading; however, MPs rejected the accompanying parliamentary resolution to provide the necessary mechanisms to conduct effective scrutiny of the implementation of judgments and further efforts aimed at reform were unsuccessful.[157]

Speaking in 2012, Oksana Klymovych (of the Westminster Foundation for Democracy–Ukraine) questioned whether the Justice Committee, as it was then constituted, was suited to take on such a role, because of its pro-government and pro-presidential stance.[158] Dmytro Kotliar has serious doubts about the sincerity of some senior political figures in considering such proposals to increase parliament's involvement in implementation: 'They have no understanding of the issue or genuine [intent], and they are doing it … to present themselves as … pro-European and pro-democratic, especially when they have all these problems with abuses in the criminal justice [system] and political persecution.'[159]

Judge Ganna Yudkivska is in favour of the government agent appearing before parliament annually in order to discuss both cases against Ukraine and relevant judgments against other states, and to inform MPs about potential violations that might occur if legislation is not amended, and violations already found in cases against Ukraine where legislative amendments need to be made as soon as possible (see 2.4).[160]

Hryhoriy Nemyria, the chair of the Human Rights Committee of the *Verkhovna Rada*, proposes to amend the remit of that committee by adding a specific responsibility to monitor the implementation of judgments of the ECtHR. He envisages introducing bi-annual or quarterly reports by the government agent to the Human Rights Committee, which would then be entitled to take follow-up measures and issue its own opinions and recommendations on questions of implementation. Mr Nemyria considers that there are various ways in which this could be achieved, 'but what is important is that there is a structural process of parliamentary oversight … to tackle it in a systematic manner'. Speaking in February 2015, Mr Nemyria was confident of being able to introduce such changes: '[I]n the new parliament, with a pro-European majority there is a good opportunity to adopt this new procedure.'[161]

5.4.4 The Ombudsman

Established in 1998, the position of Ombudsman (Parliament Commissioner for Human Rights) is provided for in the Ukrainian Constitution, which entitles individuals to appeal to the Ombudsman in order to secure the protection of their

157 Resolution 'On the Parliamentary Control of Implementation of the European Court of Human Rights Judgments' (unofficial translation provided by Dmytro Kotliar).

158 Interview, 22 May 2012.

159 Interview, 21 May 2012.

160 Interview, 27 June 2012.

161 Interview, 17 February 2015.

human rights.[162] Formally independent of any state entity, the Ombudsman is elected by secret ballot by the *Verkhovna Rada* for a term of five years. The current Ombudsman is Valeriya Lutkovska, a former government agent before the European Court, who was appointed in April 2012.[163] Her powers include the right of appeal to the Constitutional Court to challenge the constitutionality of laws, acts of parliament and acts of the president or cabinet of ministers. According to the 2006 Law on Implementation of Judgments, the Ombudsman receives a copy of every ECtHR judgment.[164]

The Ombudsman reports annually to parliament, and may publish special reports on an ad hoc basis.[165] She has advocated Ukraine's accession to human rights conventions, called for reservations to the ECHR to be lifted, and for Ukraine's reports to Council of Europe committees to be de-classified and published.[166] The first annual report, in 2000, referred to the possibility of sanctions being imposed on Ukraine should there be delays in bringing its domestic legislation into line with European standards. In 2006, she called for the PACE monitoring process to be continued until it became 'common practice' for both domestic court judgments and ECtHR judgments to be enforced.[167]

In 2010, the Ombudsman submitted a Special Report to the *Verkhovna Rada* on Ukraine's observance of European standards, which was a detailed and critical appraisal of the many human rights problems which had been encountered since its accession to the Council of Europe.[168] The report was critical of political interference with the administrative court system and the election of judges.[169] Noting that the ECtHR's judgments against Ukraine revealed 'systemic and widespread violations of human rights' and 'serious flaws' in the domestic legislative framework, the report stated that the Ombudsman had repeatedly drawn such problems to the attention of senior officials and the relevant institutions.[170] The report suggested that the failure to implement ECtHR judgments had become increasingly acute—enforcement was frequently partial or delayed, or judgments were 'completely ignored'.[171] It recommended specific measures to be implemented in order to comply with the *Ivanov* pilot judgment.[172] However, the report made no recommendations aimed at improving the domestic implementation mechanisms, or about parliament's role in the implementation process.

[162] Articles 55 and 101 of the Constitution. See also the Law on the Ukrainian Parliamentary Commissioner for Human Rights of 23 December 1997.

[163] The first Ombudsman, elected in 1998, was Nina Karpachova, who was re-elected in 2003 and 2007.

[164] Article 5 of the 2006 Law.

[165] The reports can be found on the Ombudsman's website: <http://www.ombudsman.gov.ua/en/>.

[166] Ukrainian Parliament Commissioner for Human Rights, *Special Report of the Ukrainian Parliament Commissioner for Human Rights: The State of the Observance of European Standards of Human Rights and Freedoms in Ukraine*, October 2010, 16.

[167] Ukrainian Parliament Commissioner for Human Rights (n 166) 20.

[168] Ukrainian Parliament Commissioner for Human Rights (n 166) 20.

[169] Ukrainian Parliament Commissioner for Human Rights (n 166) 29.

[170] Ukrainian Parliament Commissioner for Human Rights (n 166) 37.

[171] Ukrainian Parliament Commissioner for Human Rights (n 166) 44–6.

[172] Ukrainian Parliament Commissioner for Human Rights (n 166) 40–1.

Some of our interlocutors question whether the Ombudsman's office has sufficient clout or independence in order to be influential as regards parliament. The Ombudsman's reports have clearly placed a considerable degree of emphasis on implementation questions, which is very much to be welcomed. However, in the course of our research we found no evidence that the Ombudsman's work in this field has had any real, tangible impact on implementation processes or on particular measures instigated by the Ukrainian authorities in response to Strasbourg judgments.

In May 2015, as a result of a legislative proposal by a number of *Verkhovna Rada* deputies seeking the annulment of the decision appointing Valeriya Lutkovska as ombudsman in 2012, the Council of Europe felt it necessary to intervene publicly in order to shore up the independence of the position. The Council of Europe Commissioner Nils Muižnieks wrote to the Chair of the Parliament, Volodymyr Groysman, to express his concern about the risk of undermining the independence of the institution of the ombudsman and underlining the importance of complying with the Belgrade Principles.[173]

5.4.5 Parliament's relationship with civil society

A prevailing view amongst our interlocutors is that parliament and the legislative process take little account of the stance of civil society, whose views are routinely excluded.[174] One interviewee suggests that NGOs are considered to be competent and well-staffed, but they lack political influence. The interviewee recalls that in the Soviet era in Ukraine, 'public associations' used to be little more than extensions of political parties and suggested that some politicians still have that mindset towards NGOs today—therefore they are suspicious of them.

NGOs such as the Vinnytsya Human Rights Group (VHRG)[175] have been able to maintain collaborative links with individual MPs on particular issues. One of its specialist areas is refugee rights, on which it works in conjunction with the UNHCR,

[173] Letter from Nils Muižnieks to Volodymyr Groysman, 26 May 2015 (available on the Council of Europe Documents Database at wcd.coe.int). Muižnieks' letter drew attention to passages in the Belgrade Principles (Belgrade Principles on the Relationship Between NHRIs and Parliaments, adopted in Belgrade, Serbia, on 22–23 February 2012) relating to the role of parliaments as regards annual reports published by NHRIs: 'Parliaments should receive, review and respond to NHRI reports and ensure that they debate the priorities of the NHRI and should seek opportunities to debate the most significant reports of the NHRI promptly' (para. 16); 'Parliaments should develop a principled framework for debating the activities of NHRIs consistent with respect for their independence' (para. 17); and 'Parliaments should hold open discussions on the recommendations issued by NHRIs' (para. 18). Moreover, 'Parliaments should seek information from the relevant public authorities on the extent to which the relevant public authorities have considered and responded to NHRIs recommendations' (para. 19). Concern was also expressed by the Council of Europe's Special Adviser to the Secretary-General (SASG) on Ukraine. See: 'The SASG expresses concern on the threat to the independence of the Ukrainian Parliament Commissioner for Human Rights', 5 June 2015.

[174] Irene Fedorovych, Interview 21 May 2012; Pavlo Pushkar, Interview, 26 June 2012.

[175] The VHRG was registered in 2001, but it had existed unofficially since 1993 as a group of Amnesty International activists. VHRG specializes in refugee rights, anti-torture, and patients' rights.

but VHRG's former Director, Dmytro Groysman, said that few MPs want it to be known by the general public that they are in contact with international organizations, because of the common perceptions about having such links. According to Groysman, it can be more productive for NGOs to work with parliamentary staff, whom he considered to be often more influential than parliamentarians themselves.[176]

Oksana Klymovych (of the Westminster Foundation for Democracy–Ukraine) questions whether there is sufficient understanding within civil society of the Strasbourg pilot judgment procedure, noting that there was no public campaign behind the *Ivanov* decision. According to Klymovych, some lawyers and NGOs have good legal knowledge of ECtHR standards, but 'the knowledge should be spread to the public'.[177]

5.4.6 The role of the media

None of our interlocutors suggested to us that the Ukrainian media has an important role to play in relation to the implementation of ECtHR judgments. This is undoubtedly due to the continuing repressive media climate. In 2012, Freedom House reported on growing government control over the media in Ukraine.[178] In addition to noting the increasing politicization of the private media, Freedom House also concluded that the state media 'remained unreformed and continued to serve the interests of senior politicians and the bureaucracy'.[179] As noted at 5.1.1, by 2014, Freedom House had downgraded Ukraine's status from 'Partly Free' to 'Not Free', citing an increased concentration of print media ownership by pro-government groups, the increased politicization of private media, and that the National Television and Radio Broadcasting Council regularly applied regulations in a 'secretive and highly partisan manner'.[180]

One of our interviewees acknowledges that, as regards issues that may be the subject of Strasbourg judgments, media coverage can mobilize public opinion on a short-term basis, but the interviewee suggests that such effects are not long-lasting. Irene Fedorovych (of the Social Action Centre/No Borders Project) argues that the media rarely, if ever, cover stories arising directly from an ECtHR judgment, and that they tend to focus on the monetary implications of a decision, without understanding its significance.[181]

5.5 The Relationship between Parliament and Council of Europe Bodies

Former Minister of Justice, Serhiy Holovaty, argues that awareness of human rights amongst MPs has slowly grown during the period of Ukraine's membership of the Council of Europe. However, he points out that concepts such as

[176] Interview, 22 May 2012. [177] Interview, 22 May 2012.
[178] Freedom House, *Freedom of the Press 2012*, 28. [179] Freedom House (n 178) 350–2.
[180] Freedom House (n 178). [181] Interview, 21 May 2012.

the rule of law were alien to those brought up under the Soviet heritage.[182] This section considers to what extent Council of Europe institutions can encourage a deeper engagement by the *Verkhovna Rada* in questions of the human rights implementation.

As discussed at 5.2, Ukraine remains subject to Council of Europe monitoring procedures, and in 2012 PACE reiterated that a number of key commitments made by Ukraine on accession to the Council of Europe in 1995 had still not been fulfilled. It expressed its particular concern about politically motivated prosecutions, the lack of independence of the judiciary, deficiencies in the criminal justice process and wider systemic problems in the legal system.[183] In addition to these formal, institutional links, informal links between Council of Europe bodies and national MPs can also be influential. For example, Judge Ganna Yudkivska acknowledges the importance of developing links between the ECtHR and MPs on an informal basis. She also underlines the significance of keeping MPs informed and of making it clear to them that the quicker they act, the fewer ECHR violations will be found.[184] For her, the role of parliament is pivotal: 'The Convention is a subsidiarity mechanism—the main [responsibility] to guarantee human rights is on the parliament. The more proactive role they take, the better protection of human rights we will have.'

5.5.1 The role of the Parliamentary Assembly of the Council of Europe

Ukraine has twelve members of PACE (and twelve substitute members), and at the time of writing the Assembly's Legal Affairs Committee has three full Ukrainian members, all of whom (at the time of writing) sit on its Sub-committee on the Implementation of Judgments of the ECtHR, and two of whom sit on its Sub-committee on Human Rights. In recent years, given the increasing focus of the Legal Affairs Committee on attempting to resolve delays in the implementation of ECtHR judgments, and in view also of the particular unresolved systemic issues in Ukraine (see 5.2), PACE has sought to engage constructively with its Ukrainian members on these issues.

In July 2009, following a visit to Kiev, Christos Pourgourides, the then PACE rapporteur on the implementation of judgments of the European Court, called for greater domestic parliamentary supervision of the implementation of judgments. During his visit, a memorandum of understanding was signed as regards regular parliamentary supervision of Strasbourg judgments concerning Ukraine,[185] which recommended that the parliamentary Justice Committee (or a sub-committee of it)

[182] Interview, 28 June 2012.

[183] PACE Resolution 1862 (2012) (n 10) para. 17.

[184] Ganna Yudkivska, Interview, 27 June 2012.

[185] PACE, Committee on Legal Affairs and Human Rights, Press Release, 'Ukraine: Call for Better Implementation of Judgments of the Court', 9 July 2009.

should monitor the implementation of judgments against Ukraine, and other relevant case law.[186] The memorandum was co-signed by Serhiy Kivalov, as Chairman of the Justice Committee in the *Verkhovna Rada*. In his 2010 report on implementation of judgments, noting that, subsequently, information about parliamentary supervision, as required by the memorandum, had not been forthcoming, Mr Pourgourides proposed to call Mr Kivalov before the Committee to provide an explanation.[187] The Pourgourides report was highly critical of the failure to address the problem of the non-enforcement of judgments, and the absence of political will to resolve the issue of the excessive length of legal proceedings. In view of the large-scale and complex nature of the issues identified, Pourgourides called for a comprehensive strategy which needed co-ordination at the highest political level, subject to close monitoring by parliament, which, he advocated, should have the means to compel the government to solve the issues as a matter of priority.[188]

In 2011, Ukraine was one of nine states on which PACE decided to focus its implementation follow-up work as a result of its major structural problems.[189] In April 2012 the Legal Affairs Committee held a hearing with the head of the Ukrainian PACE delegation, Ivan Popescu, to consider the question of implementation. The minutes of that hearing do not, however, provide any evidence to suggest that there has been effective parliamentary engagement on implementation issues.[190] In its eighth report on the implementation of judgments, published in 2015, the Legal Affairs Committee noted the lack of progress as regards Ukraine, acknowledging the impact of the recent tumultuous events.[191]

There are differing views about the results of these efforts by PACE to establish an effective parliamentary dimension to Ukraine's follow-up to Strasbourg judgments. One senior government official said that resolutions from the Committee of Ministers have little impact on MPs, but argued that PACE is particularly influential when MPs are required during its meetings to provide explanations about the non-implementation of judgments, which then requires them to think about what changes are required.[192] Yuriy Zaitsev, the former Ukrainian government

[186] PACE, Committee on Legal Affairs and Human Rights, National parliaments: guarantors of human rights in Europe, Doc. 12636, 6 June 2011 (Rapporteur: Christos Pourgourides) para. 82.

[187] 7th Rapporteur Report (n 57).

[188] 7th Rapporteur Report (n 57) para. 174. See also PACE, Committee on Legal Affairs and Human Rights, Implementation of judgments of the European Court of Human Rights: Preparation of the 8th report, Addendum, AS/Jur (2013) 14 Addendum, 10 May 2013 (Rapporteur: Mr Klaas de Vries).

[189] PACE Resolution 1787 (2011), Implementation of judgments of the European Court of Human Rights, 26 January 2011. See also Recommendation 1955(2011), Implementation of judgments of the European Court of Human Rights, 26 January 2011.

[190] PACE, Committee on Legal Affairs and Human Rights, AS/Jur (2013) 13 (n 71) 2–3.

[191] 8th Rapporteur Report (n 57) para. 18: 'Almost no progress has been noted regarding Ukraine, which could be partly explained by the recent turmoil in this country, the annexation of Crimea by the Russian Federation and the violent conflict in eastern Ukraine, which recently prompted Ukraine to derogate from certain articles of the Convention under Article 15 ECHR. Ukraine is nevertheless legally obliged to implement the Court's judgments and the Council of Europe is ready to assist it in accomplishing this task.'

[192] Government Official, Interview, 22 May 2012.

agent, argues that PACE members have a particular responsibility to educate and inform others:

> … when they are back in the country, acting as members of parliament, they certainly have more opportunities to convey to all other members of parliament and to the parliament as a whole, the country as a whole, the importance of the concept of implementation of the European Court of Human Rights judgments.[193]

The benefits which may flow from involvement in PACE are acknowledged by Oksana Klymovych of the Westminster Foundation for Democracy–Ukraine: 'We see different practice, from MPs who bring information back, communicate it to staff and explain the standards, and MPs who do not.'[194]

However, Serhiy Holovaty points to the limitations of the role of PACE members. He argues that if they represent the ruling party in Ukraine then they direct their efforts not at reform, but at neutralizing criticism of Ukraine (see 2.6.2).[195] Dmytro Groysman concurs, suggesting that they use their membership of PACE 'as a reflection of internal political discussions and conflicts'.[196] Kotliar agrees with that sentiment and, speaking in 2012, considers the PACE delegation to be very inactive.[197]

5.5.2 Judgments against other states

As discussed at 2.1.1, the extent to which Strasbourg judgments ought to have effects across a number of European states (the *res interpretata* principle), has gained increasing prominence within the Council of Europe discourse.[198] Ukrainian law imposes an obligation on the courts to apply both the European Convention and its case law.[199] However, the judicial application of Strasbourg case law in practice remains highly variable. According to Dmytro Kotliar, it is very rare that non-Ukrainian judgments have any real influence on developments in Ukraine, although he acknowledges that the Constitutional Court will from time to time make reference to such cases.[200] Judge Ganna Yudkivska suggests that because of their legal background and training, it remains conceptually difficult for judges in the Ukrainian courts to accept judgments against other countries as precedents

[193] Interview, 23 July 2012 [194] Interview, 22 May 2012.

[195] Interview, 28 June 2012. A similar view is expressed by Stanislav Shevchuk; Interview, 21 May 2012.

[196] Interview, 22 May 2012. [197] Interview, 21 May 2012.

[198] See, for example, PACE, Committee on Legal Affairs and Human Rights, Contribution to the Conference on the Principle of Subsidiarity, Skopje, 1–2 October 2010: 'Strengthening Subsidiarity: Integrating the Strasbourg Court's Case law into National Law and Judicial Practice', AS/Jur/Inf (2010) 04, 25 November 2010 ('Committee on Legal Affairs and Human Rights—Skopje Conference').

[199] Article 17.1 of Law No. 3477–IV of 2006 provides: 'While adjudicating cases courts shall apply the Convention and the case law of the Court as a source of law.'

[200] Interview, 21 May 2012. See also Nußberger (n 24); Committee on Legal Affairs and Human Rights—Skopje Conference (n 198) 35–7.

which are binding on them.[201] However, Serhiy Holovaty argues there has been a gradual shift in judicial opinion on this question: 'For a long time there was a common position, especially among higher courts, that judgments against other countries are not relevant.... It was a long journey to change their minds. Now they don't object.'[202]

There are also some more recent examples of parliament taking account of non-Ukrainian judgments in the course of its legislative deliberations. Dmytro Kotliar has suggested[203] that cases against other Council of Europe states were influential on the legislature in 2010 in developing new laws regulating prisoners' correspondence[204] and the placement of children in juvenile reception centres.[205] This was, in part, a result of NGOs invoking a range of Strasbourg cases, including non-Ukrainian judgments, in lobbying parliament. For example, in the course of pushing for legislative changes in the immigration field, the Social Action Centre/No Borders Project utilized Strasbourg decisions relating to the extradition of individuals from Russia to Central Asia.[206]

5.6 Conclusion

After a decade of tumultuous political upheaval in Ukraine, and in view of the dysfunctionality of many domestic institutions and the protracted and flawed processes of constitutional and legislative reform, there is an obvious need for stronger, more independent scrutiny mechanisms. The political system has been dominated by the presidential administration, thereby severely limiting the role played by parliament, and eroding public trust in parliamentarians. The preponderance of structural or systemic violations of the Convention in Ukraine has meant that it has been, and continues to be, the subject of repeated scrutiny by PACE.

There is, nevertheless, a high level of respect for the Convention and ECtHR in Ukraine, including amongst parliamentarians (although we need to acknowledge that some of our interlocutors doubted the sincerity of some MPs in their ostensibly pro-European stance). The introduction of a law in 2006 specifically addressing the implementation of ECtHR judgments was symptomatic of such respect, but the lack of any real political will to get to grips with structural and other serious human rights violations, coupled with the insufficient clout enjoyed by the government

[201] Interview, 27 June 2012. [202] Interview, 28 June 2012.

[203] Committee on Legal Affairs and Human Rights—Skopje Conference (n 198) 35–7.

[204] Law No. 1829-VI of 21 January 2010, On Amending Certain Legislative Acts of Ukraine to Ensure the Right to Correspondence of Persons in Detention and Convicted Persons.

[205] Law No. 2507-VI of 9 September 2010, On Amending Certain Legislative Acts of Ukraine Concerning Placing Children in Juvenile Reception Centres.

[206] Irene Fedorovych, Interview, 21 May 2012. See also the discussion of the Ukrainian extradition case of *Soldatenko* at 5.2. As an example of the Russian cases referred to, see *Savriddin Dzhurayev v Russia*, No. 71386/10, 25 April 2013.

agent dealing with human rights, has meant that the law has had little impact in practice.

This chapter has highlighted the potential importance of the role which parliament could play in realizing human rights standards, but at the same time it has shown the limited influence which has actually been exerted by the *Verkhovna Rada* or its committees in recent years. Following the 2014 parliamentary elections, there may, however, be opportunities for, and some signs of, positive democratic change. Leading parliamentarians, such as Hryhoriy Nemyria, are cautiously optimistic about improving and developing domestic systems and capabilities to integrate and comply with international human rights standards, including by expanding the remit of the Human Rights Committee to take on the responsibility for monitoring the implementation of judgments of the European Court. Above all, this study of Ukraine underlines the fact that the issue of political will remains paramount, over and above the creation of suitable structures or legal powers of scrutiny.

6

Romania

6.1 The Constitutional, Legal, and Political Landscape

Romania has a semi-presidential system. Under the Constitution, adopted in 1991 and revised in 2003, the president, the formal head of state, is directly elected for up to two five-year terms. The president appoints the prime minister, subject to parliamentary approval. The parliament, comprising the Chamber of Deputies and the Senate, is the supreme representative body of the people and the sole legislative authority. Members of both chambers are directly elected for four-year terms under a mixed electoral system which creates flexibility in the number of seats.[1] Parliament is empowered to initiate legislative proposals (as are, under certain conditions, groups of at least 250,000 citizens). The government alone has the power to introduce bills, which may be introduced into either chamber. Members of the government must present any information requested by parliament, attend parliamentary proceedings if requested to do so, and answer questions or interpellations raised by deputies or senators.

The Romanian Constitutional Court (RCC), created in 1992, is the sole authority of constitutional jurisdiction in Romania, and consists of nine judges, each appointed for a single nine-year term; six are appointed by parliament and three by the president. The RCC conducts ex ante vetting of laws, treaties, and parliamentary regulations. Laws or ordinances that are found to be unconstitutional cease effect within forty-five days if, in the meantime, the elected branches cannot bring them into line with the constitution. Within Romania's civil law system, the judiciary also encompasses a hierarchy of courts of general jurisdiction, with, at its apex, the High Court of Cassation and Justice, which exists to ensure the consistent interpretation and application of law by the national courts.

The Ombudsman or 'People's Advocate' is an autonomous public authority, whose purpose is the defence of individuals' rights and freedoms in their relationship with other public authorities. The Ombudsman is appointed at a joint session of parliament. Powers and duties of the Ombudsman include investigating individual complaints against public bodies; seizing the RCC of the unconstitutionality of laws, before their promulgation; and reporting to parliament at least annually,

[1] As of October 2015, the Senate lists 165 members and the Chamber of Deputies lists 382 members.

recommending legislative reform to protect individual rights and freedoms or highlighting gaps in legislation or serious cases of corruption or violations of Romanian laws.[2] Neither the Ombudsman nor the separate Romanian Institute of Human Rights is accredited as a national human rights institution according to the Paris Principles governing the role, composition, status, and functions of such bodies.[3]

6.1.1 Political transition

The fall of Nicolae Ceaușescu in December 1989 ended more than forty years of Communist rule amid violent unrest. Crowther and Suciu argue that, possibly excepting Albania, 'at the end of the 1980s Romania was arguably less prepared than any other country in Eastern Europe to undertake democratisation. Until the very end of the Communist period, the Ceaușescu leadership systematically fostered political alienation and fractured society along class and ethnic lines'.[4]

The consequences for the post-1989 political culture were catastrophic, as 'elite-level politics resolved into a contest between forces associated with the previous regime [which won elections in May 1990] and an ineffective liberal opposition'.[5] There followed a period of highly contentious politics and civil unrest, epitomized by President Ion Iliescu's use of vigilante miners to break up opposition protests.[6] In 1996, a reformist president, Emil Constantinescu, was elected, along with a coalition of anti-Communist and ethnic minority parties. Hopes of reform were stymied, however, by corruption and political in-fighting which had become embedded in Romanian politics. Iliescu was re-elected in 2000 and his reformed Communist party (the Party of Romanian Social Democracy, later renamed the Social Democratic Party (PSD)) recaptured the Chamber of Deputies, returning Romania to a state of 'quasi-absolute domination of one party'.[7] Subsequent parliamentary elections in 2004, 2008, and 2012 saw a small number of parties form often fluid coalitions, including conservative, liberal democratic, nationalist, and ethnic minority parties, and the PSD. The 2012 election was won by the Social Liberal Union, an alliance of centre-left (PSD) and centre-right parties (the National Liberal Party (PNL) and Conservative Party) and the National Union for the Progress of Romania, a splinter group from both the PSD and PNL. The former PNL leader, Klaus Iohannis, won the presidential election in December 2014,

[2] See Ombudsman's website at <http://www.avp.ro/>.

[3] Chart of the Status of National Institutions, accredited by the International Coordinating Committee of National Institutions for the Promotion and Protection of Human Rights: Accreditation Status as of 30 December 2014.

[4] William Crowther and Oana-Valentina Suciu, 'Romania', in Sten Berglund, Joakim Ekman, Kevin Deegan-Krause, and Terje Knutsen, eds., *The Handbook of Political Change in Eastern Europe*, 3rd edn. (Cheltenham: Edward Elgar Publishing, 2013): 369, 371.

[5] Crowther and Suciu (n 4) 371.

[6] Dragoş Bogdan and Alina Mungiu-Pippidi, 'The Reluctant Embrace: the Impact of the European Court of Human Rights in Post-Communist Romania', in Dia Anagnostou, ed., *The European Court of Human Rights: Implementing Strasbourg's Judgments on Domestic Policy* (Edinburgh: Edinburgh University Press, 2013): 71.

[7] Crowther and Suciu (n 4) 389.

representing the newly merged PNL and Democratic Liberal Party. He displaced Traian Băsescu of the formerly social democratic and later centre-right Democratic Party, who had served since 2004, with periods of suspension in 2012 during parliamentary moves to impeach him for exceeding his authority.

Another key determinant of politics in this period was Romania's accession to, first, the Council of Europe and, subsequently, the European Union. Romania became a member of the Council of Europe on 7 October 1993 and ratified the European Convention on Human Rights (ECHR or 'the Convention') on 20 June 1994, a process discussed at 6.2.1. Romania applied for European Union (EU) membership in 1995 and was granted candidate status in 1999. Accession negotiations began in February 2000, the Accession Treaty was signed in April 2005, and Romania acceded to the EU in January 2007. A condition of membership was fulfilment of the Copenhagen criteria, adopted by the European Council in 1993, which required inter alia that Romania 'achieved stability of institutions guaranteeing democracy, the rule of law, human rights and respect for and protection of minorities'.[8] As Bogdan and Mungiu-Pippidi note, from the mid-1990s onwards, every government and most elite factions displayed acceptance of European standards. The EU accession process, with its regular monitoring reports,[9] 'opened the door to a new type of political change domestically, a change pushed from below but taking advantage of external conditionality'.[10] The majority of the Romanian public has a positive image of the EU, although support appears to have waned from the very high levels recorded during the accession period.[11] The impact of the EU monitoring process linked to accession is considered further at 6.6 in respect of specific human rights issues and judgments. For now, several broad observations may be made of the Romanian political system that set the context for our examination of parliament's role in the implementation of Convention standards and ECtHR judgments.

There is abundant evidence of popular distrust of, and disillusionment with, political parties and parliament as an institution which has persisted throughout the post-Communist era. One estimate, based on a composite of local and comparative surveys, suggests that in 2012, trust in parliament was barely above 10 per cent, roughly where it stood in 2000, and down from more than 60 per cent in the immediate post-Communist era.[12] Trust in the cabinet was scarcely higher, while trust in political parties was even lower.

[8] Presidency Conclusions, Copenhagen European Council, 21–22 June 1993, 7.A.iii.

[9] Regular progress reports were produced from 1998 to 2006. Since 2007, the EU has maintained a special Cooperation and Verification Mechanism in order to assist Romania to address outstanding shortcomings in the fields of judicial reform and corruption.

[10] Bogdan and Mungiu-Pippidi (n 6) 72.

[11] As a snapshot, a Eurobarometer poll published in 2014 found that 59 per cent had a positive image of the EU (Standard Eurobarometer 82, 7) while in 2004 the figure was 76 per cent (Eurobarometer 62, 12).

[12] Claudiu Tufiş, 'Changes in Institutional Trust in Post-Communist Romania', presentation to conference on 'The Crisis of Political Trust in Post-Communist Democracies', Cluj, Romania, 1 June 2013, 18. See also Roberta-Manuela Ogaru, 'The Effect of 2008 Romanian Electoral Reform on Relationship between MPs and Citizens', presentation to 'Parliaments in Changing Times: The

The roots of this mistrust are not hard to find. Political parties are widely viewed as relating narrowly to the political class rather than acting as 'vehicles of mass representation',[13] a perception accentuated by structural factors such as the lack of close or permanent connections to constituents, high levels of election spending, a heavy emphasis on personalities, and strong similarity between party platforms. Another striking factor is the frequent migration of politicians between parties, which is 'indicative of how parties attempt to reshape majorities outside of electoral processes' and has caused parliament to 'neglect its chief role as legislator'.[14] Romanian parties have been likened to 'cartels'[15] engaging in a continuous intra-elite struggle for access to state resources—access which is secured through privatization deals, public contracts awarded to political supporters and government employment for political acolytes.[16] According to Ciobanu, an 'apathetic and resigned electorate perceives politicians and institutions as actors and organisations where the fulfilment of self-interest cannot be challenged or questioned'.[17] Opposition parties have generally failed to provide a clear alternative but instead have been co-opted or marginalized.[18]

Corruption looms large in Romania. In July 2015, Prime Minister Victor Ponta was indicted for corruption. Parliament voted not to lift his immunity for charges including conflict of interest; yet other charges are not covered by immunity, such as tax evasion and money laundering. Perceptions of corruption in Romania have improved only slowly in the past decade: Transparency International's Corruption Perceptions Index (CPI), which measures the perceptions of business people and analysts, ranked Romania eighty-seventh (out of 145) in 2004 and sixty-ninth (out of 175) in 2014.[19] Public perceptions and experience are also measured using the Global Corruption Barometer, which measures, among other things, perceived corruption in parliament and among political parties and the judiciary. In 2004, corruption in parliament was ranked at 4.0, political parties at 4.2, and the judiciary at 4.1 (where one is 'not at all corrupt' and five is 'highly corrupt').[20] By 2010–11,

Inaugural General Conference of the European Consortium for Political Research Standing Group on Parliaments', Dublin, 24–27 June 2012, 14–15.

[13] Crowther and Suciu (n 4) 382.

[14] Valentina Dimulescu, Adriana Iordache, and Andrei Macsut, 'Romania', in Freedom House, *Nations in Transit 2015*: 517, 522 ('Nations in Transit: Romania').

[15] Crowther and Suciu (n 4) *passim*.

[16] Patricia T. Young, 'Political Competition and Democratic Governance in Romania', in Ronald F. King, Paul E. Sum, Lucian-Liviu Albu, and Gabriel Badescu, eds., *Romania under Basescu: Aspirations, Achievements, and Frustrations During His First Presidential Term* (Lexington Books, 2011): 135, 136. See also Oleh Protsyk and Marius Lupsa Matichescu, 'Clientelism and Political Recruitment in Democratic Transition: Evidence from Romania', *Comparative Politics* 43(2) (2011): 207.

[17] Monica Ciabanu, 'Romania's Travails with Democracy and Accession to the European Union', *Europe-Asia Studies* 59(8) (2007): 1429, 1431.

[18] Crowther and Suciu (n 4) 391.

[19] Romania's CPI score was 2.9 in 2004 (where 0 is 'highly corrupt' and 10 is 'highly clean') and 43 in 2014 (where 0 is 'highly' corrupt and 100 is 'very clean'), <http://www.transparency.org/research/cpi/>.

[20] Transparency International, *Report on the Transparency International Global Corruption Barometer 2004* (2004) 18; 2004 was the earliest year in which these questions were asked.

the scores had worsened for both parliament (4.5) and political parties (4.5), and had scarcely improved for the judiciary (4.0).[21] The latest report for 2013 uses a percentage measure which, when equated to the previous surveys, shows some improvement, especially for the judiciary, yet still gives considerable cause for concern: 68 per cent of respondents in Romania felt that parliament was corrupt or extremely corrupt; while the figures for political parties and the judiciary were 78 per cent and 58 per cent respectively.[22] Further evidence of public concern is provided by Eurobarometer polls; in the latest, published in January 2015, nine out of ten respondents in Romania said that corruption and judicial shortcomings were important problems.[23] Respondents were highly supportive (around 80%) of EU efforts to help Romania tackle these problems, suggesting a lack of faith in domestic anti-corruption mechanisms. Nevertheless, a recent report under the European Commission's Co-operation and Verification Mechanism states that judicial and anti-corruption institutions 'maintained an impressive momentum' in efforts to tackle high-level corruption in 2014, in terms of both the numbers and prominence of cases pursued.[24]

Parliament is, however, identified as a significant obstacle to these endeavours; for example, in 2014, parliament frequently refused requests by the National Anti-Corruption Directorate to lift the immunity of parliamentarians suspected of corruption, for reasons that were 'arbitrary and lacking objective criteria'[25] and, as noted above, in July 2015 refused to lift the immunity of the prime minister. Further, throughout 2014, parliament 'persistently devised legislative loopholes that facilitated corruption', including passing legislative reform that allowed mayors and county council presidents to delegate official responsibilities, such as the signing of contracts, to their subordinates, thereby hampering anti-corruption investigations.[26]

Reports further suggest that non-governmental organizations (NGOs) and the media are unable to act as strong accountability mechanisms. Recent findings conclude that NGOs are reluctant to engage in advocacy individually because they fear repercussions from powerful politicians, and that policymakers frequently ignore recommendations that originate from NGO coalitions.[27] Laws on access to information and government transparency exist but are poorly enforced, and official consultation processes are often ineffective.[28]

[21] Transparency International, Global Corruption Barometer 2010–11.

[22] Transparency International, Global Corruption Barometer 2013.

[23] Flash Eurobarometer 406, *The Cooperation and Verification Mechanism for Bulgaria and Romania: Second Wave: Report*, January 2015, 4.

[24] European Commission, Report from the Commission to the European Parliament and the Council on Progress in Romania under the Co-operation and Verification Mechanism, COM(2015) 35 final, 28 January 2015, 10, 12; see also Nations in Transit: Romania (n 14) 519.

[25] European Commission, COM(2015) 35 final (n 24) 10.

[26] Nations in Transit: Romania (n 14) 533.

[27] Nations in Transit: Romania (n 14) 525, quoting USAID, Indexul Sustenabilității Organizațiilor Societății Civile din România 2013 [Civil Society Organization Sustainability Index 2013—Romania] (2014).

[28] Nations in Transit: Romania (n 14) 525.

Freedom House's *Freedom of the Press Index* has classified the Romanian media as 'partly free' since 1992; in 2015, its score was forty-two (where 0 is the most free and 100 the least free).[29] Freedom House identifies several factors that compromise media independence, including poor economic conditions which have all but extinguished investigative journalism; a lack of transparency in media ownership; and recent attempts in parliament to introduce measures inimical to the right to freedom of expression.[30] These include an attempt by PSD Senator Şerban Nicolae—then a member of the Senate Committee on Legal, Appointments, Discipline, Immunities, and Validations—to stifle investigative reporting by amending the Criminal Code so as to make the disclosure of information from criminal cases, such as corruption investigations, punishable by imprisonment.[31] The measure passed in the Senate and was pending debate in the Chamber of Deputies when, following widespread opposition, the government reversed its earlier positive opinion on the bill and rejected it on technical grounds.[32] In a separate initiative, the Chamber of Deputies, which had in 2006 abolished Ceauşescu-era laws criminalizing defamation, made a precipitous move to restore them in December 2013, a decision that was abandoned only after a domestic and international outcry (discussed at 6.6.4). These recent examples of parliamentary behaviour demonstrate the fragility of democratic reforms, including those made as a result of Romania's obligations under the Convention.

6.2 Romania and the Convention System

As noted at 6.1.1, Romania became a member of the Council of Europe in October 1993,[33] and ratified the Convention in June 1994. Under the Constitution, international treaties ratified by parliament become part of national law.[34] Constitutional provisions concerning rights and freedoms must be interpreted and enforced in conformity with the Universal Declaration of Human Rights and international human rights treaties to which Romania is a party;[35] and where inconsistencies exist, 'the international regulations shall take precedence'.[36]

6.2.1 The accession process

The Parliamentary Assembly of the Council of Europe (PACE), which in practice took the leading role in assessing whether aspirant states were in a position to join

[29] Freedom House, Freedom of the Press CEE/Eurasia: Scores and Status 1980–2015.

[30] Nations in Transit: Romania (n 14) 526–8.

[31] 'Controversial Amendment in Romanian Laws Makes Room for Imprisonment of Journalists', *Independent Balkan News Agency*, 30 September 2014.

[32] 'Government Rejects PSD-Sponsored "Silence Law"', *Nine O'Clock*, 30 October 2014.

[33] PACE Opinion No. 176 (1993) on the application by Romania for membership of the Council of Europe, 28 September 1993.

[34] Article 11(2) of the Constitution.

[35] Article 20(1) of the Constitution.

[36] Article 20(2) of the Constitution.

the Council, adopted in 1993 an order calling on new member states to respect their commitments in respect of the Council's basic principles.[37] The order recognized that new member states may not meet all commitments at the point of entry and instructed the Assembly's Political Affairs Committee and Committee on Legal Affairs and Human Rights ('Legal Affairs Committee') to monitor progress.[38] As Peteaux observes, Romania was the first 'live test' of the order's effectiveness.[39] When Romania's proposed accession was debated by the Assembly in September 1993, one of the three rapporteurs concerned, the British delegate David Atkinson, noted that Romania 'starts from the lowest possible base in the denial of human rights, lower even than the Soviet Union'.[40] Another, Gunnar Jansson of Finland, ventured that 'Romania, which has suffered from a disastrous and ruinous regime over a period of more than 40 years, needs the Council of Europe more than our organisation needs Romania'.[41] The rapporteurs agreed that Romania should be admitted 'on certain conditions and under close surveillance'.[42] Catherine Lalumière, the (then) Secretary-General of the Council of Europe later commented that, while the Romanian authorities were known to be 'stuck in the old regime's ways', to have refused accession would have meant 'leaving all those who wanted change without hope for many years to come': 'It's true that, in a sense, we were reversing the burden of proof: allowing Romania to join and then show that it could change, instead of the other way round—but that certainly allowed it to push through the necessary reforms.'[43]

In April 1997, PACE concluded its monitoring procedure for Romania,[44] welcoming not only Romania's ratification in June 1994 of the ECHR and all its protocols, but also in October 1994 of the European Convention for the Prevention of Torture and Inhuman or Degrading Treatment or Punishment and its Protocols, and in May 1995 of the Framework Convention for the Protection of National Minorities (making Romania the first state to ratify this Convention).[45]

The Parliamentary Assembly urged Romania, however, to initiate reforms to address outstanding structural and systemic problems.[46] These included: legislative reform to ensure the independence of the judiciary, curb the powers of the Office

[37] PACE Order No. 488 (1993) on the honouring of commitments entered into by new member states, 29 June 1993.

[38] PACE Order No. 488 (1993) (n 37) para. 3.

[39] Jean Petaux, *Democracy and Human Rights for Europe: The Council of Europe's Contribution* (Council of Europe, 2009) 125.

[40] PACE, 44th Ordinary Session, Official record of debates, 28 September 1993, 1382.

[41] PACE, 44th Ordinary Session (n 40) 1381–2.

[42] Petaux (n 39) 127.

[43] Petaux (n 39) 130.

[44] PACE Resolution 1123 and Recommendation 1326 (1997), Honouring of obligations and commitments by Romania, 24 April 1997. From 2000 to 2002, the PACE Committee on the Honouring of Obligations and Commitments by Member States of the Council of Europe (the Monitoring Committee), which had been established in April 1997, conducted a 'post-monitoring dialogue' with Romania. See PACE Monitoring Committee, The monitoring procedure of the Parliamentary Assembly, AS/Mon/Inf(2013)06rev4, 24 October 2013, 4.

[45] Parliamentary Assembly, Report on the honouring of obligations and commitments by Romania, Doc. 7795, 11 April 1997 (Rapporteur: Gunnar Jansson) paras. 2–3.

[46] PACE, Doc. 7795 (n 45) paras. 7–13.

of the Public Prosecutor, and amend elements of the Criminal Code that were 'unacceptable and seriously imperil the exercise of fundamental freedoms', especially Article 200 concerning homosexual relationships, and several Articles relating to insult and defamation that interfered with press freedom (see 6.6.4).[47] The Assembly also highlighted the 'deplorable' conditions in Romanian prisons and recommended amendment of the legislative provisions permitting abuse of detention on remand. Romania was urged to improve conditions for children in state institutions, amend legislation so as to assist their adoption, and pursue policies to prevent the abandonment of children. The Assembly also implored Romania to amend legislation relating to the return of confiscated and expropriated property, so as to provide for the restitution of such property or fair compensation in lieu (see 6.6.3). Finally, the Assembly called on Romania to promote a campaign against racism, xenophobia, and intolerance and take all appropriate measures for the social integration of the Roma population.

The effects of external pressure emanating from both the Council of Europe and EU accession and monitoring processes are visible in the protracted legislative process by which Romania amended and finally repealed Ceaușescu-era laws concerning same-sex relationships. The Council of Europe noted at the time of Romania's accession that Article 200 of the Criminal Code criminalized consensual same-sex relationships, with punishment of between one and five years' imprisonment.[48] In November 1996, after the RCC gave an opinion that the prohibition contravened Romania's international treaty obligations, the Article was amended such that consensual sexual relations between adults of the same sex continued to be criminalized only if 'committed in public or producing a public scandal'.[49] Subsequent proposals to repeal Article 200 before the 2000 elections were initially rejected by deputies unwilling to jeopardize their prospects by voting for an unpopular measure: as one deputy put it, 'we want to enter Europe, not Sodom and Gomorrah'.[50] The proposed reform was revived when accession talks began with the EU in March 2000 at a time when addressing discrimination against minorities became a formal condition of accession. In June, deputies voted to decriminalize same-sex relationships in line with Council of Europe Resolution 1123, which deemed Article 200 to be discriminatory.[51] Lobbying of the Senate and President Constantinescu by Orthodox clerics threatened to derail the reform; however '[u]ltimately, the international factor decided the fate of Article 200': hours before a deadline after which the Council of Europe had threatened to renew its monitoring of Romania's human rights record, both chambers of parliament voted to repeal Article 200.[52] Despite this, as we shall see, several other problems identified by the Council of Europe

[47] Articles 205, 206, 238, and 239.

[48] Parliamentary Assembly, Report on the application by Romania for membership of the Council of Europe, Doc. 6901, 19 July 1993, para. 50.

[49] Lavinia Stan and Lucian Turcescu, *Religion and Politics in Post-Communist Romania* (Oxford: Oxford University Press, 2007) 173.

[50] Stan and Turcescu (n 49) 174.

[51] See above n 44.

[52] Stan and Turcescu (n 49) 175.

when its monitoring concluded in 1997 would later be the subject of legal challenges in Strasbourg.

6.2.2 Attitudes towards the Convention system

To the authors' knowledge, there is no polling data on public attitudes towards the Convention system in Romania. Impressionistic appraisals of public opinion are strongly favourable. Daniel Florea MP, a member of the Committee for Legal Matters, Discipline, and Immunities in the Chamber of Deputies, who chairs its sub-committee on the execution of ECtHR judgments, argues that the Court is viewed 'very positively' in Romania.[53] The comparatively high number of individual applications against Romania (see 6.2.3) is one, albeit crude, measure of public faith in the Court. Indeed, Tudor Pantiru (a former ECtHR Judge (1996–2001), who was from 2008 to 2012 a member of the Committee for Legal Matters, Discipline, and Immunities in the Chamber of Deputies) noted before a hearing of the Parliamentary Assembly that the Strasbourg Court is too often perceived as a '[fourth] instance court',[54] or, as Bodgan and Mungiu-Pippidi put it, 'some kind of panacea for all dissatisfactions related to the functioning of national courts'.[55]

Diana Hatneanu of the Association for the Defence of Human Rights in Romania (APADOR-CH) ventures that no judgment of the Court has polarized public opinion to the extent of provoking attitudes of defiance; rather, 'the Court is seen as a body providing justice to victims [and] ... enjoys a high level of appreciation from the general public'.[56] She suggests that its reputation was, however, dented by the granting of delays in the deadline for Romania to implement the pilot judgment in the case of *Maria Atanasiu and Others*,[57] which required general measures to resolve shortcomings in the system of restitution or compensation in respect of properties nationalized or confiscated by the State before 1989 (see 6.6.3), following well-publicized cases in which applicants who had waited many years died before they could receive justice.

The judiciary also increasingly sees the ECtHR as a 'force for good', according to Mihai Selegean, former director of the National Institute of Magistracy (NIM).[58] Selegean recalls that, in the years immediately after ratification, lawyers and judges were not responsive to the case law of the Court. At the time, there existed no study of ECtHR jurisprudence in Romanian and no comprehensive assessment of the compliance of Romanian legislation with the Convention. Translations of judgments in Romania were scarce. Lawyers, judges, and public officials had not been trained in the Convention and human rights were not part of university legal education. Selegean adds that,

[53] Interview, 13 May 2015.

[54] PACE, Committee on Legal Affairs and Human Rights, Implementation of judgments of the European Court of Human Rights, Extracts from the minutes of hearings, organized by the Committee, held in Strasbourg in April 2012, in June 2012, in October 2012, and in January 2013, AS/Jur (2013) 13, 28 March 2013, 8.

[55] Bogdan and Mungiu-Pippidi (n 6) 73.

[56] Interview, 24 May 2012.

[57] Nos. 30767/05 and 33800/06, 12 October 2010.

[58] Interview, 24 May 2012.

It's difficult to change suddenly your set of values. [There was a] lack of access to information and a lack of will to get that information and a different set of values that had been acquired during their professional life.... This is not an intellectual exercise which comes naturally for continental lawyers.

Judgments that directly challenged outdated practices such as the powers of prosecutors, he adds, engendered particular resistance. Bogdan and Mungiu-Pippidi argue that it was above all the numerous judgments against Romania from the late 1990s, the large amounts of damages awarded, and high-profile media coverage of these issues, that increased the pressure on the judiciary to begin to apply Strasbourg case law.[59] Former Justice Minister Monica Macovei similarly traces a shift in judicial attitudes before and after the early 2000s,

Until ... 2000, you got in the court replies from judges, including [senior] judges ... and lawyers, [saying] 'Who cares about this? We are here in Romania [with] Romanian law'. So, I wouldn't say it was xenophobia but they didn't understand that we live in an open world and we ratified the Convention and have duties. And also, when you apply something new, you have to learn it.... Then after 2002 or 2003, it started to matter ... and then [the Convention and the Court's case law] ... began to be referenced in many judgments.[60]

She adds, however, that references to case law were sometimes imprecise.

In 1999, the NIM had introduced the study of Strasbourg case law into its curricula and by the mid-2000s the first books on the Convention system in Romanian started to appear.[61] In 2012, Mihai Selegean estimates that 35 per cent of judges had received training on the Convention; however, training for lawyers had lagged behind.[62] Former ECtHR judge Corneliu Birsan detects greater receptiveness to Strasbourg case law among younger judges: 'I read judgments, especially those of young judges, which apply the ECtHR case law directly. The situation is better in the first instance courts—it's a matter of generational [change].'[63] Interviewed in 2012, Mihai Selegean added that,

I think we have a general respect for the decisions of the Court. And that is because, consistently, over the last fifteen or seventeen years now, the Court [has been] a driver for change for the better. And a lot of legislation has changed following the decisions of the Court against Romania, and they are perceived as fair ... definitely by the public and by judges.... I'm not sure about MPs.

Indeed, political attitudes towards the Court are hard to capture in generalizations. Senator Tudor Chiuariu ventures that 'there are no domestic political controversies over the application of the Convention' in Romania.[64] Interviewed in 2012, György Frunda, then a senator, observed:

No-one [in parliament] says we can ignore Strasbourg decisions. On the contrary, they take it very seriously. But of course if you're in opposition, you make curious proposals, you want

[59] Bogdan and Mungiu-Pippidi (n 6) 73.
[60] Interview, 12 June 2012.
[61] Bogdan and Mungiu-Pippidi (n 6) 73.
[62] Interview, 24 May 2012.
[63] Interview, 25 June 2012.
[64] Interview, 14 October 2013.

to be populist or appear to be patriotic—'Romania before the Court'. But when you are in the ruling party and have responsibility for decisions, it's different.[65]

Interviewees from NGOs and the Romanian Bar Association characterize political interest in ECtHR judgments variously as self-interested, partisan, and media-driven. NGOs also observe a tendency for parliamentarians to invoke judgments of the Court even when the judgment does not, in fact, substantiate the argument being advanced. For example, in a legislative proposal in 2012 (later rejected by both chambers), which would have severely restricted women's access to abortion by making 'counselling' mandatory and imposing a 'reflection' period before services could be accessed,[66] an erroneous and misleading reference to the judgment in *Vo v France* was made in its preamble in support of the proposal.[67]

Human rights activist Romanita Iordache ventures that,

It is fascinating to see that they look for Strasbourg decisions or human rights arguments as ways of selling these [proposals].... For such a long time, we [NGOs] had to explain human rights to [politicians] and now we have to explain human rights to the public because [politicians] are distorting rights or picking and choosing whatever is convenient. Or they are packaging things in a way that is a 'mish-mash'—that looks okay if you're ... not familiar with it.[68]

At other times, parliament has deliberately legislated in contradiction of Convention standards and ECtHR judgments, as explored in 6.6 in respect of specific issues and judgments.

6.2.3 Overview of applications and judgments against Romania and the state of implementation

Statistics and monitoring reports concerning Romania indicate the seriousness of the human rights problems in evidence, both in terms of their number and severity and the persistence of systemic and structural dysfunctions giving rise to repetitive applications before the Court.

As noted at 1.2.2, in December 2014, Romania accounted for 5 per cent of applications pending before the ECtHR (3,385), the fifth largest total in the Council of Europe after Ukraine, Italy, Russia, and Turkey.[69] From the point of Romania's

[65] Interview, 27 June 2012.

[66] Lege: privind înfiinţarea, funcţionarea şi organizarea cabinetelor de consiliere pentru criză de sarcină [Law on the establishment, operation, and organization of centres for pregnancy crisis counselling], No. 348/2012.

[67] The preamble to the law cites (at 10) the judgment in *Vo v France*, No. 53924/00, 8 July 2004 [GC], to support the statement that 'embryos and foetuses are not excluded' from protection under Article 2 ECHR (the right to life). In fact, the *Vo* judgment states (para. 84) that within the Council of Europe 'there is no consensus on the nature and status of the embryo and/or foetus' and (para. 85) that it is 'neither desirable, nor even possible as matters stand, to answer in the abstract the question whether the unborn child is a person for the purposes of Article 2 of the Convention'.

[68] Interview, 24 May 2012.

[69] European Court of Human Rights, *Annual Report 2014 (Provisional Version)* (2015) 167. However, in proportion to the population of the respective states, Romania fared slightly better, ranking eighth.

ratification of the ECHR in 1994 to the end of December 2014, there were 56,683 applications against Romania; again, this was the fifth highest after Russia, Ukraine, Turkey, and Poland.[70] A review of ECtHR annual reports suggests that the annual influx of applications lodged against Romania grew steadily from the early 2000s, peaking in 2012 with almost 6,800 in a single year, and falling back slightly in 2014.[71] As is the case with all states, however, the vast majority of applications is found inadmissible.[72]

In 2014, there were seventy-four adverse judgments concerning Romania, the third highest in the Council of Europe after Russia and Turkey.[73] Since Romania ratified the Convention up to the end of 2014, it was the target of 1,004 adverse judgments, or 7 per cent of all judgments that have ever found at least one violation of the Convention by a member state.[74] Around 200 of these concerned substantive or procedural violations of Article 3 ECHR (prohibition of torture and inhuman or degrading treatment or punishment). More than half arose from violations of Article 6 ECHR (the right to a fair trial).

In respect of implementation, Romania accounted for 639 cases pending before the Committee of Ministers at the end of 2014;[75] of which twenty-nine had been pending for more than five years.[76] In the Committee of Ministers' list of worst-offending states with cases under enhanced supervision (on the basis of the number of leading cases), Romania ranked seventh.[77]

The latest report of the PACE rapporteur on the execution of ECtHR judgments lists a number of cases (or groups of cases) exposing structural or systemic problems.[78] These are: outstanding issues relating to the failure to restore or compensate for nationalized property,[79] which led to the only pilot judgment to have been issued against Romania (see 6.6.3);[80] excessive length of civil[81] and criminal[82] proceedings and lack of an effective remedy; non-enforcement of domestic judicial decisions;[83] poor conditions of detention;[84] ill-treatment by police and

[70] European Court of Human Rights, *Overview: 1959–2014* (2015) 8.

[71] The earliest figures available in the Court's Annual Reports are from 1999, when 1,060 applications were lodged against Romania; in 2012 the figure was 6,790 and in 2014, 4,272. Note that the total annual figure for applications is different from the pending figure (given above for 2014; n 69), which is a snapshot of cases pending as at 31 December of the respective year.

[72] 52,012 of the 56,683 applications up to 2014; European Court of Human Rights (n 70) 8.

[73] European Court of Human Rights (n 69) 175.

[74] See 1.2.2, Table 1.2.

[75] See 1.2.2, Table 1.3.

[76] Council of Europe Committee of Ministers, *Supervision of the Execution of Judgments and Decisions of the European Court of Human Rights: 8th Annual Report of the Committee of Ministers 2014* (2015) ('8th Annual Report of the Committee of Ministers 2014') 48.

[77] 8th Annual Report of the Committee of Ministers 2014 (n 76) 41.

[78] PACE, Committee on Legal Affairs and Human Rights, Implementation of judgments of the European Court of Human Rights, Doc. 13864, 9 September 2015 (Rapporteur: Klaas de Vries) ('8th Rapporteur Report') paras. 117–43.

[79] *Străin and Others v Romania*, No. 57001/00, 21 July 2005.

[80] *Maria Atanasiu and Others v Romania* (n 57).

[81] *Nicolau v Romania*, No. 1295/02, 12 January 2006.

[82] *Stoianova and Nedelcu v Romania*, No. 77517/01, 4 August 2005.

[83] *Ruianu v Romania*, No. 34647/97, 17 June 2003; *Săcăleanu v Romania*, No. 73970/01, 6 September 2005; *Strungariu v Romania*, No. 23878/02, 29 September 2005.

[84] *Bragadireanu v Romania*, No. 22088/04, 6 December 2007.

lack of effective investigations;[85] ineffectiveness of criminal investigations into the violent suppression of anti-government demonstrations related to the fall of the Communist regime;[86] the inadequacy of the detention regime of 'dangerous' prisoners;[87] the inadequate management of psychiatric conditions of detainees in prison;[88] and the lack of appropriate judicial and social protection and medical care for a young man of Roma origin who died in a psychiatric facility.[89] Other leading cases or groups of cases under the enhanced supervision of the Committee of Ministers concern: the conviction of a whistle-blower for having disclosed information on the illegal secret surveillance of citizens by the intelligence service and lack of safeguards in the statutory framework governing secret surveillance;[90] the unjustified and disproportionate use of fire-arms by police agents, the lack of an adequate statutory and regulatory framework governing the use of fire-arms during police operations and the preparation and control of such operations, and the ineffectiveness of criminal investigations into these incidents;[91] the consequences of racially motivated violence, in one instance in 1993,[92] and in another between 1990 and 1993,[93] against villagers of Roma origin, in particular inadequate living conditions following the destruction of their homes, and the discriminatory attitude of the authorities; ill-treatment of a patient in the psychiatric unit of a hospital due to poor sanitary and hygiene conditions, overcrowding, and the impossibility of spending time outdoors;[94] and the death or ill-treatment of prisoners in penitentiary facilities and the ineffectiveness of investigations into such incidents.[95]

Notwithstanding these areas of continuing concern, judgments of the ECtHR have led to significant—albeit, in some cases, still incomplete—legal and policy reform in Romania. Bodgan and Mungiu-Pippidi identify four areas in which ECtHR judgments have had the greatest influence: prosecutorial powers, the powers of the intelligence services; the restitution of nationalized property; and freedom of expression.[96] In 6.6, we examine in detail the implementation of judgments in these areas, with a particular focus on the role of parliament. First, we discuss the system of implementation in Romania in respect both of parliament (6.3), the executive (6.4), and the implementation of judgments against other states (6.5).

[85] *Barbu Anghelescu v Romania*, No. 46430/99, 5 October 2004.

[86] *Association '21 December 1989' v Romania*, Nos. 33810/07 and 18817/08, 24 May 2011.

[87] *Enache v Romania*, No. 10662/06, 1 April 2014.

[88] *Ticu v Romania*, No. 24575/10, 1 October 2013.

[89] *The Centre for Legal Resources on behalf of Valentin Câmpeanu v Romania*, No. 47848/08, 14 July 2014 [GC]. The judgment recommends (para. 161) that Romania 'envisage the necessary general measures to ensure that mentally disabled persons in a situation comparable to that of Mr Câmpeanu, are afforded independent representation, enabling them to have Convention complaints relating to their health and treatment examined before a court or other independent body'.

[90] *Bucur and Toma v Romania*, 40238/02, 8 April 2013.

[91] *Soare and Others v Romania*, No. 24329/02, 22 February 2011.

[92] *Moldovan and Others v Romania*, No. 41138/98, 12 July 2005.

[93] *Kalanyos v Romania*, No. 57884/00, 26 April 2007.

[94] *Parascineti v Romania*, No. 32060/05, 13 March 2012.

[95] *Predică v Romania*, No. 42344/07, 7 June 2011.

[96] Bogdan and Mungiu-Pippidi (n 6) 74.

6.3 Implementation of ECtHR Judgments: The Role of Parliament

Interviewees confirm that parliament has for most of the post-accession period played a minimal role in the implementation of Convention standards and Court judgments. In the view of a former government agent from the mid-2000s:

> Parliament was one stone that I couldn't move. It was very difficult to change them; no constructive dialogue proved possible.... They seemed always to feel that our letters were illegitimate, [saying] 'Why we should we change something just because the Court or Committee of Ministers so? We are an independent country'. The awareness [of parliamentarians] was zero. The only aspect that they were interested in was the money—and who to blame. They took their expertise from the press.[97]

Roxana Rizoiu, who was government agent for two periods in the early 2000s, describes the culture shock for parliamentarians in the post-accession period:

> The early 2000s ... was the first time that parliament accepted [that it had to change] the law because of [judgments of] the ECtHR. It was very new then and very strange for parliament to have someone knocking on their door and saying things had to change; it was difficult for them to accept ... because some of the judgments changed things enormously. Now [in 2012], things are a lot better than in the early 2000s.[98]

6.3.1 National implementation legislation

Parliament has made legislative provision for the process by which ECtHR judgments are implemented.[99] The government is required to submit to parliament within three months of an adverse ECtHR judgment concerning Romania a draft law for amending, supplementing, or repealing the enactment (or part thereof) that contravenes ECtHR case law. In addition, the law requires that draft laws, legislative proposals, or other normative acts and procedures, whether originated by the government or parliament, must be accompanied by an evaluation regarding their impact on human rights and must be verified for compatibility with standards laid down in the Convention and its protocols and the case law of the Court. The law was initiated by Tudor Pantiru while he was a member of the Committee for Legal Matters, Discipline, and Immunities in the Chamber of Deputies. Interviewed in 2012, Tudor Pantiru noted that the government did not always follow the requirements of this law and that it was difficult for parliament to ensure accountability for omissions because of the sheer volume of legislation.[100]

[97] Interview (anonymous), 24 May 2012.
[98] Interview, 24 May 2012.
[99] Law No. 29/2011, which amends and supplements Law No. 24/2000 on legislative technique.
[100] Interview, 26 April 2012.

6.3.2 The Legislative Council

An expert body, the Legislative Council, advises parliament in order to ensure systematic unification and co-ordination of legislation.[101] The Legislative Council gives opinions on draft laws or ordinances submitted by the government, or legislative proposals of parliamentarians; it may also, at the request of the chairs of parliamentary committees, give opinions on draft laws, legislative proposals, or amendments received by the committee after their adoption by one of the chambers of the parliament. Tudor Pantiru notes that, at the time when the law on legislative technique was amended to provide for verification of compatibility with the ECHR, the Legislative Council possessed no specific human rights expertise and had been known to approve draft laws or legislative proposals that were incompatible with the Convention.[102] The then head of the Council had expressed the view that the jurisprudence of the ECtHR was not mandatory to follow given Romania's civil law tradition. Pantiru had proposed—unsuccessfully—that a human rights department be formed within the Legislative Council to equip it to conduct pre-legislative scrutiny for Convention compatibility. No such department has since been created. NGO representatives interviewed in 2012 concurred that, although the Legislative Council sometimes issued well-informed opinions from a human rights perspective, it lacked sufficient resources and human rights expertise, and was not immune to political pressure in respect of controversial proposals;[103] for example, the Council had approved the legislative proposal (later rejected by both chambers) which would have severely restricted women's access to abortion, even though, among other potential concerns, the proposal erroneously cited a judgment of the ECtHR in its preamble.[104] Interviewees also note that opinions of the Legislative Council are not binding on parliament and are sometimes disregarded.

6.3.3 Parliamentary committees

The Standing Bureaux which run the business of each chamber are important sites of power within parliament. Interviewees regarded the Standing Bureaux as influential bodies which can either advance draft laws or legislative proposals or obstruct them, sometimes for many years.

Each chamber of parliament sets up standing committees and may institute inquiry committees or other special committees. The chambers may also set up joint committees. Committees are made up so as to reflect the political spectrum of each chamber. The Chamber of Deputies has a Committee on Human Rights, Cults, and National Minority Issues ('Human Rights Committee').[105] It also has a

[101] See Legislative Council website at <http://www.clr.ro/en/>.

[102] Interview, 26 April 2012.

[103] Diana Hatneanu, Interview, 24 May 2012.

[104] See 6.2.2 at n 67. For the opinion of the Legislative Council, see the website of the Chamber of Deputies at <http://www.cdep.ro/pls/proiecte/upl_pck.proiect?idp=12593>.

[105] This Committee's purview includes 'human rights and citizens' rights, the problems of minorities, freedom of conscience, the problem of religious cults, and freedom of expression other than press freedom'.

Committee for Legal Matters, Discipline, and Immunities ('Legal Committee').[106] According to Daniel Florea MP, a member of the Legal Committee in the Chamber of Deputies, the Human Rights Committee deals mainly with discrimination issues and its remit and activities do not duplicate those of the Legal Committee.[107] Alina-Ştefania Gorghiu, also a member of the Legal Committee in the lower chamber, adds that it is primarily this committee—and not the Human Rights Committee—which maintains contact with Council of Europe bodies.[108]

Equivalent committees exist in the Senate. In addition, it was reported in October 2015 that the Senate's Standing Bureau had approved the establishment of a Committee on Constitutionality, Civil Liberties, and Monitoring of the Enforcement of Decisions issued by the European Court of Human Rights.[109]

Representatives of NGOs, the Romanian Bar Association and the NIM interviewed in 2012 expressed concern about the overall lack of human rights expertise among members of both the Human Rights and Legal Committees in both chambers. Expertise was viewed as being confined to certain individuals. For example, some NGOs considered that they could, as one put it, 'do business with' the Senate Human Rights Committee under the (then) chairmanship of György Frunda, who had been a senator since 1996 and was then head of the Romanian PACE delegation.

The Human Rights Committees in both chambers are viewed by interviewees as lower status than the Legal Committees, which have a more extensive remit, larger membership, and greater political influence. As one NGO interviewee explains, 'the Human Rights Committees are not of interest to mainstream politicians because they are not money-making committees'.[110] Several interviewees emphasize that leadership of committees is a vital factor in determining their credibility and effectiveness. The Human Rights Committee in the Chamber of Deputies is regarded as especially lacking in credibility since its chair since 2000, Nicolae Păun, had proposed measures which interviewees regard as, at best, displaying an idiosyncratic approach to human rights and, at worst, as being inimical to human rights protection. Păun had, for example, introduced a legislative proposal to criminalize begging (which was rejected)[111] and had sought to introduce a proposal to outlaw 'fortune-telling and witchcraft'.[112] The legislative proposal on abortion referred to at 6.2.2 was co-sponsored by Marius Dugulescu, who was at the time Vice-Chair of the Human Rights Committee in the Chamber of Deputies. Interviewees also express

[106] This Committee's purview covers 'constitutionality of bills and legislative proposals; regulations in the field of civil, criminal, administrative, civil procedure, criminal, administrative, judicial organization; other mainly legal regulations; issues of parliamentary discipline, incompatibilities and immunities'.

[107] Interview, 13 May 2015. [108] Interview, 14 October 2013.

[109] 'Senate's Standing Bureau Approves Establishment of Committee on Constitutionality, Civil Liberties, Monitoring of ECHR Decisions', Agerpres news agency, 19 October 2015.

[110] Marian Mandache, Interview, 25 May 2012.

[111] Propunere legislativa pentru reglementarea unor masuri privind cerşetoria [Legislative proposal to regulate measures on begging], Law No. 306/2012.

[112] 'Two "Witches" Detained in Romania on Extortion Charges', *The Guardian*, 14 December 2011.

disquiet about the move by a former member of the Legal Committee in the Senate, Iulian Urban, to introduce the death penalty for certain paedophiles,[113] in defiance of both Romania's Constitution and international treaty obligations. Urban had also supported a proposal (which was rejected by the Legislative Council) to revise the official term for the Roma people to 'Gypsy',[114] a word considered derogatory by many Roma people and their advocates.

6.3.4 Sub-committee on the execution of ECtHR judgments

Until 2009, no committee in either chamber had a specific institutionalized mechanism to monitor the implementation of ECtHR judgments. In 2009, the Legal Committee in the Chamber of Deputies created a sub-committee to monitor the execution of ECtHR judgments.[115] This was a direct response to a Parliamentary Assembly resolution and recommendation on the implementation of ECtHR judgments.[116] The sub-committee has up to seven members representing all parliamentary groups.[117] Tudor Pantiru was the instigator of the sub-committee and its first chair. He acknowledges that in the early years of its existence, the sub-committee lacked resources and expertise: its sole adviser was not a lawyer and no other member had specific expertise in the Convention.[118] It was also a weakness, he adds, that no equivalent sub-committee existed in the Senate (Senate committees, being smaller, do not form sub-committees).

Strikingly, almost none of the NGO representatives, former government agents, lawyers, or academics whom we interviewed in 2012 had heard of the sub-committee on the execution of ECtHR judgments, and those that had regarded it as moribund and ineffective. In its first parliamentary term, the sub-committee focused almost exclusively on a single issue: the delayed implementation of the *Atanasiu* pilot judgment of 2010 (see 6.6.3). The sub-committee has assumed a broader remit in the parliament elected in December 2012. In May 2015, its chair, Daniel Florea, reported that it meets fortnightly and has two experienced legal advisers, in addition to around twenty-five staff attached to the Legal Committee.[119] Most members of the sub-committee, he added, have a good working knowledge of the Convention system. Whereas Tudor Pantiru noted in 2012 that the sub-committee had no

[113] 'Iulian Urban propune pedeapsa cu moartea pentru pedofilii ai căror victime decedează' ['Iulian Urban Proposes the Death Penalty for Paedophiles whose Victims Die'], *Romania Libera*, 21 June 2011.

[114] 'Propunere Jurnalul Național: "Țigan" în loc de "Rom"' ['National Journal Proposes: "Gypsy" instead of "Roma"'], *National Journal*, 2 March 2009.

[115] The sub-committee had existed 'on paper' since 2007, but did not start to function until 2009; Tudor Pantiru, Interview, 26 April 2012.

[116] PACE Resolution 1516 (2006) and Recommendation 1764 (2006), Implementation of judgments of the European Court of Human Rights, October 2006.

[117] As of October 2015, six are listed on the Sub-committee's website, drawn from the twenty-six member Legal Committee.

[118] Interview, 26 April 2012.

[119] Parliament of Romania, Chamber of Deputies, Relevant Activity of Parliamentary Sub-Committee on Monitoring the Execution of ECHR [sic] Judgments (undated) (on file) 4. We are grateful to Daniel Florea, who was interviewed on 13 May 2015 and 14 October 2013 and also supplied written documentation about the work of the sub-committee and its parent Legal Committee.

competence to conduct legislative scrutiny, in 2015 Florea stated that it does now become involved in legislative scrutiny if an issue of Convention incompatibility is flagged by the Legislative Council. It sometimes does so in co-operation with other parliamentary committees. Since 2011, the sub-committee has been obliged to report regularly to the Legal Committee and at least annually to the Standing Bureau (and, on the decision of the Standing Bureau, to the plenum) on the execution of ECtHR judgments.[120]

The sub-committee regularly addresses questions and interpellations to the government agent, ministers, and state agencies such as the National Authority for Property Restitution; it also receives regular reports from the government agent, including copies of the agent's correspondence with the Department for the Execution of Judgments.[121] The sub-committee meets the government agent roughly fortnightly, and has contact in between meetings.[122] It does not, however, routinely see action plans or action reports at the time they are submitted to the Committee of Ministers; speaking in 2013, one member of the sub-committee remarked wryly that it would be 'heaven on earth if we could see them'.[123]

Discussion has begun on creating a joint standing committee on human rights in order to strengthen oversight of the executive in respect of Convention standards and ECtHR judgments. This move is endorsed by the present members of the sub-committee, but in view of the political difficulties in changing committee structures is not considered feasible until after parliamentary elections due in 2016.[124] At the time of writing, the implications for this proposed joint committee of the creation of the new Senate Committee on Constitutionality, Civil Liberties, and Monitoring of the Enforcement of Decisions issued by the ECtHR are unclear. Nor is it yet clear how the new Senate committee will co-ordinate with the sub-committee for monitoring the execution of ECtHR judgments in the lower chamber.

6.3.5 Provision of legal advice

Legal services departments exist within each chamber in the Romanian parliament, which may advise members on procedural or legal matters. As noted at 6.3.4, the Legal Committee in the Chamber of Deputies and its sub-committee to monitor the execution of judgments have a dedicated secretariat with legal expertise. In 2012, György Frunda reported that the Senate Human Rights Committee was supported by four or five staff at any one time.[125] Political groupings in parliament also employ staff; however, several interviewees doubted the quality of advice provided by political appointees. A former government agent also observes that there is insufficient stability and continuity of staff, since advisers tend to change when committee membership shifts between elections.[126] One NGO interviewee notes that

[120] Parliament of Romania, Chamber of Deputies (n 119) 4.
[121] Parliament of Romania, Chamber of Deputies (n 119) 3.
[122] Daniel Florea, Interview, 13 May 2015.
[123] Alina-Ştefania Gorghiu, Interview, 14 October 2013.
[124] Daniel Florea, Interview, 13 May 2015.
[125] Interview, 27 June 2012.
[126] Interview (anonymous), 24 May 2012.

some permanent staff of parliamentary committees are technically competent and open to engagement with external organizations, but lack authority and influence; she refers to them as the 'silent people'.[127] In summary, most interviewees concur that parliamentarians can obtain reliable advice if they require it, whether from external or internal sources, but may well have to be proactive in doing so.

6.3.6 The relationship between parliament and Council of Europe bodies

Romania has ten members of the Parliamentary Assembly (and ten substitute members). Delegates report to the Standing Bureaux in parliament and to their respective parliamentary committees. At the time of writing, the chair and secretary of the sub-committee on the execution of ECtHR judgments in the Chamber of Deputies (respectively, Daniel Florea and Alina-Ştefania Gorghiu) are members of both the PACE Legal Affairs Committee and the Committee on the Election of Judges to the European Court of Human Rights. Alina-Ştefania Gorghiu is also a member of the PACE Legal Affairs Committee's Sub-Committee on the implementation of judgments of the ECtHR. Florea considers this overlapping membership to be beneficial.[128] His predecessor as chair of the sub-committee, Tudor Pantiru, ventures that delegates to the Parliamentary Assembly are more receptive and reliable than their peers on matters relating to the Convention.[129]

Romania has come under heightened scrutiny at the Parliamentary Assembly for its record in implementing judgments. In October 2012, the PACE Legal Affairs Committee called the leaders of the Romanian delegation to a public hearing to account for the country's failure to rectify major structural problems (see 2.6.1).[130] In respect of the Romanian judge in Strasbourg, Daniel Florea reports that no formal contact is maintained, either by the Legal Committee in the Chamber of Deputies or by its sub-committee on the execution of ECtHR judgments.

6.3.7 The view of actors outside parliament

Interviewed in 2012, NGO representatives almost invariably expressed scepticism about the value of engaging with parliament on matters of human rights implementation—the exception being the Active Watch Media Monitoring Agency, which had formed working relationships with the chairs of the Committee for Culture, Arts, and Mass Media in the Chamber of Deputies and the Human Rights Committee in the Senate.[131] The human rights organization APADOR-CH had prioritized building contacts with the Ministry of Justice and individual members of parliament, rather than what it regarded as inaccessible committees or

[127] Liana Ganea, Interview, 25 May 2012.
[128] Interview, 14 October 2013.
[129] Interview, 26 April 2012.
[130] PACE, Committee on Legal Affairs and Human Rights, AS/Jur (2013) 13 (n 54) 7–8.
[131] Liana Ganea, Interview, 25 May 2012.

political groups,[132] while the Roma rights organization Romani CRISS had found it 'fruitless and inefficient' trying to engage with deputies and senators.[133]

Interviewed in 2012, Diana Hatneanu of APADOR-CH explained why, in her view, the executive was a more important actor in the implementation process:

> The main problem now is not changing the law—we had that period from 2000 to 2007. It's clear now that ... the issue is the way that Strasbourg judgments are not implemented, just in the same way that Romanian laws are not implemented. So the focus should be more on the executive and administration to implement judgments where necessary—and the parliament has little real control over the executive. That's why I don't see an important role for them.[134]

According to human rights activist Romanita Iordache, parliament is an 'unappealing venue' for pro-compliance actors, since enforcement of judgments is largely dependent on the general secretariat of the government, an advisory administrative body connected with the prime minister.

> Because they're still trying to save face with Strasbourg, you get plans of action. If the issue is serious enough to have strong actors pushing from outside, then the general secretariat of the government reacts.[135]

Speaking several months ahead of the 2012 elections, Mihai Selegean, former director of the NIM and former government lawyer, ventured that, '[t]he most important driver for change in favour of human rights is to be found in the government agent ... I still don't see a system [in parliament]. [Greater parliamentary involvement] would require a fundamental change of the work of parliament and of the whole political system'.[136]

It is to the executive system of implementation that the next section turns.

6.4 Implementation of ECtHR Judgments: The Role of the Executive

As noted at 3.5.1, the government agent in Romania is located within the Ministry of Foreign Affairs, having been moved from the Ministry of Justice in 2003, where the office had been based since its creation in 1996.[137] The government agent has the status of an under-secretary of state.[138] Monica Macovei, who was Justice Minister from 2004 to 2007, sought unsuccessfully to bring the government agent back to its former location.[139] Several interviewees, including former government

[132] Diana Hatneanu, Interview, 24 May 2012.

[133] Marian Mandache, Interview, 25 May 2012. [134] Interview, 24 May 2012.

[135] Interview, 24 May 2012. [136] Interview, 24 May 2012.

[137] Under Government Emergency Ordinance No. 64/2003.

[138] Bogdan Aurescu, 'Organizational and Procedural Aspects of the Institution of State Agent before the ECHR and ICJ: Some Romanian Perspectives', *Chinese Journal of International Law* 6(2) (2007): 363, 369.

[139] Interview, 12 June 2012.

agents, regard the move to the Ministry of Foreign Affairs as a retrograde step. This was partly because legislation can only be initiated by ministries within their specific field of competence; thus, the Ministry of Foreign Affairs cannot propose legislation that concerns judicial or other areas of domestic reform but must instead work through other relevant ministries. Mihai Selegean, former in-house lawyer at the Ministry of Justice, ventures that officials in other ministries could be obstructive, either because they were unfamiliar with the Convention and the case law of the Court, or doubted its relevance, or because judgments had not been translated or summarized to make them accessible.[140] The former senator, György Frunda, notes that the government agent lacks sufficient clout to influence ministers.[141] According to one NGO interviewee in 2012, the government agent appears like an 'orphan' in its present home.[142]

Former government agent, Bogdan Aurescu, notes, however, that the move of the agent's office to the Ministry of Foreign Affairs in 2003 involved an increase in resources (from three or four staff to fifteen) and institutional weight (since the agent was previously either a counsellor to the Minister of Justice or a secretary of state performing mainly other tasks).[143] The emphasis at that time was on reaching friendly settlements in cases where it was obvious that a violation had occurred. Subsequently, however, the volume of cases increased and the resources of the government agent decreased. A former government agent from the mid-2000s expresses great disappointment with the record of implementation during that period.[144] This failure was attributed not only to political obstruction in certain cases, but also the fact that the agent's office had at most ten (and sometimes as few as six) staff at a time when a large number of cases was being communicated. The problem of understaffing was noted by several other interviewees, along with a large turnover of government agents, some of whom had been professional and constructive, while others were political appointees who saw themselves as 'gatekeepers, trying to save the face of the Romanian government'.[145]

In September 2014, members of the Legal Committee and Human Rights Committee in the lower chamber submitted a legislative proposal stipulating an obligation for the government agent to submit annually to parliament a report on activity and progress in implementing ECtHR judgments. This proposal was rejected by both chambers in February 2015.[146] However, the sub-committee on the execution of ECtHR judgments can—and does—request the government agent to submit progress reports on implementation.[147]

140 Interview, 24 May 2012.
141 Interview, 27 June 2012.
142 Diana Hatneanu, Interview, 24 May 2012.
143 Aurescu (n 138) 371.
144 Interview (anonymous), 24 May 2012.
145 Romanita Iordache, Interview, 24 May 2012.
146 Email correspondence with Alina Grigorescu, Parliamentary Adviser, Sub-committee on monitoring the execution of ECHR judgments (Chamber of Deputies), 13 October 2015.
147 Daniel Florea, Interview, 13 May 2015. Under Article 111 of the Romanian constitution, public authorities are obliged to present information or documents requested by parliament.

6.4.1 Emergency ordinances

A long-standing matter of concern in Romania is the frequent resort to emergency ordinances—a mechanism by which legislation is adopted by the government and only retrospectively scrutinized and approved by parliament. The European Commission has consistently expressed concern about the over-use of emergency ordinances, 'which limits the opportunities for consultation and has led to a lack of legislative clarity—with consequences for the unification of jurisprudence and practice'.[148] The Commission is also concerned at the lack of effective challenge of the use of emergency ordinances. The Ombudsman is empowered to seize the Constitutional Court on the constitutionality of emergency ordinances; however, the current Ombudsman, elected in April 2014, has stated that the Ombudsman should not get involved in matters concerning the balance of powers between state authorities, 'effectively [creating] a gap, which in the current institutional setup of Romania cannot be filled by other actors'.[149] Former government agent Roxana Rizoiu echoes this concern about the frequent resort to emergency ordinances, which she describes as 'almost laws' and the executive's way of bypassing protracted parliamentary procedure.[150] In some instances, she adds, parliament subsequently adopted laws that duplicated the measures contained in emergency ordinances, leading to legislative incoherence.

6.5 Monitoring and Implementing Judgments against Other States

We received mixed accounts of the extent to which the Romanian government monitors non-Romanian judgments to assess whether the same problem of principle exists within the country's legal order. The former government co-agent, Irina Cambrea, states that all ECtHR case law is 'monitored constantly'; the agent then informs the appropriate government department and relevant judgments are translated and made available on the website of the Superior Council of Magistracy.[151] However, former Justice Minister Monica Macovei observes that there is 'no office or person to systematically look at [non-Romanian] judgments', although this might happen sporadically.

Members of the sub-committee on the execution of judgments in the Chamber of Deputies acknowledge that systematic monitoring of non-Romanian judgments is beyond the sub-committee's capacity. It had occasionally discussed such judgments if they were high profile or concerned an emergent issue that might have

[148] European Commission, COM(2015) 35 final (n 24) 5.
[149] European Commission, COM(2015) 35 final (n 24) 5.
[150] Interview, 24 May 2102.
[151] Irena Cambrea, written questionnaire, received 25 June 2012.

implications for Romanian law or practice; however, the response was unlikely to be pursued with the same urgency as a judgment against Romania.[152]

6.6 Implementation of Specific Judgments

In this section, we examine the implementation of specific judgments, with a focus on the role—sometimes facilitative, at other times laggardly or resistant—of parliament. Each involves violations of the Convention connected to the Communist era and each exposes the sluggish pace of reform, reflecting the persistence of pre-1989 structures and attitudes.

6.6.1 Prosecutorial powers

As noted at 6.2.1, the power of prosecutors was a matter of concern to the Parliamentary Assembly at the time of Romania's accession to the Council of Europe. Of especial concern were prosecutorial powers, which were retained after 1989, to challenge final and binding judicial decisions without any time limitation in both civil and criminal trials (under Article 330 of the Code of Civil Procedure). Prosecutors also had powers to arrest, intercept communications, and order and conduct searches of individuals and their homes, without the control of an independent authority.[153] In addition, seizures ordered by prosecutors during investigative procedures could not be legally contested by the individual targeted. This power was at issue in the first ECtHR judgment against Romania in 1998 in the case of *Vasilescu*, which held the lack of legal recourse to challenge seizures ordered by a prosecutor to be a violation of Article 6(1) ECHR (the right to a fair trial) and determined that prosecutors did not constitute an independent tribunal.[154]

Brumărescu v Romania in 1999 concerned the prosecutorial powers under Article 330 of the Code of Civil Procedure to quash final court decisions (in this case, a decision—already executed—to restore to the applicant his parents' house which had been nationalized without compensation; see also 6.6.3).[155] The Grand Chamber held that by allowing the application lodged under that power, the High Court of Cassation and Justice had infringed the principle of legal certainty, breaching the applicant's right to a fair trial under Article 6(1) ECHR, as well as his right to peaceful enjoyment of property under Article 1 of Protocol No. 1 to the Convention. Before *Brumărescu*, Parliament had amended Article 330 to introduce a six-month deadline by which prosecutors could apply for a decision to be quashed.[156] However, to the dismay of the European Commission, an emergency ordinance in 2000 subsequently extended the deadline to one year, allowed

[152] Alina-Ştefania Gorghiu and Daniel Florea, Interviews, 13 October 2013.
[153] Bogdan and Mungiu-Pippidi (n 6) 74.
[154] *Vasilescu v Romania*, No. 27053/95, 22 May 1998, para. 41.
[155] *Brumărescu v Romania*, No. 28342/95, 28 October 1999 [GC].
[156] *Brumărescu v Romania* (n 155) para. 33.

extraordinary appeals to be made even before all other legal avenues had been exhausted, and increased the discretion afforded to prosecutors in the exercise of their extraordinary appeal powers.[157] It was not until June 2003 that Article 330 of the Code of Civil Procedure was repealed by means of an emergency ordinance, which took almost another year to be approved by parliament.[158] Reform of the Criminal Code to remove prosecutorial extraordinary appeal powers came later still after continued pressure by the European Commission.[159]

After this period of stuttering reform, the judgment in *Pantea v Romania*[160] had a more decisive and far-reaching impact. The ECtHR held, inter alia, that the prosecutorial power of arrest violated Article 5 ECHR (the right to liberty) due to the lack of independence of prosecutors from the executive (as had already been noted in *Vasilescu*).[161] Parliament acted within a matter of days to amend the Criminal Code, transferring a raft of powers from prosecutors to judges.[162] As former government agent Roxana Rizoiu puts it,

> Overnight, some 3,000 prosecutors [lost their authority] to arrest a person; order phone tapping; or order home searches. That draft law of 2003 was a big change—it had been in parliament for around three years, moving slowly from one committee to another; one chamber to another. We knew [the law needed to be reformed] but we needed the judgment to really change things. After *Pantea*, the law changed within one month.[163]

The reformed Criminal Code also addressed the violation identified in *Vasilescu* five years earlier by introducing the right of legal recourse to contest decisions of prosecutors before a court.[164] Former Judge at the ECtHR, Corneliu Birsan, singles out the response to *Pantea* as a rare example of swift parliamentary action following a judgment of the ECtHR; nevertheless, he adds, 'the change came after the fact; it could have happened earlier'.[165]

6.6.2 Accountability of the intelligence services

Judgments of the Court have been slower to remove another legacy of the Ceaușescu era, the unaccountable power of the intelligence services. The 2000 case of *Rotaru* concerned, among other issues, interference with the applicant's right to private life under Article 8 ECHR, owing to the storage and public disclosure of information

[157] European Commission, 2001 Regular Report on Romania's Progress towards Accession, SEC(2001) 1753, 13 November 2001 ('EC Regular Report 2001') 20.

[158] Resolution CM/ResDH(2007)90, Execution of the judgments of the European Court of Human Rights—Brumărescu (Grand Chamber judgment of 28 October 1999) and 30 other cases against Romania, final between 9 July 2002 and 3 May 2005, 20 June 2007.

[159] Bogdan and Mungiu-Pippidi (n 6) 75. See also European Commission, 2004 Regular Report on Romania's Progress towards Accession, SEC(2004) 1200, 6 October 2004, 21 ('EC Regular Report 2004').

[160] *Pantea v Romania*, No. 33343/96, 3 June 2003.

[161] *Pantea v Romania* (n 160) para. 239.

[162] Law No. 281/2003.

[163] Interview, 24 May 2012.

[164] The provision was later deemed by the ECtHR to provide an effective remedy; see *Stoica v Romania*, No. 42722/02, 4 March 2008, para. 110.

[165] Interview, 25 June 2012.

on his private life by the Romanian Intelligence Service (RIS) in its capacity as custodian of the archives of the pre-1989 intelligence services; the lack of an effective remedy to refute this information, which wrongly accused the applicant of being a member of an extreme right-wing organization (Article 13); and failure by the domestic court to consider the applicant's claims for non-pecuniary damage and costs in proceedings brought against the RIS (Article 6(1)).[166]

The European Commission noted in its 2004 monitoring report that the required reforms had not been made.[167] In 2005, the Committee of Ministers issued an interim resolution calling on the Romanian authorities rapidly to adopt the legislative reforms necessary to respond to *Rotaru*.[168] The government had reported to the Committee of Ministers that several bills concerning the reform of the impugned law had been submitted to parliament, but the legislative process had not yet led to the necessary reform 'in view of the complexity and of the sensitive nature of the subject matter'. The Committee of Ministers reiterated the need for legislative reform in 2007.[169] The Parliamentary Assembly, too, expressed concern. In 2006, PACE stated in respect of Romania's failure to execute *Rotaru* that 'the prolongation of such situations of non-compliance puts at stake the effectiveness of the ECHR system'.[170] The PACE rapporteur's report of 2010 deplored the continued failure to reform the law governing the RIS a decade after *Rotaru*.[171] An NGO submission to the Committee of Ministers in 2012 lamented that '[c]ivil society remains concerned about the possible extent of government surveillance of civilians, but it has no instruments to identify, let alone correct, abuses'.[172]

In an emergency ordinance in 2008, approved by parliament in the same year, Romania had revised the legal framework governing the processing of information contained in the archives of the former intelligence services.[173] However, in 2009 in *Haralambie v Romania*, the ECtHR had identified shortcomings in the operation of the revised framework, including the excessive length of procedure for gaining access to the archives, instances of incomplete access to relevant files, problems with the transfer of files from the RIS to a body established in 1999, the National Council for the Study of the Archives of the Securitate, and non-compliance by the authorities with the procedure to be followed in cases where the RIS maintains that information is related to national security.[174]

[166] *Rotaru v Romania*, No. 28341/95, 4 May 2000 [GC].

[167] EC Regular Report 2004 (n 159) 28.

[168] Interim Resolution ResDH(2005)57, 5 July 2005.

[169] 997th meeting (DH), 5–6 June 2007.

[170] PACE Resolution 1516(2006), Implementation of judgments of the European Court of Human Rights, para. 12.

[171] PACE, Committee on Legal Affairs and Human Rights, Implementation of judgments of the European Court of Human Rights, 7th report, AS/Jur (2010)36, 9 November 2010, para. 7.6.

[172] Request to the Committee of Ministers for enhanced supervision of the judgment in *Association 21 December 1989 and Others v Romania* (Applications No. 33810/07 and 18817/08) made by the Open Society Justice Initiative and the Romanian Helsinki Committee (APADOR-CH), 6 February 2012.

[173] Emergency Regulation No. 24/2008 on citizens' access to their personal files held by the Securitate.

[174] *Haralambie v Romania*, No. 21737/03, 27 October 2009.

Rotaru was finally closed by the Committee of Ministers in November 2014,[175] on the basis of assurances provided by the Romanian government that, within the framework of the execution of the *Haralambie* group of cases, and another case, *Bucur and Toma*,[176] it would continue its efforts to remedy the shortcomings identified by the Court in the implementation of the mechanism created by the 2008 reform and to bring the legal framework governing the organization and functioning of the RIS into compliance with Convention requirements.

Interviewees identify recalcitrance among both the executive and Parliament leading to the prolonged, and still incomplete,[177] process of legislative reform following *Rotaru*. Former government agent Roxana Rizoiu states,

> While I was agent [in the early 2000s] there were five or more drafts to change [the law] and we never managed to go to parliament with it. There was huge resistance. At some point, we thought that subject was so sensitive it was just easier not to do it.[178]

Mihai Selegean, an in-house lawyer at the Ministry of Justice between 1997 and 2002, attributes the delay partly to the fact that it was the Ministry of the Interior, and not the Ministry of Justice, that held the initiative with the legislative reform post-*Rotaru*.

> The only thing the government agent at the time could do was to say, 'this draft law needs to be further amended before we can say yes to it'. So it wouldn't go ahead with the initiative [which would have needed to be] approved by the government and sent to parliament.... But nor was there a possibility to make a different, compliant ... draft law.... We would keep sending them letters asking for meetings and explaining the need to make a change but the initiative ... [stayed with the Ministry of Interior or even the secret service].[179]

A former MP, speaking anonymously, notes in addition that the intelligence services 'had too much influence' on the parliamentarians tasked with monitoring and reforming them, including members of the Joint Standing Committee of the Chamber of Deputies and the Senate for the exercise of parliamentary control over the activity of the RIS.

[175] Resolution CM/ResDH(2014)253, 26 November 2014.

[176] *Bucur and Toma v Romania* (n 90), concerning, inter alia, the criminal conviction of Constantin Bucur, an RIS employee, for revealing irregularities in a government wiretapping intelligence programme (in violation of Article 10 ECHR, the right to freedom of expression), and the public disclosure of private conversations of a journalist, Micea Toma, and his daughter, which had been obtained by wiretapping (in violation of Article 8 ECHR, the right to respect for private life).

[177] In its latest examination of the execution of Bucur and Toma in 2014, the Committee of Ministers noted that Law No. 255/2013 introduced certain safeguards for the respect for private life to remedy the shortcomings found by the ECtHR in this case and also in the cases of *Rotaru, Dumitru Popescu (No. 2) v Romania*, No. 71525/01, 26 April 2007 (concerning the lack of sufficient safeguarding against arbitrariness in the interception of the applicant's telephone calls) and *Association '21 December 1989' and Others v Romania* (n 86). The latter case involved several violations arising from the violent crackdown on protests connected to the fall of the Communist regime, including (paras. 171–2) the lack of safeguards in Romanian legislation applicable to secret surveillance measures based on national security grounds.

[178] Interview, 24 May 2012. [179] Interview, 24 May 2012.

6.6.3 Nationalized property

Central and eastern European states have variously pursued either restitution or compensation mechanisms for property nationalized during the Communist period. In Romania, the property issue has proved particularly intractable for a combination of reasons: the wide-scale nature of the original nationalization; corruption and political instability; a slow and disjointed approach to reform; and the weakness of the institutions tasked with implementing it.[180] In the early years of the post-Communist transition, the Romanian authorities vacillated in their approach to the property issue: the former Communist President Ion Iliescu opposed any restitution and declared that the courts were not competent to determine claims, while anti-Communist parties championed the rights of former owners.[181] The resulting legislative incoherence, compounded by fluctuating and politically influenced judicial decisions, created uncertain and overlapping entitlements—and continuing social and political friction—between former owners seeking to reclaim confiscated properties and former tenants who had bought properties from the state.[182]

Legislative reform in 1995[183] exacerbated the problem, since it permitted the sale of tens of thousands of nationalized properties to tenants at discounted prices even where legal challenges by former owners were pending; controversially, politicians who had passed the law were among the beneficiaries.[184] In 1997, the Council of Europe urged Romania to, among other steps, amend the 1995 law so as to provide for the restitution of such property *in integrum* or fair compensation in lieu.[185] A new property law in 1998[186] confirmed the courts' competence to adjudicate former owners' claims regarding confiscated property, but did not provide for an administrative path for restitution.[187] In 2000, the European Commission highlighted the resulting legal chaos, noting that proposed legislation to clarify those instances where restitution or compensation was due had been blocked in the Senate, while judicial practice in that area was cumbersome and lacked uniformity.[188]

The chaotic design and implementation of reform, and consequent legal uncertainty, ensured that a large volume of applications was lodged at the ECtHR. The Court has very often found violations of both Article 1 of Protocol No. 1 and Article 6 ECHR. The *Brumărescu* judgment in 1999 proved to be a landmark. Bogdan and Mungiu-Pippidi note that although the case principally concerned prosecutorial powers to lodge extraordinary appeals in civil cases (see 6.6.1), the

[180] European Parliament, *Private Properties Issues following the Change of Political Regime in Former Socialist of Communist Countries* (Directorate General for Internal Policies—Policy Department: Citizens' Rights and Constitutional Affairs, 2010) 96; Lavinia Stan, 'The Roof over Our Heads: Property Restitution in Romania', *Journal of Communist Studies and Transition Politics* 22(2) (2006): 180.

[181] Bogdan and Mungiu-Pippidi (n 6) 80.

[182] Bogdan and Mungiu-Pippidi (n 6) 80–1.

[183] Law No. 112/1995.

[184] European Parliament (n 180) 104.

[185] Committee of Ministers (ResDH(1997)1123) and Parliamentary Assembly (1123 (1997)) (n 44) para. 14.4.

[186] Law No. 213/1998.

[187] European Parliament (n 180) 105; Stan (n 180) 193–4.

[188] European Commission, 2000 Regular Report from the Commission on Romania's Progress towards Accession, 8 November 2000, 22.

fact that it concerned a property claim caused it to be regarded by former owners, their political backers, and the media as an endorsement of claims for the restitution of property in kind.[189]

The accumulation of applications at the ECtHR, and external pressure from the European Commission,[190] led in 2001 to the first law regulating the administrative restitution of nationalized property.[191] In the view of the European Commission, the law exceeded the requirements of the ECHR by covering almost all confiscations between 1945 and 1989, as well as satisfying many of the restitution demands of Jews who suffered from anti-Semitic laws adopted between 1940 and 1945.[192] However, the principle of *restitutio in integrum* was not followed in practice since in cases where properties had been sold to the tenants occupying them; former owners were only entitled to compensation. As Stan observes, promises of financial compensation remained unfulfilled in the absence of a special law, and no national budget adopted after 2001 included compensation funds.[193] Moreover, administrative procedures for calculating and awarding compensation were inadequately defined, triggering another wave of domestic lawsuits between former owners and new owners (former tenants). Again, politicians who sponsored the law were among the direct beneficiaries of it.[194]

Further reform from 2005 onwards created and subsequently amended a compensation mechanism, with the frequent use of emergency ordinances. From 2007, payment of financial compensation in cash was capped at approximately €125,000, while any amount above that ceiling was to be compensated with shares in a new, state-established Property Fund.[195]

Throughout this period, the ECtHR repeatedly drew attention to the systemic flaws in Romania's property restitution system.[196] By 2010, hundreds of repetitive cases were pending before the Court and in the case of *Maria Atanasiu and Others*, it applied the pilot judgment procedure for the first time in a Romanian case. The Court stated that, in spite of previous judgments in which it had indicated that general measures were needed in order to guarantee the right to restitution in an effective and rapid manner, the 'ineffectiveness of the compensation and restitution mechanism continues to pose a recurrent and large-scale problem in Romania'—one which also represented 'a threat to the future effectiveness of the Convention machinery'.[197] The Court set a deadline of eighteen months (12 July 2012) for

189 Bogdan and Mungiu-Pippidi (n 6) 81.

190 European Parliament (n 180) 96.

191 Law No. 10/2001.

192 EC Regular Report 2001 (n 157) 27.

193 Stan (n 180) 197.

194 Susie Alegre, Ivanka Ivanova, and Dana Denis-Smith, *Safeguarding the Rule of Law in an Enlarged EU: The Cases of Bulgaria and Romania* (Brussels: Centre for European Policy Studies, 2009) 62–3.

195 European Parliament (n 180) 105–6.

196 *Străin and Others v Romania*, No. 57001/00, 21 July 2005; *Păduraru v Romania*, No. 63252/00, 1 December 2005; *Viaşu v Romania*, No. 75951/01, 9 December 2008; *Faimblat v Romania*, No. 23066/02, 13 January 2009; *Katz v Romania*, No. 29739/03, 20 January 2009; *Tudor Tudor v Romania*, No. 21911/03, 24 March 2009; *Matieş v Romania*, No. 13202/03, 8 June 2010.

197 *Maria Atanasiu and Others v Romania* (n 57) paras. 216–17.

Romania to reform the system, during which time it adjourned examination of all similar applications.[198]

Immediately after *Atanasiu*, the president and other officials of the ECtHR visited Bucharest at the invitation of the Ministry of Foreign Affairs, meeting the Minister of Justice and members of parliament.[199] In December 2010, the Romanian government formed an inter-ministerial commission to draft legislation in response to the pilot judgment.[200] The sub-committee on the execution of ECtHR judgments in the Chamber of Deputies held public hearings with the commission and engaged in correspondence with the government agent on the matter. Indeed, as noted at 6.3.4, in the early years of the sub-committee's existence this was the only case on which it actively pursued the question of implementation.

In January 2011, the Property Fund was listed on the stock exchange in order to ensure that shares in the fund could be sold at market prices. However, within months the fund ran short of money (in part because it had been raided to meet other state obligations), while the low value of shares created a de facto ceiling on compensation, resulting in further legal claims.[201] The Romanian government sought, and was granted, two extensions of the deadline imposed in *Atanasiu*, up to May 2013.[202] On 5 April 2013, the government held consultations with officials from the Department for the Execution of Judgments and the Registry of the Court on a draft law which provided, as a general rule, for the restitution of property and created a mechanism for compensation for cases in which restitution is impossible.[203] On 22 April 2013, the Romanian parliament adopted the law.[204] A year later, the ECtHR delivered a follow-up judgment in which it held that the new law provided, in principle, an accessible and effective framework of redress for the vast majority of situations arising in the reparation process.[205] However, the judgment identified outstanding problems such as the lack of provisions affording redress in cases involving multiple documents of title for the same building, and failure to address the situation of former owners who were unable to obtain restitution but had

198 *Maria Atanasiu and Others v Romania* (n 57) operative paras. 6 and 7.

199 Andrei Popovici, *Romania's Coming Property Reform: Nine Months Left to Solve a 21 Billion Euro Problem* (Romanian Centre for European Policies, 2011) 23.

200 This comprised the Office of the Prime Minister, the National Restitution Authority, the Authority for State Assets Recovery, and the Ministries of Justice, the Interior, Finance, Agriculture and Rural Development, Environment and Forests, and Foreign Affairs.

201 Bogdan and Mungiu-Pippidi (n 6) 82–3; Popovici (n 199) 20.

202 Committee of Ministers 1144th (DH) meeting, CM/Del/Dec(2012)1144/13, 4–6 June 2012.

203 The law envisages that the authorities should, by 1 January 2016, resolve all claims of restitution, issue property titles and ensure that the beneficiaries take possession of their respective properties. Where restitution is impossible, a points-based compensation system permits claimants either to bid for alternative state-owned properties or to receive (via a new National Fund) financial compensation in instalments over seven years starting in 2017. The law sets binding time-limits for each administrative stage of the process and provides for the possibility of judicial review. See Străin and Others against Romania and Maria Atanasiu and Others against Romania (and 266 similar cases) group, Memorandum prepared by the Department for the Execution of Judgments of the European Court of Human Rights, in close co-operation with the Registry of the European Court, H/Exec(2013)1, 10 April 2013.

204 Law No. 165/2013.

205 *Preda and Others v Romania*, No. 9584/02, 29 April 2014, para. 129.

missed an earlier deadline for claiming compensation.[206] At the time of writing, the implementation of the new reparation mechanism and the outstanding issues identified by the Court remain under the enhanced supervision of the Committee of Ministers.[207]

The protracted failure to resolve the property issue comprehensively is attributed by interviewees to a range of obstacles. These include the political sensitivity of the issue, which ensured that legislation was shaped spasmodically under the force of competing electoral interests and profound social tensions between former owners and those who had rented or bought their properties. In between electoral cycles, there was a persistent lack of will due to the financial and political costs involved, particularly after the financial crash of 2008.[208] As one NGO interviewee remarks, 'With the pace of the European Court of Human Rights, it was cheaper for the state just to keep paying [compensation in] 100 cases per year.'[209]

Interviewees also point to corruption and the financial interest of some politicians, judges, and prosecutors in nationalized properties as reasons for the long-delayed implementation of ECtHR judgments. Elite actors had profited both by buying properties at advantageous rates and by purchasing litigious rights over restitution files, securing large compensation payments where the former owners had failed to do so.[210] The use of emergency ordinances which were insufficiently consulted upon or scrutinized was also criticized. Former Justice Minister Monica Macovei notes, in addition, that contradictory judgments in domestic courts had compounded the problem, revealing the lack of judicial commitment to unified jurisprudence during the post-1989 transition. Political commitment to fulfilling Convention obligations in respect of nationalized properties was highly contingent throughout the post-Communist transition. When former owners began applying to the ECtHR in 1995, 'Romanian politicians claimed that, by seeking justice in Strasbourg, the owners exposed the country to the criticism of the international community during negotiations for accession to the European Union'.[211]

While EU pressure was a catalyst for the restitution law in 2001, the law was undermined by sluggish and inconsistent implementation; former Prime Minister Adrian Năstase, for example, remarks that the ECtHR 'was not a real estate agent'.[212] The application of the pilot judgment procedure in *Atanasiu* and the imposition of a deadline undoubtedly had a galvanizing effect on the executive and parliament in fashioning a legislative response after years of delay. With some 200,000 restitution claims outstanding, however, further litigation cannot be ruled out.

[206] *Preda and Others v Romania* (n 205) para. 124.

[207] 8th Annual Report of the Committee of Ministers 2014 (n 76) 177.

[208] As one measure of the costs involved, the new fund created by Law 165/2013 is worth some €10 billion. See 'Romania Plans Another National Fund for Property Restitution, with Landplots and Forestry as Main Assets', *Romania Insider*, 19 March 2013.

[209] Diana Hatneanu, Interview, 24 May 2012.

[210] Stan (n 180) 200; 'Romanian PM: Property Restitution Became Lucrative Real Estate Business for 1,000 Intermediaries', *Romania Insider*, 15 April 2013.

[211] Stan (n 180) 199.

[212] Stan (n 180) 198.

6.6.4 Freedom of expression

In the Ceauşescu era, criticism of the state apparatus was severely restricted: insult and calumny were criminal offences punishable by imprisonment (Articles 205 and 206 of the Criminal Code dating back to 1968) and those accused of libel were obliged to prove the truth of their statements or allegations (Article 207). In addition, insult and calumny against civil servants ('offence against authority' under Article 238) and 'verbal outrage' (Article 239) were criminal offences. After the fall of Ceauşescu, the media rapidly liberalized, but establishing a new ethical and legal framework aligned to European standards was a slower process.[213] After sustained pressure by the European Union,[214] the Council of Europe,[215] and Romanian media and civil society,[216] which referred to case law of the ECtHR,[217] a draft bill was introduced that would have abolished prison sentences for insult and libel and eliminated the offences of 'offence against authority' and 'verbal outrage'. However, the bill was rejected by the Chamber of Deputies.[218] In 1999, in *Dalban v Romania*, the ECtHR held that issuing a suspended prison sentence to a journalist convicted of calumny in 1994 amounted to violation of Article 10 (the right to freedom of expression), and noted that 'it would be unacceptable for a journalist to be debarred from expressing critical value judgments [sic] unless he or she could prove their truth'.[219] In June 2000, the Chamber of Deputies adopted a draft bill repealing Articles 238 and 239 of the Criminal Code and reducing the prison sentence for insult and defamation; however, the Senate delayed voting on it and following the parliamentary election of November 2000 and presidential election of December 2000, the Ministry of Justice sought to reverse the reforms which had been adopted by the Chamber of Deputies (and were still awaiting a vote in the Senate).[220] In May 2002, following further pressure from Brussels,[221] the government introduced an emergency ordinance, which restored most, but not all, of the reforms passed by the Chamber of Deputies.[222] This measure, too, was deemed inadequate by the European Commission, which noted that maintaining calumny against officials as a specific offence and leaving unreformed

213 Bogdan and Mungiu-Pippidi (n 6) 77–9.

214 European Commission, Regular Report from the Commission on Romania's Progress towards Accession (1998) 11.

215 See Resolutions issued on 24 April 1997 by the Committee of Ministers (ResDH(1997)1123) and Parliamentary Assembly (1123 (1997)) (n 44) on the honouring of obligations and commitments by Romania.

216 In 1997, ten NGOs made various proposals for reform aimed at protecting freedom of expression, including making insult and libel civil offences and introducing into Article 207 (on the burden of proof) the notion of public interest. See Association for the Defence of Human Rights in Romania (APADOR-CH), Report of 1997 (on file).

217 See, for example, *Lingens v Austria*, No. 9815/82, 8 July 1986, para. 46.

218 Bogdan and Mungiu-Pippidi (n 6) 78.

219 No. 28114/95, 28 September 1999 [GC] para. 49.

220 Association for the Defence of Human Rights in Romania (APADOR-CH), Report of 2001.

221 EC Regular Report 2001 (n 157) 26.

222 Emergency Ordinance No. 58/2002.

Article 207 on the burden of proof was incompatible with the Convention and the case law of the ECtHR.[223] In the face of this pressure, President Ion Iliescu returned the ordinance to parliament and in June 2004, a new Criminal Code was adopted which repealed the crime of 'insult', removed the possibility of a prison sentence for slander, and aligned requirements on the burden of proof with those of the Convention.[224] The Code did not enter into force as the new reformist Minister of Justice, Monica Macovei, sought to instigate more thoroughgoing reform, and it was only after the parliamentary elections of November 2004 that further partial reform took place (repealing the offence of outrage and eliminating prison sentences for calumny),[225] before full decriminalization was achieved in 2006.[226]

The legislative saga was not over, however. Legislative and judicial moves to repeal criminal libel were overruled in 2007 and 2013 by the Romanian Constitutional Court,[227] and on 10 December 2013, the Chamber of Deputies voted unexpectedly and without public consultation to recriminalize insult and defamation.[228] The reinstatement by the Chamber of Deputies of the previously abolished provisions of the Criminal Code would have meant, among other things, reintroducing the standard for the burden of proof (Article 207) which had been expressly rejected by the Court in *Dalban* more than fifteen years earlier. A report for Index on Censorship ventured that:

> Of particular concern is that parliamentarians have misused the recent European Commission cooperation and verification mechanism report[229] that called for 'freedom of the press [to be] accompanied by a proper protection of institutions and of individuals' fundamental rights as well as to provide for effective redress' to justify these measures.[230]

Following international pressure, and rejection of the measure by the Senate, the new Criminal Code, adopted in February 2014, did not include criminal sanctions for libel and slander.[231]

223 European Commission, 2002 Regular Report on Romania's Progress towards Accession, SEC(2002) 1409, 9 October 2002, 33.

224 EC Regular Report 2004 (n 159) 26.

225 Law No. 160/2005.

226 Law No. 278/2006.

227 'OSCE Media Freedom Representative Urges Romanian Authorities to Finalize Decriminalization of Libel', Organization for Security and Co-operation in Europe, 7 May 2013.

228 'Romanian President Urged to Counter Recriminalisation of Libel', IFEX, 11 December 2013. According to IFEX, the global network promoting and defending freedom of expression, the move occurred 'under very suspicious circumstances' by means of radical overnight redrafting of an innocuous Bill (Pl-x 680/2011) introduced in 2011 to repeal of a single article of the Criminal Code (Article 74/1).

229 Report from the Commission to the European Parliament and the Council On Progress in Romania under the Co-operation and Verification Mechanism, COM(2013) 47 final, 30 January 2013.

230 Mike Harris, *Time to Step Up: The EU and Freedom of Expression* (Index on Censorship, 2013) 9–10.

231 Nations in Transit: Romania (n 14) 528.

6.7 Conclusion

The account of implementation of ECtHR judgments in this chapter reveals the uneven pace and trajectory of reform in the post-1989 era. Substantial reform has been achieved, such as the decriminalization of same-sex relationships and libel, and curbs on the power of prosecutors, but only after tortuous legislative battles which suggest that progress made remains insecure. In other areas, such as the restitution of nationalized properties or compensation in lieu, and reform of the legislative framework governing the intelligence services, implementation remains under the enhanced supervision of the Committee of Ministers. Still other systemic and structural problems remain unresolved or only partially resolved, such as inhuman or degrading treatment in Romanian detention facilities;[232] the excessive length of civil and criminal proceedings;[233] the consequences of racially motivated violence against villagers of Roma origin in the early 1990s;[234] and the lack of adequate investigation into the suppression of protesters during the fall of the Ceaușescu regime.[235]

These and other judgments remain on the agenda of the sub-committee on the execution of ECtHR judgments in the Chamber of Deputies. This sub-committee was by all accounts dormant and severely under-resourced in its first few years of existence after 2009; however, in the parliament elected in 2012 it appears to have developed more systematized working methods and to be monitoring a broader range of judgments, whilst at the same time building links with the Council of Europe. There is little evidence, however, that this knowledge and commitment extends much beyond the sub-committee's (currently) six members. After elections due in 2016, parliamentary oversight of the implementation of Convention norms may be strengthened with the proposed creation of a joint committee of the Chamber of Deputies and the Senate.

In addition to their complexity and resource demands, many judgments of the Court have struck at the core of sensitive matters connected to Romania's emergence from the Communist era. As Bogdan and Mungiu-Pippidi observe, '[i]n this conflict between old mentalities and new democratic values, there has been huge domestic resistance to the latter'.[236] Parliamentarians have at times perceived both political and material incentives to resist legislative reform required by Strasbourg judgments.

Accession to the EU and continuous monitoring by the European Commission has provided 'the principal driving force in pushing implementation of the ECtHR's decisions', in tandem with pressure from domestic pro-compliance

[232] 8th Annual Report of the Committee of Ministers 2014 (n 76) 116.
[233] 8th Annual Report of the Committee of Ministers 2014 (n 76) 142.
[234] 8th Annual Report of the Committee of Ministers 2014 (n 76) 188, which 'deplored the significant and persistent delay' in the adoption and implementation of the required general measures.
[235] 8th Annual Report of the Committee of Ministers 2014 (n 76) 100–1.
[236] Bogdan and Mungiu-Pippidi (n 6) 86.

constituencies.[237] However, a report in 2009 noted that the Romanian authorities had become adept at 'mimicking progress in the areas they consider important for the EU', such as anti-corruption, with the risk that corrupt or ineffective structures might become ossified beneath a veneer of reform.[238] As noted at 6.1.1, parliament is viewed as a corrupt institution enjoying minimal public trust. The precipitous, albeit unsuccessful, move to recriminalize libel in 2013 in defiance of Convention standards and the case law of the ECtHR exemplifies the fragility of democratic reform—and the manifest need to strengthen further the oversight conducted by the nascent, and still evolving, pro-compliance structures within parliament.

[237] Bogdan and Mungiu-Pippidi (n 6) 86–7.
[238] Alegre, Ivanova, and Denis-Smith (n 194) 82.

7

The United Kingdom

7.1 The Constitutional, Legal, and Political Landscape

The constitutional system of the UK, developed incrementally over centuries, is derived from a variety of written and unwritten sources, including statutes, treaties, case law, and constitutional conventions (informal and uncodified procedural agreements that establish the day-to-day rules and expectations for the exercise of state power). Three fundamental principles are woven into the constitutional fabric of the UK: the presumption of liberty, the doctrine of parliamentary sovereignty, and the rule of law, which together 'ensure that the exercise of public power is subject to various forms of legal and political accountability, and provide a normative framework which shapes how political debate and decision-making proceeds' in the UK.[1] Oliver argues that the doctrine of parliamentary sovereignty is accompanied by a pragmatic recognition by both politicians and the courts that responsibility for preventing unconstitutionality and upholding the rule of law rests on every organ of state—the executive, parliament, and the courts—and not solely or primarily on the Supreme Court.[2] Thus, despite the political character of the UK's constitutional system, it is subject to 'very significant normative constraints'.[3]

O'Cinneide identifies various factors that have eroded the sovereign authority of the Westminster parliament. These include the delegation of authority from the late 1990s to the devolved assemblies in Scotland, Wales, and Northern Ireland.[4] In addition, the introduction of the Human Rights Act (HRA) 1998, along with the influence of both the European Convention on Human Rights (ECHR or 'the Convention') and European Union law, 'have played a key role in infusing human rights values into UK law and, in tandem with other developments, have ensured that a better balance has been struck between "legal" and "political" elements of the UK constitutional order'.[5] The nature of that balance, however, remains a source of continuing tension, as manifested by the sometimes intense hostility in UK public discourse towards both the HRA and the European Court of Human Rights

[1] Colm O'Cinneide, *The Human Rights Act and the Slow Transformation of the Political Constitution*, UCL Institute for Human Rights Working Paper No. 01 (2012) 2–3.

[2] Dawn Oliver, 'Parliaments and the Courts: A Pragmatic (or Principled) Defence of the Sovereignty of Parliament', in Alexander Horne, Gavin Drewry, and Dawn Oliver, eds., *Parliament and the Law* (Oxford: Hart Publishing, 2013): 309, 310.

[3] O'Cinneide (n 1) 3. [4] O'Cinneide (n 1) 16. [5] O'Cinneide (n 1) 17.

(ECtHR or 'the Court') for their perceived disturbance of the principle of parliamentary sovereignty.

7.2 The UK and the Convention System

Politicians and lawyers from the UK greatly influenced the creation of the Council of Europe and the European Convention in the aftermath of World War Two.[6] As Bates and others have documented, British ministers were concerned from the outset at the potential loss of national sovereignty entailed by participation in the Convention system.[7] The UK, Bates observes, ratified the Convention in 1951 'primarily to set an example for others, and not with the expectation that it would be found in violation itself, at least not regularly', and safe in the knowledge that the right of individual petition to the (then) European Commission of Human Rights (ECommHR) and the jurisdiction of the (not yet established) Court were optional for member states.[8] In 1966, the UK accepted the jurisdiction of the Court—which had been constituted in 1959—along with the right of individual petition. It renewed its acceptance of these optional clauses on successive occasions in the 1970s, 1980s, and early 1990s, before, in 1994, ratifying Protocol No. 11 to the Convention which created the full-time, permanent Court.[9] Ministerial discussions in the 1980s reveal disquiet about the implications of the ECtHR for national sovereignty; yet despite this, and in full awareness of the steady expansion of the Court's jurisprudence since the late 1970s, Prime Minister Margaret Thatcher declared in 1989 that the UK 'was committed to, and supported, the principles of human rights' in the Convention and her successor, John Major, reiterated this commitment in 1993.[10]

7.2.1 The Human Rights Act 1998

Despite having international obligations under the Convention since it entered into force in 1953, for decades UK judges and public authorities were not bound to observe these human rights as a matter of domestic law.[11] This changed with the introduction of the Human Rights Act 1998, which came into force across

[6] Ed Bates, *The Evolution of the European Convention on Human Rights: From Its Inception to the Creation of a Permanent Court of Human Rights* (Oxford: Oxford University Press, 2010); A.W. Brian Simpson, *Human Rights and the End of Empire: Britain and the Genesis of the European Convention* (Oxford: Oxford University Press, 2004).

[7] Bates (n 6) 77–8, 116–17; Elizabeth Wicks, 'The United Kingdom Government's Perceptions of the European Convention on Human Rights at the Time of Entry', *Public Law* (2000): 438.

[8] Ed Bates, 'The UK and Strasbourg: A Strained Relationship—The Long View', in Katja S. Ziegler, Elizabeth Wicks, and Loveday Hodson, eds., *The UK and European Human Rights: A Strained Relationship?* (Oxford: Hart Publishing, 2015): 39, 42.

[9] Bates (n 6) 316–18.

[10] Bates (n 6) 317–18.

[11] In essence, the courts had to do no more than 'have regard' to the ECHR when interpreting ambiguous statutes, the presumption being that Parliament intended to legislate in conformity with the Convention (*R v Secretary of State for the Home Department ex parte Brind* [1991] 1 AC 696).

the UK in 2000.[12] The aim of the HRA is to 'give further effect' in UK law to the fundamental rights and freedoms in the Convention, thereby making available in domestic courts a remedy for the breach of a Convention right.

The Act has three main dimensions. First, it makes it unlawful for public authorities to act in a way that is incompatible with a Convention right unless primary legislation requires otherwise, and provides a remedy to individuals for breaches of Convention rights.[13] Secondly, it requires that domestic courts 'take into account' judgments of the ECtHR in so far as they are relevant in any case concerning a Convention right.[14] This means that domestic courts are required to take account of all ECtHR jurisprudence, not merely judgments against the UK, but are not bound by it.[15] In practice, domestic courts have sometimes expressly departed from ECtHR judgments in comparable cases.[16]

The third dimension concerns the framing and interpretation of legislation. Unlike constitutional bills of rights, the HRA has no entrenched status and can be revised or repealed on the basis of a simple parliamentary majority. Thus, the Act does not fundamentally disturb the UK's tradition of representative parliamentary democracy. As Hiebert notes, the HRA is politically oriented in that it provides for rights-based scrutiny at four stages, three of which relate to the legislative rather than the judicial process.[17] First, ministers introducing draft legislation are required to attach a statement as to its compatibility with the Convention.[18] This provides a legal basis for the second stage of the process—parliamentary rights-based scrutiny of legislation. This is exercised principally by the Joint Committee on Human Rights (JCHR), which was established in 2000 and has twelve members drawn equally from the House of Commons and House of Lords, thereby ensuring its independence from the executive.[19] The third stage is judicial review: courts are empowered to read legislation in a way that is compatible with Convention rights, but only 'so far as it is possible to do so'.[20] If such an interpretation is not possible, the higher courts may issue a declaration of incompatibility, which signals to the executive and legislature the inconsistency between the domestic statute and Convention rights.[21]

[12] The devolved administrations in Scotland, Wales, and Northern Ireland were bound by the HRA from their inception in 1999.

[13] HRA 1998, s. 6.

[14] HRA 1998, s. 2.

[15] Roger Masterman, 'The Mirror Crack'd', UK Constitutional Law blog, 13 February 2013.

[16] Notably, in *R v Horncastle and Others (Appellants)* [2009] UKSC 14, the Supreme Court opted not to follow a Chamber decision of the ECtHR relating to whether allowing criminal convictions based solely or decisively on hearsay evidence automatically breached Article 6 ECHR (the right to a fair trial). Subsequently, the Grand Chamber essentially agreed with the domestic courts, in what the (then) UK judge Nicolas Bratza described as 'a good example of the judicial dialogue between national courts and the European Court on the application of the Convention' (see *Al Khawaja and Tahery v UK*, Nos. 26766/05 and 22228/06, 15 December 2011, Concurring Opinion of Judge Bratza, para. 2).

[17] Janet Hiebert, 'The Human Rights Act: Ambiguity about Parliamentary Sovereignty', *German Law Journal* 14(12) (2013): 2253.

[18] HRA 1998, s. 19.

[19] Janet Hiebert, 'Parliament and the Human Rights Act: Can the JCHR Help Facilitate a Culture of Rights?', *International Journal of Constitutional Law* 4(1) (2006): 1.

[20] HRA 1998, s. 3(1).

[21] HRA 1998, s. 4.

In this event, the fourth stage empowers ministers to introduce a remedial order, a form of delegated legislation by which a minister may choose to amend primary legislation following a declaration by a UK court that it is incompatible with the ECHR or a judgment of the ECtHR in a case concerning the UK.[22] Remedial orders must be laid before parliament for an affirmative resolution and are subject to scrutiny by the JCHR as part of its formal remit.[23] Crucially, it is left to the elected branches of government to decide whether they agree that there is an incompatibility and, if so, whether and how to remedy it. In practice, domestic courts have made few declarations of incompatibility. There were twenty-nine between 2000, when the HRA came into force, and December 2014, and in every case the incompatibility was either remedied by primary or secondary legislation or a remedial order, or overturned on appeal.[24] As King notes, despite considerable delays in some cases, and with the possible exception of prisoner voting (see 7.6.1), 'there has been no case to date where Government or Parliament affirmatively chose not to remedy incompatible legislation'.[25] This leads King towards the tentative conclusion that, while it is not possible to conclude that there is a constitutional convention in favour of legislative amendment following a judicial declaration of incompatibility, 'evidence is mounting that one is perceived by the Government and some legislators to exist'.[26]

7.2.2 Attitudes towards the Convention system

As noted in 1.1.2, public discourse about the Convention system and about human rights law in the UK has become increasingly critical and at times intemperate in recent years. The HRA has been lambasted for being a 'villains' charter', purportedly creating an individualistic and socially irresponsible culture; in 2011, Prime Minister David Cameron went so far as to identify the HRA as a contributory cause of riots in several English cities.[27] Certain politicians, judicial figures, and sections of the press have been persistently critical of judgments of both the ECtHR (see 1.1.2) and of domestic courts under the HRA.[28] A recent analysis of parliamentary

[22] HRA 1998, s. 10 and Schedule 2.

[23] See the JCHR website at <http://www.parliament.uk/business/committees/committees-a-z/joint-select/human-rights-committee/role/>.

[24] Apart from one that was still subject to appeal; see Ministry of Justice, *Responding to Human Rights Judgments: Report to the Joint Committee on Human Rights on the Government Response to Human Rights Judgments 2013–14*, CM 8962 (2014) ('Ministry of Justice Report 2013–14') 32.

[25] Jeff King, 'Parliament's Role Following Declarations of Incompatibility under the Human Rights Act', in Murray Hunt, Hayley Hooper, and Paul Yowell, eds., *Parliaments and Human Rights: Redressing the Democratic Deficit* (Oxford: Hart Publishing, 2015): 167.

[26] King (n 25) 182–6.

[27] Prime Minister David Cameron, 'Speech on the Fight-Back after the Riots', Witney, 15 August 2011.

[28] For example, following the judgment in *R (F and Thompson) v Home Secretary* [2010] UKSC 17, in which the Supreme Court ruled that the law concerning the Sex Offenders Register breached the right to respect for private life under Article 8 ECHR since it failed to provide an opportunity for independent review of the indefinite requirement to be on the Register, the Home Secretary said: 'It is time to assert that it is Parliament that makes our law, not the courts; that the rights of the public come before the rights of criminals; and, above all, that we have a legal framework that brings sanity to cases such as these'; HC Deb, 16 February 2011, vol. 523, col. 961. Nevertheless, the Government complied with the judgment by introducing the Sexual Offences Act 2003 (Remedial) Order 2012.

debates in 2013 suggests that 'the ECtHR is depicted as a biased institution that poses a risk to the human rights of large sections of the UK population', with such 'negative and hostile' attitudes providing a 'powerful discursive "tool"' with which to advance competing political objectives.[29]

In 2012, a majority of members of the Commission on a Bill of Rights, formed in 2011 to explore the creation of a new Bill of Rights to replace the HRA, recommended this step principally on the ground of the perceived degree of public alienation from the Act, which, it suggested, calls for a 'fresh beginning'.[30] This was despite the fact that a majority of the more than 2,000 respondents to the Commission's public consultations favoured retaining the HRA.[31] Moreover, attitudes are not uniform across the UK: higher levels of political support for both the HRA and the ECtHR are evident in the devolved nations of Scotland, Wales, and Northern Ireland.[32]

In respect of the ECtHR, opinion polls in the UK appear to show a fall in public support in the past twenty years.[33] Surveys further suggest that antipathy towards the Court—a Council of Europe institution—is fuelled by, and frequently confused with, scepticism about the European Union.[34] Nevertheless, opinion about the Court and the Convention system should not be assumed to be uniformly negative. In a qualitative survey of opinion among politicians, judges, and lawyers undertaken in 2008–2011, only one out of twenty-one interviewees in the UK assessed the constitutive legitimacy of the Court negatively (see 4.1).[35] UK respondents were deemed to have '[set] the legitimacy bar high' compared to the other states under review, suggesting that in the UK the Court 'does not start with a large legitimacy surplus but that it needs to gain legitimacy through its performance'—a performance which was, however, positively appraised by around two-thirds of interviewees.[36]

[29] Paul Johnson, 'Beliefs about the European Court of Human Rights in the United Kingdom Parliament', in Anthony Amatrudo and Regina Rauxloh, eds., *Law in Popular Belief: Myth and Reality* (Manchester: Manchester University Press, forthcoming in 2016). Johnson analyses debates in the House of Commons and House of Lords relating to the Marriage (Same Sex Couples) Act 2013.

[30] Commission on a Bill of Rights, *A UK Bill of Rights? The Choice Before Us*, Volume 1 (December 2012) 30.

[31] In their minority report, two Commissioners, Baroness Helena Kennedy and Philippe Sands QC, observe (178): 'Whilst in the minority on the Commission, our views are aligned with the views of respondents to our two consultations, as this report recognises, in the sense of overwhelming support to retain the system established by the Human Rights Act (and very considerable opposition, for now at least, to the idea of a UK Bill of Rights).'

[32] The majority report of the Commission on a Bill of Rights acknowledged that there was 'little or no call' for reform in Scotland, Wales, or Northern Ireland. See Commission on a Bill of Rights (n 30) 15.

[33] See 4.1 at n 20.

[34] For example, in a national survey, 'interference by Europe' was the second most common association with human rights, and 60 per cent of those surveyed thought that the ECtHR was part of the European Union; see Equality and Diversity Forum, *Public Attitudes to Human Rights: A Summary of Research Commissioned by the Equality and Diversity Forum* (2012) 6.

[35] Başak Çalı, Anne Koch, and Nicola Bruch, *The Legitimacy of the European Court of Human Rights: The View from the Ground* (Department of Political Science, University College London, 2011): 25.

[36] Çalı, Koch, and Bruch (n 35) 26. The other states under review were Ireland, Germany, Turkey, and Bulgaria.

Opprobrium towards the ECtHR, which has intensified since 2010, has been based on various grounds, relating to its alleged judicial activism;[37] the supposedly poor quality[38] or undemocratic character[39] of its personnel and procedures; its perceived intent to impose uniform standards on member states;[40] and its purported cost to the UK.[41] The President of the Supreme Court, Lord Neuberger, traces the origins of these suspicions to the fact that the Convention seems 'far more revolutionary' in the UK than in other European states that have written and coherent constitutions, in which '[t]here is little danger of the Convention leading to ... public suspicion of judicial aggrandisement ... particularly in the light of their history which gives rise to rather less confidence in the democratic process than that of the UK'.[42] The British are, as a consequence, 'peculiarly averse to, and particularly suspicious of, being told what they can and can't do by pan-European bodies'.[43]

Even allowing for the historical origins of British exceptionalism, there is a twofold paradox at the heart of the strife surrounding the UK's relationship with the Convention system. First, the statistics do not bear out the assertion—whether explicit or implicit—that the ECtHR is increasingly or disproportionately prone to overrule decisions taken by UK authorities. The UK's 'rate of defeat' in Strasbourg is extremely low. Between 1959 and 2014, of the 22,781 applications against the UK, only 1.3 per cent (301) resulted in an adverse judgment.[44] As explained at 1.2.2, this figure reflects the Court's strict admissibility criteria, which mean that only a few applications of substantial merit proceed to a judgment. To be sure, compared to the small numbers of judgments in 1970s and 1980s, the frequency of judgments against the UK increased markedly after the entry into force of Protocol No. 11 to the ECHR in 1998, after which individuals had the right of direct petition to the Court without having to apply initially to the ECommHR.[45] However, criticism of the ECtHR in recent years cannot be explained by any increasing tendency on its part to find violations in UK cases. On the contrary, there has been a downward trend: in 2013, there were eight adverse judgments concerning the

[37] Lord Sumption, 'The Limits of Law', 27th Sultan Azlan Shah Lecture, Kuala Lumpur, 20 November 2013.

[38] See, for example, 'Europe's Court Jesters', *The Times*, 19 April 2012.

[39] The incorrect but often-repeated assertion that judges of the ECtHR are unelected has been made in numerous press reports (see, for example, 'Unelected Euro Judges are Bringing Terror to the Streets of Britain', *Daily Mail*, 18 January 2012) and by a senior judicial figure (Lord Judge, 'A View from London', *Counsel*, October 2014).

[40] Lord Hoffmann, 'The Universality of Human Rights', Judicial Studies Board Annual Lecture, 19 March 2009.

[41] Lee Rotherham, *Britain and the ECHR* (Taxpayers' Alliance, 2010).

[42] Lord Neuberger, 'The Role of Judges in Human Rights Jurisprudence: A Comparison of the Australian and UK Experience', conference at the Supreme Court of Victoria, Melbourne, 8 August 2014, para. 17.

[43] Lord Neuberger, 'The British and Europe', Cambridge Freshfields Annual Law Lecture, 12 February 2014, para. 10.

[44] See 1.2.2, Table1.2.

[45] House of Commons Library, *UK Cases at the European Court of Human Rights since 1975*, SN/IA/5611, 30 April 2013.

UK;[46] and in 2014, only four.[47] This compared to an average of around sixteen adverse judgments annually in the previous decade. Even allowing for natural fluctuations in the annual statistics, these figures appear to bear out the expectation that, as a consequence of the HRA, national authorities consider human rights more explicitly and intensively than before and therefore the ECtHR is, in turn, more likely to follow their reasoning and conclusions. Indeed, greater controversy about the UK's relationship with Strasbourg might have been expected in previous decades when, despite the lower numbers overall, the UK, having accepted the right of individual petition comparatively early, accounted for a significantly higher proportion of applications and judgments than other states. As a snapshot, in 1983, the UK accounted for a third of all applications registered by the ECommHR;[48] three decades later, in the context of a greatly enlarged Council of Europe (up from twenty-one member states in 1983 to forty-seven in 2013), it accounted for just 2 per cent of applications.[49]

The second contradiction about the furore surrounding the Court is that the UK has a comparatively strong record in implementing its judgments. Bates observes that from the 1970s onwards, despite the fact that the Convention was an irritant to British politicians, at least a minimal attempt was made to give effect to adverse judgments of the Court (and decisions of the ECommHR) in every case.[50] Notable judgments and decisions from the early decades concerned the right of British passport holders of Asian descent in East Africa to enter or settle in the UK;[51] the use of interrogation techniques in Northern Ireland;[52] judicial corporal punishment;[53] the criminalization of homosexuality;[54] and the interception of communications by law enforcement and intelligence agencies.[55] Even judgments which initially provoked defiance from the UK government were ultimately implemented; for example, *McCann v UK*, which concerned the fatal shooting in Gibraltar of three members of the Irish Republican Army by British Special Air Service officers in violation of the right to life under Article 2 ECHR.[56] The (then) Deputy Prime Minister, Michael Heseltine, said that the ruling would encourage a 'terrorist mentality' and that the UK would 'ignore it and do nothing about it'.[57] Media reaction, too, was hostile.[58] However, over time, the standards established by the judgment

46 European Court of Human Rights, *Annual Report 2013* (2014) 201.

47 European Court of Human Rights, *Annual Report 2014* (2015) 175.

48 European Commission of Human Rights, *Stock-Taking on the European Convention on Human Rights: The First Thirty Years 1954–1984* (Strasbourg, Council of Europe, 1984): 325.

49 See 1.2.2, Table 1.1.

50 Bates (n 6) 317.

51 *East African Asians v UK*, Nos. 4403/70–4419/70, 4422/70, 4434/70, 4443/70, 4476/70–4478/70, 4486/70, 4501/70, and 4526/70–4530/70, Report of the European Commission of Human Rights, 14 December 1973. See also Bates (n 6) 242–7.

52 *Ireland v UK*, No. 5310/71, 18 January 1978.

53 *Tyrer v UK*, No. 5856/72. 25 April 1978.

54 *Dudgeon v UK*, No. 7525/76, 22 October 1981.

55 *Malone v UK*, No. 8691/79, 2 August 1984.

56 No. 18984/91, 27 September 1995 [GC].

57 D. Wilson Jackson, *The United Kingdom Confronts the European Convention on Human Rights* (Gainesville: University Press of Florida, 1997): 57.

58 Bates (n 6) 437.

for the control and planning of operations gained acceptance, and are enshrined in guidance for police on the management, command and deployment of armed officers.[59] Socially-sensitive judgments concerning, for example, corporal punishment in schools[60] and in the family[61] also led to far-reaching, if belated, legislative reform.

The Ministry of Justice ventures that the UK's implementation of judgments has historically been 'timely and effective'.[62] At the end of 2014, the UK was responsible for twenty-six pending cases before the Committee of Ministers, a mere 0.3 per cent of the total caseload.[63] Of these, five were 'leading' cases which had been pending for at least two years.[64] In March 2015, the JCHR commended the government for its 'generally very good record' on implementing Court judgments, in particular its swift implementation of several recent judgments and its success in resolving some older cases which had been under supervision by the Committee of Ministers for many years.[65] However, it noted that there were a few cases in which there had been unacceptable delays in implementation.[66] These were a group of historic cases from Northern Ireland concerning the inadequacy of the investigation of the use of lethal force by state agents;[67] the non-implementation in Northern Ireland of certain judgments which had been implemented elsewhere in the UK;[68] and, most glaringly, the protracted failure to implement judgments on the right of convicted prisoners to vote.[69]

The Parliamentary Assembly of the Council of Europe (PACE) has identified the UK as having 'significant implementation problems' stemming largely from the prisoner voting saga.[70] As a consequence, the leaders of the UK delegation were

[59] Association of Chief Police Officers and National Policing Improvement Agency, *Manual of Guidance on the Management, Command and Deployment of Armed Officers* (2009) 17.

[60] *Campbell and Cosans v UK*, Nos. 7511/76 and 7743/76, 25 February 1982. Corporal punishment was banned in state-funded schools from 1987 and in privately funded schools from 1999.

[61] *A v UK*, No. 25599/94, 23 September 1998. As a consequence, in England and Wales, section 58 of the Children Act 2004 removed the defence of 'reasonable chastisement' for those with parental responsibility and replaced it with one of 'reasonable punishment', which may be used only in relation to charges of common assault, where the injury suffered is transient or trifling.

[62] Ministry of Justice, *Responding to Human Rights Judgments: Report to the Joint Committee on Human Rights on the Government Response to Human Rights Judgments 2011–12*, CM 8432 (2012) ('Ministry of Justice Report 2011–12') 15.

[63] See 1.2.2, Table 1.3.

[64] Committee of Ministers, *Supervision of the Execution of Judgments and Decisions of the European Court of Human Rights: 8th Annual Report of the Committee of Ministers 2014* (2015) 48.

[65] Joint Committee on Human Rights, Seventh Report of Session 2014–15, *Human Rights Judgments*, HL Paper 130, HC 1088 (2015), para. 2.12.

[66] JCHR, Seventh Report of Session 2014–15 (n 65) para. 2.13.

[67] *Jordan v UK*, No. 24746/94, 4 May 2001; *McKerr v UK*, No. 28883/95, 4 May 2001; *Kelly v UK*, No. 30054/96, 4 May 2001; *Shanaghan v UK*, No. 37715/97, 4 May 2001; *Finucane v UK*, No. 29178/95, 1 July 2003; *McShane v UK*, No. 43290/98, 28 May 2002.

[68] The most serious delay related to the judgment in *S and Marper v UK*, Nos. 30562/04 and 30566/04, 4 December 2008 [GC], concerning the retention of fingerprints and DNA profiles and samples (see 7.6.2).

[69] *Hirst v UK (No. 2) v UK*, No. 74205/01, 6 October 2005 [GC]; *Greens and MT v UK*, Nos. 60041/08 and 60054/08, 23 November 2010.

[70] PACE, Committee on Legal Affairs and Human Rights, Implementation of judgments of the European Court of Human Rights, Doc. 12455, 20 December 2010 (Rapporteur: Christos Pourgourides), para. 9.

called before the Assembly's Committee on Legal Affairs and Human Rights ('Legal Affairs Committee') in January 2013 to account for the UK's failure to comply with its obligations, finding themselves in the ignominious position of being subject to the same heightened scrutiny as delegations from states such as Russia, Turkey, Ukraine, and Moldova.[71] Yet despite the high-profile 'brinkmanship'[72] with the Court over prisoners' voting rights, the UK's overall record of compliance with judgments is among the best in the Council of Europe. An empirical study of states' compliance with ECtHR judgments found that the UK's overall compliance rate was 71 per cent, behind only Ireland and the Netherlands.[73]

How are we to explain the paradox between, on the one hand, the UK's comparatively strong implementation record and, on the other hand, the contentiousness of the ECtHR in public discourse? One explanation for the apparent contradiction lies in the contingent and politicized nature of the debate about the Court in the UK. Its frequently populist tone and the extent to which it appears at times wilfully misinformed[74] suggest that characterizations of the Court as incompetent and/or illegitimate are driven as much by opportunism as by principled reservations about the constitutional propriety of review by a supranational human rights court. The inconsistent nature of the anti-Strasbourg discourse is explored in 7.6 in respect to specific judgments. Here, it is submitted that a politically driven negative discourse about the Court has taken hold at the same time as, away from the public gaze, institutional arrangements for implementing ECtHR judgments have become *more* systematic and robust. It is to these institutional arrangements that this chapter now turns.

7.3 Implementation of ECtHR Judgments: The Role of Parliament

7.3.1 The Joint Committee on Human Rights

As noted at 3.4.1, human rights oversight in the UK parliament is principally conducted by the Joint Committee on Human Rights, the epitome of the 'specialized' approach to parliamentary human rights work. The JCHR's remit is broad, covering 'matters relating to human rights' in the UK, excluding consideration

[71] See 2.6.1 at n 164.

[72] Ed Bates, 'Analysing the Prisoner Voting Saga and the British Challenge to Strasbourg', *Human Rights Law Review* 14(3) (2014): 503.

[73] Courtney Hillebrecht, *Domestic Politics and International Human Rights Tribunals: The Problem of Compliance* (Cambridge: Cambridge University Press, 2014): 48.

[74] For example, it has frequently been stated that the ECtHR banned the imposition of whole life tariffs even for the gravest crimes as being incompatible with Article 3 ECHR (prohibition of torture and inhuman or degrading treatment or punishment); see, especially, Conservative Party, *Protecting Human Rights in the UK: the Conservatives' Proposals for Changing Britain's Human Rights Laws* (2014) 3. In fact, in *Vinter v UK*, Nos. 66069/09, 130/10, and 3896/10, 9 July 2013, the Court stated (paras. 119–20) that, to be compatible with Article 3 ECHR, whole life tariffs must be subject to review after a suggested period of no more than twenty-five years.

of individual cases.[75] Since its inception in 2000, the Committee has interpreted its mandate expansively to include pre-legislative scrutiny, thematic inquiries, and scrutiny of the government's compliance with all the UK's international human rights obligations.[76] In addition, the Committee conducts scrutiny of government responses to adverse judgments of the ECtHR (in addition to declarations of incompatibility by domestic courts under the HRA), a function which it decided to assume some two years after its creation.[77]

In the early 2000s, whenever ECtHR judgments required general measures, the JCHR wrote to the relevant minister to request information about the proposed response.[78] In 2006, it published its first progress report to parliament on the implementation of Strasbourg judgments.[79] Following a review of its working practices in 2006, the Committee decided to integrate its monitoring of Strasbourg judgments, whether or not they might potentially give rise to remedial orders, with enhanced scrutiny of declarations of incompatibility by domestic courts, leading to its first integrated report in 2007.[80] This report also recommended improvements to the way in which the UK government responded to judgments, including a co-ordinating role for the Ministry of Justice.[81] In addition, the JCHR committed itself to a more coherent approach to its own scrutiny work in this area.[82] In its 2008 report, the JCHR lamented the government's failure to provide a substantive response to the Committee's recommendations, which were reiterated and expanded to include an annual report by the executive to the JCHR on the implementation of human rights judgments.[83]

In its monitoring report published in 2010, the JCHR recommended further improvements in order to facilitate parliamentary scrutiny.[84] The Committee also produced guidance, including the stipulation of deadlines, for government responses to human rights judgments, given what it viewed as inconsistent and opaque practice across departments.[85] At the beginning of the 2010–15 parliament, the

[75] See 7.2.1 at n 23.

[76] For detailed accounts of the JCHR's work, see David Feldman, 'Can and Should Parliament Protect Human Rights?', *European Public Law* 10(4) (2004): 635; Murray Hunt, 'The Joint Committee on Human Rights', in Horne, Drewry, and Oliver (n 2): 223.

[77] David Feldman, Interview, 25 April 2012.

[78] JCHR, Nineteenth Report of Session 2004–05, *The Work of the Committee in the 2001–2005 Parliament*, HL Paper 112, HC 552 (2005).

[79] JCHR, Thirteenth Report of Session 2005–06, *Implementation of Strasbourg Judgments: First Progress Report*, HL Paper 133, HC 954 (2006).

[80] JCHR, Sixteenth Report of Session 2006–07, *Monitoring the Government's Response to Court Judgments Finding Breaches of Human Rights*, HL Paper 128, HC 728 (2007).

[81] JCHR, Sixteenth Report of Session 2006–07 (n 80) paras. 151–63.

[82] JCHR, Sixteenth Report of Session 2006–07 (n 80) para. 162.

[83] JCHR, Thirty-First Report of Session 2007–08, *Monitoring the Government's Response to Human Rights Judgments: Annual Report* 2008, HL Paper 173, HC 1078 (2008) para. 14.

[84] JCHR, Fifteenth Report of Session 2009–10, *Enhancing Parliament's Role in Relation to Human Rights Judgments*, HL Paper 85, HC 455 (2010) para. 175.

[85] JCHR, Fifteenth Report of Session 2009–10 (n 84) 69–76 (Annex: Guidance for Departments on Responding to Court Judgments on Human Rights). The JCHR requires notification of judgments within fourteen days, detailed plans as to what the Government's response will be within four months, and a final decision as to how the incompatibility will be remedied within six months.

Committee reaffirmed these requirements and announced that it would continue its predecessor's practice of scrutinizing the government's responses to human rights judgments made both by UK courts and the ECtHR.[86] Between 2011 and 2014, the JCHR produced no further detailed periodic reports; rather, it sought to integrate its work on human rights judgments into other aspects of its work, mainly by scrutinizing the government's response to certain judgments in the context of its legislative scrutiny.[87] This shift in approach reflects the way in which parliamentary oversight mechanisms evolve over time due both to differences in the priorities of committees between parliamentary terms and, in the JCHR's case, to fluctuations in the number of legal advisers attached to the Committee (which fell from three to one for much of the 2010–2015 parliament). In March 2015, the Committee produced its first report on human rights judgments for five years. The Committee noted that it had actively sought to encourage more input from civil society into its work on human rights judgments.[88] In addition, it had for the first time heard oral evidence from the (then) President and Registrar of the ECtHR (see 2.4).[89] Members of the Committee had also visited Strasbourg to meet representatives of the Court, Committee of Ministers, and Parliamentary Assembly.[90]

The Committee observed that the relatively strong institutional mechanisms and practices that have been developed in the UK place it in a good position to provide strong leadership on this question within the Committee of Ministers, and urged the government to become a 'champion of increasing parliamentary involvement in the ECHR system'.[91] As noted at 2.9, the JCHR also highlighted the implications for parliament of Protocol No. 15 to the Convention, which in its view signifies a new emphasis on the primary responsibility of member states to secure Convention rights and freedoms and 'casts a greater onus on government departments to conduct detailed assessments of the Convention compatibility of their laws and policies and on Parliament to subject the government's assessment to careful scrutiny and debate'.[92]

7.3.2 The JCHR and other actors

The JCHR collaborates with other institutional human rights actors in its monitoring of human rights judgments. A case in point is the liaison between the Committee

[86] JCHR Press Notice, 'JCHR to review Government's response to judgments identifying breaches of human rights in the UK', 10 September 2010.

[87] For example, the JCHR's report on the Protection of Freedoms Bill scrutinized the government's response in England and Wales to the ECtHR's judgment on the legal framework for the retention of biometric data in *Marper v UK* (n 68); Eighteenth Report of Session 2010–12, *Legislative Scrutiny: Protection of Freedoms Bill*, HL Paper 195, HC 1490 (2011) paras. 6–87.

[88] JCHR, Seventh Report of Session 2014–15 (n 65) para. 1.2.

[89] JCHR, Uncorrected Transcript of Oral Evidence from Sir Nicolas Bratza and Erik Fribergh on Human Rights Judgments, 13 March 2012.

[90] JCHR, Seventh Report of Session 2014–15 (n 65) para. 1.12.

[91] JCHR, Seventh Report of Session 2014–15 (n 65) para. 5.5.

[92] JCHR, Seventh Report of Session 2014–15 (n 65) para. 5.4. See also Fourth Report of Session 2014–15, *Protocol 15 to the European Convention on Human Rights*, HL Paper 71, HC 837 (2014).

and the Independent Reviewer of Terrorism Legislation in their respective scrutiny of the government's response to *Gillan and Quinton v UK*,[93] which concerned the stop and search powers under section 44 of the Terrorism Act 2000 of two individuals near an armaments fair. The ECtHR had found that the law was too broadly defined and contained insufficient safeguards to act as a curb on the wide powers afforded to the executive, amounting to a violation of the right to respect for private life under Article 8 ECHR. The government's response was to issue an urgent remedial order to repeal and replace the offending provisions with new, more circumscribed powers.[94] Both the JCHR[95] and the Independent Reviewer of Terrorism Legislation[96] reported to parliament welcoming the government's willingness to change the law but recommending amendments to the remedial order and accompanying Code of Practice, since the discretion conferred on officers remained too broad to remove the risk of arbitrariness. The government initially rejected the amendments as unnecessary.[97] However, following public consultation in 2012 on the revised draft Code of Practice, changes were made to satisfy some of the concerns raised by the JCHR and the Independent Reviewer.[98]

Another important relationship is that between the JCHR and the Equality and Human Rights Commission (EHRC).[99] The EHRC engages selectively with Court judgments in various ways. It makes submissions to government consultations on the appropriate response to judgments; produces briefings for parliament on the human rights or equality implications of legislation, including in respect of relevant judgments; advises public authorities on the implications of judgments for their policy or practice; and writes to the Committee of Ministers highlighting its concerns.[100] In addition, the EHRC can, and fairly frequently does, intervene in human rights proceedings taken by others, including at the ECtHR.[101] Our interlocutors in both the JCHR and EHRC highlighted the Belgrade Principles on the

[93] No. 4158/05, 12 January 2010.

[94] Ministry of Justice, *Responding to Human Rights Judgments: Report to the Joint Committee on Human Rights on the Government's Response to Human Rights judgments 2010–11*, CM 1862 (2011) ('Ministry of Justice Report 2010–11') 15–17.

[95] JCHR, Fourteenth Report of Session 2010–12, *The Terrorism Act 2000 (Remedial) Order 2011: Stop and Search Without Reasonable Suspicion*, HL Paper 155, HC 1141 (2011); Seventeenth Report of Session 2010–12, *The Terrorism Act 2000 (Remedial) Order 2011: Stop and Search Without Reasonable Suspicion (Second Report)*, HL Paper 192, HC 1483 (2011).

[96] David Anderson (Independent Reviewer of Terrorism Legislation), *Report on the Operation in 2010 of the Terrorism Act 2000 and of Part 1 of the Terrorism Act 2006* (2011).

[97] *Gillan & Quinton v the United Kingdom* (application no. 4158/05): Updated Information Submitted by the United Kingdom Government on 10 October 2011, DH-DD(2011)851E.

[98] David Anderson, *The Terrorism Acts in 2011: Report of the Independent Reviewer on the Operation of the Terrorism Act 2000 and Part 1 of the Terrorism Act 2006* (2012) para. 8.19.

[99] The EHRC, which was created in 2007, is the national human rights institution for England and Wales and also covers non-devolved policy areas in Scotland.

[100] For example, the EHRC undertook each of these activities in response to the *Marper* judgment on the retention of biometric data.

[101] The Commission 'seeks out public interest cases which raise issues affecting vulnerable groups, seeking to clarify or challenge important questions of law, involving serious matters of public policy or general public concern, and/or concerning systematic default or abuse by a public body'. See the EHRC website at <http://www.equalityhumanrights.com/legal-and-policy/commission/legal-powers>.

relationship between national human rights institutions and parliaments, which were elaborated under UN auspices in 2012, and welcomed their explicit call for co-operation in monitoring the implementation of human rights judgments.[102] There is regular informal contact between legal specialists of the two bodies, in addition to the Commission's periodic formal submissions of evidence to the Committee.[103]

Across all strands of its work, the JCHR invites civil society actors and legal experts to submit evidence and legal opinion about the continued effect of judicially impugned laws or the potential effect of proposed legislation. Such submissions are frequently cited as authoritative sources in JCHR reports. For example, the JCHR's consultation on the Gender Recognition Bill, prompted in part by the judgment in *Christine Goodwin v UK*,[104] drew submissions from transsexual people; organizations working with or representing transsexual people; and professionals with expertize about the medical and legal issues involved, as well as opponents of any recognition of gender reassignment. The JCHR's recommendations for revision of the bill were grounded in part on the weight of these various submissions.[105]

Legal advisers to the JCHR acknowledge the value of maintaining external contacts. Angela Patrick, a former assistant adviser to the Committee, ventures that seeking external sources of advice and evidence is a legitimate function for a parliamentary committee: 'JCHR members like being able to have their ear to the ground and not being detached from organisations … working at the coalface'.[106] She cites by way of example the JCHR's scrutiny of the government's response to a declaration of incompatibility and subsequent ECtHR judgment concerning an indiscriminate scheme requiring immigrants without settled status to pay large fees to obtain permission from the Home Office to marry anywhere other than in an Anglican church.[107] The Committee's legal advisers had sought advice from immigration law practitioners and specialist charities about mounting numbers of compensation claims, in order to challenge the government's justification for its prolonged inaction on the matter.

7.3.3 Provision of legal advice

Parliamentarians in the UK do not receive human rights training as such, and human rights are not included in the induction for new MPs.[108] However, our interviewees noted that any member of parliament who has a question about human

[102] Belgrade Principles on the Relationship between National Human Rights Institutions and Parliaments, Belgrade, Serbia, 22–23 February 2012.

[103] John Wadham, Interview, 12 July 2012.

[104] No. 28957/95, 11 July 2002 [GC].

[105] For example, the JCHR's recommendation that the bill should have retrospective effect was informed by submissions which argued that it would be demeaning to require existing 'married' couples to undergo a gender recognition process and a further wedding ceremony; Nineteenth Report of Session 2002–03, *Draft Gender Recognition Bill*, HL Paper 188-I, HC 1276-I (2003), para. 36 and recommendations 3–5, 34–5.

[106] Interview, 8 March 2012.

[107] *R (Baiai) v Secretary of State for the Home Department* [2009] 1 AC 287; *O'Donoghue and Others v UK*, No. 34848/07, 14 December 2010.

[108] Angela Patrick, Interview, 8 March 2012.

rights will invariably be able to get an answer. The libraries of each House produce research briefings, either proactively or upon request of MPs or peers; these do not constitute legal advice. MPs may also seek ad hoc advice from lawyers in the Scrutiny Unit.[109] They may also submit written questions to ministers. MPs are, in addition, more likely than peers in the House of Lords to receive research assistance from among their own, albeit limited staff. [110]

The JCHR is one of a small number of committees in the UK parliament which is serviced by its own permanent, specialized legal advisers (in recent years, the number has fluctuated between one and three and presently stands at two). In relation to ECtHR judgments, the legal advisers variously provide Committee members with: a summary of the judgment; analysis as to its significance; advice about the options for implementation; draft correspondence that the Committee may send to the executive; and advice about the adequacy of the government's response.[111] Several interviewees note that the specialized remit of the JCHR had helped it to attract and retain legal advisers of exceptional quality, enhancing both the productivity and credibility of the Committee (see also 3.4.3). The former Liberal Democrat MP and JCHR member, Evan Harris, notes that the provision of bespoke legal advice is a model that should be nurtured, since it provides Committee members with 'workable' information, rather than relying on them to read purely legalistic documents.[112] The first Chair of the JCHR, Jean Corston, recalls that the respect accorded to its first adviser, David Feldman, meant that he became a 'de facto legal adviser' not only to the Committee but also to government departments'.[113] Angela Patrick identifies several benefits of servicing the Committee with independent legal advice.[114] These include drawing members' attention to judgments that have important policy implications but risk 'passing by unnoticed if they are not particularly controversial' and, conversely, providing a corrective to prevalent misinformation about judgments that are contentious. Where there are multiple options for implementing a particular judgment, she adds:

> It can be a useful democratic engagement—looking at a range of options and discussing which is most desirable. What is important is that [members] get really good legal advice that they can trust is politically neutral. The minute they think the advice reflects [the adviser's] own take on politically important questions, they start to distrust [it].

7.3.4 'Mainstreaming' human rights in parliament

The JCHR is the natural focal point of parliament's human rights work. Nevertheless, as noted at 3.4.2, there are limits to what a committee of twelve members can achieve. Murray Hunt, legal adviser to the JCHR since 2004, advocates

[109] The Scrutiny Unit is part of the Committee Office in the House of Commons and exists to strengthen the scrutiny function of the House.

[110] David Feldman, 'Parliamentary Scrutiny of Legislation and Human Rights', *Public Law* Summer (2002): 323, 325.

[111] Angela Patrick, Interview, 8 March 2012.

[112] Interview, 6 July 2012.

[113] Interview, 4 July 2012.

[114] Interview, 8 March 2012.

a programmatic and anticipatory approach to human rights among legal advisers to committees other than the JCHR.[115] Such an approach, he suggests, would require lawyers in parliament working in collaboration with both clerks from the two Houses and research and information services to bring to the attention of other committees any relevant human rights standards or rule of law considerations, including treaty obligations, court judgments, and recommendations by UN treaty bodies. Hunt adds that 'mainstreaming' of this kind would also confer a 'legitimation advantage' by countering the tendency for politicians to view human rights as 'standards articulated and imposed on Parliament and government by outside actors, judges and lawyers in particular, who lack democratic legitimacy'.[116]

It is highly unusual for a judgment of the ECtHR to be debated on the floor of the House of Commons. One such instance was the backbench debate in the House of Commons in February 2011 on a motion about the *Hirst* judgment on prisoner voting rights (see 7.6.1). However, the JCHR faces an uphill struggle in extending parliamentary interest beyond such exceptions. In respect of ECtHR decisions against the UK, debate in either House has very rarely cited JCHR reports or recommendations on specific judgments.[117] Francesca Klug, who interviewed parliamentarians both within and outside the JCHR in her review of the Committee's working practices in 2006, observes: 'Most of the parliamentarians I spoke to outside of the [JCHR] were barely aware of the Council of Europe and its mechanism, let alone its judgments. They ... had no real sense of having a role in it whatsoever.'[118]

7.3.5 The relationship between parliament and Council of Europe bodies

As noted at 2.6.2, the JCHR has commended the approach of having overlap, or at least co-ordination, between the Committee and members of the UK delegation to the Parliamentary Assembly. However, there is no mechanism to ensure either overlapping membership or co-ordination: MPs are elected to parliamentary select committees by their peers within each party, while PACE delegates are appointed by the Prime Minister following a more informal process involving party whips (and, in the case of the Labour members, an internal party election).[119] The method of selection of PACE delegates became controversial within the UK parliament in November 2015 following the non-renewal of the mandate of three Conservative members of the delegation (Christopher Chope, Sir Edward Leigh, and Cheryl Gillan). Chope alleged that they had been 'purged' for defying the Conservative

[115] Hunt (n 76) 247–8. [116] Hunt (n 76) 247.

[117] JCHR reports or recommendations relating to five judgments (including *Hirst*) were referred to between 2000 and 2010; Murray Hunt, Hayley Hooper, and Paul Yowell, *Parliaments and Human Rights: Redressing the Democratic Deficit* (Arts and Humanities Research Council Public Policy Series No. 5, 2012) 39.

[118] Interview, 8 March 2012.

[119] Arabella Lang, *UK Delegation to the Parliamentary Assembly of the Council of Europe*, House of Commons Library, Briefing Paper No. 7378, 16 November 2015, 6.

government by voting for a purdah period in advance of the referendum on the UK's membership of the European Union.[120] On 16 November 2015, MPs debated a backbench motion calling for parliament to adopt, with immediate effect, the same system for nomination of PACE delegates as it has for nomination, following party elections, of membership of select committees. Moving the motion, Owen Paterson MP asked '[h]ow … members of PACE from the UK's governing party [can] express independent opinions in Strasbourg if there is a covert threat that their appointment will not be renewed if they step out of line with the Government's wishes?'[121] The motion, although it was unsuccessful,[122] attracted support among both Conservative and opposition MPs. Moreover, it provided a rare opportunity for MPs to debate the role of delegates to the Parliamentary Assembly. According to Labour MP Geraint Davies,

> In the exchanges of [backbenchers] from across the nations there is a different sort of dialogue going on whereby we can suggest, 'Why don't we do this in our Parliament and your Parliament?', and begin a campaign. Those in positions of power may be conservative with a small 'c' in terms of change or may not want to cross-fertilise culturally in terms of policy, but these sorts of forums enable us to move forward on human rights through free thinking, freedom of expression, and new ideas.[123]

Such debate is welcome in view of the hitherto low profile of PACE members within the UK parliament—and their inconsistent record in promoting the implementation of ECtHR judgments (see 2.6.2 and, in respect of prisoner voting rights, 7.6.1).

In respect of contact with the Court, in March 2012, in the first session of its kind in the UK—or, as far as we are aware, any Convention member state—the (then) UK Judge and President of the Court, Sir Nicolas Bratza, appeared before the JCHR, along with the Court's Registrar at the time, Erik Fribergh.[124] This exercise has not been repeated; however, as discussed at 2.4, such evidence sessions could prove a useful means of strengthening interaction between the Court and national parliaments.

7.4 Implementation of ECtHR Judgments: The Role of the Executive

In 2010, the Ministry of Justice assumed co-ordination of the executive response to ECtHR judgments, as had been recommended by the JCHR. The role was previously performed by the deputy head of the UK mission to the Council of Europe,

[120] HC Deb, 3 November 2015, vol. 601, col. 887.

[121] HC Deb, 16 November 2015, vol. 602, col. 411.

[122] MPs voted on an amendment which would have delayed the introduction of elections in order to avoid a hiatus during which there would have been no UK delegation to PACE; however, after it was defeated, MPs did not back the main motion.

[123] HC Deb, 16 November 2015, vol. 602, col. 417.

[124] See 2.4 at n 82.

who was ill-placed to liaise with Whitehall departments. The first stage is for the Foreign and Commonwealth Office (FCO) to alert the government department(s) responsible for the violation(s) to the judgment and to provide advice about, for example, the possibility of referring a Chamber judgment to the Grand Chamber of the ECtHR. Co-ordination of the executive response then passes to the Ministry of Justice, which sends the lead policy team(s) within the department(s) concerned a standardized form, in order to elicit within a set time frame what action they intend to take in response to the judgment (see 3.5.1).[125] This in turn forms the basis of the government's action plan in response to the judgment (see 2.5.2). The Ministry also acts as the conduit for information to the secretariat of the Committee of Ministers and the UK deputy head of mission in Strasbourg. The department responsible for the violation(s) acts as the lead in the event of questions or debate in parliament about the government's proposed response. The JCHR notes that the government's systems for responding promptly and fully to Court judgments concerning human rights generally work well.[126]

Depending on the nature of the violation, co-ordination across government departments may be necessary, and this may significantly affect the speed of implementation. Two cases which the JCHR reported on in its early years illustrate this effect: *Christine Goodwin v UK*, concerning the legal recognition of transsexuals, and *Grieves v UK*,[127] concerning the independence and impartiality of naval courts martial. *Christine Goodwin* entailed considerable administrative complexity, as well as extensive review and debate in both Houses, and it was two years before the Gender Recognition Act 2004 made provision for the legal recognition of gender reassignment. In contrast, *Grieves*, which concerned the Ministry of Defence alone, was implemented within one month by means of an urgent remedial order.[128]

7.4.1 Reporting mechanisms

The JCHR has welcomed the 'very significant improvement' in the information provided to parliament about human rights judgments in recent years.[129] The first step is for the FCO to notify the Committee of adverse ECtHR judgments, while government departments notify it of any declarations of incompatibility in their area of departmental responsibility. Attention then passes to the government's action plan or action report. The JCHR has attached importance to regular scrutiny at the earliest possible stage of action plans or reports and has secured a commitment in principle from the Ministry of Justice to send it these documents at the same time as they are submitted to the Committee of Ministers. The JCHR has occasionally corresponded with the executive *before* an action

125 Ministry of Justice Report 2010–11 (n 94) 27.
126 JCHR, Seventh Report of Session 2014–15 (n 65) para. 6.1.
127 No. 57067/00, 16 December 2003 [GC].
128 The Naval Discipline Act 1957 (Remedial) Order 2004.
129 JCHR, Seventh Report of Session 2014–15 (n 65) para. 6.3.

plan is published.[130] In addition, the JCHR has argued for domestic parliamentary and other scrutiny of government responses to be reported routinely within action plans in accordance with the principle of subsidiarity.[131] Following *Gillan*, the JCHR deplored the fact that the government's action plan, as submitted to the Committee of Ministers, made no mention of the scrutiny conducted by the JCHR and the Independent Reviewer of Terrorism Legislation (see 7.3.2).[132] A revised action plan later rectified this omission.

In 2011, the government initiated the production of an annual report on its response to human rights judgments, as had been requested by the JCHR since 2008, emulating the practice in the Netherlands and Germany. This proactive provision of information replaced the previous government practice of responding to the JCHR's own monitoring reports on human rights judgments. The reports are not debated in parliament but form the basis of the Committee's evidence sessions with the Lord Chancellor and Secretary of State for Justice.[133] A government official, speaking anonymously, notes that the reports had created a 'public, ongoing dialogue' between the JCHR and the executive; the fact that the Ministry of Justice provided information proactively for scrutiny was a 'big step forward' and had encouraged a less defensive governmental stance.[134] The JCHR notes that the annual reports have greatly assisted its work. It welcomes the recent addition to the report of details of ECtHR judgments in UK cases finding *no* violation of the Convention, since such information brings to parliamentarians' attention the sorts of cases in which Convention-compatibility issues were raised, but the Court upheld the law or policy in question as being compatible with the ECHR.[135] The JCHR recommends further improvement to the current format, suggesting that it should be turned into an 'Annual Human Rights Report' to parliament, covering not only responses to human rights judgments but also the UK's reporting to UN treaty monitoring bodies and wider human rights developments.[136] In addition, the Committee suggests including in the report significant judgments against other states which may have implications for

[130] As happened, for example, within five days of the judgment in *Marper v UK* (n 68). See Twenty-Seventh Report of Session 2008–09, *Retention, Use and Destruction of Biometric Data: Correspondence with Government*, HL Paper 182, HC 1113 (2009) (Letter from the Chair of the Committee to Rt Hon Jacqui Smith MP, Home Secretary, 9 December 2008).

[131] JCHR, Seventh Report of Session 2014–15 (n 65) para. 6.4.

[132] JCHR, Seventeenth Report of Session 2010–12 (n 95) para. 10.

[133] JCHR, Seventh Report of Session 2014–15 (n 65) para. 1.4.

[134] Interview (anonymous), 10 July 2012.

[135] JCHR, Seventh Report of Session 2014–15 (n 65) para. 6.6. One example of a judgment finding no violation in the preceding year was *National Union of Rail, Maritime and Transport Workers v UK*, No. 31045/10, 8 April 2014. While the Ministry of Justice Report 2013–14 notes (at 13) that the Court found no violation in this case concerning a ban on secondary strike action, it would have been more informative for parliament to have been alerted to the Court's reasoning (para. 89), which rested partly on the fact that 'by virtue of their direct knowledge of their society and its needs, the national authorities, *and in particular the democratically elected parliaments*, are in principle better placed than the international judge to appreciate what is in the public interest on social or economic grounds and what are the legislative measures best suited for the conditions in their country' (emphasis added); see also 4.5.2 at n 147.

[136] JCHR, Seventh Report of Session 2014–15 (n 65) para. 6.8.

UK law, as already happens in the Netherlands (8.4) and Germany (9.5), an area discussed in the next section.[137]

7.5 Monitoring and Implementing Judgments against Other States

The JCHR has expressed concern that the impact of Strasbourg judgments is limited in practice by states taking an 'essentially passive approach' to compliance with the ECHR.[138] The Committee recommended in 2010 that the Ministry of Justice, working with the FCO, should give systematic consideration to whether ECtHR judgments against other countries have implications for the UK and inform parliament accordingly.[139] The government rejected this approach, arguing that primary responsibility for identifying relevant judgments lies with individual government departments and that the Ministry of Justice plays only a supplementary and supportive role.[140] Officials at the Ministry of Justice and FCO defend this approach on the basis that departmental legal teams have both the expertise and, under the HRA, the responsibility to identify implications for their policy area arising from a judgment of the ECtHR.[141]

The Ministry of Justice produces a cross-departmental information bulletin highlighting significant domestic and international human rights judgments, which may include non-UK judgments at the ECtHR. Current and former advisers to the JCHR have requested that the bulletins be shared with the Committee, redacted if necessary, in order that it can understand the type of information included. However, an official at the Ministry of Justice explains that the information is confidential, since it may have guiding effect for arguing future cases.[142] A non-UK judgment of the ECtHR would be drawn to the JCHR's attention only if it had 'direct, immediate and obvious' implications for UK law or policy, as in the cases of *VgT Verein Gegen Tierfabriken v Switzerland* in respect of the Communications Bill 2003 (see also 7.6.3); and *Salduz v Turkey*,[143] concerning the right of access to a lawyer prior to being interviewed by the police, which led to legislative change in Scotland.[144]

The Ministry of Justice monitors systematically all referrals to the Grand Chamber in case a decision is made that the UK government should intervene. The JCHR has recommended that the government commit to informing it at the earliest opportunity whenever it plans to intervene in a case against another state, and to making available to parliament the reasons for its intervention and the

137 JCHR, Seventh Report of Session 2014–15 (n 65) para. 6.7.
138 JCHR, Fifteenth Report of Session 2009–10 (n 84) para. 188.
139 JCHR, Fifteenth Report of Session 2009–10 (n 84) paras. 191–2.
140 Ministry of Justice Report 2011–12 (n 62) 10.
141 Interviews (anonymous), 10 July 2012.
142 Interview (anonymous), 10 July 2012.
143 No. 36391/02, 27 November 2008 [GC].
144 The Criminal Procedure (Legal Assistance, Detention and Appeals) (Scotland) Act 2010.

substance of its argument (see also 2.2).[145] However, government officials argue that the Court's tight timescales for would-be third-party interveners to request permission to intervene (twelve weeks from the date that the case is communicated) preclude such a commitment; and that, in any case, scrutiny of UK government interventions is properly made by the Court rather than parliament or other interested parties.[146] One exception was the UK's intervention in the case of *Saadi v Italy*,[147] which was, according to our interlocutor in the Ministry of Justice, brought to parliament's attention because of the political sensitivity of the principle at stake:[148] the question of whether governments should be able to balance the risk that a deportee might suffer torture or inhuman or degrading treatment in a receiving state against the risk they are deemed to pose to the national security of the host state.[149] The JCHR had previously argued strongly[150] that the absolute nature of the prohibition on torture and inhuman or degrading treatment precludes any such balancing exercise, as had been established in the earlier case of *Chahal v UK*[151] and was subsequently reaffirmed by the Court in *Saadi*.[152] The House of Commons Foreign Affairs Committee also later criticized the UK government's stance as seeking to 'water down' the prohibition of torture, and found it 'disturbing and surprising' that such arguments were made in the name of the UK.[153] Another case in which the UK government intervened on the basis of arguments disputed by parliament was *Scoppola v Italy (No. 3)* (on prisoner voting rights).[154] The JCHR also considered that the government's intervention arguing against the applicants in *Schalk and Kopf v Austria*,[155] concerning the rights of same-sex couples to marry, demonstrated the need for a 'mechanism for ensuring the transparency of the UK Government's position in such interventions, and [the] ... opportunity to hold the Government accountable for the arguments it makes'.[156] Our interlocutors in the UK government acknowledge that there is a lack of accessible and timely information about third-party interventions. As proposed at 2.2, this apparent scrutiny gap could be addressed, at least retrospectively,

[145] JCHR, Fifteenth Report of Session 2009–10 (n 84) para. 180.

[146] Interviews (anonymous), 10 July 2012.

[147] *Saadi v Italy*, No. 37201/06, 28 February 2008 [GC]. The UK government had earlier intervened, along with the governments of Lithuania, Portugal, and Slovakia, in the case of *Ramzy v Netherlands* No. 25424/05, 27 May 2005, with the same arguments (paras. 125–30) and requested that the Court include its intervention in *Ramzy* for consideration in *Saadi*.

[148] Interviews (anonymous), 10 July 2012.

[149] The Grand Chamber rejected the UK government's argument (*Saadi v Italy* (n 147) paras. 138–39).

[150] JCHR, Nineteenth Report of Session 2005–06, *UN Convention on Torture*, HL Paper 185-I, HC 701-I (2006) paras. 19–27 and, on the issue of diplomatic assurances, paras. 126–31; Third Report of Session 2005–06, *Counter-Terrorism Policy and Human Rights: Terrorism Bill and Related Matters*, HL Paper 75-II, HC 561-II (2005) para. 149.

[151] *Chahal v UK*, No. 22414/93, 15 November 1996 [GC].

[152] *Saadi v Italy* (n 147) paras. 138–42.

[153] Foreign Affairs Committee, Ninth Report of Session 2007–08, *Human Rights Annual Report 2007*, HC 533 (2008) para. 72.

[154] No. 126/05, 22 May 2012 [GC], paras. 75–80.

[155] *Schalk and Kopf v Austria*, No. 30141/04, 24 June 2010, paras. 45–6, 81–3.

[156] JCHR, Fifteenth Report of Session 2009–10 (n 84) para. 180.

by including in government annual reports to parliament information on interventions made in the previous year and their reasoning.

For its part, the Committee does not routinely monitor non-UK judgments, due to its lack of capacity for such a task, and the fact that the monitoring of non-UK judgments is not proximate enough to garner sufficient interest among MPs to warrant the necessary investment of resources.[157] A former member of the JCHR, Evan Harris, recalls that Committee members would tend to take an interest in a non-UK judgment only if it happened to coincide with an area of existing focus—as happened, for example, when the case of *Ramzy*, concerning the *Chahal* principle referred to above, coincided with the Committee's consideration of the UK's compliance with the UN Convention against Torture and Other Cruel, Inhuman or Degrading Treatment.[158]

7.6 Implementation of Specific Judgments

The JCHR has argued that, given the discretion inherent in the Convention's supervision mechanism, the process of implementing Strasbourg judgments is an 'unavoidably political process'. Parliamentary involvement, the JCHR argues,

> raises the political visibility of the issues at stake and provides an opportunity for public scrutiny of the justifications offered by the Government for its proposed response to the judgment or for its delay in bringing such a response forward.[159]

The Committee adds that '[i]n so doing it helps both to ensure a genuine democratic input into legal changes following Court judgments and to address the perception that changes in law or policy as a result of Court judgments lack democratic legitimacy'.[160]

This chapter has already alluded to the politicization of debate about human rights in the UK since the early 2000s. Since its inception, then, the JCHR has operated against the backdrop of dissensus about fundamental questions concerning human rights protection. This section examines how Parliament, and especially the JCHR, has managed these constraints. It focuses on the political responses to ECtHR judgments concerning three issues: the right of convicted prisoners to vote (7.6.1); the retention, use, and destruction of biometric data (7.6.2); and the prohibition of political advertising on radio and television (7.6.3). These were selected not because they are necessarily representative of ECtHR judgments against the UK, but because they reveal, in the contrasting political responses at play, the contingent and politicized nature of the implementation process.

[157] Murray Hunt, Interview, 10 September 2012.
[158] See above n 147.
[159] JCHR, Fifteenth Report of Session 2009–10 (n 84) para. 15.
[160] JCHR, Fifteenth Report of Session 2009–10 (n 84) para. 17.

7.6.1 The voting rights of convicted prisoners

The right of convicted prisoners to vote has become, according to the former Justice Secretary, Chris Grayling, 'totemic' for those who assert the primacy of parliament over the Strasbourg Court.[161] Christopher Chope, a Conservative MP, and former chair of the Committee on Legal Affairs and Human Rights of the Parliamentary Assembly, observes that,

> In many ways, the issue of giving prisoners the vote is *de minimis*.... But it's attracted a symbolism because it makes it seem as though the UK parliament is no longer in charge of mundane issues.... The question is, why shouldn't parliament be allowed to decide these things in its own national context?[162]

Referring to the intensification of the prisoner voting debate under the Conservative-led coalition government from 2010, the former Deputy Registrar of the Court, Michael O'Boyle, argues that:

> The Court has never, in its 50-year history, been subject to such a barrage of hostile criticism as that which occurred in the United Kingdom in 2011.... The issue of prisoners' voting rights was transformed into a national interrogation in the UK about the legitimacy of the ECtHR.[163]

A brief chronology of the prisoner voting saga (and in particular its parliamentary dimension) runs as follows.[164] The Grand Chamber of the ECtHR ruled in 2005 that the automatic and indiscriminate ban on the right of convicted prisoners to vote under the Representation of the People Act 1983 breached Article 3 of Protocol No.1 to the Convention on the right to free elections.[165] Notably, the Grand Chamber found 'no evidence that Parliament had ever sought to weigh the competing interests or to assess the proportionality of a blanket ban on the right of a convicted prisoner to vote'.[166] In November 2010, the Court issued a pilot judgment (see 2.3.1) in the case of *Greens and MT*, which stipulated an obligation of parliamentary involvement by requiring that the UK government must, within six months of the judgment becoming final, 'bring forward ... legislative proposals' to render the law Convention compliant.[167] Subsequently, the UK was granted an extension of this deadline, to take account of the referral of *Scoppola* (a case similar to *Greens*) to the Grand Chamber and the UK's intervention in that case.[168] The Court granted an extension of six months from the date of the *Scoppola* judgment, which was handed down on 22 May 2012 and

[161] The Joint Committee on the Draft Voting Eligibility (Prisoners) Bill, Uncorrected Transcript of Oral Evidence, Session II, 20 November 2013 (QQ 206–40), Q223.

[162] Interview, 27 June 2012.

[163] M. O'Boyle, 'The Future of the European Court of Human Rights', *German Law Journal* 12 (2011): 1862, 1862.

[164] For detailed accounts, see Bates (n 72); Colin Murray, 'A Perfect Storm: Parliament and Prisoner Disenfranchisement', *Parliamentary Affairs* 66(3) (2012): 511.

[165] *Hirst v UK (No. 2)* (n 69).

[166] *Hirst v UK (No. 2)* (n 69) para. 79.

[167] *Greens and MT v UK* (n 69) operative para. 6(a).

[168] See 7.5 at n 154.

in which the Grand Chamber upheld its decision in *Hirst.* On 22 November 2012, the government published the Voting Eligibility (Prisoners) Draft Bill,[169] which was sent for pre-legislative scrutiny by a Joint Committee of both Houses (considered further below). In October 2013, some 2,500 clone cases before the ECtHR, which had been frozen since *Greens*, were reinstated due to the failure to repeal the blanket prohibition. The Court subsequently found a violation in all of these applications that were deemed admissible, given that the impugned legislation remained unreformed, but declined to award either damages or costs to the applicants.[170]

How, then, has the JCHR responded to this protracted saga? From 2006, the Committee issued several reports and engaged in protracted correspondence with ministers on the prisoner voting issue.[171] The JCHR repeatedly deplored executive inaction on the matter and, from 2006, characterized the need for a solution, by means either of a remedial order or amendments to other Bills, as urgent. It reiterated that the continued failure to remove the blanket ban was unlawful, tarnished the UK's reputation, and burdened the ECtHR with repetitive applications. The Committee also criticized ministers' failure to keep it informed of its communications with the Committee of Ministers, including the government's revised action plan of March 2008 which indicated that it was still undecided as to whether a legislative solution was necessary.[172]

The JCHR has at no point proposed a specific remedy or options for remedying the violation identified in *Hirst.* The closest it came to expressing a view on the adequacy of any particular remedy was in 2010, when it argued that the Labour government was taking a 'very limited' approach to the judgment by consulting on a proposal to disenfranchise all prisoners sentenced to four years' imprisonment or more in any circumstances. At the time, the JCHR was not persuaded that automatic disenfranchisement based upon a set period of custodial sentence provided the discernible link between the conduct and circumstances of the individual and necessity for the removal of the right to vote required by the Grand Chamber in

[169] Voting Eligibility (Prisoners) Draft Bill, Cm 8499, November 2012.

[170] *Firth and Others v UK*, No. 47784/09, 12 August 2014; *McHugh and Others v UK*, No. 51987, 10 February 2015.

[171] JCHR, Eleventh Report of Session 2005–06, *Legislative Scrutiny: Fifth Progress Report*, HL Paper 115, HC 899, (2006) paras 1.40–1.42; Thirteenth Report of Session 2005–06 (n 79) paras. 51–3; Sixteenth Report of Session 2006–07 (n 80) paras. 67–79; Thirty-First Report of Session 2007–08 (n 83) paras. 47–63; Fourth Report of Session 2008–09, *Legislative Scrutiny: Political Parties and Elections Bill*, HL Paper 23, HC 204 (2009) paras. 1.10–1.19; Seventeenth Report of Session 2008–09, *Government Replies to the Second, Fourth, Eighth, Ninth and Twelfth reports of Session* 2008–09, HL Paper 104, HC 592 (2009) 36; Fifteenth Report of Session 2009–10 (n 84) paras. 99–119; Sixth Report of Session 2010–11, *Legislative Scrutiny: (1) Superannuation Bill; (2) Parliamentary Voting System and Constituencies Bill*, HL Paper 64, HC 640 (2010) paras. 2.7–2.15; Uncorrected Transcript of Oral Evidence, Minutes of Evidence taken before the Joint Committee on Human Rights: The Government's Human Rights Policy, Rt Hon Chris Grayling MP, 12 February 2013, Q13; Uncorrected Transcript of Oral Evidence, Minutes of Evidence taken before the Joint Committee on Human Rights: The Government's Human Rights Policy, Rt Hon Chris Grayling MP and Rosemary Davies, 18 December 2013.

[172] JCHR, Thirty-First Report of Session 2007–08 (n 83) para. 50.

Hirst.[173] Nevertheless, the Committee's 'overriding disappointment' was the government's failure to introduce *any* remedial measures.[174]

Current and former members and advisers of the JCHR observe that its reluctance to propose specific options for remedy betrayed the lack of consensus on the matter within the Committee, before and especially after the 2010 election. Nevertheless, the controversy did not ignite immediately. According to Evan Harris, a member of the JCHR from 2005 to 2010, in the years immediately following the judgment,

> I don't remember it being considered … We didn't do anything on prisoner voting other than within the reports on Strasbourg judgments and some of us thought that there were other matters that were more important. It has only been made an issue by people who use it to bash the Court.[175]

Later, according to Jean Corston, who chaired the JCHR from its inception until 2005, the Committee was 'particularly harried over prisoner voting rights because senior figures in both main parties led campaigns on it'.[176] Murray Hunt, legal adviser to the JCHR since 2004, notes that prisoner voting was 'probably the most divisive issue' of the parliament elected in 2010.[177] Nevertheless, Hunt adds, the Committee came close at different points to identifying those options that were 'off limits' and those that would be likely to meet the requirements of the judgment, without prescribing a particular option. David Feldman, a former adviser to the JCHR, argues that the Committee should have pursued such an approach:

> I think that a human rights committee does have a responsibility to try to foster a culture of respect for rights within parliament. You can't do that if you go into your shell as soon as the pack starts baying … Otherwise [the JCHR] will just pick off the easy cases and not make any contribution on the tough ones … But it's not a natural thing for politicians to be doing—swimming against the tide … It does take a certain degree of moral and political courage to do it.[178]

Another approach to such a contentious matter, Hunt ventures, would have been for the Committee, if it found that it could not agree, to have issued a majority report and one or more minority reports, with each position being justified by reference to reasoned arguments. However, as discussed at 7.6.4, the Committee's approach has almost invariably been to produce unanimous and non-partisan reports.[179]

[173] JCHR, Fifteenth Report of Session 2009–10 (n 84) para. 107. The JCHR's response reflects in part the 'mixed messages' in *Hirst*, which, as Bates notes, is capable of both a minimalist and expansive reading as to what the judgment required; Bates (n 72) 509–11. The judgment in *Scoppola* removed this ambiguity, reaffirming (para. 102) states' wide margin of appreciation to decide either to leave it to the courts to determine the proportionality of a measure restricting convicted prisoners' voting rights, or to incorporate provisions into their laws defining the circumstances in which such a measure should be applied.

[174] JCHR, Fifteenth Report of Session 2009–10 (n 84) para. 108.

[175] Interview, 6 July 2012.

[176] Interview, 4 July 2012.

[177] Interview, 10 September 2012.

[178] Interview, 25 April 2012.

[179] Dawn Oliver, 'Constitutional Scrutiny of Executive Bills', *Macquarie Law Journal* 33(4) (2004): 33, 48.

In addition to the JCHR's scrutiny of the government's response to *Hirst*, other parliamentary actors have also become involved. In February 2011, the House of Commons Political and Constitutional Reform Committee issued a report of evidence it had heard as to whether extending the right to vote to convicted prisoners in certain circumstances would be justifiable. The Committee concluded that 'however morally justifiable it might be, this current situation is illegal under international law founded on the UK's treaty obligations'.[180] The Committee addressed its report to MPs preparing to take part in a backbench debate on a parliamentary motion on prisoner voting tabled by two MPs, Conservative member David Davis and Labour's Jack Straw, the former Secretary of State for Justice who had presided over the Labour government's non-implementation of *Hirst*.[181] The motion noted the ECtHR's view that there had been no substantive debate in parliament on the continued justification for the general restriction on the right of convicted prisoners to vote and acknowledged the treaty obligations of the UK. It expressed support for the status quo with respect to the indiscriminate ban and asserted that 'legislative decisions should be a matter for democratically-elected lawmakers'.[182] Neither the government nor opposition front benches voted on the motion, which carried by 234 votes to twenty-two.

The backbench debate on prisoner voting has been differently appraised by different authors. What *is* clear is that, as Danny Nicol observes, the debate 'did not conform to the templates of Strasbourg analysis'.[183] A mere handful of MPs engaged with the substantive human rights issue—the scope of the right at stake and the proportionality of options for restricting it—while the majority invoked broader constitutional principles of the sovereignty of parliament and the separation of powers, and questioned whether the ECtHR had violated these principles in *Hirst*.[184] As Colin Murray observes, the majority of MPs who spoke in the debate were seized by 'a confluence of penal populism, Euro-scepticism and widespread concerns over a decline in Parliament's authority' in asserting that this was a struggle between a 'foreign' Court and a 'long-established feature of democracy in the UK', neglecting to acknowledge that there was, in fact, widespread prisoner enfranchisement between 1948 and 1969.[185] Dominic Raab MP (later appointed as Parliamentary Under-Secretary of State at the Ministry of Justice) argued that the UK should simply ignore the Court's judgments since '[t]he worst that can happen is that we remain on a very long list of unenforced judgments to be reviewed by the Committee of Ministers.... There is no risk of a fine and no power to enforce compensation, and absolutely no chance of being kicked out of the Council of Europe'.[186]

[180] House of Commons Political and Constitutional Reform Committee, Fifth Report of Session 2010–11, *Voting by Convicted Prisoners: Summary of Evidence*, HC 776 (2011), para. 22.

[181] HC Deb, 10 February 2011, vol. 523, cols. 493–584.

[182] HC Deb, 10 February 2011, vol. 523, col. 493.

[183] Danny Nicol, 'Legitimacy of the Commons Debate on Prisoner Voting' Public Law Oct (2011): 681. See also Aruna Sathanapally, *Beyond Disagreement: Open Remedies in Human Rights Adjudication* (Oxford: Oxford University Press, 2012): 216–21.

[184] Nicol (n 183) 691. [185] Murray (n 164) 533.

[186] HC Deb, 11 February, vol. 523, col. 583.

A regrettable feature of the debate which has largely escaped comment is the role played by the UK's delegates to the Parliamentary Assembly.[187] Only two out of the twelve MPs who were at the time full members of the UK delegation spoke in the Davis-Straw debate; both (including the leader of the delegation, Conservative MP Robert Walter) opined that the ECtHR had erred in *Hirst* and that it should not be implemented (see 2.6.2).[188]

Indeed, the (then) Attorney General, Dominic Grieve, felt the need to remind MPs during the debate of the binding nature of the UK's obligation to implement judgments of the ECtHR and implore them to focus on the proportionality of the ban in the national context and not merely the question of the Court's authority.[189] Nevertheless, some MPs argued that there mere fact that the debate had taken place,[190] and the 'clear demonstration' of parliamentary disapproval of *Hirst*,[191] should be decisive in ensuring acceptance of the UK government's stance should the ECtHR consider the matter again.

For Nicol, MPs' decision to focus on constitutional principles is unproblematic since 'to expect parliamentarians to engage with constitutional matters in identical terms to the courts would be to deny Parliament credit for having an interpretive role distinct from the judicial role'.[192] However, Fredman ventures that the debate was 'conducted in highly emotive terms with little supporting evidence or justification for many of the assertions made'.[193] Hiebert questions whether 'the democratic character of the initial legislative debate and the post-judicial review sequel justify Parliament's insistence on the primacy and virtue of its judgment', and suggests that parliament's response to *Hirst* would struggle to satisfy a quality criterion (of the type discussed at 4.5.2) since it focused more on the desire to maintain a historical position rather than on a reassessment of the justification of the legislation.[194] Moreover, Hiebert adds, in asserting its superior democratic credentials vis-à-vis the ECtHR, Parliament failed to confront a 'serious legitimacy problem'—namely, its claim to represent the people when the matter at issue was the deliberate *dis*enfranchisement of a specific category of the population.[195] She adduces in support of this view evidence by Jeremy Waldron to the JCHR, in which he argued that the justification of parliamentary sovereignty rests not on abstract or historical convention but, rather, on the legitimacy of the democratic process,

[187] Eighteen MPs and Lords are appointed by the Prime Minister to the UK delegation to PACE (see also 2.6.2).

[188] HC Deb, 10 February 2011, vol. 523, cols. 527–8 (Robert Walter MP) and 567–8 (Brian Binley MP). Robert Walter described the judgment as 'wrong … illogical and unfair', but added that for the UK to withdraw from the Convention because of it would be 'counter-productive, if not dishonourable'.

[189] HC Deb, 10 February 2011, vol. 523, col. 514: 'In order for the views of this House to be helpful, we need to demonstrate that we are engaging with the concerns of the Court and that we are not just expressing our frustrations.'

[190] Alan Johnson MP, HC Deb, 10 February 2011, vol. 523, col. 500.

[191] Stephen Phillips MP, HC Deb, 10 February 2011, vol. 523, cols. 573–4.

[192] Nicol (n 183) 681.

[193] Sandra Fredman, 'From Diaolgue to Deliberation: Human Rights Adjudication and Prisoners' Right to Vote', in Hunt, Hooper, and Yowell, eds. (n 25): 447, 465.

[194] Hiebert (n 17) 2272.

[195] Hiebert (n 17) 2270.

of which the right to vote—the 'right of rights'—is an integral requirement. For Waldron, democratic arguments against judicial review 'run into their deepest challenge when the majoritarian institution is actually addressing the basis of its own electoral credentials'.[196]

It is notable that this discussion involves authors who reject a predominantly court-centric approach to rights protection. In that sense, the discussion reflects differences within the political constitutionalist position as to the processes or criteria (and the *need* for processes or criteria) by which to assess the justification for governmental inaction or parliamentary refusal to amend or repeal judicially impugned legislation (see also 4.6).[197] Responses to the prisoner voting judgments reveal the extent to which this question is unresolved within political discourse in the UK.

Murray Hunt suggests that one conclusion to be drawn from the backbench debate is the imperative to maximize both opportunities and incentives for parliamentary consideration of the substantive issues at stake in human rights judgments. He suggests the ECtHR could have gone further to bring about such consideration of the substance of the prisoner voting issue by being more prescriptive as to timescales and rejecting the UK government's request for an extension of the deadline stipulated in *Greens*, thereby obliging it to introduce and invite parliamentary scrutiny of (at least) a draft bill by the original deadline. Hunt describes this as a missed opportunity to get proper parliamentary deliberation started:

> On an issue like this, parliamentary consideration can only improve matters because there are so many fixed positions.... If you have committees crawling over a draft bill and forcing [parliamentarians] to engage with justificatory arguments, the debate can only get better informed.... The longer parliament can be ... engaging with the substantive issues at stake before they actually have to legislate, the better.[198]

In the event, as noted above, in November 2012 the government introduced the Voting Eligibility (Prisoners) Draft Bill, which proposed three options: options A and B were to give the vote to prisoners sentenced to fewer than four years or fewer than six months respectively, while option C restated the existing indiscriminate ban—a proposal which would plainly leave the UK in outright breach of *Hirst*.[199] In December 2013, a majority of members of the Joint Committee formed to scrutinize the draft bill recommended that the government bring forward a bill at the start of the 2014–15 parliamentary session giving the vote to all prisoners serving sentences of twelve months or fewer, and those within six months of their

[196] JCHR, Human Rights Judgments: Oral Evidence, 15 March 2011, Q 53. This view directly contradicts the opinion expressed by some MPs in the Davis-Straw debate that parliamentarians are especially *well*-placed to decide who should have the vote. See, for example, remarks by Karen Bradley MP (Conservative) that it was 'particularly difficult to accept that the will of Parliament should be challenged on this matter of all things in the way we find it challenged today'; HC Deb, 10 February 2011, vol. 523, col. 534.

[197] Hiebert (n 17) 2266–74.

[198] Interview, 10 September 2012.

[199] Voting Eligibility (Prisoners) Draft Bill, Cm 8499, November 2012.

release date.[200] The report stated that the UK was under a binding international law obligation to comply with *Hirst* and it would be unprecedented for any state that has ratified the Convention to legislate in defiance of a binding judgment of the ECtHR.[201] While the UK remains part of the Convention system, the majority of the Committee argued, it incurred obligations that could not be the subject of 'cherry picking'.[202] It is noteworthy that the report, published almost a decade after *Hirst*, is the first by a parliamentary body advancing a reasoned argument for a specific remedy. The government did not respond formally to the report before the dissolution of parliament ahead of the general election in May 2015. In its monitoring report issued shortly before the election, the JCHR recommended that the new government introduce legislation (whether primary legislation or a remedial order) at the earliest opportunity in the new parliament to give effect to the recommendation of the Joint Committee on the Draft Voting Eligibility (Prisoners) Bill, given the near inevitability that the May 2015 elections and elections to the devolved legislatures in 2016 will trigger further waves of repetitive applications in Strasbourg to which the UK would have no defence.[203]

7.6.2 The retention, use, and destruction of biometric data

In political terms, a startling contrast to the prisoner voting controversy is presented by the case of *S and Marper*, which concerned the UK's policy (in place since 2003) of retaining indefinitely fingerprints and DNA profiles and samples of everyone arrested for a recordable offence.[204] The UK's National DNA Database contained around five million profiles, making it the largest in the world, both per capita and in absolute terms.[205] Around one million of these profiles belonged to people who had never been charged with or convicted of a criminal offence. The applicants in *S and Marper*, a child and an adult, fell into this category. In 2008, the Grand Chamber of the ECtHR unanimously held that the 'blanket and indiscriminate nature' of powers of retention of biometric data of persons suspected but not convicted of offences, failed to strike a fair balance between competing public and private interests.[206] The retention of such information was held to constitute

[200] Joint Committee on the Draft Voting Eligibility (Prisoners) Bill, Session 2013–14, *Draft Voting Eligibility (Prisoners) Bill: Report*, HL Paper 103, HC 924 (2013) ('Joint Committee on the Draft Voting Eligibility (Prisoners) Bill Report') 25.

[201] Joint Committee on the Draft Voting Eligibility (Prisoners) Bill Report (n 200) para. 229.

[202] Joint Committee on the Draft Voting Eligibility (Prisoners) Bill Report (n 200) para. 112.

[203] JCHR, Seventh Report of Session 2014–15 (n 65) paras. 3.21, 3.26. In December 2015, the Committee of Ministers expressed its 'profound concern' that the blanket ban on prisoner voting remained, and pledged to resume consideration of the relevant cases in December 2016 at the latest in the light of the UK's commitment to report regularly on the steps taken to abide by the judgment; Interim Resolution CM/ResDH(2015)251, Execution of the judgments of the European Court of Human Rights Hirst and three other cases against the United Kingdom, 9 December 2015.

[204] *S and Marper v UK* (n 68). DNA, or deoxyribonucleic acid, is the carrier of genetic information about an individual. A recordable offence is any offence under UK law in respect of which the police must keep records of convictions and offenders on the Police National Computer.

[205] Eric Metcalfe, *Freedom from Suspicion: Surveillance Reform for a Digital Age* (JUSTICE, 2011) 9.

[206] *S and Marper v UK* (n 68) para. 125.

a disproportionate interference with the applicants' right to respect for private life under Article 8 ECHR.

In response, in the final days of the Labour government, the Crime and Security Act 2010 was passed (but not enacted) to restrict the retention of innocent people's DNA to six years for adults and three years, in most cases, for children. This response was considered inadequate by the JCHR,[207] as well as by the Home Affairs Committee,[208] and the Committee of Ministers.[209] The JCHR criticized the government's 'very narrow approach' to the judgment, which was deliberately 'pushing the boundaries' of the Court's decision in order to maintain the thrust of its original policy on DNA retention.[210] In the Committee's view, the blanket six-year retention period remained disproportionate and potentially arbitrary and carried a significant risk of further litigation.

In the case of *Marper*, the JCHR was able to be unusually specific in its proposed remedy since an alternative regime for DNA retention already existed: the model used in Scotland, which the Grand Chamber had identified as achieving a more proportionate balance between, on the one hand, public protection through the investigation and prevention and crime, and, on the other, respect for a person's private life.[211] Lord Lester, a member of the JCHR from 2000 to 2015, recalls the 'especially thorough and comprehensive' engagement of the JCHR with the *Marper* judgment.[212] As noted at 7.4.1, the Committee first wrote to the government within five days of the judgment, asking, inter alia, whether the government intended to bring forward proposals similar to those which apply in Scotland (and if not, why not) and whether it proposed to remove the breach by means of a remedial order or—the JCHR's recommended approach—primary legislation.[213] The JCHR subsequently engaged in protracted correspondence with ministers and conducted detailed scrutiny of the responses proposed both by the Labour government before 2010,[214] and the Conservative-led coalition government after 2010.[215] The incoming coalition introduced the Scottish model to England and Wales (but not Northern Ireland[216]) as part of the Protection of Freedoms Act 2012.

[207] Twenty-Seventh Report of Session 2008–09, *Retention, Use and Destruction of Biometric Data: Correspondence with the Government*, HL 182, HC 1113 (2009); Twelfth Report of Session 2009–10, *Legislative Scrutiny: Crime and Security Bill etc*, HL 67, HC 402 (2010) paras. 1.4–1.76; Fifteenth Report of Session 2009–10 (n 84) paras. 41–58.

[208] The Committee recommended a three-year retention period for adults; House of Commons Home Affairs Committee, Eighth Report of Session 2009–10, *The National DNA Database*, HC-222-I (2010), Conclusions and recommendations, 20 (para. 9).

[209] 1072nd (DH) meeting, 1–3 December 2009, Decisions adopted at the meeting, CM/Del/Dec(2009)1072, 7 December 2009; 1078th meeting (DH), 2–4 March 2010, Decisions adopted at the meeting, CM/Del/Dec(2010)1078, 8 March 2010.

[210] JCHR, Twelfth Report of Session 2009–10 (n 207) para. 1.10.

[211] JCHR, Twelfth Report of Session 2009–10 (n 207) paras. 1.64–1.74.

[212] Interview, 12 March 2012.

[213] See 7.4.1 at n 130.

[214] JCHR, Tenth Report of Session 2008–09, *Legislative Scrutiny: Policing and Crime Bill*, HL Paper 68, HC 395 (2009) paras. 1.111–1.119; see also reports cited at n 207.

[215] JCHR, Eighteenth Report of Session 2010–12 (n 87) paras. 6–87.

[216] See 7.2.2 at n 68.

Unlike *Hirst*, *Marper* was 'widely applauded in British political and legal circles'.[217] Perhaps motivated by the opportunity to develop a pro-civil liberties narrative in opposition to the Labour government, the (then) Conservative shadow Security Minister, Baroness Pauline Neville-Jones, had pressed for its speedy implementation and was 'gratified' that the ECtHR had obliged the Labour government to revise its position.[218] Speaking less than a year after the judgment, Baroness Neville-Jones complained that 'the UK, in the face of great criticism of the legislation in this country, is taking an excessive time to amend its legislation to conform to a judgment of the European court'.[219] The (then) shadow Home Secretary, Chris Grayling, also referred to the urgency of remedial measures.[220] In a parliamentary debate initiated by a Labour backbencher in 2009, while some members backed Labour's minimalist approach to implementation, none questioned the authority or legitimacy of the ECtHR's judgment or suggested that it should not be implemented.[221] Press reporting, too, was largely favourable, even among newspapers generally antipathetic to the Court.[222]

The respect accorded to the judgment in *Marper* is all the more remarkable given that the Grand Chamber resoundingly rejected (17–0) the position of both the UK government and the Law Lords.[223] Moreover, the judgment implicitly rejected the position of parliament, which had introduced the offending provision (via amendments to section 64(1A) of the Police and Criminal Evidence Act 1984) following public disquiet about cases in which, for example, DNA evidence linking one suspect to a rape and another to a murder had not been able to be used because the law as it stood had required that their samples be destroyed and disregarded.[224] Yet, despite these considerations, *Marper* excited nothing like the opprobrium directed at *Hirst*. Moreover, as the former Attorney General Dominic Grieve reminded MPs during the backbench debate on prisoner voting discussed in 7.6.1, other judgments, such as *Gillan and Quinton* on police powers to stop and search individuals without reasonable suspicion, had been applauded in the House of Commons: 'We therefore need to be careful about too much picking and choosing of what we might think is desirable or not.'[225]

[217] Nicolas Bratza, 'Britain Should Be Defending European Justice, Not Attacking It', *The Independent*, 24 January 2012.

[218] Baroness Neville-Jones, HC Deb, 20 October 2009, vol.713, col. 666.

[219] HC Deb, 20 October 2009, vol. 713, col. 668.

[220] 'Conservatives Drop Opposition to DNA Proposals following Alan Johnson Ultimatum', *The Guardian*, 7 April 2010.

[221] HC Deb, 9 December 2009, vol. 502, cols. 104WH-127WH.

[222] See, for example, 'One Million Innocent People Could Have Their Profiles Wiped from Britain's "Orwellian" DNA Database after Court Ruling', *Daily Mail*, 5 December 2008.

[223] The House of Lords, in *R (S) v The Chief Constable of South Yorkshire Police and R (Marper) v The Chief Constable of South Yorkshire Police* [2004] UKHL 3, held by a majority of 2:1 that that the value of retained fingerprints and samples taken from suspects was considerable, while the mere retention of fingerprints and DNA samples did not constitute an interference with the right to respect for private life, or at most a very modest, and proportionate, interference (*S and Marper v UK* (n 68) paras. 14–25).

[224] *S and Marper* (n 68) para. 15.

[225] Dominic Grieve MP, HC Deb, 10 February 2011, vol. 523, col. 512.

As noted at 3.6.1.2, *Marper* (and *Gillan*) thus illustrate well the contingent and politicized nature of the implementation process; factors related to timing, political opportunity and the nature of the underlying issue (limiting state interference in civil liberties rather than extending positive rights) may explain the contrasting political responses.

7.6.3 The prohibition of political advertising on radio and television

Another counterpoint to the political handling of *Hirst* is the way in which the UK government and parliament took ECtHR decisions into account in the framing of the Communications Bill (which became the Communications Act 2003), which aimed radically to reform the regulation of electronic and broadcast media in England and Wales. The JCHR's legislative scrutiny highlighted several human rights concerns arising from the Bill, the most serious of which, the Committee said, concerned the maintenance of a blanket prohibition on political advertising in the broadcast media, which had originally been imposed at the advent of commercial broadcasting in 1954.

At issue was the ECtHR judgment in 2001 in the case of *VgT Verein Gegen Tierfabriken v Switzerland*,[226] which had held that a ban on political advertising on national broadcast media in Switzerland violated the right to freedom of expression under Article 10 ECHR. Notwithstanding this judgment, in its first scrutiny report on the Communications Bill in July 2002, the JCHR urged caution in reversing the prohibition in England and Wales given its important rationale: 'fear of the annexation of the democratic process by the rich and powerful', to which the Court had alluded in *VgT*.[227] The JCHR acknowledged the difficulty of devising a more circumscribed solution and saw merit in waiting for the jurisprudence in this area to mature before deciding on the appropriate legislative response. Nevertheless, the Committee considered that the maintenance of a total prohibition on political advertising on radio and television was likely, if challenged, to be held to be incompatible with Article 10,[228] a risk that the government had itself acknowledged in its Explanatory Notes to the Bill.[229] The JCHR recommended that the government examine ways in which workable and Convention-compatible restrictions could be included.

In its next scrutiny report on the matter in December 2002, the JCHR noted that the government had, for the first time since the HRA was enacted, felt unable to make a statement of compatibility under section 19 of the Act (see also 7.2.1).[230]

[226] No. 24699/94, 28 June 2001.

[227] JCHR, Nineteenth Report of Session 2001–02, *Draft Communications Bill*, HL Paper 149, HC 1102 (2002) para. 63.

[228] JCHR, Nineteenth Report of Session 2001–02 (n 227) para. 64.

[229] Department of Trade and Industry, *Draft Communications Bill: Explanatory Notes*, Cm. 5508-II (2002) para. 365.

[230] JCHR, First Report of Session 2002–03, *Scrutiny of Bills: Progress Report*, HL Paper 24, HC 191 (2002) para. 11.

The Committee recognized that it may sometimes be legitimate to legislate in ways which are known to be potentially incompatible with Convention rights, but only when certain criteria are met.[231] These include that the statement of incompatibility does not evince a lack of respect for human rights standards; that the reasons for risking incompatibility are sufficiently compelling and consistent with the general aim of maintaining respect for rights; and that the government does not consider that the legislation *is* incompatible, merely that it cannot state with confidence that it is more likely than not to be held compatible. The Committee had written to the government pressing it to explain why it had not included a more circumscribed prohibition in the Bill.[232] In February 2003, the JCHR reported that correspondence with ministers had satisfied it that the government had met the Committee's criteria.[233]

David Feldman, adviser to the JCHR at the time, explains that Committee members were highly cognisant of the political factors at play and adamant in refusing to take a position that the *VgT* judgment precluded a complete ban on political advertising on radio and television in the UK: 'They thought that, simply as a matter of practical politics, giving way on that point would leave big business in control of the … debate.'[234] Therefore, rather than pronouncing definitively on whether it considered the proposed legislation incompatible in the light of *VgT*, the Committee had assessed the *risk* of such a ruling being made in future, and had challenged the government to justify its position and explain what it would do in the event of a declaration of incompatibility or an adverse judgment in Strasbourg. According to Feldman, the Committee decided that maintaining the blanket ban, 'was a legitimate thing for a democratically accountable government to do because they weren't flouting the rule of law or human rights. They were saying, "We think we have a decent argument here and if we lose we'll think again"'.

In the event, the UK's position was subsequently scrutinized by the Grand Chamber, which (as discussed at 4.5.2) placed considerable weight on the detailed parliamentary scrutiny of the Communication Bill in finding by a narrow majority (9–8) that the UK's ban on political advertising on broadcast media was a necessary interference with the right to free expression.[235]

7.6.4 The JCHR and the politics of implementation

The dissonance between the political responses to the judgments discussed in this chapter illustrate that, as the JCHR observes, the implementation of ECtHR decisions is not only a legal and technical, but also an intensely political process.

[231] JCHR, First Report of Session 2002–03 (n 230) paras. 14–15.

[232] An ad hoc Joint Committee on the Draft Communications Bill had also reported on this aspect of the Bill in a similar vein; see Joint Committee on the Draft Communications Bill, *Draft Communications Bill*, HL Paper 169-I, HC 876-I (2002) para. 301.

[233] JCHR, Fourth Report of Session 2002–03, *Scrutiny of Bills: Further Progress Report*, HL Paper 50, HC 397 (2002) paras. 9–16.

[234] Interview, 25 April 2012.

[235] *Animal Defenders International v UK*, No 48876/08, 22 April 2013 [GC].

Sometimes, as in the case of *Grieves*, implementation encounters no political or administrative obstacles and is swift and comprehensive. Yet other judgments have provoked highly-charged debate about how, or even whether, they should be implemented. How may we characterize the approach of parliament, and especially the JCHR, to managing these constraints?

A recurrent feature of the JCHR's monitoring reports has been to insist that the government adopt an expansive rather than minimal approach to implementation.[236] A minimal approach, the JCHR has argued, exacerbates the problem of repetitive cases because it leads to future litigation which can culminate in foreseeable findings of violation. The Committee identified such an approach in the Labour government's response to *Marper*. It made similar criticisms of ministers' 'narrow' response to the decision in *A and Others v UK* about the unfairness caused by the use of secret evidence and special advocates in the context of legislation which authorized the detention of foreign nationals suspected of terrorism;[237] and its 'passive and minimalist' approach following judgments in the domestic courts and the ECtHR concerning control orders, which permitted the Home Secretary to impose a wide range of restrictions on any person suspected of involvement in terrorism.[238]

Conversely, the JCHR commended the government for its implementation of *B and L v UK*, concerning the prohibition on a parent-in-law from marrying their child-in-law unless their respective spouses had died, in violation of Article 12 ECHR.[239] The Marriage Act 1949 (Remedial Order) 2006 went wider than removing the incompatibility found by the ECtHR in the particular case, and removed an age restriction on the right of a parent- and child-in-law to marry which, though not at issue in the case itself, would in the government's view inevitably have been found to be incompatible with Article 12 as a result of the Court's reasoning. Another example of expansive implementation concerns the *Christine Goodwin* judgment on the legal recognition of transsexuals. Sathanapally notes that, while legislative reform was prompted by the ECtHR judgment, and a declaration of incompatibility in a comparable domestic case,[240] the government made the case for the legislation 'as a matter of ethical imperative, not simply compliance', as did MPs from all major parties.[241] Moreover, the Gender Recognition Bill provided a more comprehensive framework to deal with gender change than was strictly required by the legal judgments; for example, recognition was not limited to post-operative transsexuals, as in some jurisdictions, but instead provided a system of certification

[236] JCHR, Fifteenth Report of Session 2009–10 (n 84) paras. 168–70.

[237] JCHR, Fifteenth Report of Session 2009–10 (n 84) paras. 40, referring to *A and Others v UK*, No. 3455/05, 19 February 2009 [GC].

[238] JCHR, Ninth Report of Session 2009–10, *Counter–Terrorism Policy and Human Rights (Sixteenth Report): Annual Renewal of Control Orders Legislation 2010*, HL 64, HC 395 (2010) para. 53.

[239] JCHR, Fifteenth Report of Session 2009–10 (n 84) para. 169, referring to *B and L v UK*, No. 36536/02, 13 September 2005.

[240] *Bellinger v Bellinger* [2003] UKHL 21.

[241] Sathanapally (n 183) 167–8.

by a specialized Gender Recognition Panel, in which a range of factors could be considered in evaluating gender change.[242]

While the JCHR has consistently advocated a comprehensive approach to implementation, it has generally avoided being either definitive in identifying potential breaches of the Convention or prescriptive in its proposed remedies. Rather, it has tended to direct open-ended questions to ministers about proposed responses to judgments and their justification, paraphrased by David Feldman as asking ministers to 'tell parliament what you are doing or not doing—and explain why'.[243] The JCHR has habitually framed its conclusions in terms of the *risk* that a provision would be found incompatible with the Convention by a domestic court or in Strasbourg.[244] This risk-assessment approach reflects the Committee's reluctance, as a matter of constitutional propriety, to assume ultimate interpretive authority. Pragmatic considerations also favour such a strategy: a prescriptive approach is likely to make it harder to achieve cross-party consensus. Moreover, a definitive pronouncement by the Committee that a legislative provision breaches the Convention runs the risk of being contradicted by a subsequent judicial finding, to the detriment of the Committee's credibility. A non-prescriptive approach also preserves flexibility for the Committee to advocate particular options that may rely on arguments *other* than strict legal compliance.[245]

A change of tone was signalled in 2006 when the JCHR commissioned a review of its working practices. This advocated that the Committee find its own 'less technical voice' when appropriate—in particular, where proportionality considerations apply—based on the examination of witnesses and evidence, rather than necessarily determining the risk of incompatibility by 'second guessing' the courts.[246] The Committee pledged to give further consideration to this question, while also pledging to be less exhaustive in its pre-legislative scrutiny in order to focus on the most significant human rights issues raised by a bill and thereby exert greater influence on the legislative agenda.[247] Following the review, the JCHR also adopted a strategy of proposing amendments to Bills to give effect to its recommendations.[248]

As noted at 7.3, the review prompted the Committee to make more systematic its monitoring of the implementation of human rights judgments. Aside from the greater regularity of the JCHR's subsequent reports to parliament, it does not appear that the 2006 review marked a substantive departure in the Committee's approach to this aspect of its work. Our interlocutors among both the pre- and

[242] Sathanapally (n 183) 170–2. However, the JCHR's concerns about retrospective relief for the litigants were overlooked in both Houses.

[243] Interview, 25 April 2012.

[244] JCHR, Nineteenth Report of Session 2004–05 (n 78) paras. 44–5.

[245] For example, in its reviews of the introduction and continuation in force of the legislation that brought about control orders, the JCHR went beyond the application of judicial standards and made demands that were more exacting and expansive than those made by the courts; see Sathanapally (n 183) 208–9.

[246] JCHR, Twenty-Third Report of Session 2005–06, *The Committee's Future Working Practices*, HL Paper 239, HC 1575 (2006) Appendix 1 ('the Klug Report') 78–9.

[247] JCHR, Twenty-Third Report of Session 2005–06 (n 246) para. 77.

[248] Hunt, Hooper, and Yowell (n 117) 22.

post-2006 members and advisers of the Committee concur that for the JCHR, responding to human rights judgments is rarely a 'zero-sum' game aimed at producing one particular outcome; rather, the Committee's role is to promote informed deliberation of the alternative options and their respective merits, while consistently arguing that judicial decisions are to be treated as providing a minimum required to protect human rights.

While the Committee has eschewed the role of Platonic guardian in respect of identifying and remedying human rights violations, it has on occasions taken a more directive approach. As we have seen, it did so in the case of *Marper*, in response to which it was able to propose an existing alternative scheme (the Scottish model of DNA retention) which had been commended by the ECtHR. The JCHR has also regularly castigated ministers for their inaction in response to a judgment when the Committee deemed that their justification for delaying remedial action was inadequate or where no justification was forthcoming.

The Committee's freedom of manoeuvre is determined in part by the extent to which judgments become politically controversial. Hunt observes that the JCHR has always contained a wide range of intellectual conceptions of human rights, stretching from libertarianism to a strong adherence to positive rights.[249] Notwithstanding this diversity of views, the Committee has almost invariably sought to work by consensus and to produce unanimous and non-partisan reports.[250] This has occasionally led the Committee to avoid inquiring into, or issuing recommendations about, a particular issue (such as prisoner voting) on which consensus is likely to be elusive. Nevertheless, Hunt suggests, 'the capacity for human rights discourse to transcend political partisanship never ceases to surprise'.[251]

The former JCHR Chair Jean Corston reflects upon the difficulty facing elected members of parliament as they seek to balance competing pressures in formulating a response to ECtHR judgments. She acknowledges that politicians may be scorned for adopting what appear to be populist responses. However, she argues:

> That is to misunderstand what it is that MPs get on a daily, even hourly basis, from the people they represent and [the difficulty of] trying to distil and make sense of those views and set them against what's proposed either in Westminster or from Strasbourg. [MPs] do genuinely try to square that circle.[252]

Angela Patrick ventures that, while the starting point of the JCHR (unlike that of parliament as a whole) has always been to do justice to the UK's obligations under the Convention, 'there's nothing to tie them to that'. In this context, she suggests, the provision of consistent and politically neutral advice is paramount, since it provides 'political cover' for MPs if they move away from their party line or advocate positions that run against the tide of public opinion (see also 3.4.3.1).[253]

[249] Hunt (n 76) 243. [250] Oliver (n 179) 48. [251] Hunt (n 76) 243.
[252] Interview, 4 July 2012. [253] Interview, 8 March 2012.

7.7 Conclusion

Within the UK parliament, the JCHR is the principal site of engagement with human rights judgments. The attention devoted by the Committee to systematic monitoring of the executive's response to human rights judgments has varied over time, peaking between 2006 and 2010. How may we assess the effectiveness of this monitoring work in relation to the Council of Europe's imperative for full and rapid implementation of judgments?

In respect of the JCHR's legislative scrutiny, Hiebert points to the severe limitations on parliament's ability to influence or constrain the executive; principally, government domination of parliament and the centrality of disciplined political parties in the Westminster system.[254] These limitations apply equally to the post-judicial phase of the JCHR's monitoring work, which is further dependent on the timely provision of information by the executive in order that parliament may seize the opportunity to influence the executive's response to judgments within the timeframe stipulated by the Committee of Ministers.

It is sometimes possible to identify the substantive influence of the JCHR in the sense of executive uptake of specific recommendations made by the Committee as to the means of remedying a violation (as in the case of *Gillan*). However, causality remains an open question, especially where other actors have made the same recommendations.[255] Similarly, it is difficult to say definitively that the JCHR's scrutiny has hastened implementation of judgments in particular instances. Multiple factors are likely to influence the timing of executive action, most obviously a change of government and a greater willingness by incoming ministers to remedy violations that occurred under their predecessors (as in the cases of *Marper* and *Gillan*). Where a judgment requires legislative reform, and the JCHR (or another parliamentary committee) is able to scrutinize draft legislation and propose changes prior to the proposal's formal introduction into parliament, its capacity to influence both parliamentary deliberation of the matter and the eventual outcome is likely to be greater than when this opportunity is lacking, as evidenced by the expansive approach of both the government and parliament to implementing judgments on transgender rights.[256]

The JCHR's effectiveness in respect of its work in monitoring judgments should not be measured solely by executive uptake of recommendations relating to specific judgments, but also by the 'system-wide' improvements its pressure has helped to secure. The instigation of more systematic arrangements for co-ordinating the government's response to judgments; the timely and routine provision of information

[254] Janet Hiebert, 'Governing Under the Human Rights Act: The Limitations of Wishful Thinking', *Public Law*, January (2012): 27.

[255] See Hunt, Hooper, and Yowell (n 117) 43–4 for discussion of this methodological challenge in respect of the JCHR's legislative scrutiny.

[256] Sathanapally (n 183) 166–72.

by the executive to parliament; and improvements in the quality and timeliness of the UK government's action plans submitted to the Committee of Ministers—all these may be regarded as a vindication of the JCHR's rigorous approach to monitoring up to 2010. Interviewees also suggest that the JCHR's scrutiny work has galvanized ministers to provide in the statements of compatibility attached to bills an increasingly thorough treatment of the human rights issues identified and justification for the positions taken.[257] In addition, the Committee's monitoring work has fostered the creation of an accessible public record of adverse ECtHR judgments (and declarations of incompatibility by domestic courts) and executive responses to them, including the reasoning behind those responses, and has thereby provided a regular burden of justification upon ministers for their action or inaction.

These improvements to the executive system of implementation, and its increased responsiveness to parliament, have occurred at the same time as the anti-Strasbourg rhetoric has become more strident at Westminster and in sections of the press. Under changed political conditions, these contradictions, which have—with certain high-profile exceptions—permitted implementation of judgments to proceed smoothly, may become increasingly exposed. In this sense, the UK's institutional arrangements for responding to ECtHR judgments, which are among the most robust and respected in the Council of Europe, may be vulnerable to revision or erosion by any government which seeks to weaken the UK's ties to Strasbourg.

[257] David Feldman, Interview, 25 April 2012; Lord Lester, Interview, 12 March 2012.

8

The Netherlands

8.1 The Constitutional, Legal, and Political Landscape

The Netherlands has the status of a constitutional monarchy, with a parliamentary democracy. Its bicameral parliament, the States General (*Staten-Generaal*), is made up of the Senate (the upper house: the '*chambre de reflection*'), and the House of Representatives (the lower house). The seventy-five members of the Senate, who sit on a part-time basis, are elected by the twelve States-Provincial every four years. The 150 members of the House of Representatives are elected every four years by proportional representation.

The Council of State (*Raad van State*) is an independent body, comprising eminent jurists and former politicians.[1] It has two primary functions.[2] Through its Advisory Division it advises the government and parliament on draft legislative bills (the majority of which are submitted by the government),[3] including compliance with international law, especially the ECHR. It also acts as the country's highest general administrative court—through its Administrative Jurisdiction Division. The government and parliament also receives advice from the Advisory Council on International Affairs (*Adviesraad Internationale Vraagstukken* (AIV)), on foreign policy issues, including human rights, peace and security, development co-operation, and European integration.[4]

As regards the incorporation of international law into the domestic polity, the Netherlands is a monist state, and the Dutch Constitution explicitly recognizes the supreme position of international law.[5] The substantive rights in the European

[1] It has a maximum of ten members, in addition to its President (the King) and Vice-President.

[2] See Articles 73–75 of the Constitution of the Kingdom of the Netherlands 2008.

[3] Janneke Gerards and Joseph Fleuren, 'The Netherlands', in Janneke Gerards and Joseph Fleuren, eds., *Implementation of the European Convention on Human Rights and of the Judgments of the ECtHR in National Case-Law: A Comparative Analysis* (Antwerp-Oxford-Portland: Intersentia, 2014): 217, 217–218.

[4] See <http://aiv-advice.nl/63l/home>. The AIV has four permanent committees, one of which is the Human Rights Committee. Its recent reports include *The Rule of Law—Safeguard for European Citizens and Foundation for European Cooperation*, Advisory Report No. 87, January 2014.

[5] Articles 93 and 94 of the Constitution of the Kingdom of the Netherlands 2008. See also Gerards and Fleuren (n 3) 220–5. Article 90 of the Constitution (which provides that the government shall promote the development of the international legal order) was introduced in 1953 at the instigation of the parliamentarian (and judge) Jos Serrarens. See Barbara Oomen, 'Small Places: The Home-coming of Human Rights in the Netherlands', Inaugural Lecture, Utrecht University, 2 December 2011, 24.

Convention on Human Rights (ECHR or 'the Convention') are considered to have acquired self-executing status, and the Supreme Court's development of its 'incorporation theory' means that, in practice, Dutch state organs are required to apply the case law of the European Court of Human Rights (ECtHR or 'the Court') relating to the other Council of Europe States (as well as the Netherlands), as the provisions of the ECHR must be interpreted in the light of all the relevant ECtHR jurisprudence.[6] The Dutch courts have the power to review primary legislation as against the provisions of international human rights treaties (although not against human rights provisions in the Constitution).[7] De Wet has argued that the introduction of the concept of the supremacy of international law 'marked the beginning of a significant change in the relationship between the courts and the legislature, as ... the courts and not Parliament had the final say in matters touching upon ... human rights'.[8] Nevertheless, Gerards and Fleuren have discerned the development, since the 1980s, of a certain judicial prudence as regards human rights questions. They argue that the growing practice of the ECtHR to impose 'positive obligations' on states (applying its 'living instrument' doctrine; see 1.1.2), and the Netherlands' accession to the International Covenant on Civil and Political Rights (ICCPR) in 1979, 'prompted the Supreme Court to create a doctrine of judicial restraint in cases where the removal of inconsistencies between Dutch law and self-executing provisions of the ICCPR and the ECHR would involve political choices that should preferably be made by the legislature'.[9] In practice, this means that in circumstances where legislation is already being prepared, the Supreme Court 'seems to be reluctant to run ahead of things'.[10] Cases which lead to the setting aside of an Act of Parliament, because of a Convention violation, are rare.[11]

Changes were made to the Council of State, in the light of the ECtHR judgment in *Procola v Luxembourg*[12] in which the Court found the similarly constituted body in Luxembourg to be incompatible with Article 6 ECHR (the right to a fair trial) because of its dual role as both an advisory body during the legislative process, and a judicial body during administrative litigation.

8.2 The Netherlands and the Convention System

The Netherlands ratified the ECHR in 1954 and instituted the right of individual petition in 1960.[13] The first adverse Dutch judgments were handed down in the

[6] Erika de Wet, 'The Reception Process in the Netherlands and Belgium', in Helen Keller and Alec Stone Sweet, eds., *A Europe of Rights: The Impact of the ECHR on National Legal Systems* (Oxford: Oxford University Press, 2008): 229, 235–7.

[7] A situation which Gerards and Fleuren (n 3 (231)) acknowledge appears to be paradoxical.

[8] De Wet (n 6) 235–40.

[9] Gerards and Fleuren (n 3) 225.

[10] Gerards and Fleuren (n 3) 226.

[11] Gerards and Fleuren (n 3) 239.

[12] No. 14570/89, 28 September 1995. See also *Kleyn and Others v Netherlands*, Nos. 39343/98, 39651/98, 43147/98, and 46664/99, 6 May 2003.

[13] It has ratified all the protocols to the ECHR, save for Protocol No. 7. The ECHR and the relevant protocols are also applicable in the Caribbean parts of the Kingdom of the Netherlands.

1970s: *Engel and Others v Netherlands*[14] (concerning military disciplinary law) and *Winterwerp v Netherlands*[15] (which led to reform of the law concerning the rights of detained psychiatric patients). In 1979, the Court published its judgment in *Marckx v Belgium*,[16] concerning discriminatory treatment of children born outside marriage, which Gerards and Fleuren have noted had a 'tremendous impact' on Dutch court decisions in the field of family law.[17] In its 1985 judgment in *Benthem v Netherlands*,[18] the ECtHR found that the Dutch administrative law system—providing for proceedings before the Administrative Litigation Division of the Council of State, and the Crown—did not comply with the right to a fair hearing under Article 6(1) ECHR.

It is evident that Strasbourg decisions, including many non-Dutch cases, have had a significant impact on developments in law and policy in the Netherlands, reaching back to the 1970s and 1980s. For example, de Wet cites a series of such influential judgments, including: *Öztürk v Germany*[19] (the classification of tax law penalties as 'criminal charges'), *Lingens v Austria*[20] and *Goodwin v UK*[21] (protection of the rights of journalists), *Colozza v Italy*[22] and *Unterpertinger v Austria*[23] (rights of defendants in criminal proceedings), *Gaskin v UK*[24] (a 'right of personality'), and *Abdulaziz, Cabales and Balkandali v UK*[25] (the facilitation of family life in the immigration context). These judgments led directly to changes introduced by the Supreme Court and the Council of State, and, less frequently, by legislative amendments in parliament. Martin Kuijer (Senior Legal Adviser on Human Rights at the Dutch Ministry of Security and Justice) refers, inter alia, to the major changes that were made to the criminal procedural law as a result of judgments such as *Brogan and Others v UK*[26] and the *Kostovski*,[27] *Lala*,[28] and *Pelladoah*[29] judgments against the Netherlands.[30] As a result, says Kuijer, the Court and its case law became 'mainstream' in Dutch political debate: 'the main political parties realized that international human rights norms provided for a powerful political weapon in parliamentary debate with the Government'.[31] Another more recent case which led to a major reform in the domestic system was the 2008 judgment in *Salduz v Turkey*,[32]

[14] Nos. 5100/71; 5101/71; 5102/71; 5354/72; 5370/72, 8 June 1976.

[15] No. 6301/73, 24 October 1979.

[16] No. 6833/74, 13 June 1979.

[17] Gerards and Fleuren (n 3) 236. See also Martin Kuijer, 'Guaranteeing International Human Rights Standards in the Netherlands: The Parliamentary Dimension', in Murray Hunt, Hayley Hooper, and Paul Yowell, eds., *Parliaments and Human Rights: Redressing the Democratic Deficit* (Oxford: Hart Publishing, 2015): 300 (text at n 21).

[18] No. 8848/80, 23 October 1985.

[19] No. 8544/79, 21 February 1984.

[20] No. 9815/92, 8 July 1986.

[21] No. 17488/90, 27 March 1996 [GC].

[22] No. 9024/80, 12 February 1985.

[23] No. 9120/80, 24 November 1986.

[24] No. 10454/83, 7 July 1987.

[25] No. 9214/90 et al., 28 May 1985.

[26] Nos. 11209/84, 11234/84, 11266/84, and 11386/85, 29 November 1988.

[27] No. 11454/85, 20 November 1989.

[28] No. 14861/89, 22 September 1994.

[29] No. 16737/90, 22 September 1994.

[30] Martin Kuijer, 'The Impact of the Case Law of the European Court of Human Rights on the Political Debate in the Netherlands Concerning the Court', in Marjolein van Roosmalen, Ben Vermeulen, Fried van Hoof, and Marten Oosting, eds., *Fundamental Rights and Principles. Lieber Amicorum Pieter van Dijk* (Cambridge: Intersentia, 2013): 99.

[31] Kuijer (n 17) 301.

[32] No. 36391/02, 27 November 2008 [GC].

concerning the right of access to a lawyer for detainees in police custody (which is discussed further at 8.3 below). The notable frequency with which the Convention is invoked before, and by, the national courts, has been attributed to the clarity of its provisions and the depth of the ECtHR case law.[33]

The Dutch government may also intervene as a third party in ECtHR litigation concerning other states, as it did, for example, in *M.S.S. v Belgium and Greece*[34] (concerning the protection of asylum-seekers) and in *Ahorugeze v Sweden*[35] (concerning the proposed deportation of the applicant to Rwanda). Roeland Böcker, the Netherlands government agent in Strasbourg (from the Ministry of Foreign Affairs), explains that the government intervened in the *M.S.S.* case because of the parallels as regards the asylum system between the position of Belgium and the Netherlands, and in *Ahorugeze* in order to provide information to the Court about the situation in Rwanda: the Court concluded that extradition would violate neither Article 3 ECHR (prohibition of torture and inhuman or degrading treatment or punishment) nor Article 6 ECHR (the right to a fair trial).[36]

8.2.1 Attitudes towards the Convention system

Expert observers, such as Martin Kuijer, have underlined the strength of the usually prevalent 'pro-Strasbourg' view in the Netherlands:

> The almost unconditional support to the Convention system in the political domain in the Netherlands was striking. The Court could do no wrong, or so it seemed ... the Convention mechanism was not seen as intruding on the domestic legal order (or political sovereignty in the national parliament), but as a welcome addition to the constitutional order of the Kingdom.[37]

In recent years, however, the Strasbourg Court has frequently found itself in the firing line—as the target of political attacks. A number of our interlocutors described something of a shift in attitudes, revealing a relative lack of concern at the domestic level for the rule of law at the Council of Europe level. Thus, the Convention has latterly more frequently been seen as a nuisance or an irritant;[38] and MPs are less interested in it than before, especially those who are directly elected,

[33] Gerards and Fleuren (n 3) 236–7.

[34] No. 30696/09, 21 January 2011 [GC]. Third party interventions in that case were also submitted by the UK government, the AIRE Centre, Amnesty International, the Council of Europe Commissioner for Human Rights, the Office of the United Nations High Commissioner for Refugees (UNHCR), and the Greek Helsinki Monitor.

[35] No. 37075/09, 27 October 2011

[36] Interview, 22 March 2012. Professor Rick Lawson notes, however, that there have been far more Dutch government third-party interventions at the Court of Justice of the European Union than at the Strasbourg Court; Interview, 22 March 2012.

[37] Kuijer (n 17) 301.

[38] Such sentiments would appear to be over and above the more general fear of 'juridification' and the rise of a 'claim culture' which some commentators have detected in parliamentary debates in recent years. See, for example, Barbara Oomen, 'The Rights for Others: The Contested Homecoming of Human Rights in the Netherlands', *Netherlands Quarterly of Human Rights* 31(1) (2013): 41, 67–8.

and therefore dependent on local support. The question of the implementation of Strasbourg judgments used to be more or less automatic and not questioned, but by 2012, it was not a question of 'how to' implement but 'why should we?'.[39] There also seemed to be a discernible shift in the Government's position. Ministerial correspondence in October 2011 relating to the reform of the ECtHR invoked the notion of subsidiarity in order to 'warn off' the Court: 'the principle of subsidiarity means that constant vigilance is required on the part of the Court … in order to do full justice to its subsidiary role…. The Court should also respect the decision of the national (judicial) authority on the facts or the competing interests, unless the decision is manifestly unreasonable'.[40] Earlier that year, the Dutch Minister of Foreign Affairs suggested that 'the Court should not weaken its authority by rendering judgments which are only peripherally related to human rights'.[41]

The 'backlash' in the Netherlands reached its height between 2010 and 2012, coinciding with the increasing influence of Geert Wilders and the Party for Freedom (PVV), promoting populist anti-European, anti-immigration and anti-judicial policies (see 1.1.2).[42] As a result, more politicians showed a greater interest in cases which would previously have fallen below the domestic political radar, resulting in political resentment at the perceived constraining influence of courts vis-à-vis a democratically elected parliament and also international treaties being reframed as restricting Dutch policy. For example, the plans of the People's Party for Freedom and Democracy (VVD) to reduce entitlement to social security benefits (as a response to the general situation of austerity) were held up by decisions of the Dutch courts, which found that the proposals violated ECtHR case law on property rights (Article 1 of Protocol No. 1). This led to some MPs blaming the Strasbourg Court for its supposed undue judicial interference.[43] The VVD MP Stef Blok (subsequently, Minister of Security and Justice, and Minister for Housing and the Central Government Sector) suggested in 2011 that Strasbourg judges had become 'politicians in judicial robes'.[44] Furthermore, a private members' bill was presented to the

[39] Frans Timmermans, Interview, 13 June 2012.

[40] The correspondence is cited at Kuijer (n 17) 302.

[41] Kuijer (n 17) 302.

[42] Gerards and Fleuren have suggested that this critical debate was fuelled in particular by a 2010 newspaper opinion piece by Thierry Baudet which argued that the Court had strayed unacceptably beyond its remit: Thierry Baudet, *Het Europees Hof voor de Rechten van de Mens vormt een ernstige inbreuk op de democratie* ['The European Court of Human Rights Represents a Serious Breach of Democracy'], *NRC Handelsblad*, 12 November 2010. See Gerards and Fleuren (n 3) 251 (and the articles they cite at n 137). In 2013, the PVV presented a parliamentary resolution calling for the denunciation of the ECHR, but it was rejected by the other parties in the Lower House. See also Oomen (n 5) 42–3; Egbert Myjer, 'The Success Story of the European Court: The Times They are A-Changin'?', *Netherlands Quarterly of Human Rights* 30(3) (2012): 264, 270–1; Jasper Krommendijk, *The Domestic Impact and Effectiveness of the Process of State Reporting under UN Human Rights Treaties in the Netherlands, New Zealand and Finland: Paper-Pushing or Policy Prompting?* (Cambridge: Intersentia, 2014): 81–2. Martin Kuijer notes that although a high proportion of the Strasbourg *applications* (approximately 80%) have related to asylum or immigration law in recent years, there were only six such *judgments* against the Netherlands from 2008 to 2014. He does though acknowledge a perception that the Court's case law has an increasing influence on immigration policy. See Kuijer (n 17) 301.

[43] Gerards and Fleuren (n 3) 252.

[44] *Volkskrant*, 7 April 2011, as cited in Kuijer (n 17) 302.

House of Representatives in September 2012 (the 'Taverne Proposal'; see 1.1.2) which sought to amend the Constitution by strengthening the powers of the legislature over the courts vis-à-vis the application of self-executing treaty law provisions (which would include the ECHR).[45]

One reason for this is perceived to be the influence of debates in the UK. Speaking in 2012, the Dutch politician Frans Timmermans (a former Labour Party MP and Minister for Foreign Affairs, who took up office as Vice-President of the European Commission in November 2014) detected the UK tradition of emphasizing parliamentary sovereignty seeping into Dutch politics, but he argued that 'mixing systems' in such a way could be dangerous.[46] Professor Rick Lawson (University of Leiden) identifies a worrying lack of respect for courts generally—a prevalent notion that 'the will of the people' should have its preferences realized.[47] Roeland Böcker criticizes as 'simplistic' the view expressed by some MPs that courts are constraining their ability to take decisions.[48]

Nevertheless, by 2012, the anti-Strasbourg debate was reaching its saturation point, at which point, suggests Rick Lawson, the Senate and the Ministry of Justice reasserted themselves in support of the Strasbourg Court.[49] Indeed, a number of our interlocutors emphasized the role played, in general terms, by the Senate in standing up for human rights norms.[50] For example, the former European Court Judge, Egbert Myjer, argues that the Senate played a vital role in stemming the unjustified attacks on the Court: there was a long debate which had real impact, leading to the adoption of two motions proposed by senators who were also members of PACE—one by Marie-Louise Bemelmans-Videc in April 2011,[51] urging the Dutch government to stop attacking the Court, and another by Senator Hans Franken in March 2012, calling on the government to observe its obligations under the ECHR.[52] In contrast to the increasingly radical position taken by certain politicians on immigration questions, according to Myjer, the Senate is a bulwark for tolerance, democracy, and human rights.[53]

It is notable that, in spite of some politicians' criticisms seeking to undermine the ECtHR, the Dutch parliament has never *refused* to implement a judgment. For Marie-Louise Bemelmans-Videc (the former Senator and member of the Parliamentary Assembly of the Council of Europe (PACE)), the core Convention values are 'untouchable', as they are fundamentally concerned with protecting minorities against majorities.[54] Roeland Böcker of the Ministry of Foreign Affairs

[45] See also, for example, Stef Blok, Klaas Dijkhoff, and Joost Taverne, 'Verdragen mogen niet langer rechtstreeks werken' ['Treaties Can No Longer Have Direct Effect'], *NRC Handelsblad*, 23 February 2012.

[46] Interview, 13 June 2012.

[47] Interview, 22 March 2012.

[48] Interview, 22 March 2012.

[49] Interview, 22 March 2012.

[50] Marie-Louise Bemelmans-Videc, Interview, 22 March 2012.

[51] See 2.6.2 at n 176.

[52] Egbert Myjer, 'Why Much of the Criticism of the European Court of Human Rights is Unfounded', in Spyridon Flogaitis, Tom Zwart, and Julie Fraser, eds., *The European Court of Human Rights and Its Discontents: Turning Criticism into Strength* (Cheltenham: Edward Elgar Publishing, 2013): 37, 37–8.

[53] Interview, 27 June 2012.

[54] Interview, 22 March 2012.

argues that the appropriate response to the attacks on the Court is to encourage parliamentarians to get more involved with international processes, such as negotiations on draft conventions and the follow up to judgments, rather than closing themselves off from international law.[55] Rick Lawson suggests that if you want to involve parliamentarians in the implementation of judgments, they should be involved at an earlier stage, when the legal issues are being decided by the ECtHR, for example, by the government engaging with parliament as to the line it is going to take in cases in which it intervenes as a third party. That would mean, argues Lawson, that MPs would have more ownership of the jurisprudence.[56]

8.3 Implementation of ECtHR Judgments: The Role of Parliament

The Dutch parliament adopts a cross-cutting approach to human rights work (see 3.4.1). No committee has human rights within its remit; rather, human rights issues are handled by different committees as they arise within their respective mandates. Although, historically, the Dutch parliament was an active player in promoting compliance with international human rights standards (e.g., as an impetus for the Netherlands ratifying the ECHR) more recently the question of human rights implementation has essentially become an executive-driven system. Parliamentary involvement is rather more ad hoc and dependent upon pressing political priorities—for example, when there is pressure from constituents. Frans Timmermans observes that parliamentary involvement tends to be issue-driven and that MPs may 'jump on the bandwagon' (giving the example of MPs supporting women's rights in order to critique Islam). Interviewees at the Dutch section of the International Commission of Jurists (*Nederlands Juristen Comité voor de Mensenrechten* (NJCM)) were unable to cite a single example of parliament pushing for legislation to be *more* faithful to the Convention, rather than advocating for more *restrictive* laws (especially in the field of immigration).[57] Professor Barbara Oomen (Utrecht University) is highly critical that there is so little parliamentary ownership. According to her, MPs do not consider themselves as responsible human rights actors domestically—rather, they see human rights as an 'export product', and as a result they are either ignorant or wilfully neglectful of human rights issues.[58] Oomen has also been disapproving

[55] Interview, 22 March 2012. [56] Interview, 22 March 2012.

[57] Friederycke Haijer, Franka Olujic, Antoine Buyse, and Lize Glas, Interview, 22 March 2012. The NJCM has about 1,000 members (primarily lawyers and jurists). It frequently engages with the Dutch parliament through its reports and bulletins, and provides speakers for events in parliament.

[58] Interview, 12 June 2012. Oomen notes that, historically, there was far more parliamentary involvement in discussion about human rights—for example, the impetus to sign up to the ECHR came from parliament; many Dutch parliamentarians were in favour of the development of a supranational system of fundamental rights, but there was resistance from government. See also Oomen (n 5). Her research reveals that human rights were raised in the House of Representatives more often in 2010 than in 1995, but 73 per cent of those references related to foreign rather than domestic policy, and that human rights are more often mentioned in documents sent to parliament by the government, rather than in parliamentary debates.

of the apparent disconnection between international human rights standards and the nature and level of parliamentary debates (in the context of a discussion about domestic violence):

> What is striking here is that, even where there is a clear relation with international developments and international human rights law and its enforcement, this is not explicated in the policy documents and the parliamentary discussions. Combating domestic violence is presented, in short, as a policy concern, not a response to a state obligation under international human rights law. In the parliamentary discussions the question as to whether the Netherlands could pass the 'Opuz-test'[59] was raised once but never generated a response.[60]

Martin Kuijer of the Ministry of Security and Justice is rather more positive about the parliamentary role, on the basis of the high volume of parliamentary questions submitted to his office. He does acknowledge, however, that MPs' questions are not systematic and that they are not always followed up.[61] Barbara Oomen suggests that the heavy workload faced by individual parliamentarians (whom she describes as 'one-stop-shops') is not conducive to their active engagement with human rights questions: 'This enables the administration to "hide" information by leaving it out of the summaries, or sending it [to] parliament too late for the parliamentarians to read.'[62]

Dr Jan-Peter Loof (Leiden University) underlines the important roles played by both government and civil society in ensuring human rights compliance, as a result of which 'big accidents don't happen'.[63] However, he regrets the fact that there is no real debate about improving 'systems' for human rights compliance and the prevailing assumption that informal channels will suffice; if the culture changes, he warns, there may be nothing to fall back on. Kuijer agrees that parliaments often have a tendency to put the onus for providing a sufficient human rights structure exclusively on the government, without contemplating how to increase its own responsibility in this regard.[64]

Interviewees at the NJCM suggested that once a judgment has been issued by the ECtHR, both the executive and civil society act more quickly than parliament in respect of its implementation.[65] Roeland Böcker confirms that the first opportunity for parliamentary involvement is to raise questions, sometimes even within a few days of an adverse judgment, but parliamentarians' engagement is far from systematic. Almost invariably the relevant minister will be asked what steps will be taken, to which the usual response—at least with regards to general measures—is that it is too early to say.[66] Our interlocutors told us that, in essence, the legislative initiative lies with the government; MPs *can* introduce bills but rarely do.[67]

[59] A reference to the ECtHR judgment of *Opuz v Turkey*, No. 33401/02, 9 June 2009—a leading precedent on how states should respond to domestic violence.
[60] Oomen (n 5) 17.
[61] Interview, 23 March 2012.
[62] Oomen (n 5) 39.
[63] Interview, 22 March 2012.
[64] Interview, 23 March 2012.
[65] Friederycke Haijer, Franka Olujic, Antoine Buyse, and Lize Glas, Interview, 22 March 2012.
[66] Interview, 22 March 2012.
[67] Laurien Koster, Interview, 23 March 2012.

Important ECtHR judgments are translated by the Council of State or by the government, but they are usually only published *after* the Government has submitted a bill to parliament (which allows the government to take a position first). However, translations of the judgments are not in fact needed by the courts, which are able in practice to consider and apply them in their original English or French.

Jan-Peter Loof suggests that, within the Dutch parliament's cross-cutting approach to human rights oversight, the Justice Committee is in practice the main venue for discussion of human rights issues in parliament, but argues that the quality of the discussion is not high.

There is no parliamentary scrutiny of action plans, as such (see 2.5.2) (nor by the Council of State). Although actions plans are not at present sent to parliament systematically, Roeland Böcker confirms that they are not secret and that he would not object to their being circulated to parliament. However, he is not convinced of the *need* to do so, since parliament is by definition involved in legislative measures taken as a result of a Court judgment.[68]

A number of our interviewees describe the more sophisticated approach of the Senate to human rights questions, and its more institutionalized and reflective methodologies (including, e.g., an annual human rights debate). That contrasts with the position of the House of Representatives—although it has more political clout, its debates on human rights issues are often short and formulaic. Jasper Krommendijk has suggested that the perfunctory nature of the human rights scrutiny performed by the lower house is attributable to the limited legal expertise, the considerable turnover of MPs and accordingly their limited experience, the absence of any collective or institutional memory, and the limited popularity of involvement in the technical scrutiny of legislation.[69] Eva Rieter has argued that a Dutch parliamentary committee should be given a direct mandate for involvement in the implementation process, by creating a forum and establishing a process for consultation between victims and their legal representatives, and government and civil society representatives, as regards both individual and general measures which need to be implemented following a judgment of the ECtHR.[70]

The pre-legislative scrutiny process in the Netherlands is considered to be effective, although it is the Council of State which has the pre-eminent role in this, rather than parliament. The Council of State provides a non-binding advisory opinion to parliament on all draft bills, to which the government is required to respond.[71] Martin Kuijer suggests that the Justice Committee in both houses 'place considerable emphasis on compliance with human rights instruments like the Convention' when examining draft legislation, although there is no specific

[68] Interview, 22 March 2012. [69] Krommendijk (n 42) 76–7.

[70] Eva Rieter, 'Het EHRM ontlasten: de rol van de nationale parlementen bij het toezicht op de naleving van het EVRM' ['Unburdening the ECtHR: The Role of National Parliaments in Monitoring Compliance with the ECHR'] in Ashley Terlouw and Janneke Gerards, eds, *Amici Curiae: Adviezen aan het Europees Hof voor de Rechten van de Mens* (Nijmegen: Wolf Legal Publishers, 2012): 1.

[71] However, Gerritjan van Oven notes that the Council of State does not review the compatibility of *amendments* which are tabled to bills: Interview, 2 August 2012.

parliamentary procedure for the verification of the compatibility of draft laws with the Convention.[72] Kuijer also emphasizes the specific instructions to drafters within ministries to ensure conformity with international law, and the requirement that explanatory memoranda should contain a justification of the legislation in question. The NJCM also frequently submits opinions to parliament on the human rights compatibility of draft legislation.[73] Marie-Louise Bemelmans-Videc evaluates the process in positive terms—the Senate in particular maintains a critical eye—and there is generally a high degree of consensus.[74] Frans Timmermans agrees that the Council of State's advice is generally accepted.[75]

A number of our interlocutors suggested that the parliamentary debate itself frequently adds little or nothing to the process: save for a small number of particular senators, parliamentarians lack adequate knowledge to scrutinize compatibility with human rights norms.

In some instances, there will be a clear 'political dimension' to questions of implementation which may influence the nature or the timing of the reactions by the various domestic players. In the often-contested field of immigration, in particular, there have been heated debates about *how* to implement a judgment—whether to do so expansively or restrictively. Some cases, such as *Salah Sheekh v Netherlands*[76] (in which the Court found that the proposed expulsion of the applicant to Somalia would violate Article 3 ECHR), may be seen as controversial and receive a high media profile.[77] As a result, they may provoke many parliamentary questions even though there may be no legislative implications.[78]

Martin Kuijer argues that many judgments do not require changes to the domestic law, but when legislative amendments are required, it is often the interested groups that are most active in pushing for change—as an example he cites the involvement of the journalists' associations in the aftermath of the Grand Chamber judgment in the *Sanoma* case[79] as regards the disclosure of journalistic sources.[80] Gerritjan van Oven, a former member of the House of Representatives, argues that the question of the *cost* of implementation will often also be an important consideration for MPs.[81]

8.3.1 Provision of legal advice

Gerritjan van Oven ventures: 'You can't expect parliamentarians to have a regular overview of the Court. It will come to them through the press, practitioners, voters, or channels from ministries.'[82]

[72] Kuijer (n 17) 303. [73] Kuijer (n 17) 303. [74] Interview, 22 March 2012.
[75] Interview, 13 June 2012. [76] No. 1948/04, 11 January 2007.
[77] Kuijer ((n 17) 302) suggests that the Government took a 'loyal stance' as regards the *Salah Sheekh* judgment, although he states that the then opposition leader, Mark Rutte, argued that the judgment should be ignored.
[78] Roeland Böcker, Interview, 22 March 2012.
[79] *Sanoma Uitgevers B.V. v Netherlands*, No. 38224/03, 14 September 2010 [GC].
[80] Interview, 23 March 2012. [81] Interview, 2 August 2012.
[82] Interview, 2 August 2012.

As parliamentarians' knowledge and understanding of human rights is often limited,[83] interviewees underlined the importance of the need for the effective provision of advice. Interlocutors noted that parliamentarians often seek information from multiple sources, including academics, NGOs, the Council of State, the Netherlands Institute for Human Rights (the country's national human rights institution), and the bureau of legislation in parliament, and a number underlined that there is no shortage of advice.[84] However, Martin Kuijer acknowledges the benefits of having a centralized focal point for such advice and information—as is provided, for example, by the Joint Committee on Human Rights (JCHR) in the UK (see 7.3.1).[85] Jan-Peter Loof is concerned that MPs have to trust the accuracy of government information because the majority have few staff with legal expertise.[86]

8.3.2 Human rights as a 'cross-cutting' issue in parliament

Differing views are expressed by our interviewees as to the pros and cons of attempting to 'mainstream' human rights across parliament or establishing a specialist human rights parliamentary committee (see 3.4.2). NJCM representatives acknowledge the arguments in support of a specialized committee (such as improved awareness raising), but also note that such a committee would have no 'partner' ministry and could be used by other committees to buck responsibility. They are in favour of having greater systematization (such as an annual parliamentary debate), because otherwise there was a danger that agendas would be set by individuals' personal 'hobby horses'.[87] The former Dutch judge in Strasbourg, Egbert Myjer, also expresses concern that a specialized human rights committee would become 'an excuse committee': 'People would say we have a human rights committee, so we no longer need to be involved.'[88]

There is some support for an equivalent body to the JCHR model in the UK (see 7.3.1), especially if it were properly staffed.[89] Martin Kuijer acknowledges that the Dutch system lacks a specialized human rights impact assessment procedure comparable to that of the JCHR, but he argues that the more mainstreamed Dutch model can be equally effective.[90] Laurien Koster (the Chair of the Netherlands Institute for Human Rights, and a former President of its predecessor body, the Equal Treatment Commission) agrees that mainstreaming is the 'ideal', but also acknowledges that a specialized committee would be beneficial because the particular

[83] For example, Gerritjan van Oven (Interview, 2 August 2012) noted that the majority of parliamentarians are not jurists.

[84] Marie-Louise Bemelmans-Videc, Interview, 22 March 2012; Frans Timmermans, Interview, 13 June 2012.

[85] Interview, 23 March 2012.

[86] Interview, 22 March 2012.

[87] Friederycke Haijer, Franka Olujic, Antoine Buyse, and Lize Glas, Interview, 22 March 2012.

[88] Interview, 27 June 2012.

[89] Marie-Louise Bemelmans-Videc, Interview, 22 March 2012; Jan-Peter Loof, Interview, 22 March 2012; Frans Timmermans, Interview, 13 June 2012.

[90] Interview, 23 March 2012.

human rights aspects of certain issues, such as health and pensions, can get lost in the discussions of the wider policy committees.[91]

There is no parliamentary debate of the Ministry of Justice's annual human rights report (see 8.4 below), a situation which Gerritjan van Oven, the former member of the House of Representatives (and subsequently a Court of Appeals judge in the Hague), describes as deplorable, and a lost opportunity to make the government accountable.[92] A number of interviewees point to the inevitable delays involved with a report produced annually, which means that the process is too slow to ensure timely debate; MPs often get information about Dutch judgments more quickly from the media and other sources.[93] The 'added value' of the report is queried, given that follow up is rare and individual judgments can be debated separately. Roeland Böcker acknowledges that the Senate refers to the annual report, but notes that it rarely leads to questions in either House and is never debated as such.[94] Writing in 2015, Martin Kuijer ventured that the annual reports 'may prove a useful tool, facilitating parliamentary debate on Convention-related matters'. [95] This observation points to the potential, if not proven utility of the reporting exercise.

8.3.3 The role of members of the Parliamentary Assembly of the Council of Europe

There are divergent views about the contributions made by the Dutch parliamentarians who also sit on the Parliamentary Assembly. For example, as members of the PACE Committee on Legal Affairs and Human Rights, Dutch politicians such as Marie-Louise Bemelmans-Videc and Klaas de Vries (a former member of both the House of Representatives and Senate, and former Home Affairs Minister), have acted as rapporteurs in respect of the Committee's work on the ECHR and the implementation of ECtHR judgments.[96]

Some interlocutors suggest that PACE members were always better informed than their parliamentary colleagues[97] and were more 'Europe-oriented'.[98] PACE delegates are seen as an important pro-Strasbourg voice, especially amongst senators who tend to have more time than their counterparts in the House of Representatives and who are not subject to the additional pressures of seeking re-election.[99] Bemelmans-Videc also suggests that, within the Dutch PACE delegation, to a

[91] Interview, 23 March 2012.

[92] Interview, 2 August 2012.

[93] Rick Lawson, Interview, 22 March 2012; Laurien Koster, Interview, 23 March 2012; Barbara Oomen, Interview, 12 June 2012.

[94] Interview, 22 March 2012.

[95] Kuijer (n 17) 304.

[96] See, for example: PACE, Committee on Legal Affairs and Human Rights, Report, Guaranteeing the authority and effectiveness of the European Convention on Human Rights, Doc. 12811, 3 January 2012 (Rapporteur: Marie-Louise Bemelmans-Videc); PACE, Committee on Legal Affairs and Human Rights, Report, Implementation of judgments of the European Court of Human Rights, Doc. 13864, 9 September 2015, (Rapporteur: Klaas de Vries).

[97] Gerritjan van Oven, Interview, 2 August 2012. Marie-Louise Bemelmans-Videc (Interview, 22 March 2012) stresses the importance of the knowledge, integrity, and commitment of the staff of the Committee on Legal Affairs and Human Rights of the Parliamentary Assembly.

[98] Laurien Koster, Interview, 23 March 2012.

[99] Frans Timmermans, Interview, 13 June 2012; Barbara Oomen, Interview, 12 June 2012.

certain extent human rights issues raised in Strasbourg would transcend domestic political differences: 'Everyone was always very independent of their political colour.... These are such vital, crucial fundamental rights that we all stand up for [them], no matter whether you are on the left or right.'[100]

However, Rick Lawson argues that membership of PACE is viewed by some as being esoteric and low profile.[101] Laurien Koster believes that it is easier for parliamentarians to be pro-human rights at the more 'abstract' level of PACE, or the European Parliament, but rather more difficult in specific national situations, as a result of party pressures and coalition arithmetic (see 2.6.2).[102]

8.4 Implementation of ECtHR Judgments: The Role of the Executive

There are three Dutch Ministries which are primarily concerned with liaison with the ECtHR and handling cases: Foreign Affairs, Justice, and Interior. The Ministry of Foreign Affairs acts as the primary interface with the Court; the substance of the cases usually relates to the Ministry of Security and Justice, and, to a lesser extent, other ministries and offices. In practice, senior officials at the Ministry of Foreign Affairs and the Ministry of Security and Justice work very closely, sharing or dividing specific responsibilities.[103]

Since 1996, the Ministry of Justice has produced an annual report to parliament on pertinent case law of the ECtHR. Since 2006 the Ministry's report has included commentary on the supervision of the execution of judgments, and since 2009 it has incorporated discussion of judgments delivered against other states which have implications for the Netherlands.[104] The reports also cover cases in which the Netherlands has intervened as a third party (see 8.2). Whenever an MP needs more specialized technical advice (e.g., on Convention-related matters, mostly in the course of initiating their own bill) they may call upon the Ministry of Justice who will, as a rule, agree that one of its civil servants will assist the MP on these matters.[105]

Interviewees at the NJCM recall that there had been limited dissemination by the government as regards UN human rights materials (such as government reports to UN treaty monitoring bodies or UN bodies' concluding observations). Accordingly, the NJCM raised this with parliament, which resulted in a parliamentary resolution

[100] Interview, 22 March 2012. [101] Interview, 22 March 2012.

[102] Interview, 23 March 2012.

[103] Roeland Böcker, Interview, 22 March 2012; Martin Kuijer, Interview, 23 March 2012. A number of our interlocutors suggested that Dutch officials have been very visible within the Council of Europe arena, where they have 'punched above their weight': Rick Lawson, Interview, 22 March 2012; Jan-Peter Loof, Interview, 22 March 2012.

[104] Since 2010, the reports have also analysed reasoned inadmissibility decisions in Dutch cases and those cases which have been struck out.

[105] Martin Kuijer, Interview, 23 March 2012.

obliging the government to share such materials with parliament (and this also ensured that the reports would be more publicly accessible).[106]

Roeland Böcker suggests that, even though the annual reports on international human rights case law are never as such discussed in parliament, overall there is a 'rich interaction' between the government and parliament in relation to both Dutch and non-Dutch cases.[107] Martin Kuijer explains that MPs' questions about particular cases will usually amount to a 'quick response from the political arena'. Such interactions may take place very quickly after a judgment—in the case of *Salduz v Turkey* (concerning a detainee's right of access to a lawyer in police custody; see 8.2). Kuijer recalls that, within a few days of the decision, the Minister of Justice acknowledged that the Dutch practice was not in conformity with the ECHR and said that a draft bill would therefore be presented to parliament. He also notes that MPs have also asked questions about other non-Dutch cases (such as the 'Abu Qatada case' (*Othman v UK*[108]), *Sufi and Elmi v UK*,[109] and *M.S.S. v Belgium and Greece*[110]).[111] According to Kuijer, MPs of all hues have come to realize that the ECHR can be a powerful political weapon—a way of building an argument—as the authority of Court and its nuanced jurisprudence are widely recognized.[112]

Both Erik Jurgens (the Dutch politician and jurist, and a former PACE rapporteur on the implementation of ECtHR judgments) and Rick Lawson advocate in favour of an improved system of inter-ministerial/departmental co-ordination (at civil servant level), to push matters ahead even if the relevant minister is recalcitrant. They note that there is such a committee for European Union affairs but not for the Strasbourg Court.[113]

8.5 The Netherlands Institute for Human Rights

Established in October 2012, the Netherlands Institute for Human Rights (*College voor de Rechten van de Mens* (NIHR)) is an independent, statutory body with a very broad human rights mandate, whose roles include providing advice to public authorities on human rights issues, conducting investigations, publishing thematic reports, and providing information to the general public.[114] The NIHR was established to be the Dutch national human rights institution, and to attain 'A' status in accordance with the Paris Principles, which it was indeed conferred with in 2014.[115]

[106] Friederycke Haijer, Franka Olujic, Antoine Buyse, and Lize Glas, Interview, 22 March 2012.
[107] Interview, 22 March 2012. [108] No. 8139/09, 17 January 2012.
[109] Nos. 8319/07 and 11449/07, 28 June 2011. [110] See 8.2 at n 34.
[111] Interview, 23 March 2012. [112] Interview, 23 March 2012.
[113] Rick Lawson, Interview, 22 March 2012; Erik Jurgens, Interview, 23 March 2012.
[114] See <http://www.mensenrechten.nl/>. It is the successor body to the Equal Treatment Commission.
[115] Explanatory Memorandum, Establishment of the Netherlands Institute for Human Rights (Netherlands Institute for Human Rights Act), Appendix 2 to ref. nr. 2011-2000054729, House of Representatives of the States General 2009–2010, session 32 467. See also Netherlands Institute for Human Rights, *Annual Report 2014* (2015) 7.

Its statutory duties include: advising on acts, bills, orders in council, draft orders in council, ministerial orders, and drafts of ministerial orders relating (directly or indirectly) to human rights, and pressing for the ratification, implementation, and observance of human rights treaties.[116] Its strategic objectives include ensuring that the government, parliament, organizations, and individuals take active responsibility in relation to human rights.[117]

Speaking in 2012, Laurien Koster (the first President of the NIHR) notes that the Institute considers it does have a role in educating and informing parliamentarians, because the concept of human rights is still seen as an 'export product' relevant to faraway places and because many MPs do not fully understand human rights principles.[118] In her foreword to the NIHR's 2014 Annual Report, Koster made this point emphatically:

> Are human rights solely an issue outside the Netherlands? This annual report proves the contrary. During the past year the Dutch debate was dominated by racism, discrimination, the accommodation of asylum seekers who have been denied refuge, ... and the decentralisation of government duties to municipalities. The Institute's 50 recommendations to the Government also confirm the need for constant attention to human rights issues in the Netherlands.[119]

According to Koster, the main priority of the NIHR is more general awareness raising about human rights standards, rather than to engage MPs specifically in relation to ECtHR judgments.[120] However, the NIHR's annual report to parliament includes analysis of measures taken in response to judgments. Koster believes that the NIHR can be especially useful in improving the *speed* of implementation—it can take a role similar to that of a parliamentary committee. She would also welcome being informed in advance about proposed governmental third-party interventions at the Court.[121]

8.6 Monitoring and Implementing Judgments against Other States

One of the significant strengths of the domestic legal and political system in the Netherlands is an acceptance of the relevance and applicability of non-Dutch decisions from Strasbourg (see 2.1.1). As regards the courts, Gerards and Fleuren have argued that they 'generally accept the *res interpretata* of the ECtHR's judgments. They usually do not distinguish between judgments against the Netherlands and judgments rendered against other states, but generally accept that all the Court's precedents have equal interpretative force'.[122]

[116] See, respectively, sections 5 and 3(g) of the Netherlands Institute for Human Rights Act 2011.

[117] See the NIHR's 'mission and ambition' at <http://www.mensenrechten.nl/mission-and-ambition>.

[118] Interview, 23 March 2012.

[119] Netherlands Institute for Human Rights (n 115) 4.

[120] Interview, 23 March 2012.

[121] Interview, 23 March 2012.

[122] Gerards and Fleuren (n 3) 237.

At the executive level, Rick Lawson notes that there is an inter-departmental committee reviewing judgments from the Court of Justice of the European Union and their implications for the Netherlands, but there is no equivalent review of human rights decisions. There is also no formal structure within parliament for it to be alerted to judgments against other Council of Europe states which may have a bearing on the equivalent situation in the Netherlands.[123] However, in practice, Martin Kuijer explains that both he and the government agent's office consider themselves to be responsible for tracking Strasbourg case law for implications for the Netherlands, and when an important new decision is published they will inform the ministry which has the relevant policy responsibility and other executive agencies.[124]

Non-Dutch cases have made an impact in recent years in a number of areas, such as the length of proceedings cases (from, inter alia, Italy and Poland).[125] Marie-Louise Bemelmans-Videc recalls that the ECtHR judgments of *M.S.S. v Belgium and Greece*[126] (concerning the treatment of asylum-seekers), and *Salduz v Turkey*[127] (concerning the right of detainees to have prompt access to a lawyer; see 8.2) excited a significant level of political debate, and that the relevant minister was questioned about how the cases would be implemented.[128] Rick Lawson agrees that the case of *Salduz* made headlines in the Netherlands and was picked up very quickly by multiple actors.[129] Following *Salduz*, it was not necessarily clear to the Dutch authorities precisely what the Strasbourg standards required, but in any event the Dutch judiciary took the initiative to tell the prosecuting authorities what they believed was needed. Lawson suggests that the 'correct' implementation of *Salduz* has been an ongoing process of trial and error.[130]

8.7 Relationship between Parliament and Council of Europe Bodies

Frans Timmermans argues that the Council of Europe needs more active political communication[131] and Rick Lawson suggests that more could be done to ensure that national parliaments and national judges are aware of the most important 'must read' judgments.[132] Gerritjan van Oven argues that both the Court and the Committee of Ministers should invite national MPs, or their staff, to Strasbourg, to help foster a better understanding of the Convention system.[133]

[123] Interview, 22 March 2012. [124] Interview, 23 March 2012.

[125] As regards the changes introduced in the Dutch system as a result of the case-law on length of proceedings, see Martin Kuijer, 'The Right to a Fair Trial and the Council of Europe's Efforts to Ensure Effective Remedies on a Domestic Level for Excessively Lengthy Proceedings', *Human Rights Law Review* 13(4) (2013): 777, 791–2.

[126] See 8.2 at n 34. [127] See 8.2 at n 32. [128] Interview, 22 March 2012.

[129] Interview, 22 March 2012. [130] Interview, 22 March 2012.

[131] Interview, 13 June 2012. [132] Interview, 22 March 2012.

[133] Interview, 2 August 2012.

Lawson believes that parliamentarians *should* be incentivized to debate human rights considerations, so as to earn a wider 'margin of appreciation' (see 4.5), but notes that they often resent the very idea of being reviewed by a court. Martin Kuijer notes that in defending a Strasbourg case, the government will always review any relevant parliamentary debate: a debate which explicitly balances rights and recognizes proportionality will 'help a great deal'. Kuijer also believes that the Court's acknowledgement of domestic debates would, in addition, help gain domestic-level acceptance of judgments.[134]

Marie-Louise Bemelmans-Videc is supportive of the notion of 'earned deference' and she would also welcome advisory opinions from the ECtHR which might prevent new cases from arising.[135] The former PACE rapporteur Erik Jurgens, however, advises that the Court should be very careful about commenting on the *quality* of parliamentary consideration of an issue, unless there has been *no* debate at all—he believes that judges should presume that legislators are trying to abide by the rule of law.[136]

As discussed at 2.3, it is arguable that the facilitation or incentivization of greater parliamentary involvement is strengthened by the Court's developing tendencies to show a greater degree of precision in its judgments as regards measures of redress, and to indicate minimum 'general measures' that need to be taken in order to comply with a judgment where a systemic human rights problem has been identified. Such 'indications' or 'recommendations' (often developed by the Court invoking Article 46 ECHR) are likely to aid parliamentarians' understanding of what the Court and the Convention require.

8.8 Conclusion

The positive impact of the jurisprudence of the ECtHR on legal and policy developments in the Netherlands has been evident since the 1970s and 1980s. Consequently, it became a mainstream element of Dutch political debate, as MPs' realized its political potency. However, in recent years, there has been a significant political backlash against the Strasbourg Court (which reached its zenith in 2012), riding on a tide of populist anti-European, anti-immigration, and anti-judicial policies, which questioned the constraints perceived to be imposed by the Court on the democratically elected parliament. After 2012, however, the wave of populism was turned back, with the Senate taking a pivotal role in reasserting the primacy of governmental obligations to comply with human rights norms.

Nevertheless, matters of human rights implementation remain essentially controlled and dominated by the executive in the Netherlands; parliamentary involvement in human rights questions is not systematic, but tends to be ad hoc, perfunctory, and overly dependent upon prevalent political priorities. There is a

[134] Interview, 23 March 2012.

[135] Interview, 22 March 2012.

[136] Interview, 23 March 2012.

greater level of systematized attention in the Senate, but even its annual human rights debate may not have sufficiently discernible, tangible impacts.

One legitimate response to concerns expressed by some parliamentarians about the perceived expansionism of the ECtHR would be to invest in giving parliamentarians a greater sense of responsibility in, and for, the implementation process, which would then act as a counterweight to ill-informed discussion. The human rights scrutiny and reporting roles played by civil society, and the Netherlands Institute for Human Rights, have also exposed a worrying viewpoint which is all too prevalent amongst parliamentarians—that human rights are still considered to be an 'export product'. If parliament has relatively recently woken up to the extent of the influence of the Court, it should in turn become more active in the processes relating to the translation of Convention standards into Dutch law and policy. This chapter has shown that parliamentary involvement may sometimes have a 'negative' effect, in the sense that MPs may not be seeking to develop and enhance human rights standards, as such, but our interlocutors were clear that that is no argument against keeping parliamentarians informed and active. As Barbara Oomen has argued, if human rights implementation is treated purely as a 'government project', it becomes technocratic, erodes support, and fuels ignorance.[137] If the attitude of the executive is to keep parliament at arm's length, MPs will not understand and engage with the human rights system and they are also unlikely to see the human rights dimensions of broader policy questions. Clearly, where 'general measures' are required in response to a judgment, or a systemic problem has been identified, parliament should play a significant role in establishing the legal and policy response. We detected, however, no clear consensus in favour of either maintaining the Dutch parliament's cross-cutting approach, in the hope of achieving an effective 'mainstreaming' of human rights across parliament, or establishing a specialist human rights parliamentary committee. Arguably, it would be beneficial to introduce a practice of holding a parliamentary debate in response to the Ministry of Justice's annual human rights report. Although they appear to have had limited discernible impact to date, the Dutch annual reports are the most comprehensive of any in the Council of Europe (including coverage of other states, and inadmissibility decisions) and are therefore regarded as a model.

Referring to Article 1 ECHR (laying down an obligation on states to secure the Convention rights within their jurisdiction), Egbert Myjer, the former Dutch judge at the ECtHR argues that 'it should be the task of parliamentarians to remind the government of its own promises—it's all about promises'.[138]

[137] Interview, 12 June 2012.

[138] Interview, 27 June 2012. Egbert Myjer referred in that respect to Egbert Myjer and Peter Kempees, *Jack and the Solemn Promise, A Cautionary Tale* (Nijmegen: Wolf Legal Publishers, 2010).

9

Germany

9.1 The Constitutional, Legal, and Political Landscape

As a mature democracy with a strong domestic human rights culture, founded on the Basic Law (*Grundgesetz*) which incorporates rights similar to those enshrined in the European Convention on Human Rights (ECHR or 'the Convention'), as Christian Tomuschat has noted, Germany has not generally had difficulties in complying with the Convention.[1] One of the core pillars of the German constitutional system is the Federal Constitutional Court (*Bundesverfassungsgericht* ('BVerfGE')) which was established in 1951 (in the city of Karlsruhe), half of whose judges are elected by the *Bundestag* and half by the *Bundesrat*.[2] In accordance with the Basic Law, the role of the Federal Constitutional Court is to assess the constitutionality of laws and the actions of the legislature, executive, and judiciary. The Federal Constitutional Court has the power to annul domestic legislation if it is not in compliance with the Basic Law or national court decisions (although it does not have the power to award pecuniary damages, unlike the European Court of Human Rights ('ECtHR' or 'the Court')). It also has the power to create temporary 'legislation' through an edict, in order to prevent lacunae in the law once a statute is declared unconstitutional. The Basic Law and the Federal Constitutional Court have established a sophisticated level of domestic human rights protection. For example, the authors of the JURISTRAS project argued that,

> ... the Federal Constitutional Court plays an integral role in protecting, promoting, and developing human rights ... Public opinion and politicians highly acknowledge and respect judgments made by the Federal Constitutional Court, even if the findings are received controversially. Over the last decades, the Federal Constitutional Court has grown into the role of a safeguard for human rights and fundamental rights contained in the German Basic Law or Federal Constitution.[3]

[1] Christian Tomuschat, 'The Effects of the Judgments of the European Court of Human Rights According to the German Constitutional Court', *German Law Journal* 11 (2010): 513, 514–15.

[2] In both chambers, a two-thirds majority is required.

[3] Christoph Gusy and Sebastian Müller, *Strasbourg Court Jurisprudence and Human Rights in Germany: An Overview of Litigation, Implementation and Domestic Reform*, JURISTRAS report, October 2007.

The Federal Constitutional Court has confirmed that all state bodies are subject to the binding effect of Strasbourg judgments. Exceptionally, state entities may deviate from an ECtHR judgment when its implementation would mean that the Basic Law is violated, but, as Gusy and Müller have noted, the similar scope of the Basic Law and the European Convention 'excludes almost completely any possible situation in which a deviation might be justifiable'.[4] Elisabeth Lambert Abdelgawad and Anne Weber argue that the human rights protections within the German domestic system are even higher than those at the European level.[5] Accordingly, Tomuschat has suggested that 'little is left for correction by the Strasbourg Court'.[6] Speaking at the opening of the judicial year in Strasbourg in January 2014, Andreas Voßkuhle, the President of the Federal Constitutional Court, suggested that, on occasions, the Basic Law provides a higher level of protection than the Convention, citing as an example the case law relating to the bar on successive adoption by same-sex couples.[7]

The principle of judicial review of legislation is clearly a very well-established element of the German constitutional system.[8] Nevertheless, Voßkuhle argues that democratic principles are at the heart of the Constitutional Court's jurisdiction: 'German constitutional jurisdiction was born of the democratic idea of the

[4] Christoph Gusy and Sebastian Müller, 'The Interrelationship between Domestic Judicial Mechanisms and the Strasbourg Court Rulings in Germany', in Dia Anagnostou, ed., *The European Court of Human Rights: Implementing Strasbourg's Judgments on Domestic Policy* (Edinburgh: Edinburgh University Press, 2013): 27, 32.

[5] Elisabeth Lambert Abdelgawad and Anne Weber, 'The Reception Process in France and Germany', in Helen Keller and Alec Stone Sweet, eds., *A Europe of Rights: The Impact of the ECHR on National Legal Systems* (Oxford: Oxford University Press, 2008): 107, 112. They also suggest (at 136) that 'the idea that rights protection under the national system is better, compared with the ECHR, is widespread, the view being that the substantive guarantees of the Basic Law are in general wider in scope and more effectively monitored than the rights enshrined in the ECHR'.

[6] Tomuschat (n 1) 515. Tomuschat cites four cases where Strasbourg notably found Convention violations, though the Federal Constitutional Court had not: *Vogt v Germany*, No. 17851/91, 26 September 1995 [GC] (concerning a ban on civil servants' involvement in politics); *Von Hannover v Germany*, No. 59320/00, 24 June 2004 (concerning the publication by the German press of photographs of Princess Caroline of Monaco); *Brauer v Germany*, No. 3545/04, 28 May 2009 (concerning the rights of children born outside marriage); and *M v Germany*, No. 19359/04, 17 December 2009 (concerning preventive detention).

[7] Professor Dr Andreas Voßkuhle, 'Pyramid or Mobile?—Human Rights Protection by the European Constitutional Courts', Speech on the occasion of the opening of the judicial year, 31 January 2014; ECtHR, *Annual Report 2014* (2015): 39, 43. In *X and Others v Austria*, No. 19010/07, 19 February 2013 [GC], the ECtHR held that there had been no violation of Article 14 ECHR (prohibition of discrimination) taken in conjunction with Article 8 ECHR (right to respect for family life) when comparing the situation of the unmarried, same-sex applicant couple with married opposite-sex couples, whereas the Federal Constitutional Court found that the bar on successive adoption by registered (same-sex) civil partners constituted a violation of the principle of equality before the law (BVerfGE, judgment of the First Division (Senat) of 19 February 2013, 1 BvL 1/11, NJW 2013: 847, 855). Nevertheless, we would note that in *X and Others v Austria*, the ECtHR *did* find a violation of Article 14 ECHR together with Article 8 ECHR (by ten votes to seven) as a result of the difference in treatment between the applicant couple and an *unmarried* opposite-sex couple.

[8] Between 1951 and 2014, the Federal Constitutional Court declared 697 pieces of legislation to be unconstitutional: Speech by Dr Almut Wittling-Vogel, 'Parliaments and the European Court of Human Rights', report of conference organized by Middlesex University and the Helsinki Foundation for Human Rights at the Senate, Warsaw, 12 May 2015 ('Warsaw Conference Report') 7.

primacy of the Constitution, whose fundamental rights bind all state authorities as directly applicable and enforceable law.'[9]

Voßkuhle has described an internationalized constitutional system for the protection of fundamental rights in Germany, with a Federal Constitutional Court whose jurisdiction has been 'embedded in a sphere of international and European references'.[10]

A legal culture in Germany with strong rights protection provided by the Basic Law[11] and the Federal Constitutional Court has therefore meant a lower profile for the ECtHR, but at the same time, the prevailing domestic rights culture has ensured the *acceptability* of the Court. Eckart Klein perceives no fundamental or widespread public criticism of the role of the Court (other than what arises from time to time resulting from individual judgments).[12] Indeed, Scribner and Slagter argue that the Court is accepted 'to such a degree that it is not at all contentious'.[13] The German government lawyer who handles the cases brought against Germany at the Strasbourg Court, Dr Almut Wittling-Vogel, concurs with such a view. According to Dr Wittling-Vogel,[14] there is little or no culture of hostility towards the ECtHR for being perceived to be too interventionist—and the reason for that is the prevailing practice of the Federal Constitutional Court which can issue judgments which are very prescriptive towards parliament, setting down in detail what follow-up steps are required, and stipulating time limits. Wittling-Vogel acknowledges that parliamentarians may not like certain 'prescriptive' judgments, whether from Karlsruhe or Strasbourg, but they know that there is no way to avoid them and they must respond. Therefore, she believes that attitudes are more conducive to compliance than in countries which have no comparable judgments at the domestic level.

Legal and constitutional debate in Germany has tended to focus more on the respective powers of the European Courts (both the ECtHR and the Court of

[9] Andreas Voßkuhle, 'Multilevel Cooperation of the European Constitutional Courts: *Der Europäische Verfassungsgerichtsverbund*', *European Constitutional Law Review* 6 (2010): 175, 178–9.

[10] Voßkuhle (n 9) 179.

[11] Eckart Klein has suggested that the Basic Law 'tries to draw legal consequences from the experiences of the first half of the 20th century, the two World Wars, the failed Weimar Republic, the totalitarian Nazi regime based on excessive nationalism, racism and a complete denial of the individual's dignity, finally culminating in the Holocaust. By contrast, the Basic Law founds the German State on the respect for the dignity and fundamental rights of all human beings, on organisational principles such as democracy, separation of powers and the rule of law, and on the repudiation of nationalistic exclusivity by declared openness to international law and the international community': Eckart Klein, 'Germany', in Janneke Gerards and Joseph Fleuren, eds., *Implementation of the European Convention on Human Rights and of the Judgments of the ECtHR in National Case-Law: A Comparative Analysis* (Antwerp-Oxford-Portland: Intersentia, 2014): 185.

[12] Klein (n 11) 211.

[13] Druscilla Scribner and Tracy Slagter, 'Domestic Institutions and Supranational Human Rights Adjudication: The ECtHR and the IACtHR Compared', ASPA 2009 Toronto meeting paper, 20. See also Başak Çalı, Anne Koch, and Nicola Bruch, *The Legitimacy of the European Court of Human Rights: The View from the Ground* (Department of Political Science, University College London, 2011) 28–9.

[14] Interview, 20 March 2012. Dr Wittling-Vogel is the Representative of the Federal Government for Matters Relating to Human Rights, and Director of Ministry's Directorate-General IV (Constitutional, Administrative, EU, and International Public Law).

Justice of the European Union (CJEU)) and the Federal Constitutional Court,[15] than on any question of conflict between courts and parliament. Reflecting on the respective roles of the ECtHR, the CJEU, and the Federal Constitutional Court, Andreas Voßkuhle has described a 'multilevel cooperation' and a 'composite multilevel structure of constitutional jurisdictions which entertain complementary and cooperative relationships'.[16] A 2009 study by Druscilla Scribner and Tracy Slagter demonstrated that there was far greater awareness amongst members of the *Bundestag* of the judgments of the Federal Constitutional Court, as compared to those of the ECtHR.[17] They also suggested that the parties in government had little incentive to refer to the ECtHR, because of its lower status and issues of timing:

> ... because there is little risk that a current government policy will be brought before the ECtHR during the legislative session, a government might be less likely to consider the ECtHR's jurisprudence if it thinks the costs of compliance are too high and the chances of being reprimanded are too low. Indeed, because the ... Court's rulings do not have direct effect in Germany, there is even less incentive for the government to consider the Court too seriously because there are virtually no ramifications for not doing so.[18]

However, Scribner and Slagter draw a distinct contrast with the position of smaller political parties outside government, for whom the Court and Convention 'can become part of the legislative toolkit for achieving policy outcomes', citing in particular the question of partnership rights for gays and lesbians.[19]

[15] See, for example, Tomuschat's discussion of the *Görgülü* case (*Görgülü v Germany*, No. 74969/01, 26 February 2004): Tomuschat (n 1) 520–6. See also Mads Andenas and Eirik Bjorge, 'National Implementation of ECHR Rights', in Andreas Føllesdal, Birgit Peters, and Geir Ulfstein, eds., *Constituting Europe: The European Court of Human Rights in a National, European and Global Context* (Cambridge: Cambridge University Press, 2013): 181, 218–37; Birgit Peters, 'Germany's Dialogue with Strasbourg: Extrapolating the *Bundesverfassungsgericht*'s Relationship with the European Court of Human Rights in the Preventive Detention Decision', *German Law Journal* 13 (2012): 757; Corinna Coors, 'Headwind from Europe: The New Position of the German Courts on Personality Rights after the Judgment of the European Court of Human Rights', *German Law Journal* 11 (2010): 527; Nico Krisch, 'The Open Architecture of European Human Rights Law', *Modern Law Review* 71(2) (2008): 183; Grischa Merkel, 'Incompatible Contrast? Preventive Detention in Germany and the European Convention on Human Rights', *German Law Journal* 11 (2010): 1046; Almut Wittling-Vogel, 'The Role of the Legislative Branch in the Implementation of the Judgments of the European Court of Human Rights', Conference at the Paulinerkirche, Georg-August-University, Göttingen, 20–21 September 2013. Press coverage following the *Görgülü* case also reflected this debate; see, for example, 'Das Letzte Wort' ['The Last Word'], *Frankfurter Allgemeine Zeitung*, 23 October 2004; 'Im Ausland Mißverständlich' ['Prone to Misconception Abroad'], *Frankfurter Allgemeine Zeitung*, 23 October 2004.

[16] Voßkuhle (n 9) 184. See also Voßkuhle (n 7).

[17] Druscilla Scribner and Tracy Slagter, 'Supranational Human Rights Adjudication and National Legislative Politics', Paper presented at the 2011 Annual Meeting of the International Studies Association, Montreal, Quebec. Having reviewed the *Bundestag* legislative database in the period from 2005 to 2009, the authors found far more references to the Federal Constitutional Court than the ECtHR, pointing to the greater political salience of the former and the non-contentious nature of the ECtHR in German political discourse. Minority parties were more likely than parties in the ruling coalition to invoke the Strasbourg Court and its judgments, the notable example during this time period being calls for executive action on partnership rights for gays and lesbians.

[18] Scribner and Tracy Slagter (n 17) 17.

[19] Scribner and Tracy Slagter (n 17) 18. They also explain that in 2008 the Green party submitted a 'major interpellation' (see 9.4 below) relating to registered civil partnerships, and specifically to the

Sebastian Müller, an academic in the Law Faculty of the University of Bielefeld, argues that '[t]he Federal Constitutional Court … is very well respected by the citizens—even more than parliament. [It] is seen as the guarantor of our liberties, with good reason. There is a strong belief that the legal system works well …'.[20]

In his study of *The Politics of Constitutional Review in Germany*, Georg Vanberg demonstrates the extent to which there are very high levels of public support for the Constitutional Court, which explains the authoritative position it enjoys and which, in turn, creates a momentum in favour of compliance with its decisions. He also suggests that 'legislators are candid about the fact that the potential for a public backlash is a primary motivating factor in complying with [its] decisions'.[21]

Some would argue that there is too great a culture of deference, or of passivity, towards the Federal Constitutional Court. Scribner and Slagter cite the Social Democratic Party (*Sozialdemokratische Partei Deutschlands* (SPD)) MP Christine Lambert lambasting her colleagues in the legislature: 'We could use a little more courage in politics! One can't always wait to find out what the Constitutional Court is going to say.'[22]

The SPD MP and Federal Government's Commissioner for Human Rights Policy and Humanitarian Aid Christoph Strässer—a former member of the Committee on Human Rights and Humanitarian Aid ('Human Rights Committee') and the Committee on Legal Affairs and Consumer Protection ('Legal Affairs Committee') (within the *Bundestag*) and also of the Committee on Legal Affairs and Human Rights of the Parliamentary Assembly of the Council of Europe (PACE)—emphasizes the strict separation in Germany of the three arms of the state, and also underlines the strength of the independence of the judiciary within courts in the *Länder*: 'If the courts say they won't accept [a contentious Strasbourg decision], the legislature and executive can do nothing.'[23]

These various factors have accordingly created a strong culture of compliance in Germany with human rights norms and judgments. By way of example, Sebastian Müller cites the response to the 2006 ECtHR Grand Chamber judgment in *Jalloh v Germany*,[24] which concerned the forcible administration of emetics by the police in order to obtain evidence of a drugs offence. Mr Jalloh was a Sierra Leonean national living in Cologne who had been seen by police officers taking a tiny plastic bag out of his mouth (a 'bubble') and handing it over to other people. When the police approached him, he swallowed a bubble which was in his mouth, and the police

ECtHR judgments in *Karner v Austria*, No. 40016/98, 24 July 2003 and *Salgueiro Da Silva Mouta v Portugal*, No. 33290/96, 21 December 1999.

[20] Interview, 20 March 2012.

[21] Georg Vanberg, *The Politics of Constitutional Review in Germany* (Cambridge: Cambridge University Press, 2005) 124. There is a general consensus as to the powerful position of the Federal Constitutional Court, but not necessarily agreement as to the basis of the Court's authority. For example, Hailbronner emphasizes its legal expertise, over 'popular sovereignty'. See Michaela Hailbronner, 'Rethinking the Rise of the German Constitutional Court: From Anti-Nazism to Value Formalism', *International Journal of Constitutional Law* 12(3) (2014): 626.

[22] Scribner and Slagter (n 13) 19.

[23] Interview, 21 March 2012.

[24] No. 54810/00, 11 July 2006 [GC].

found no drugs on him. The public prosecutor then authorized the use of emetics. Mr Jalloh was taken to hospital where he was held down by four police officers. A doctor then forcibly administered a salt solution and emetic syrup through a tube which was introduced into his stomach through his nose. He was also injected with another emetic. As a result, Mr Jalloh regurgitated a bubble containing cocaine. By ten votes to seven, a majority of the Grand Chamber of the ECtHR found that this amounted to inhuman and degrading treatment, in violation of Article 3 ECHR. In reaching this decision, the Court took account of the potential health risks of the use of a nasogastric tube to administer emetics by force, which had caused the deaths of two people in Germany. The Court also noted in its judgment that since 1993, five of the sixteen *Länder* in Germany (Berlin, Bremen, Hamburg, Hesse, and Lower Saxony) had regularly employed the forcible administration of emetics. Sebastian Müller comments that, after the judgment, the Ministry of Justice instructed every interior ministry at the state level to cease administering emetics, and on that basis the issue was indeed resolved.[25]

Almut Wittling-Vogel does not consider there is any perceived lack of 'democratic legitimacy' in Germany as regards the execution of Strasbourg judgments: 'The Convention system went through parliament, and they said "yes, that's what we want". So I don't need additional democratic legitimation—on the contrary, I am *obliged* to do what the Court tells me.'[26]

Dr Wittling-Vogel adds that the notion of a 'democratic override' (see 4.6) is inimical to human rights because the overriding objective of the concept of human rights is to protect the rights of minorities—to support those who do not have a majority in parliament.

Scribner and Slagter note that when the opposition Green Party put down a motion (in 2007) calling for the strengthening of the ECtHR, it received the support of all parties.[27] Christoph Strässer describes the Court as having a 'very high value'. He suggests that there may be disagreement about specific judgments, but he does not accept that the Strasbourg Court meddles in domestic systems and considers that there should not be political deals over something so valuable. Strässer has expressed his surprise over the position taken by the UK government relating to prisoner voting rights. In his view, if there is an adverse decision of a court, 'we have to respect it whether we like it or not'.[28]

Sebastian Müller emphasizes the differing settings in the UK and Germany: 'I can understand the debate about legitimacy in the UK context. But we have a [different context] and we have a good experience of [having] a strong Federal Constitutional Court. The Federal Constitutional Court is widely accepted and it has earned its merits.'[29]

25 Interview, 20 March 2012. See also Gusy and Müller (n 4) 32–3.
26 Interview, 20 March 2012.
27 Scribner and Slagter (n 13) 21. See Deutscher Bundestag, Drucksache 16/4405, 28 February 2007.
28 Interview, 21 March 2012.
29 Interview, 20 March 2012. See also Çalı, Koch, and Bruch (n 13) 28–9.

The former Deputy Chair of the *Bundestag* Human Rights Committee, Holger Haibach, is in agreement about the differing contexts between the two countries and suggests that this was evident from the attitudes of the respective Parliamentary Assembly delegations: 'The British delegation has always been very outspoken ... trying to limit the influence of the Court and the Council of Europe on such domestic issues. That is a different mindset.... The German delegates are more internationally minded.'[30]

Marina Schuster (a former Free Democratic Party (FDP) MP and a former Deputy Chair of the PACE Committee on Legal Affairs and Human Rights) suggests that questions about compliance with the Strasbourg Court which have arisen in the UK have not been an issue in Germany: 'With our history, we know Europe is our future and it's the only one. We have to comply, even if the judgments are sometimes very difficult.'[31]

9.2 Germany and the Convention System

Although the Convention is not incorporated into German law by way of the Constitution, but by ordinary statute law,[32] the fundamental rights provisions in the Basic Law (Articles 1–19) are very similar to those in the Convention.[33] Mads Andenas and Eirik Bjorge argue that the risk of divergence between German domestic law and the Convention is obviated by the national courts' tendency to reach interpretations which conform to the Convention, aided by the principle of openness of the Basic Law towards international law (*Völkerrechtsfreundlichkeit*).[34] According to Holger Haibach, because of the status of Strasbourg judgments as 'ordinary' law, the way in which domestic courts have taken account of ECtHR decisions has varied greatly. This has improved because of the increased availability of Strasbourg judgments translated into German. Haibach notes that most German judges can speak English, but suggests that it is quite another thing to be able to work in English.[35]

The first Strasbourg judgment concerning Germany was handed down in 1968 (*Wemhoff v Germany*, concerning pre-trial detention[36]) and the first judgment finding Germany to be in violation of the Convention was *König v Germany* in 1978,[37] concerning the length of administrative proceedings. According to Dr Almut Wittling-Vogel,[38] there was little interest in the ECtHR at that time, because judgments tended to concern relatively minor questions and any consequential changes

[30] Interview, 15 June 2012. [31] Interview, 21 March 2012.

[32] Gesetz über die Konvention zum Schutze der Menschenrechte und Grundfreiheiten (Act on the Convention for the Protection of Human Rights and Fundamental Freedoms), 7 August 1952, Federal Law Gazette (Bundesgesetzblatt—BGBl) II, 685. For an overview of the status of the ECHR in the German domestic legal system, see Lambert Abdelgawad and Weber (n 5) 118–20.

[33] See, for example, Klein (n 11) 187–8.

[34] Andenas and Bjorge (n 15) 219–20; Klein (n 11) 192–3, 200.

[35] Interview, 15 June 2012. [36] No. 2122/64, 27 June 1968.

[37] No. 6232/73, 28 June 1978. [38] Interview, 20 March 2012.

required related almost exclusively to the individual applicants, rather than reforms affecting the wider society ('individual measures' rather than 'general measures').[39] However, that changed once the judgments against Germany started to become more prominent, and where questions of legislative change arose.

Until the 2000s, there were very few adverse judgments against Germany: just fourteen in the period between 1978 and 1998.[40] The rate of such judgments then increased: there were sixty from 1999 to 2007. In these decades, the most significant generic issues to come before the Court were the dismissal of civil servants for political activity,[41] the legislation enabling secret surveillance,[42] and the tensions between the freedom of the press and the right to privacy.[43] Gusy and Müller suggest that this low rate was a consequence not only of the strength of domestic human rights protections, but was also due to a lack of awareness within Germany, notably amongst practising lawyers (*Rechtsanwälte*), of the European Court system.[44] There was a marked increase in the number of adverse ECtHR judgments against Germany in the late 2000s.[45] There were seven adverse judgments in 2007 and six in 2008. The number then increased to eighteen (2009), twenty-nine (2010), and thirty-one (2011).[46] This upward trend was due, at least in part, to an increase in repetitive violation cases (there were, e.g., nineteen judgments in 2011 relating to the length of domestic proceedings).[47] Sebastian Müller is clear that this increase has had a political impact in Germany: 'If the Court is not well known and there are few judgments, why bother about it on the political level? ... Now, with the European Court delivering more cases, it's getting more interesting for politicians to refer to it.'[48]

9.3 The Politics of Implementation

Although Germany's implementation record has reflected a high level of compliance, there is undeniably a political aspect to the process, which is especially evident

[39] An early exception was the judgment in *Luedicke, Belkacem and Koç v Germany*, Nos. 6210/73, 6877/75, and 7132/75, 28 November 1978, concerning the obligation to provide state-funded interpretation in criminal proceedings.

[40] See also the various tables at 1.2.2 setting out, inter alia, the number of judgments by state from 1959 to 2014 and pending cases before the Committee of Ministers (as at 31 December 2014).

[41] *Vogt v Germany*, No. 17851/91, 26 September 1995 [GC].

[42] *Klass and Others v Germany*, No. 5029/71, 6 September 1978; *Weber and Saravia v Germany*, No. 54934/00, 29 June 2006.

[43] See, for example, *Von Hannover v Germany* (n 6).

[44] Christoph Gusy and Sebastian Müller, *JURISTRAS Report: Supranational Rights Litigation, Implementation and the Domestic Impact of Strasbourg Court Jurisprudence: A Case Study of Germany* (Bielefeld University, June 2008) 4.

[45] By referring to 'adverse judgments' we mean a judgment in which there was at least one finding of a violation of the ECHR. The figures are obtained from the Annual Reports of the European Court, available at the Court's website at <http://echr.coe.int>.

[46] There were eleven adverse judgments against Germany in 2012 and just three in both 2013 and 2014.

[47] Gusy and Müller (n 4) 30.

[48] Interview, 20 March 2012.

as regards the more contentious areas of public policy. Gusy and Müller underline the role played by the parliamentary opposition in bringing forward legislative proposals in response to ECtHR judgments against Germany and indeed other states, citing as examples (in the 2009–13 parliamentary term) the cases of *Heinisch v Germany*[49] (the protection of whistle-blowers) and *M.S.S. v Belgium and Greece*[50] (the rights of asylum-seekers).[51]

Speaking in 2012, the SPD MP Christoph Strässer argued that Germany's record on implementation is strong:

> In nearly every case, implementation is done rapidly.... I can say this even though we are in opposition—all governments since I became an MP in 2002 have been very engaged in implementing judgments.... There is no ... fundamental difference between the political parties on this.[52]

One of the most difficult areas to resolve in Germany in recent years has been the question of preventive detention (*Sicherungsverwahrung*), which is often applied in cases concerning sex offenders or violent crimes, in order to protect society from future harm.[53] In *M v Germany* in 2009 the ECtHR found that the retroactive application of preventive detention (beyond a ten-year maximum period) violated Article 5 ECHR (right to liberty) and Article 7 ECHR (no punishment without law).[54] Unlike the position taken by the German courts, the ECtHR found that preventive detention amounted to a 'penalty' and accordingly the principle of the prohibition of retroactivity was applicable to it. For Andenas and Bjorge, that decision 'cast a veil of doubt over the whole German system of preventive detention'.[55] Christoph Strässer confirms that extensive attempts were made within the *Bundestag* Legal Affairs Committee to come up with a solution which would comply with the Strasbourg judgment in *M*, and that it was far from easy to reach a consensus.[56] Silvia Grundmann, a former adviser to the Council of Europe Human Rights Commissioner, is more sceptical of the extent of the involvement of parliamentarians in responding to the issue of preventive detention:

> Parliament could have played a stronger role but it seems that at the time there were also other topics in addition to this very controversial and complex one. There is a lot on MPs' plates and probably for complex issues they think it's safer to leave it to the experts to come up with a draft law—so the involvement of parliamentarians in this matter appears limited.[57]

[49] No. 28274/08, 21 July 2011.
[50] No. 30696/09, 21 January 2011 [GC].
[51] Gusy and Müller (n 4) 39.
[52] Interview, 21 March 2012.
[53] See, for example, Merkel (n 15); Grischa Merkel, 'Case Note: Retrospective Preventive Detention in Germany: A Comment on the ECHR Decision *Haidn v Germany* of 13 January 2011', *German Law Journal* 12 (2011): 968; Peters (n 15).
[54] See 9.1 at n 6. There were similar judgments in 2011: *Schummer v Germany (No. 1)*, Nos. 27360/04 and 4222207, 13 January 2011; *Mautes v Germany*, No. 20008/07, 13 January 2011; *Kallweit v Germany*, No. 17792/07, 13 January 2011; and *Jendrowiak v Germany*, No. 30060/04, 14 April 2011.
[55] Andenas and Bjorge (n 15) 225, 233.
[56] Interview, 21 March 2012.
[57] Interview, 27 June 2012.

According to Dr Wittling-Vogel, at the time of the judgment in *M*, legislative proposals were already being drafted and discussed, because it was part of the coalition's programme after the election. Stefan von Raumer, of the German Bar Association, agrees that the parliament reacted quickly in deciding how to respond to the judgment in *M*, especially given the complexity of the task.[58] However, Wittling-Vogel acknowledges that it is a difficult and contentious subject,[59] potentially pitting the Ministry's legal experts against the press and the public: 'It is difficult for a politician to say that, even if there is a risk to children ... we have to free these people because this is a major issue of the rule of law and we cannot have retrospective application of laws.'[60]

Grischa Merkel has acknowledged the extent to which some politicians responded to the media's lead on this issue:

> [T]he media have enforced strong tendencies to polarize between the allegedly 'virtuous' citizen on the one hand and the dangerous 'sex-monster' on the other, thereby creating an antagonism that has been aptly exploited and further accentuated by politicians, too rarely working at stemming such tides of populist belief.[61]

In spite of the undoubted difficulties, however, according to the former FDP MP Marina Schuster, '[t]here was no discussion about *whether* we should deal with it'.[62]

Christoph Strässer argues that there was no parliamentary resistance to the judgments as such, but rather that some of the proposals put forward by the government were not necessarily compliant with the Strasbourg decision, and so it required an extensive debate in order to try to find compatible solutions.[63] However, in any event, the Strasbourg decision was subsequently backed up by a judgment of the Federal Constitutional Court in 2011 on the same issue, which may have 'tipped the balance' for MPs, as it led to legislative changes at both the Federal and *Länder* levels in 2013.[64] Dr Wittling-Vogel recalls that 'from that day on, the situation

[58] Interview, 19 March 2012.

[59] For example, the then Bavarian Minister of Justice, Beate Merk (Christian Social Union), was quoted in press coverage of the case arguing that the ECtHR's judgment was problematic and potentially dangerous for the public, should dangerous perpetrators be released. See, for example, 'Nachträgliche Verlängerung der Sicherungsverwahrung—Deutschland muss Häftling 50.000 Euro Zahlen' ['Retrospective Extension of Preventive Detention—Germany Must Pay Detainee 50,000 Euros'], *RP Online*, 17 December 2009, and 'Streit über Sicherungsverwahrung: Im Zweifel für die Dauerhaft' ['Dispute over Preventive Detention: In Favour of Continuous Detention if in Doubt'], *Spiegel Online*, 8 February 2011.

[60] Interview, 20 March 2012.

[61] Merkel (n 15) 1065.

[62] Interview, 21 March 2012.

[63] Interview, 21 March 2012. The use of electronic tags was championed by the then Federal Minister of Justice, Sabine Leutheusser-Schnarrenberger (of the FDP), whereas the then Minister of Interior, Thomas de Maiziere (of the CDU), supported the introduction of 'preventive housing': Merkel (n 15) 1055.

[64] *Bundesverfassungsgericht*, Case No. 2 B v R 2365/09, May 4, 2011, 2011 NJW 1931, 88. See also *Schmitz v Germany*, No. 30493/04, 9 June 2011. Dr Almut Wittling-Vogel has noted that the decision of the Federal Constitutional Court led to the preparation of seventeen draft bills: one federal bill and sixteen *Länder* bills. Each was then debated by the respective parliament (Warsaw Conference Report (n 8) 7). Subsequently, the Act to Effect Implementation under Federal Law of the Distance Requirement in the Law Governing Preventive Detention came into force on 1 June 2013, setting out guiding principles regarding the treatment and placement of 'preventive detainees', and the

was more or less clear. The political problems remained, but with several judgments of the Strasbourg Court and now this fundamental decision of the Federal Constitutional Court, there was no other way'.[65]

Another controversial human rights case in Germany was the ECtHR's judgment in 2000 in *Gäfgen v Germany*.[66] In that case, the police threatened to use torture against a man who had been arrested for abducting an eleven-year-old boy (he had in fact already suffocated the boy and hidden his corpse, but this was unknown to the police at the time). In an attempt to save the boy's life, police officers threatened to inflict 'intolerable pain' on him if he refused to disclose the boy's whereabouts. As a result, the applicant told the police where he had hidden the body. The interrogation under threat of ill-treatment lasted for about ten minutes, and the Court found that this would have caused him considerable fear, anguish, and mental suffering, and therefore that it amounted to inhuman treatment, in violation of Article 3 ECHR (but that it did not constitute torture). Two police officers were subsequently convicted of coercion committed in the course of their duties, but they were only subjected to minor suspended fines (of €60 per diem for sixty days and €120 per diem for ninety days, respectively). Recognizing that the police were motivated by the desire to save the boy's life, the Court nevertheless reiterated the absolute nature of the prohibition of treatment violating Article 3: '[T]he prohibition on ill-treatment of a person applies irrespective of the conduct of the victim or the motivation of the authorities. Torture, inhuman or degrading treatment cannot be inflicted even in circumstances where the life of an individual is at risk.'[67]

As a result of the case there was a public debate in Germany as to whether in some cases it could be justified to put more pressure on suspects (the 'ticking bomb' scenario).[68] There was a parliamentary debate and the responsible minister appeared before the Human Rights Committee to say that there are no instances where it would be justified. Holger Haibach describes the *Gäfgen* case as one which 'broke the ice' about public debate on domestic human rights issues:

We came up with a resolution in the German parliament saying that we condemn every kind of torture. We got some fire for that and I always responded that if I were the parent of that

relevant laws in the *Länder* were then amended. See also Committee of Ministers Resolution CM/ResDH(2014)290, Execution of the judgments of the European Court of Human Rights in thirteen cases against Germany, 17 December 2014.

65 Interview, 20 March 2012.

66 No. 22978/05, 1 June 2010 [GC].

67 *Gäfgen v Germany* (n 66) para. 107.

68 See, for example, the following press reports and/or letters, which reflected, broadly, a critical view of the judgment: 'Das Recht ist stärker als Rache, Posteingang' ['Inbox: Right is more powerful than revenge'], *Frankfurter Allgemeine Zeitung*, 8 August 2011; 'Leserbriefe zum Fall Gäfgen' ['Letters to the Editor on the Gäfgen Case'], *Frankfurter Allgemeine Zeitung*, 9 August 2011; 'Nicht zwingend—Wiedergutmachung im Fall Gäfgen' ['Redress in the Gäfgen case—Not Necessarily'], *Frankfurter Allgemeine Zeitung*, 13 August 2011; 'Leserbriefe' ['Letters to the Editor'], *Frankfurter Allgemeine Zeitung*, 14 August 2011; 'Briefe an die Herausgeber' ['Letters to the Editors'], *Frankfurter Allgemeine Zeitung*, 17 August 2011; 'Trauer, Wut und Verachtung sind Geblieben' ['Sadness, Anger and Contempt Remain'], *Frankfurter Allgemeine Zeitung*, 26 September 2012.

child I would beat the hell out of that man, but as a politician and lawmaker I cannot allow it because if you give in on one point, where do you stop?[69]

According to Almut Wittling-Vogel, problems have only rarely arisen in relation to the implementation of cases against Germany. She acknowledges, however, that on occasion, there has been reluctance amongst parliamentarians to take steps to implement a judgment, for political reasons.[70] Such a situation arose in relation to the problem of overly lengthy domestic legal proceedings in Germany. Officials in the Ministry of Justice had started to work on a draft bill before the first Strasbourg judgment against Germany on the question, but there was a lot of scepticism amongst parliamentarians about the need for new legislation, who said 'this is a fantasy of bureaucracy': according to Dr Wittling-Vogel,[71] it was clear to the Ministry that new legislation was required, in the light of the Grand Chamber judgment in *Kudła v Poland*[72] in 2000. Following the 2006 Grand Chamber judgment on the same issue in *Sürmeli v Germany*,[73] the Ministry of Justice proposed to introduce a new remedy akin to that which had been introduced in Austria (a right of appeal to a higher court), but there was opposition on the basis that the judiciary was functioning effectively and so there was no need to make changes. Sebastian Müller suggests that this resistance also reflected a prevailing view within German legal culture that judges are independent and therefore their work cannot be externally scrutinized.[74] The Ministry originally proposed the introduction of a special application to a higher court in order to speed up the case; however, at a seminar of judges and academics, it became clear that there was insufficient support for it. So, the Ministry developed a second option—the possibility to apply for compensation. According to Sebastian Müller, this was deemed acceptable, as it did not affect the work of the judges, as such.[75] The line taken by the Ministry was aided by successive judgments being issued in Strasbourg on the same question, culminating in the pilot judgment in *Rumpf v Germany* in 2010.[76] Marten Breuer describes this as the only situation of which he is aware in which there was resistance in parliament to giving effect to a Strasbourg judgment.[77] Wittling-Vogel suggests that the position changed after the 2009 federal elections, which

[69] Interview, 15 June 2012. See Committee of Ministers Resolution CM/ResDH(2014)289, Execution of the judgment of the European Court of Human Rights Gäfgen against Germany, 17 December 2014. In official liability proceedings, the Frankfurt am Main Regional Court ordered the Land of Hesse to pay the applicant compensation of €3,000 as a result of the threat to use force against him.

[70] Interview, 20 March 2012. See also Wittling-Vogel (n 15) 6–7.

[71] Interview, 20 March 2012.

[72] No. 30210/96, 26 October 2000 [GC].

[73] *Sürmeli v Germany*, No. 75529/01, 8 June 2006 [GC].

[74] Interview, 20 March 2012. See also Gusy and Müller (n 4) 41–3.

[75] In fact, the Act on Legal Redress for Excessive Length of Court Proceedings and of Criminal Investigation Proceedings (which came into force on 3 December 2011) provides for both acceleratory and compensatory remedies. See Committee of Ministers Resolution CM/ResDH(2013)244, 71 cases against Germany—Execution of the judgments of the European Court of Human Rights, 5 December 2013, and the Court's subsequent inadmissibility decisions in *Taron v Germany*, No. 53126/07, 29 May 2012 and *Garcia Cancio v Germany*, No. 19488/09, 29 May 2012.

[76] No. 46344/06, 2 September 2010.

[77] Interview, 4 May 2012.

saw the introduction of new members of parliament who were more open to the need for change.[78]

Rumpf was the first pilot judgment concerning Germany, and indeed it was the first directed at a western European country. Sebastian Müller emphasizes the significance of the domestic impact of the pilot judgment procedure applied by the ECtHR: 'The pilot judgment was like a red line. If you have one, parliamentarians realise they have to do something.'[79]

The time limit laid down by the Court in *Rumpf* was one year, within which Germany was required to introduce an effective remedy to provide sufficient redress for excessively long legal proceedings. Almut Wittling-Vogel comments that such a timescale was only possible because a draft bill on the issue had already been prepared (which she said the Court was aware of).[80] Wittling-Vogel is supportive in principle of deadlines being imposed by the Court—as reflecting a balance between the human rights demands for immediate implementation, and the democratic requirement for adequate legislative time. However, in her view, periods of only one year are unrealistic if legislative change is required.[81] On the other hand, Stefan von Raumer, of the German Bar Association, welcomed the imposition of a time limit in *Rumpf*, as it put pressure on the government to meet the deadline. In the *Rumpf* judgment itself, the Court noted that over a period of several decades it had delivered judgments in more than forty cases against Germany finding legal proceedings to be excessively long, and yet no measures had been put in place to remedy the situation.[82] Such delays would undoubtedly have strengthened the Court's hand in imposing a tight time limit.

In general, Wittling-Vogel would not wish to see the ECtHR becoming more prescriptive about what implementation requires, because in her view the authorities in the state are better placed than the Strasbourg Court to assess the possible options. She also argues that deciding on what measure to take to give effect to an adverse judgment from Strasbourg should be left to parliamentarians: 'If you are a member of parliament you are independent and you have a direct source of legitimation.'[83]

That position is shared by Christoph Strässer who makes a comparison with previous situations in which the Federal Constitutional Court has made some very specific recommendations in its judgments: 'It's our job to see what they say and respect it—and on this basis we do our legislative job.'[84]

Stefan von Raumer, of the German Bar Association, believes that it is a matter of subsidiarity—there may be a wide range of possibilities to remedy a situation, and it is up to the German parliament and state to decide what to do.[85] Nevertheless, Wittling-Vogel acknowledges that a greater degree of prescription may be helpful in some situations for some states: 'I have the impression that ... some eastern

[78] Interview, 20 March 2012. [79] Interview, 20 March 2012.

[80] Interview, 20 March 2012; Wittling-Vogel (n 15) 11–12.

[81] Wittling-Vogel (n 15) 12–15. [82] *Rumpf v Germany* (n 76) paras. 64–72.

[83] Interview, 20 March 2012. [84] Interview, 21 March 2012.

[85] Interview, 19 March 2012.

countries tend to say "tell us clearly what to do". They may have many more problems than we have and not many staff. You might be grateful [for some direction] and any room for debate just makes it harder.'

9.4 Implementation of ECtHR Judgments: The Role of Parliament

We turn in this section to the parliamentary structures and processes. The German parliament is bicameral: the *Bundestag* (the lower house) currently has 631 members, who are directly elected for four-year terms; the *Bundesrat* (the upper house) has sixty-nine members, who are delegated by the sixteen *Länder* (states) governments. As regards general scrutiny mechanisms within the *Bundestag*, individual members may put down oral or written questions for a response by the government. 'Minor interpellations' are submitted in written form, and the government responds in written form. 'Major interpellations' generally carry more weight, requiring 5 per cent of members to call on the government to 'clarify' a particular political issue. This then gives rise to a debate on the issue. The most serious is a call for a Committee of Inquiry, which requires 25 per cent of the vote.

Plenary sessions of the *Bundesrat* are usually held every three weeks. The federal government is required to present all of its legislative proposals to the *Bundesrat* first, which may give its opinion on the draft law, after which a proposal (appended to which will be the *Bundesrat's* opinion and the government's response) may be passed to the *Bundestag*. The *Bundesrat* must approve all legislation relating to policy areas for which the Basic Law grants the *Länder* concurrent powers and for which the *Länder* must administer federal regulations. Against all other legislation the *Bundesrat* has a suspending veto, which can be overridden by the *Bundestag* passing the law again.

Although, during the course of our research, we have detected reluctance from some government representatives in some states to facilitate parliamentary involvement in questions of human rights implementation, this was not the case in Germany. Dr Wittling-Vogel argues that 'it is important for our Federal Government's human rights work to receive feedback from ... the ... Bundestag', identifying four methods of co-operation, notably involving parliamentary committees (which are discussed at 9.4.1): (i) written reports on the decisions of the ECtHR and their implementation in Germany; (ii) the involvement of, and provision of information to, parliamentary committees in drafting the state reports to the United Nations; (iii) the submission of a report by the government to the parliament every two years on its human rights policies, both domestic and international (including a national action plan for human rights); and (iv) oral and written reports by the government on human rights issues on an ad hoc basis (primarily to the Human Rights Committee in the German *Bundestag*).[86]

[86] Intervention of Almut Wittling-Vogel, 'National Parliaments: Guarantors of Human Rights in Europe', Hearing of the Committee on Legal Affairs and Human Rights of the Parliamentary Assembly

9.4.1 Parliamentary committees

There are currently twenty-three permanent committees within the *Bundestag*, which are formed by a decision of the *Bundestag* for the duration of the electoral term. The committee structure is intended, in essence, to be parallel to the federal government structure. The committees deliberate on bills in their particular fields, and may call for information or evidence from government representatives or independent experts. The permanent committees may set up sub-committees to examine particular topics. The two committees of the *Bundestag* which primarily deal with human rights questions are the Human Rights Committee, which has sixteen members, and the Legal Affairs Committee, which has thirty-nine members.[87]

The Legal Affairs Committee leads on all matters relating to the Ministry of Justice. If legislation needs to be revised as a result of an ECtHR judgment, this will be considered by the Legal Affairs Committee, and in order to do so the latter will frequently summon representatives of the Ministry of Justice. The Human Rights Committee has, until recently, rarely been the lead committee on a particular issue, as it is not aligned with a specific ministry.[88] However, Roman Schmidt-Radefeldt detects a recent tendency for the plenary of the Bundestag increasingly to entrust the Human Rights Committee with the leading role in the framing of legislation.[89] The Committee discusses human rights issues from a broad perspective—both on an international basis and in relation to Germany. It was originally established as a sub-committee of the Committee on Foreign Affairs (one of four committees which are provided for on a permanent basis by the Basic Law). Therefore, it was initially primarily focused on international issues, but it has subsequently shifted its focus to consider, in addition, domestic human rights questions. According to Holger Haibach, the former Deputy Chair of the Human Rights Committee, that shift was due to high profile cases such as *Von Hannover* (concerning the publication by the German press of photographs of Princess Caroline of Monaco), and the judgments on property restitution in East Germany, as well as, more recently, the cases concerning length of proceedings and preventive detention.[90] Its recent

of the Council of Europe, 14 April 2011, 2–3 (on file). According to Wittling-Vogel, the *Bundestag* had a decisive influence on the compilation of the government's human rights policy report, leading to its inclusion of coverage of domestic issues as well as foreign policy questions, and to its inclusion of a national action plan. See also: PACE, Committee on Legal Affairs and Human Rights, National parliaments: guarantors of human rights in Europe, Doc. 12636, 6 June 2011 (Rapporteur: Christos Pourgourides) paras. 71–7.

[87] Parliamentary Project Support Division, 'The Role of Parliaments in Implementing ECHR Standards: Overview of Existing Structures and Mechanisms: Background Memorandum', prepared by the Secretariat with the assistance of Dr Alice Donald, PPSD (2014) 22 rev., 8 September 2015, 7.

[88] Christoph Strässer, Interview, 21 March 2012.

[89] Email correspondence with Roman Schmidt-Radefeldt, Parliamentary Research Services (*Wissenschaftliche Dienste*), *Bundestag*, 29 June 2015. During the fifteenth electoral term, the Human Rights Committee was the lead committee for just thirty-six draft bills. This increased to 114 in the sixteenth electoral term and 175 in the seventeenth. See the Human Rights Committee Report *Bilanz der Arbeit des Ausschusses für Menschenrechte und humanitäre Hilfe in der 17. WP des Deutschen Bundestages*, available on the *Bundestag* website at <http://www.bundestag.de>.

[90] Interview, 15 June 2012.

practice has been to hold two or three thematic hearings annually, and to invite politicians, officials, and non-governmental organization (NGO) and academic human rights experts to address it.[91]

It is generally considered that the Human Rights Committee has a lower status than other committees, because it has until recently rarely had the role of leading on the framing of legislation.[92] However, Holger Haibach argues that 'Although its capacity and influence is limited, the … Human Rights Committee has some influence, even if it's only to bring issues to the attention of the public, which most of the time is quite an appropriate means to get government to act on something.'[93]

Neither the Human Rights Committee nor the Legal Affairs Committee has an explicit agreed mandate to consider the implementation of ECtHR judgments—their involvement will depend on the particular topic and questions of timing.[94]

Holger Haibach acknowledges that parliament has much less of a role in implementation than either the executive or the judiciary:

> [T]hat is quite logical within the German political system, because there is no direct link between the judiciary and parliament….[95] It's really more between the government and the judiciary. But I always look at it as being part of our … function [of] … overseeing government actions.[96]

Haibach explains the justification for parliament's role in this way:

> To a certain extent it will always be a more rhetorical exercise—they cannot goad anyone into doing anything. But I see parliament as a watchdog and it's a field where civil society can co-operate and try to raise awareness of certain issues. So parliamentary involvement is necessary and useful—not in a legalistic way, but really by making a point.[97]

Marina Schuster, a former MP and member of the Human Rights Committee, explains that in practice the onus lies with the Ministry of Justice to instigate implementation measures:

> Judgments can be very long and detailed. It's not the primary task of parliamentarians to read them systematically—we are not all lawyers and I admit that I don't understand them all. It's the job of the government to check what the judgment means and how we should respond. So the first proposal usually comes from the government side.[98]

Gusy and Müller have contrasted German legislators' growing awareness of the European Union with their understanding of the Strasbourg Court: 'The ECtHR simply does not have an important role in the daily work of a member of parliament.

[91] Thematic meetings have covered, for example, religious freedom and human trafficking: Marina Schuster, Interview, 21 March 2012; email correspondence with Roman Schmidt-Radefeldt, Parliamentary Research Services (*Wissenschaftliche Dienste*), *Bundestag*, 29 June 2015.

[92] Sebastian Müller, Interview, 20 March 2012; Holger Haibach, Interview, 15 June 2012. See also Gusy and Müller (n 4) 38–9.

[93] Interview, 15 June 2012.

[94] Marina Schuster, Interview, 21 March 2012.

[95] With the exception of the election of judges of the federal courts, as Haibach acknowledges.

[96] Interview, 15 June 2012.

[97] Interview, 15 June 2012.

[98] Interview, 21 March 2012.

This limited consciousness of the salience of the ECtHR can influence the willingness to execute judgments and lead to their tardy implementation.'[99]

Depending on the nature of the judgment, more than one parliamentary committee may be involved in considering how to respond. Where new or revised legislation is required to implement a judgment, then the issue will also be considered by the Legal Affairs Committee. In those circumstances it is common for the Committee to summon representatives of the Ministry of Justice to attend to explain why they consider it is necessary, and why the draft law is considered to be sufficient to implement the judgment.

Marina Schuster confirms that there is no special procedure as regards the implementation of ECtHR judgments: '[W]e treat [laws responding to Strasbourg] judgments in the same way as responses to [domestic] judgments or any other parliamentary initiatives.'[100]

Parliamentarians are not sent a copy of the government's action plans which set out how the government proposes to respond to a judgment of the Strasbourg Court (see 2.5.2). According to Dr Wittling-Vogel,[101] the Ministry of Justice is not asked to provide copies of action plans, although it would not be averse to doing so. She acknowledges that, in relation to cases which require legislative change, it could be useful for parliamentarians to find out what is being proposed at an earlier stage, by being provided with action plans, depending on whether they incorporate sufficiently detailed proposals at that stage of the process. Marina Schuster suggests that following any Strasbourg judgment, information about the ruling should *automatically* be provided to the relevant committees.[102]

Holger Haibach supports the role of a specialist human rights committee. Within the Bundestag he believes that there is no need to change the remit of the Human Rights Committee, but he would advocate investing it with more powers, or leverage, so that it is in a stronger position to oversee legislative changes, in general, and the implementation of Strasbourg judgments, in particular.[103]

9.4.2 Provision of legal advice

The importance of parliamentarians engaging with both civil society and the media is widely recognized. Christoph Strässer explains that MPs have good contacts with NGOs and acknowledges their vital role in the parliamentary process: 'We'd be lost without civil society input.... Sometimes we ask them to draft questions and motions—we can't know about every issue.'[104]

Another significant domestic player is the German Institute for Human Rights, which is the national human rights institution in Germany. Sebastian Müller describes the Institute as a 'very important actor' and a 'focal point in Germany', as it is an independent and effective body which produces thematic materials which

[99] Gusy and Müller (n 4) 36.
[100] Interview, 21 March 2012.
[101] Interview, 20 March 2012.
[102] Interview, 21 March 2012.
[103] Interview, 15 June 2012.
[104] Interview, 21 March 2012.

are readily absorbed by politicians and are accessible within their time constraints. Furthermore, according to Müller, the Institute has 'created awareness that human rights are an issue in Germany'.[105] The Institute carries out monitoring functions for the UN Convention on the Rights of Persons with Disabilities, but it does not have any direct function as such in respect of judgments of the ECtHR.

Marina Schuster also recognizes the importance of media coverage for MPs: 'If there is no coverage, or discussion in the constituency, you may not even know that there has been a case.'[106]

The case of *M v Germany* (see 9.3) prompted an intensive media debate because of public concerns that as a result of the decision, serious criminals might be released. There was rather more media coverage of the ECtHR as a result of the *Von Hannover* case, because its subject matter was considered to be of interest to the public, than a case like *Rumpf*, concerning the reform of legal procedures.

Nevertheless, although there may be input from civil society or the media which influences particular human rights questions, Holger Haibach still identifies a prevailing feeling among MPs that the question of human rights is an area for 'experts'. Various factors tend to militate against their involvement, including MPs' workloads, the fact that most constituents do not welcome, or have any real interest in, their engagement in foreign affairs, as well as the raw politics of cases that involve 'unpopular' minority groups or issues.

Marina Schuster considers that MPs' knowledge and awareness of human rights issues is hugely variable, and that those most informed are the members of the Human Rights Committee, the Legal Affairs Committee, and the PACE delegation.[107] Almut Wittling-Vogel suggests that knowledge and understanding of human rights questions, and the Strasbourg system in particular, is high among those in the PACE delegation.[108] Sebastian Müller argues that only a few parliamentarians are very well informed about human rights in general. However, some have good knowledge about specific rights, because they or their staff tend to work on specific thematic issues (such as data protection, asylum, or lesbian, gay, bisexual, and transgender rights).[109] Holger Haibach suggests that there is relatively little awareness within the *Bundestag* about the Council of Europe, other than within the PACE delegation or the Human Rights Committee.[110]

MPs can seek advice from the *Bundestag*'s Parliamentary Research Services (*Wissenschaftliche Dienste*), as well as from advisers to political groups and clerks to committees.[111] Former MP Marina Schuster is highly complimentary of the independent, expert advice provided to MPs by the Parliamentary Research Services,

[105] Interview, 20 March 2012.
[106] Interview, 21 March 2012.
[107] Interview, 21 March 2012.
[108] Interview, 20 March 2012.
[109] Interview, 20 March 2012.
[110] Interview, 15 June 2012.
[111] The Research Services comprise a directorate with ten research sections, sixty-four specialists with various academic backgrounds, and about thirty lawyers. It supports the work of MPs in the field of human rights by submitting expert studies, dossiers, overviews, briefing notes, and expert contributions, as well as case law of the ECtHR (both cases against Germany and other important cases); email correspondence with Roman Schmidt-Radefeldt, Parliamentary Research Services (*Wissenschaftliche Dienste*), *Bundestag*, 29 June 2015.

including on matters of international law.[112] Schuster argues that there is more than sufficient information available to MPs on topics they are debating—in fact, there can be information overload, as happened in the follow up to the case concerning the rights of biological fathers to have contact with their children (*Anayo v Germany*).[113] She notes that discussions on that case went on for two years, not because of the lack of information, but because there was a political problem that could not be resolved. Sebastian Müller also emphasizes the importance of parliamentarians having access to independent advice:

> In 2007–8, the federal parliament opened an office in Brussels with their own staff to get their own information from Brussels and not be dependent on the government. They had woken up to the importance of being independently informed. You should ask the MPs whether they have someone sitting in Strasbourg [doing the same thing].[114]

9.4.3 Engagement with the Parliamentary Assembly of the Council of Europe

The *Bundestag* sends eighteen representatives to the Parliamentary Assembly of the Council of Europe. The PACE Committee on Legal Affairs and Human Rights has four representatives from Germany, two of whom are on its Sub-committee on Human Rights.

The German MP Christoph Strässer was formerly a member and Vice-Chair of the PACE Committee on Legal Affairs and Human Rights. Strässer describes a productive dialogue between the German members of PACE and the German Judge at the ECtHR, whom they meet annually to discuss the issues arising in German judgments.[115] He also believes it is useful for members of PACE to be made aware about the problems relating to implementation of judgments in other Council of Europe states.

As we note above, both Marina Schuster and Almut Wittling-Vogel acknowledge that amongst German MPs those who are also members of PACE (and in particular of its Committee on Legal Affairs and Human Rights) have the most awareness and understanding of human rights issues. At 2.6.2, we discuss the potential of the 'dual role' played by MPs who are also members of PACE. In Germany, at present, five members of the Human Rights Committee in the Bundestag are also either full or alternate members of the German PACE delegation, while one member of the Legal Affairs Committee is an alternate member of the PACE delegation. There are examples of German parliamentarians who have filled the 'dual role' expressing

[112] Interview, 21 March 2012.

[113] No. 20578/07, 21 December 2010. The ECtHR found a violation of Article 8 ECHR (the right to respect for private family life). In 2006 the Karlsruhe Court of Appeal had found against the applicant, and in 2007 the Federal Constitutional Court had declined to consider his constitutional complaint. The essential difference was that the domestic courts did not consider whether contact between the applicant and his biological children, who were living with their biological mother and her husband, would be in the children's best interests.

[114] Interview, 20 March 2012.

[115] Interview, 21 March 2012.

strong political support for the Court, such as Herta Däubler-Gmelin;[116] however, as is the case for our other country studies in this book, there is little evidence to establish to what extent this dual role has led to quicker or more effective responses at the national level in order to implement judgments of the Court.

9.5 Implementation of ECtHR Judgments: The Role of the Executive

A number of our interlocutors emphasize the significant influence which the office of the government agent has in practice. According to Sebastian Müller, for example, the current post-holder, Dr Almut Wittling-Vogel, has the authority to get things done. He is also intrigued by what he describes as the 'dual function' of the role (see 3.5.1): 'She defends Germany at the European Court of Human Rights, but once a judgment is there, she does absolutely everything to get it implemented. Her predecessors were all also quite critical and open-minded, and spoke their minds.'[117]

Dr Wittling-Vogel herself confirms that the Ministry will take further action to facilitate implementation where difficulties arise.[118] For example, that was the case following the Court's 2004 judgment in *Görgülü v Germany*[119] which proved problematic for both the local authorities and the higher courts in the constituent states. The applicant in *Görgülü* was the father of a child born out of wedlock. As the mother had lost contact with him, he was not involved when she gave the child up for adoption. When he subsequently found out, he brought legal proceedings in order to obtain access to, and custody of, the child. He was unsuccessful in the national courts, but the ECtHR found a violation of Article 8 ECHR (the right to respect for private and family life). When the case was then reconsidered at the national level, there were diverging opinions from the Court of First Instance and the Court of Appeal as to what the effect of the Strasbourg decision should be, leading to a further intervention from the Federal Constitutional Court finding that it was for 'the authorities and courts of the Federal Republic of Germany ... under certain conditions, to take account of the European Convention on Human Rights as interpreted by the Strasbourg Court in making their decisions'.[120] However, the Constitutional Court found that the lower courts had not been bound by the Strasbourg Court as regards the actual outcome, as such. This then led to the lower courts finding against the applicant again, before a further judgment from the

[116] See, for example, PACE, Committee on Legal Affairs and Human Rights, The future of the Strasbourg Court and enforcement of ECHR standards: reflections on the Interlaken process: Conclusions of the Chairperson, Mrs Herta Däubler-Gmelin, of the hearing held in Paris on 16 December 2009, AS/Jur (2010) 06, 21 January 2010. Mrs Däubler-Gmelin is a former German Minister of Justice, and a former Chair of both the Bundestag Human Rights Committee and the PACE Committee on Legal Affairs and Human Rights.

[117] Interview, 20 March 2012.

[118] Interview, 20 March 2012.

[119] *Görgülü v Germany* (n 15).

[120] BVerfGE 111, 307 (315).

Constitutional Court found in his favour.[121] There was clearly a very complex legal backdrop, but according to Dr Wittling-Vogel, the Ministry invited some interlocutors to Berlin to discuss the matter, and it became clear that the local authorities would undertake further efforts to remove the logjam.

Since 2004, both the Human Rights Committee and the Legal Affairs Committee have received an annual report from the Ministry of Justice on judgments of the ECtHR.[122] The extent of the coverage of the reports has evolved to respond to emerging questions. Initially, it simply covered judgments and decisions in that year against Germany. In 2006, the Parliamentary Assembly passed a resolution on the implementation of ECtHR judgments which urged all national parliaments to introduce specific mechanisms and procedures to ensure effective parliamentary oversight of the implementation of the Court's judgments, on the basis of regular reports by the responsible ministries. As a result, from 2007 the Ministry's annual reports also covered measures undertaken to implement judgments against Germany.

In addition to being made available to parliament, the report is published on the Ministry of Justice's website. Dr Almut Wittling-Vogel emphasizes that other audiences are important too—including lawyers, judges, civil society, and potential applicants to the Court—given also that not every judgment will be made available in German. The MP and Federal Government's Commissioner for Human Rights Policy and Humanitarian Aid Christoph Strässer (a former member of the Human Rights Committee and of PACE), believes that the regular provision of such reports are an important source of information for parliamentarians about ECtHR judgments and their implementation. Sebastian Müller argues that the provision of annual reports has been a significant development in making Strasbourg case law more accessible within Germany, because of the language barrier.[123] It is also important for lawyers and the judiciary, he argues, that the reports are officially authorized by the Ministry of Justice.

There is, however, no formalized procedure to respond to the submission of the Ministry's annual report.[124] The parliamentary committees may put it on to their agenda for discussion (although this is not routinely the case) and they may call in Government representatives to question them about it. According to Dr Wittling-Vogel, follow-up steps of this sort are less likely in respect of the more routine judgments, which may only require the payment of damages to the applicant, and the translation, publication, and dissemination of the judgments (to judges, lawyers, and the *Länder*).[125]

[121] BVerfGE, 1 Bv R 2790/04.

[122] For the latest report, see Bundesministerium der Justiz und für Verbraucherschutz (Federal Ministry of Justice and Consumer Protection), *Bericht über die Rechtsprechung des Europäischen Gerichtshofs für Menschenrechte und die Umsetzung seiner Urteile in Verfahren gegen die Bundesrepublik Deutschland im Jahr 2013* [*Report on the Case Law of the European Court of Human Rights and the Implementation of its Judgments in Cases against Germany in 2013*], 6 June 2014.

[123] See also Gusy and Müller (n 4) 33–4.

[124] Christoph Strässer, Interview, 21 March 2012.

[125] Interview, 20 March 2012.

Since 2010, in response to a formal request from the *Bundesrat*, an annual report has also been commissioned which covers judgments against other Council of Europe states which have potential implications for Germany (see 2.1.1).[126] The reports are compiled by independent academics,[127] because the Ministry of Justice has insufficient resources to do so. The aim of these reports is to provide an overview of judgments against other states which might be relevant to, or have consequences for, German legislation or practice.[128] Marten Breuer (who was initially commissioned to write the reports) confirms that the focus of those reports is not necessarily significant cases in their own right, but judgments which might have particular relevance for Germany, or developing trends in the Court's jurisprudence which might have domestic implications in the future. For example, Breuer included reference to the *Greens* case (prisoner voting rights; see 7.6.1) in his 2010 report, even though it did not require an automatic change to German law, because of the Court's apparent tendency to take voting rights more seriously.[129] This is no easy task:

> The question is always, 'Is it exactly the same situation in Germany; is it exactly comparable; can we draw immediate conclusions from the case; if it had been a German case, would the Court have come to a different conclusion?' One has to be very careful ...[130]

[126] Such judgments are considered by the courts in Germany to have the same status as judgments directed against Germany, on the basis that in all cases the judgments reflect the current understanding of the Convention rights: Klein (n 11) 203–6.

[127] Initially they were written by Professor Marten Breuer (University of Konstanz), and latterly by Professor Heiko Sauer (University of Bonn).

[128] See, for example, the 2012 report: Dr Heiko Sauer, *Bericht über die Rechtsprechung des Europäischen Gerichtshofs für Menschenrechte in Verfahren gegen andere Staaten als Deutschland im Jahr 2012* [*Report on the Case Law of the European Court of Human Rights in Cases against States other than Germany in 2012*] (2013). The 2012 report includes reference, inter alia, to the following cases and issues: a ban on prisoner voting rights (*Scoppola v. Italy (No. 3)*, No. 126/05, 22 May 2012 [GC]); the refusal to grant a long-term cohabitee the right in criminal proceedings not to testify against their partner (*Van der Heijden v the Netherlands*, No. 42857/05, 3 April 2012 [GC]); the retention of a caution on criminal record for life (*M.M. v UK*, No. 24029/07, 13 November 2012); evidence obtained by torture and used in criminal proceedings (*El Haski v. Belgium*, No. 649/08, 25 September 2012); a ban preventing healthy carriers of cystic fibrosis from screening embryos for in vitro fertilization (*Costa and Pavan v Italy*, No. 54270/10, 28 August 2012); the inability of a child abandoned at birth to gain access to information (*Godelli v Italy*, No. 33783/09, 25 September 2012); the obligation to pay compensation to a child victim of sexual abuse for revealing her identity in a newspaper article (*Kurier Zeitungsverlag und Druckerei GmbH v Austria*, No. 3401/07, 17 January 2012); the limited effectiveness of a remedy available to an asylum-seeker to challenge a deportation order (*I.M. v. France*, No. 9152/09, 2 February 2012); the containment of peaceful demonstrators within a police cordon for over seven hours (*Austin and Others v* UK, Nos. 39692/09, 40713/09, and 41008/09, 15 March 2012 [GC]); the imposition of a fine for displaying a flag with controversial historical connotations in protest against an anti-racist demonstration (*Fáber v. Hungary*, No. 40721/08, 24 July 2012); the non-fatal shooting of a waiter by a police officer on unauthorized leave of absence and the liability of state for acts of the police officer (*Sašo Gorgiev v The former Yugoslav Republic of Macedonia*, No. 49382/06, 19 April 2012); retroactive legislative interference in litigation between private parties (*Arras and Others v Italy*, No. 17972/07, 14 February 2012); restrictions on the volume of a church bell at night (*Schilder v The Netherlands*, No. 2158/12, 16 October 2012); the prohibition, under legislation implementing UN Security Council Resolutions, on travel through country surrounding an enclave (*Nada v Switzerland*, No. 10593/08, 12 September 2012 [GC]); and torture and inhuman and degrading treatment during and following an applicant's extraordinary rendition by the US Central Intelligence Agency (*El-Masri v The former Yugoslav Republic of Macedonia*, No. 39630/09, 13 December 2012 [GC]).

[129] Interview, 4 May 2012.

[130] Interview, 4 May 2012. To illustrate the inherent difficulties, Wittling-Vogel cites the differing conclusions reached by the Chamber and the Grand Chamber judgments in *Herrmann v Germany*

In drafting reports in 2010 and 2011, Breuer cites the case of *Salduz v Turkey*[131] (right of suspect in police custody to a lawyer) as requiring a change in the domestic law, and two examples where he had to carefully scrutinize the implications for Germany: *S.H. v Austria*[132] (discrimination in the availability of IVF treatment) and *Enerji Yapı-Yol Sen v Turkey*[133] (civil servants' right to strike).[134] Roman Schmidt-Radefeldt agrees that it is difficult to identify cases which have led to specific changes in law or policy in Germany, but he argues that important ECtHR cases are taken into account during policy debates, one example being the references made to the case of *Pretty v UK*[135] in recent discussions about assisted suicide.[136]

Holger Haibach acknowledges that during his time as a member of the *Bundestag* (from 2002 to 2011), ECtHR judgments against states other than Germany were not considered by MPs—primarily because of their heavy workloads. Haibach also argues that it is a complex task to evaluate the impact of such judgments within the German system (or that of any other country).[137] Christoph Strässer also accepts that as regards the Strasbourg Court, MPs in Germany do not take account of judgments against other countries.[138] As we note at 2.1.1, it is increasingly important for Council of Europe states to consider the relevance of ECtHR judgments in cases brought against other states, and the publication of these reports by the Ministry of Justice has set a precedent which should be followed elsewhere. However, we do also have to acknowledge that, aside from the example of *Salduz v Turkey*, we have not uncovered any evidence to suggest that these reports have led to any other specific changes in law or policy in Germany.

9.6 Conclusion

The strength of domestic human rights norms and machinery in Germany has led to the development of a legal and political culture which has little trouble in accepting and incorporating decisions from Strasbourg. The prevailing attitudes, including amongst parliamentarians and the public, are generally very conducive to compliance. The higher rate of adverse ECtHR judgments against Germany witnessed in the late 2000s increased the political salience of Strasbourg decisions, but even as regards the most contentious issues politically, debates have still concerned

(No. 9300/07, 20 January 2011 and 26 June 2012 [GC]) as to the application to Germany of the Court's established case law relating to hunting rights, as had been expressed in *Chassagnou and Others v France* (No. 25088/94, 29 April 1999 [GC]) and *Schneider v Luxembourg* (No. 2113/03, 10 July 2007). See Wittling-Vogel (n 15) 11–12.

131 No. 36391/02, 27 November 2008 [GC].

132 No. 57813/00, 1 April 2010 (Chamber judgment) and 3 November 2011 (Grand Chamber).

133 No. 68959/01, 21 April 2009.

134 Interview, 4 May 2012.

135 No. 2346/02, 29 April 2002.

136 Email correspondence with Roman Schmidt-Radefeldt, Parliamentary Research Services (*Wissenschaftliche Dienste*), *Bundestag*, 29 June 2015.

137 Interview, 15 June 2012.

138 Interview, 21 March 2012.

how to comply with ECtHR judgments, not *whether* to do so. Nor have conceptions of a perceived lack of democratic legitimacy, or the need for any form of 'democratic override', gained any traction.

The executive continues to take very seriously its role in having the primary responsibility in practice for ensuring compliance with Strasbourg decisions, and the current German government agent is widely credited with having both the will and the capability to ensure that there is an effective and efficient process. Institutionally within parliament, none of the committees has an explicit mandate to monitor and scrutinize the implementation of ECtHR decisions. There is, nevertheless, support for the earlier provision of information to parliamentarians about the government's intentions in responding to individual judgments, for example, by disseminating the government's 'action plans'. Members of parliament have access to ample advice and information on human rights topics, both from within (from the Parliamentary Research Services) and from the German Institute for Human Rights, and from NGOs.

Like the Netherlands, Germany has pioneered the provision of governmental annual human rights reports to parliament which are credited with improving the accessibility of Strasbourg decisions, to parliamentarians, judges, and lawyers. These have been supplemented to include coverage of judgments against other states which may have relevance to Germany. Nevertheless, as laudable as these developments are, there is no formalized parliamentary response to the annual reports (such as a debate) and it is difficult to establish to what extent, if at all, such reports have led to specific changes in domestic law or policy. There is still potential, we suggest, for parliamentary involvement in implementation matters to be considerably enhanced.

10
Conclusion

The introduction to this book identified a confluence of concerns about perceived deficiencies in both the effectiveness and legitimacy of the system of human rights protection under the European Convention on Human Rights and the related problems of 'backlog' and 'backlash'. We have established, too, that the obligations created under international human rights law rest on all arms of the state—executive, legislative, and judicial—as has been reinforced by the Council of Europe (including, belatedly, its inter-governmental arm) and United Nations bodies, among others. These developments have created an unprecedented focus on national implementation of Convention standards and judgments of the European Court of Human Rights and, in particular, the role of parliaments in the shared obligation of human rights protection.

Accordingly, this book has explored the institutional, legal, and political dimensions of the implementation of Convention norms and judgments of the Court—the effectiveness of which, we have argued, is determined by the capacity and political will of state actors. This insight is premised on empirically grounded accounts that explain compliance—whether full, partial, or non-compliance—with international human rights norms as being, to a significant extent, the outcome of domestic political bargaining. This approach rests in turn upon a characterization of the state not as a unitary actor, but as a collection of actors which, through their relative power and interactions, determine whether, and to what extent, compliance occurs. At the same time, we do not discount transnational processes and influences and we have therefore examined the interaction, and *potential* for interaction, between national parliaments and Council of Europe bodies—in particular, the Court, the Committee of Ministers, and the Parliamentary Assembly (PACE).

Viewed in this way, the Convention system may be understood as a complex web of interaction and interdependence between institutional actors, both domestic and supranational, each of which has different functions, expertise, competence, and claims to legitimacy—and none of which can secure the objective of the Convention[1] alone, but only through their inter-relationships, whether of collaboration, co-ordination, competition, or oversight. We have proposed, then, that the effectiveness or legitimacy of any single actor must be assessed contextually,

[1] That objective being expressed in the obligation on states (under Article 1 ECHR) to 'secure to everyone within their jurisdiction the rights and freedoms' enshrined in the Convention.

with regards to the effectiveness and legitimacy of other actors, and of the system as a whole.

Against this background, this chapter offers concluding reflections on the role of national parliaments as an essential component of the Convention system. We summarize the 'state of play' with respect to parliamentary capacity to implement Convention standards and ECtHR judgments, and suggest priorities for strengthening it (10.1). We examine options for increasing interaction between national parliaments and the Convention 'machinery' (10.2). We also look forward, from the vantage point of both parliaments and Council of Europe institutions, in order to address questions relating to the legitimacy of the Convention system (10.3).

10.1 The Question of Capacity

Parliamentary capacity to conduct human rights oversight is highly uneven across the Council of Europe. A few states have well-established parliamentary structures and processes to, among other functions, scrutinize legislation systematically for Convention compliance and to monitor the implementation of ECtHR judgments—the UK Joint Committee on Human Rights (JCHR) being the standout example. Most have structures and processes which are at best embryonic and at worst ineffective due to a combination of neglect, misuse, under-resourcing, and/or political enfeeblement. Still others effectively have no structures or processes at all.

Where at least some degree of parliamentary monitoring of human rights occurs, the institutional models adopted for this purpose vary considerably: some are wholly decentralized (the 'cross-cutting' model; e.g., the Netherlands and several Nordic states), while others have allocated the role to a single committee (the 'specialized' model; e.g., the UK) or to more than one committee (the 'hybrid' model; e.g., Germany, Ukraine). A few domestic systems of implementation—in Italy, Romania, Macedonia, and Ukraine—have a basis in national legislation that stipulates the roles and duties of different state actors; however, as the record of these states attests, the mere existence of such legislation is no guarantee of effectiveness in the absence of political commitment.

Aside from the cross-cutting approach adopted by the unicameral parliaments of several Nordic states, there is no distinctive pattern in the models adopted by parliaments in the Council of Europe. Rather, what emerges is a patchwork of different approaches to conducting human rights oversight, reflecting in part the incremental and ad hoc nature of their development—a process that has frequently relied on the initiative of individual parliamentarians (usually members of the Parliamentary Assembly).

The Parliamentary Assembly has declined to endorse a specific model for institutionalizing parliamentary human rights work. Whilst its approach is non-prescriptive, the Assembly's Committee on Legal Affairs and Human Rights has, in its various reports, resolutions, and recommendations, indicated a preference for either a specialized or hybrid approach over a cross-cutting model—at least for parliaments that are initiating human rights oversight or developing it from a low base. At the same time, it is important not to fixate on structures, since parliamentary bodies that have a stated human rights remit may, in practice, be moribund due to lack of expertise, resources, or political will. Further, concentrating human rights expertise within a specialized committee or sub-committee runs the concomitant risk of discouraging the integration of human rights and related rule of law issues across the entire range of a parliament's functions and structures. The risk of creating a human rights 'silo' within a national parliament is exacerbated by the fact that parliamentary human rights committees, where they exist, tend to be viewed by parliamentarians as being of lower status than some other committees (such as committees on justice or legal affairs), as reflected in their size, formal powers, and informal standing.

These findings suggest several priorities for the strengthening of parliamentary capacity. The first is to foster the development within national parliaments of a body of professional staff capable of providing independent and expert advice on matters related to human rights and the rule of law. While certain staff may be attached to a specific committee, such advice should be made available to all parliamentary bodies that may need to take account of human rights or rule of law issues within their work. The critical role of parliamentary advisers has been repeatedly recognized by the Parliamentary Assembly and reflected in its own capacity-building work. Our research vindicates this approach, highlighting the multiple functions of parliamentary advisers as 'mediators' between parliamentarians and the Convention system (as well as other international human rights bodies). These functions include screening the outputs[2] of Council of Europe bodies and selectively drawing parliamentarians' attention to them; analysing the meaning and significance of these outputs in the domestic context; and briefing parliamentarians as to the range of Convention-compliant options open to them. In this way, parliamentary advisers should facilitate, rather than constrain, democratic deliberation on human rights questions and empower parliamentarians to fulfil their interpretive role—a role that, our research suggests, the great majority of parliamentarians lack the motivation, confidence, or expertise to assume (many viewing human rights as an 'export product' rather than a framework that generates obligations for parliament at the domestic level). Indeed, a degree of realism is required as to the extent to which elected politicians can be expected to grapple with the legal, technical, and moral issues that may be raised in human rights judgments—hence the importance of the role of politically neutral parliamentary advisers who can provide political cover for parliamentarians in matters that are contentious, and provide continuity between parliaments by creating an

[2] The need for this mediating role is apparent if one considers the sheer range of outputs that parliamentarians might potentially need to be apprised of, including not only adverse judgments of the Court, but also no-violation judgments, reasoned inadmissibility decisions, friendly settlements, unilateral declarations, interim measures, derogations, third-party interventions, judgments against other states that might have implications for the domestic legal order, and additional protocols to the Convention requiring debate about ratification. Added to this are the outputs of the Parliamentary Assembly and Committee of Ministers, such as reports, resolutions, and recommendations.

institutional memory in relation both to substantive issues and the working methods of parliamentary committees.

Nor is the 'mediating' role of advisers limited to the relationship with international bodies: they may also perform that function in relation to executive actors (ministers, government departments, and government lawyers)—screening, analysing, summarizing, and signposting the significance of, among other outputs, statements of Convention-compatibility, action plans and reports, annual reports on ECtHR judgments, and ministerial correspondence. Further, well-serviced parliamentary committees will have greater capacity to engage with civil society by means of hearings, calls for evidence, and thematic inquiries. Civil society actors (such as legal practitioners, academics, non-governmental organizations (NGOs), and individuals or groups that are able to represent the experience of particular communities) also 'mediate' parliamentarians' understanding of the meaning and significance of human rights judgments and the impact of legislation and policy on the realization of human rights. The dialogical capacity of parliamentary bodies is thus crucial to their effectiveness—and, we suggest, to the legitimacy of the Convention system to the extent that openness and transparency are prerequisites of both social and normative legitimacy.

In summary, if, as proposed above, we view the Convention system as interactional and collaborative, then the role of independent advisers assumes an even greater importance than might at first be apparent—indeed, they appear uniquely well placed to facilitate dialogue, exchanges of information, and mutual understanding between different actors within the system, thereby reinforcing the shared normative framework created by the Convention. The challenges presented by this role underline the importance—both for Council of Europe bodies and national parliaments—of ensuring that parliamentary advisers are politically independent, sufficiently numerous and well-resourced, and afforded ample opportunities to develop their own capacity in relation to the Convention system. Further, the centrality of the advisory role implies the need to ensure that human rights expertise is not confined to a single committee in parliament but is, as far as possible, 'mainstreamed' across the full range of parliamentary activity.

The interactional nature of the Convention system brings us to the second priority for strengthening parliamentary capacity—improving the quality and regularity of executive reporting and information sharing. Since executives are the main interlocutors with Council of Europe bodies, and therefore the gatekeepers of information, some form of executive reporting to parliament is a prerequisite of parliamentary involvement in the implementation process. This imperative was elaborated and reinforced by the Brussels Declaration of March 2015.[3] Governments are, however, inconsistent and equivocal in their approaches to facilitating parliamentary involvement through the systematic provision of information at critical junctures in the implementation process—and most have no mechanism for doing so. Where such mechanisms exist, they generally take the form of an annual report

[3] See 1.1.3 at n 79.

to parliament on the implementation of human rights judgments; such reports are provided in around one-third of Convention states. Such reporting mechanisms appear to yield few tangible results in respect of the implementation of specific judgments. They are rarely, if ever, debated by parliaments. However, we have identified several advantages of such mechanisms which suggest that they are a potentially valuable tool in the implementation process. They may galvanize executive bodies to systematize co-ordination of implementation and increase its efficiency, in part by ensuring that the government agent (or equivalent body) is sufficiently empowered to influence and obtain information from other arms of the executive. Regular executive reporting to parliament may also have the beneficial effect of normalizing the implementation process and preventing it from becoming unduly politicized. Annual reports also provide a cumulative public record of a state's compliance performance which may be used both by parliamentarians and civil society actors as a basis for invigorating implementation, both in respect of specific judgments and the system as a whole. We suggest, therefore, that regular reporting mechanisms should be instituted by states that lack them—emulating the approaches adopted by Germany, the Netherlands, and the UK. It is important, too, that parliaments use such reports as a practical basis for human rights oversight, lest they become a mere paper exercise. Nor is there any reason why reporting mechanisms should be confined to Convention compliance: the JCHR has proposed that this aspect of reporting should form part of an 'Annual Human Rights Report' to parliament, covering not only responses to human rights judgments (both of domestic courts and the ECtHR) but also the UK's reporting to UN treaty monitoring bodies and wider human rights developments.

Whatever their advantages, annual reporting mechanisms do not facilitate 'real time' human rights scrutiny of executive action—or inaction—by parliamentarians. For this reason, we also propose that action plans or action reports that spell out what steps the executive proposes to take (or has taken) in response to an adverse judgment should be routinely shared with parliament at the same time as they are submitted to the Committee of Ministers. To our knowledge, only the UK government regularly does so. This is despite the fact that action plans and action reports are now regarded as the central feature of the process of supervision conducted by the Committee of Ministers—and can (and should) reflect parliamentary input on the implementation matters at stake, either in the initial submission or subsequent updates. This lacuna in the information-sharing process is, we suggest, the result of both parliamentary inertia and reluctance on the part of governments to include parliaments in what has hitherto been seen as an executive domain. This appears increasingly outdated, in light of the Committee of Ministers' view that action plans and reports are 'the practical expression of the principle of subsidiarity'[4] and a 'key tool' for facilitating dialogue with national parliaments.[5]

A third, and overarching, priority is to equip parliamentarians to recognize and act upon the obligations and opportunities afforded by their role within the

[4] See 2.5.2 at n 110. [5] See 2.5.2 at n 112.

Convention system. This is no easy task. Parliamentarians may have political or material disincentives to comply with judgments of the ECtHR, or be ignorant of or indifferent towards them. Not surprisingly, then, executive, judicial, and NGO actors—and indeed some parliamentarians—are dubious about the feasibility or merit of increasing parliamentary monitoring of human rights norms. However, we have argued that to disparage parliamentary involvement in the interests of 'depoliticization' is to be overly pessimistic about the longer-term advantages of developing structures and processes that require parliamentarians to engage with reasoned, justificatory arguments about the meaning and scope of rights and their application in the domestic context. Structures which embed parliamentary consideration of ECtHR judgments and promotion of Convention standards, rather than relying on reactive or sporadic responses, may, in the longer term, help both to strengthen implementation and pre-empt opportunistic attacks on the Strasbourg system.

As noted above, we should be realistic about the extent to which, in particular, elected members of parliament are likely to be able or willing to spend time or political capital engaging with matters of human rights implementation. Nevertheless, we have detected in the course of our research growing appetite among some parliamentarians (and parliamentary advisers) to instigate or strengthen structures and processes for conducting human rights oversight; these include the establishment of human rights committees or sub-committees, clarification or expansion of the remit of existing committees, initiatives to ensure more reliable and systematic information sharing by the executive, and attention to the means by which implementation is co-ordinated at the domestic level. This impetus is especially evident among some members of the Parliamentary Assembly, demonstrating the important role of PACE as a catalyst of developments at the national level, and the potential that is inherent in the—still under-exploited—'dual mandate' of PACE delegates.

The time is ripe for further efforts to strengthen the capacity of parliamentarians and their advisers to recognize and fulfil their obligations under the Convention, including by sharing effective practice between different national contexts. We hope this book will increase momentum in this direction. Further, we suggest that a priority for future research is to enquire into the effectiveness—and the methods of determining the effectiveness—of parliaments in respect of their human rights obligations. This is not, however, a straightforward endeavour. Parliaments are political bodies whose overarching purpose cannot be reduced to mere technocratic goals, but extends, we suggest, to strengthening the state's compliance with human rights norms and standards in accordance with the principle of subsidiarity, and legitimizing those norms and standards by engaging in reasoned debate about the interpretation and application of human rights in the domestic context.

We recommend also that the Draft Principles and Guidelines on the Role of Parliaments in the Protection and Realisation of the Rule of Law and Human Rights[6] that have been initiated by Murray Hunt, legal adviser to the Joint Committee on Human Rights in the UK, are disseminated and debated, leading

[6] See 3.4.3 at n 126.

to the endorsement of a set of Principles and Guidelines by national, regional, and international parliamentary bodies and international organizations (such as the UN, Council of Europe, and Inter-Parliamentary Union). Such a development would be, as Hunt ventures, of 'real practical benefit to parliaments and parliamentarians everywhere' in devising 'the appropriate structures, mechanisms and practices which are required in order for them to discharge their important obligations and responsibilities in relation to human rights'.[7] Indeed, the utility of the Draft Principles and Guidelines is demonstrated by the fact that they are already being used as a tool with which to assess parliamentary human rights work.[8]

10.2 Interaction between Parliaments and Council of Europe Bodies

National parliaments may be influenced by direct interaction with Council of Europe institutions, which may apply pressure towards compliance and help to shape parliamentarians' understanding of the meaning and significance of judgments. Such influence depends in part upon the nature and extent of contact between parliamentarians and Council of Europe bodies. In practice, such contact is uneven and, for the most part, minimal.

In respect of the Court, in the five states reviewed in this book, there is little regular contact between members of relevant parliamentary committees (where they exist) and judges or officials of the Court. Exceptionally, the JCHR in the UK held an evidence hearing in 2012 with the UK judge and the Registrar of the ECtHR, demonstrating that such appearances before parliament need not, as might be feared, unduly politicize the judicial role or undermine its independence. At a more general level, the Court may wish to consider how it can become more adept at communicating with parliamentarians (among other audiences) in order to, for example, correct common misconceptions about its role and to raise their awareness and understanding of the Convention system. The Jurisconsult of the Court, whose role is to ensure the quality and consistency of its case law, is well-placed to perform such a role.[9] A strategic approach to communications might include drawing attention to judgments that have found *no* violation of the Convention, especially where a wide margin of appreciation has been applied out of deference to

[7] Murray Hunt, 'Enhancing Parliaments' Role in the Protection and Realisation of Human Rights', in Murray Hunt, Hayley Hooper, and Paul Yowell, eds., *Parliaments and Human Rights: Redressing the Democratic Deficit* (Oxford: Hart Publishing, 2015): 469, 483.

[8] In 2015–16, the Westminster Foundation for Democracy and Oxford University's 'Parliaments, the Rule of Law, and Human Rights' project are using the Draft Principles and Guidelines as a framework to assess six parliaments (in Georgia, Macedonia, Serbia, Uganda, Ukraine, and Tunisia) in terms of their capacity and effectiveness in scrutinizing the government against human rights and rule of law standards (email correspondence with Murray Hunt, 10 December 2015).

[9] See, e.g., European Court of Human Rights (Case-law Information and Publications Division, Jurisconsult's Department), *Finding and Understanding the Case-law of the European Court of Human Rights* (December 2015).

the quality of domestic democratic deliberation on the matter in question. Such an approach might also include 'signposting' in media releases and other outputs the Court's role in standard-setting and the significance of judgments to states other than the respondent state. Indeed, it is to be welcomed that the Court has already begun to communicate in this way.[10]

There is naturally more scope for direct contact between parliamentarians and the Parliamentary Assembly. PACE has used both 'carrot' and 'stick' in its interactions with parliamentarians. The Assembly conducts important work to strengthen the capacity of both parliamentarians and parliamentary staff. Our interlocutors suggest that PACE reports, resolutions, and recommendations have in some instances been influential in galvanizing the creation of more robust arrangements for conducting human rights oversight within national parliaments. At the same time, the Assembly has played an increasingly assertive role in exposing and pursuing accountability for failures in implementation. Delegates from some states have, for example, been called to give evidence to its Committee on Legal Affairs and Human Rights ('Legal Affairs Committee') to account for such shortcomings. In addition, the PACE rapporteur on the implementation of ECtHR judgments conducts visits to states with poor records, among other activities. The visibility of the rapporteur looks set to increase with the appointment to the role in 2015 of Pierre-Yves Le Borgn', an outspoken defender of the Convention system.[11] The sub-committee on the implementation of judgments (established in 2015 under the Legal Affairs Committee) may also be expected to intensify the Assembly's engagement with national parliaments.

These developments are welcome in view of our argument that the 'dual mandate' of members of the Assembly remains under-exploited. While some members have been highly active and visible at the domestic level, many appear to regard the role as being remote from domestic priorities, or have treated the Assembly principally as a venue within which to negate criticism of their respective states. In a political body such as the Assembly, such problems are unavoidable—yet are mitigated by the existence of a strong secretariat attached to the Legal Affairs Committee and, as noted above, increasingly assertive mechanisms to respond to failures in implementation of Convention standards and judgments of the Court. Other measures—such as the suspension of voting rights of national delegations when their parliaments do not exercise effective control over the executive in cases of non-compliance with judgments, or the summoning of government ministers to explain serious failures in implementation—have also been proposed, but not utilized. Given the problems of non-compliance which continue to bedevil the Convention system, such

[10] See, e.g., European Court of Human Rights, 'Q & A: Roman Zakharov v. Russia, Grand Chamber judgment', 4 December 2015, which highlights the consequences for other states of *Roman Zakharov v Russia*, No. 47143/06, 4 December 2015, which held that the arbitrary and abusive secret surveillance of mobile telephone communications in Russia violated the right to respect for private life and correspondence under Article 8 ECHR.

[11] See, e.g., Pierre-Yves Le Borgn', 'Stop aux Attaques à l'Encontre de la Cour Européenne des Droits de l'Homme!' ['Stop Attacks Against the European Court of Human Rights!'], *Huffington Post*, 26 November 2015.

measures would be a natural extension of the Parliamentary Assembly's de facto role in the supervision process—with states' elected representatives in effect being called to account by parliamentarians from across the Council of Europe.

In respect of the Committee of Ministers, we detected minimal contact with national parliaments. MPs rarely take part in thematic or regional seminars organized by the Committee of Ministers. When dialogue takes place at national level, the Department for the Execution of Judgments of the ECtHR (the secretariat body of the Committee of Ministers) confines its discussions with parliamentary bodies to procedural issues. Interlocutors within the Committee of Ministers indicate that no inherent value is placed on the involvement of parliament in the execution process; the Committee is, in this sense, neutral about which state actor is involved in the execution process—the executive, parliament, or the courts. These findings are perhaps unsurprising: the executive is the main interlocutor of the Committee of Ministers and there are good reasons for the Department to retain flexibility in the supervision process. However, this pragmatic approach should not be permitted to obscure instances in which, for example, executive bodies respond to judgments by means of decrees or ordinances which effectively bypass parliamentary procedure. These concerns underline the need for sensitivity within the execution process to the (potential) role of parliamentarians as actors who may both initiate remedies and scrutinize executive action or inaction following judgments of the Court.

10.3 The Question of Legitimacy

The 'democratic critique' of the Court has intensified in recent years. Obloquy directed at the Court has not been confined to the UK, but has also surfaced elsewhere, including France, the Netherlands, and several Nordic states. Yet the UK stands out both for the vehemence of the criticism of the Court expressed by government ministers, among others, and because proposals to weaken its authority have become a staple of mainstream political discourse, rather than being, as elsewhere, largely sporadic or confined to the political margins. Attitudes towards the Court are not static, however, and the risk of contagion is ever present. At the time of writing, there are alarming signs that challenges to the Court's adjudicatory authority are gathering force within the Russian parliament.[12]

At the same time, criticism of the Court emanating from national authorities—executive, legislative, or judicial—does not necessarily indicate an underlying crisis of legitimacy. On the contrary, the *absence* of resistance would be equally concerning if it meant that the Convention system was regarded as toothless or ineffective. Moreover, stridently negative voices should not be permitted to obscure the resilience and achievements of the Convention system in protecting fundamental rights and freedoms over the past half century, in the face of tumultuous political events leading to the dramatic eastwards expansion of the Council of Europe.

[12] See 1.1.2 at n 36.

We have proposed some 'ground rules' for discussion of the legitimacy of the Convention system—that it should be evidence-based rather than conducted in purely abstract terms; inclusive and participative, rather than monopolized by powerful voices; cosmopolitan rather than parochial, so as to capture the distinct value of the Convention as a supranational human rights system; and sensitive to context and institutional interaction, rather than invoking hard-edged or comprehensive claims to legitimacy on behalf of any single actor.[13]

These precepts in turn highlight priorities for future research. First, there is a dearth of research which enquires into public attitudes towards the Convention system in different member states, including not only representative surveys of opinion but also qualitative research which probes the basis of normative expectations that different audiences have of the Convention system and their assessment of how far those expectations are met in practice.[14] Such research would provide an empirical basis for discussion of legitimacy within the Convention system, thereby acting as a counterweight to the present, largely abstracted debate in which (at least in the UK) legitimacy is invoked as part of a zero-sum game in which any ceding of authority to the Court is perceived as entailing a corresponding (and, for some, unacceptable) loss of sovereignty domestically. In our view, it is imperative that this debate becomes more connected to the experience of applicants (and would-be applicants), litigators, and civil society actors—not only in the domestic jurisdiction but also across the Convention system as a whole.

A second priority for research of both an empirical and normative nature is to elucidate the—as yet under-explored—role of the Parliamentary Assembly. The increasingly assertive role of the Assembly in matters of human rights implementation merits greater attention and visibility than it has received heretofore, both in relation to the effectiveness and democratic legitimacy of the Convention system.

Thirdly, the Court's developing jurisprudence, and its implications for the allocation of authority between the supranational and domestic levels, presents opportunities for further research of relevance to national parliaments. We have identified two emergent areas of both risk and opportunity for the Court. First, its increasing willingness to be directive in its judgments both as to substance and timing (by means of the pilot judgment procedure and 'Article 46' judgments) opens up an area of inquiry as to the effectiveness of such an approach at galvanizing implementation—and the attendant risks of political 'pushback' if the Court is seen to intrude unduly into the sphere of domestic decision-making. Secondly, the Court's developing approach to the way in which it structures—and makes explicit—the deference paid to domestic democratic deliberation should also be of

[13] The extent to which debate in the UK departs from these ground rules is evidenced by the statement by the Lord Chancellor and Secretary of State for Justice in the UK, Michael Gove to the House of Lords Constitution Committee on 2 December 2015: 'We have a conflict between two principles: respect for the [ECtHR] judgment and for parliamentary sovereignty. I would err on the side of democratic sovereignty.' See 'Plan to Scrap Human Rights Act Delayed Again', *The Guardian*, 2 December 2015.

[14] Such research would follow the 'legitimacy-in-context' approach proposed by Beetham as a means of assessing both the social and normative legitimacy of institutions; see 4.2 at n 48.

interest to parliaments since it offers them the possibility of 'earning' deference from the Strasbourg Court through the quality of the parliamentary process. Moreover, this trend in the Court's case law sends a signal to executives, which have every incentive to facilitate legislative deliberation (by inviting parliamentary scrutiny of legislative proposals at an early stage and ensuring that parliaments are fully informed about the executive's proposed response to adverse judgments) and to provide the Court with relevant evidence of parliamentary consideration of the human rights compatibility of laws which are the subject of applications. Applicants, litigators, and third-party interveners may likewise contribute through their submissions to the Court's qualitative assessment of the parliamentary process.

The potential of the Court (and the international human rights judiciary in general) to promote the quality of parliamentary process raises a host of questions, which, building on the work of others, we have begun to address in this book.[15] From the Strasbourg perspective, it may be asked whether the Court has a mandate to seek to influence the quality of the parliamentary process. If so, what qualitative criteria might it apply across the forty-seven states of the Council of Europe, and by what modalities should Strasbourg judges operate vis-à-vis national authorities in what some have termed this new 'age of subsidiarity'? From the national perspective, to what extent will parliaments, executives, courts, and other domestic actors 'hear' the signals sent by the Court in its developing case law? Will they be incentivized by, or resistant to, those signals? How, if at all, will their interactions with the Convention system be affected? What will be the result in respect of the effectiveness and (perceived) legitimacy of the Convention system? These are questions which will require both normative and empirical inquiry to be addressed—and present a rich agenda for both scholars and practitioners who are concerned with the success of the European Convention on Human Rights in its next half century.

[15] Two international workshops of scholars and legal practitioners were held at the University of Oslo in March 2015, and Middlesex University in November 2015, on 'The International Human Rights Judiciary and National Parliaments'. We are grateful to Matthew Saul of the University of Oslo for the opportunity to collaborate on these events, which hold the promise of future work in this area.

Appendix: Interviewees

The list below contains the names of those interviewed during the course of the research for this book. Affiliations are given as they were at the time of the interview. Where interviewees are cited within the book, more recent affiliations are also given.

1. Anonymous, Department for the Execution of Judgments of the European Court of Human Rights, Council of Europe, 26 June 2012.
2. Anonymous, Council of State (Netherlands), 22 March 2012.
3. Anonymous, former government agent (Romania), 24 May 2012.
4. Anonymous, government official (UK), 10 July 2012.
5. Anonymous, government official (UK), 10 July 2012.
6. Anonymous, government official (Ukraine), 22 May 2012.
7. Professor Myroslava Antonovych, National University 'Kyiv–Mohyla Academy' (Ukraine), 21 May 2012.
8. Katja Behr, Head of Unit IV C 1, Human Rights Protection, Government Agent before the European Court of Human Rights (Netherlands), 20 March 2012.
9. Marie-Louise Bemelmans-Videc, former Senator (Netherlands), 22 March 2012.
10. Corneliu Birsan, Judge of the European Court of Human Rights (Romania), 25 June 2012.
11. Roeland Böcker, Agent for the Government of the Netherlands, Ministry for Foreign Affairs, 22 March 2012.
12. Professor Marten Breuer, University of Konstanz (Germany), 4 May 2012.
13. Arkadiy Bushchenko, Executive Director, Ukrainian Helsinki Human Rights Union, 21 May 2012.
14. Dr Antoine Buyse, Associate Professor, Netherlands Institute of Human Rights, Utrecht University, 22 March 2012.
15. Irina Cambrea, Co-agent of the Government of Romania before the European Court of Human Rights, 25 June 2012 (written questionnaire).
16. Giancarlo Cardinale, Deputy to the Director of the Office of the Council of Europe Commissioner for Human Rights, 27 June 2012.
17. Tudor Chiuariu, Chair of the Committee on Legal Appointments, Discipline, Immunities and Validations of the Senate of Romania, 14 October 2013.
18. Christopher Chope MP (UK), Chair of the Committee on Legal Affairs and Human Rights of the Parliamentary Assembly of the Council of Europe, 27 June 2012.
19. Jean Corston, former Chair of the Joint Committee on Human Rights (UK), 4 July 2012.
20. Damian Draghici, member of the Committee on Human Rights, Cults, and Minorities of the Senate of Romania, 14 October 2013.
21. Andrew Drzemczewski, Head of the Legal Affairs and Human Rights Department of the Parliamentary Assembly of the Council of Europe, 27 June 2012.
22. Anne van Eijndhoven, Policy Officer, Equal Treatment Commission (Netherlands), 23 March 2012.
23. Irene Fedorovych, Social Action Centre/No Borders Project (Ukraine), 21 May 2012.
24. Professor David Feldman, Cambridge University, 25 April 2012.

25. Daniel Florea, member of the Committee for Legal Matters, Discipline, and Immunities of the Chamber of Deputies of Romania, and Chair of its Sub-committee on Monitoring the Execution of European Court of Human Rights Judgments, 14 October 2013 and 13 May 2015.
26. Petra Follmar-Otto, Head of Department of Human Rights Policies (Germany/Europe), German Institute for Human Rights, 20 March 2012.
27. Olga Frayshteter, Deputy Representative of the Secretary General of the Council of Europe in charge of the co-ordination of the Council of Europe co-operation programmes/Head of Operations, 21 May 2012.
28. Georgiy Frunda, Chair of the Committee on Human Rights, Religion, and Minorities of the Senate of Romania, 27 June 2012.
29. Alexander Galkin, Hebrew Immigrant Aid Society (Ukraine), 21 May 2012 (written questionnaire).
30. Liana Ganea, Programme Director, FreeEx, Active Watch Media Monitoring Agency, 25 May 2012.
31. Professor Conor Gearty, London School of Economics and Matrix Chambers, 24 April 2012.
32. Christos Giakoumopoulos, Director of Human Rights I, Directorate General Human Rights and Rule of Law of the Council of Europe, 27 June 2013.
33. Lize Glas, Radboud University (Netherlands), 22 March 2012.
34. Alina-Ştefania Gorghiu, member of the Committee for Legal Matters, Discipline, and Immunities of the Chamber of Deputies of Romania, 14 October 2013.
35. Dmytro Groysman, Director, Vinnytsya Human Rights Group, 22 May 2012.
36. Silvia Grundmann, Adviser to the Council of Europe Commissioner for Human Rights, 27 June 2012.
37. Holger Haibach, former Deputy Chair of the Committee on Human Rights and Humanitarian Aid of the German *Bundestag*, 15 June 2012.
38. Friederycke Haijer, President of the Dutch section of the International Commission of Jurists (*Nederlands Juristen Comité voor de Mensenrechten*), 22 March 2012.
39. Evan Harris, former member of the Joint Committee on Human Rights (UK), 6 July 2012.
40. Diana Hatneanu, Executive Director of the Association for the Defence of Human Rights in Romania (APADOR-CH), 24 May 2012.
41. Professor Robert Hazell, University College London (UK), 5 March 2012.
42. Professor Janet Hiebert, Queen's University (Canada), 11 June 2012.
43. Serhiy Holovaty, former Minister of Justice, former member of the Committee on Legal Policy and Justice of the *Verkhovna Rada* (Ukraine), 28 June 2012.
44. Murray Hunt, Legal Adviser, Joint Committee on Human Rights (UK), 10 September 2012.
45. Romanita Iordache, Chair of the Romania Helsinki Committee, 24 May 2012.
46. Georgiana Iorgulescu, Executive Director of the Centre for Legal Resources (Romania), 25 May 2012.
47. Erik Jurgens, former member of House of Representatives and Senate (Netherlands); former Rapporteur on the Implementation of European Court of Human Rights Judgments of the Parliamentary Assembly of the Council of Europe, 23 March 2012.
48. Francesca Klug OBE, Human Rights Futures project, London School of Economics, 8 March 2012.
49. Oksana Klymovych, Westminster Foundation for Democracy–Ukraine, 22 May 2012.

50. Laurien Koster, President of the Equal Treatment Commission (Netherlands), 23 March 2012.
51. Dmytro Kotliar, former Deputy Minister of Justice (Ukraine), 21 May 2012.
52. Martin Kuijer, Senior Legal Adviser on Human Rights, Ministry of Security and Justice (Netherlands), 23 March 2012.
53. Elisabeth Lambert-Abdelgawad, CNRS-University of Strasbourg, 28 June 2012.
54. Professor Rick Lawson, University of Leiden, 22 March 2012.
55. Lord Lester of Herne Hill QC, member of the Joint Committee on Human Rights (UK), 12 March 2012.
56. Dr Jan-Peter Loof, University of Leiden, 22 March 2012.
57. Lord Mackay of Clashfern, former Lord Chancellor (UK), 14 March 2012.
58. Monica Macovei, Member of the European Parliament, former Minister of Justice (Romania), 12 June 2012.
59. Marian Mandache, Interim Director, Romani CRISS (Romania), 25 May 2012.
60. Tetyana Montyan, human rights legal consultant (Ukraine), 21 May 2012.
61. Dr Sebastian Müller, Bielefeld University, 20 March 2012.
62. Egbert Myjer, Judge of the European Court of Human Rights, 27 June 2012.
63. Hryhoriy Nemyria, former Deputy Prime Minister; Chair of the Committee on Human Rights, National Minorities, and Interethnic Relations of the *Verkhovna Rada* (Ukraine), 17 February 2015.
64. Michael O'Boyle, Deputy Registrar, European Court of Human Rights, 14 October 2013.
65. Dr Colm O'Cinneide, University College London, 4 May 2012.
66. Franka Olujic, Secretary of the Dutch section of the International Commission of Jurists (*Nederlands Juristen Comité voor de Mensenrechten*), 22 March 2012.
67. Professor Barbara Oomen, University College Roosevelt (Utrecht University) (Netherlands), 12 July 2012.
68. Gerritjan van Oven, former member of the House of Representatives (Netherlands), 2 August 2012.
69. Tudor Pantiru, former Judge of the European Court of Human Rights; member of the Committee for Legal Matters, Discipline, and Immunities in the Chamber of Deputies of Romania, and founding Chair of its Sub-committee on Monitoring the Execution of European Court of Human Rights Judgments, 26 April 2012.
70. Angela Patrick, Director of Human Rights Policy, JUSTICE; former Assistant Legal Adviser, Joint Committee on Human Rights (UK), 8 March 2012.
71. Olena Petsun, Adviser to the Council of Europe Commissioner for Human Rights, 27 June 2012.
72. Pavlo Pushkar, Senior Lawyer, Registry of the European Court of Human Rights, 26 June 2012.
73. Stefan von Raumer, German Bar Association, 19 March 2012.
74. Vladimir Ristovski, Representative of the Secretary General of the Council of Europe in charge of the co-ordination of the Council of Europe co-operation programmes/Head of Office (Ukraine), 21 May 2012.
75. Roxana Rizoiu, National Institute of Magistracy; former Government Agent for Romania before the European Court of Human Rights, 24 May 2012.
76. Marina Schuster, member of the Committee on Human Rights and Humanitarian Aid of the German *Bundestag*; former Deputy Chair of the Committee on Legal Affairs and Human Rights of the Parliamentary Assembly of the Council of Europe, 21 March 2012.

77. Mihai Selegean, former government lawyer; former director of the National Institute of Magistracy (Romania), 24 May 2012.
78. Maxim Shcherbatyuk, Ukrainian Helsinki Human Rights Union, 21 May 2012.
79. Halyna Shevchuck, Westminster Foundation for Democracy, 22 May 2012.
80. Professor Stanislav Shevchuk, National University 'Kyiv–Mohyla Academy', former ad hoc Judge of the European Court of Human Rights (Ukraine), 21 May 2012.
81. Elina Shyshkina, member of the *Verkhovna Rada* (Ukraine), 5 July 2012.
82. Christoph Strässer, member of the Committee on Human Rights and Humanitarian Aid and the Committee on Legal Affairs and Consumer Protection of the German *Bundestag*; member of the Committee on Legal Affairs and Human Rights of the Parliamentary Assembly of the Council of Europe, 21 March 2012.
83. Mariia Synenka, Head of the Unit for International Co-operation and International Law, Ombudsman (Parliament Commissioner for Human Rights) (Ukraine), 22 May 2012.
84. Oksana Syroyid, Deputy Speaker of the *Verkhovna Rada* (Ukraine), 17 February 2015.
85. Valentyna Telychenko, lawyer (Ukraine), 18 June 2012.
86. Frans Timmermans, former Minister of Foreign Affairs; member of the House of Representatives (Netherlands), 13 June 2012.
87. Adrian Vasiliu, Romanian Bar Association, 11 June 2012.
88. Klaas de Vries, Senator (Netherlands); Rapporteur on the Implementation of European Court of Human Rights Judgments of the Parliamentary Assembly of the Council of Europe, 24 July 2012 (written questionnaire).
89. John Wadham, Group Director, Legal, Equality and Human Rights Commission (UK), 12 July 2012.
90. Dr Almut Wittling-Vogel, Representative of the Federal Government for Matters Relating to Human Rights, and Director of Ministry's Directorate-General IV (Constitutional, Administrative, EU, and International Public Law), 20 March 2012.
91. Ganna Yudkivska, Judge of the European Court of Human Rights, 27 June 2012.
92. Yuriy Zaitsev, former Government Agent of Ukraine before the European Court of Human Rights, 23 July 2012.

Index

Please see under entries for specific countries for topics relating to that country